Why Nobody is Searching for God

by Roland Jutras

xulon PRESS

Why Nobody is Searching for God
by Roland Jutras

Printed in the United States of America

ISBN 9781626977914

www.xulonpress.com

Contents

*To my loving wife Rita, whose undying love
propels me forward.*

*To my Aunt Lillian, who has loved me with the heart of my
Memere and whose love for Christ stood as an example for me.*

Acknowledgements

Thanks to Denise whose endless hours in the first editing run through taught me how "redundant" I was.

Thanks to all the song writers that put song titles and lyrics to the many chapters of so many lives.

Thanks to all my friends who listened to me as I relived some of those painful days.

Thanks to Rick who graciously helped a complete stranger, finalize this manuscript.

A Note from the Author

Everyone sees the world differently. We all interpret our surroundings in varying degrees. Some of us walk to the edge of a cliff and immediately jump back and thank God we saw it before we ventured too far. Others go the edge of the cliff and see how close they can get, seemingly teetering on the edge of disaster while appreciating the heights they absorb through their senses. Two entirely different views of the same cliff. Then you have the people at the bottom of the cliff looking up. One admires how impressive it is and gazes upon it in amazement, while the other sees, almost instinctively, the hand holds all the way to the top. Now put these same people next to a river, and the roles could be reversed. Those who held back from the cliff are now ready to jump in because they know exactly how to make it across without the fear of drowning.

This is life. We all have ways of looking at things and the images and ideas that were pressed upon us from our earliest beginnings form who we are. The child who was raised around motorcycles has a natural respect for them and does not see them as harmful. He begins riding at an early age, suffering from the occasional bumps and bruises as though second nature. Take the same child, raise him in a home where a family member has a fear of motorcycles and it may imbed in the child a fear of getting hurt.

Resolutely, we are a product of our environment to a certain degree. No one can get away from this fact of life. That which we see, interpret and internalize forms the personality that we were born with outside of our natural tendencies. We are born into something and it is from there that we become the sum of all our experiences. Some would argue that what we thought we saw was not even true, but we proceed believing what we thought we saw or experienced. As we journey through old age, we develop prejudices, likes and yearn for something based on all we know or think we know. We finally see the world around us through our own set of glasses and many wonder, how did I get here and why am I?

That has been the question Man has been asking since the beginning of time. Unfortunately, the answer is much deeper than 'I am me and I came from the union from my mother and father.' No, that answer has never satisfied the hunger in the depths of a man's soul. There has to be meaning. There has to be an answer that makes sense of it all as we walk into the next moment of our lives.

Similarly, many people want God to provide the additional proof to satisfy their doubts and signs and wonders tailored to them. If given the essential proof, they somehow believe they won't be disappointed or hurt if they believe in Him. When it comes to God, many want a relationship they can control with outcomes that can be foreseen. Once feeling satisfied they understand how the relationship will work, then and only then will they believe. Many travel that path, a method of religiosity where good behavior and routines bring structure to a relationship with God, but it turns out to be a one-way relationship.

What you do with your life and how you respond to the world will fulfill you or leave you wanting. There is a voice inside all of us wanting to be heard, but so often we cover it up with the external noise of life. You are about to embark on a journey with a man we shall call 'Nobody' who had wanted to be somebody else, a feeling many of us have felt at one point in all of our lives. You will see the world through his eyes and hopefully feel the honesty in which he views his surroundings. Hopefully, you might even see yourself through him. We are all on journey and like mine, I found many dead ends and was discouraged, however I never gave up and I am a better man for it.

So I hope you will enjoy the raw truth that surrounds all of us from our earliest memories to our later years as we find out "Why Nobody is Searching for God."

Roland Jutras

Part I

The Foundation

Episode 1

You're Having My Baby

In a land far far away, there was placed on this Earth a man we will call Nobody. He came into this world no different than anyone else. He had parents that loved him, and a string of relatives that supported him in the Catholic traditions. His mother was from a family of five and was the middle child. She was the daughter of a construction worker, a religious man. His mother attended a Catholic school. When he was baptized, his mother's brother and wife became his Godparents. They vowed they would care for Nobody should something happen to his parents.

Nobody's father was the older of two sons, 10 years apart and their father was an alcoholic. This grandfather was a blue-collar worker and had worked in the shoe factories most of his life. There was always a lot of talk about how he threw Nobody's mother out of the house in the early years. Nobody never got the whole story, but he did hear his parents say they did not like his grandfather or better yet he heard his mother say it. However, when Nobody began to understand things, he was sure that his father vowed he would never be like his dad and did not drink. When Nobody visited his father's parents house, it was always a short visit. He thought it was strange that his grandmother and grandfather, on his father's side, slept in different bedrooms. He remembered hearing early on what a real man was supposed to be, according to his grandfather. Nobody's father worked hard, became educated, had a career and passed on the rest of those family traditions and behaviors from his generation to this one. Somehow, Nobody knew that his father did not become the man his grandfather wanted his son to become as he heard bits and pieces of those stories growing up.

Like every other child growing up in this world, Nobody was introduced to a lot of rules one must follow so he would not get in trouble. He learned at a very early age that if he would follow the rules he would not get punished. Nobody believed that if he was a good boy he would be loved. The problem was that the rules always changed in his house, and they were based on the mood of the household at that time. He had to spend a lot of time figuring out which rule applied to which situation, then apply that rule, weigh it against the atmosphere of the house. Most of the time he found that it was best to be quiet. 'Leave me alone or else.' If he could only understand what sort of mood his mother was in it would be easier. Sometimes he would get in trouble and sometimes he would not for doing the same thing. He just had to be careful and not make a mistake. So Nobody asked on many occasions if what he was doing was OK. He always heard that you must listen to your mother, be a good boy so she wouldn't have to worry about him.

Myth #1 Nobody needs to be a good boy all the time.

One time his aunt came for a visit. That was one afternoon Nobody enjoyed. It was on this old metal framed rocking chair, with a vinyl foam cushion that his aunt rocked him with his arms around her neck. It seemed like all afternoon. That was the first time Nobody remembered he was safe; he loved being held there on her chest. It was absolute Heaven. That was one day that Nobody did not want to be anybody else and wished he could stay there forever.

It wasn't long after his aunt left, that Nobody didn't know if he was dreaming or if he saw it from his hiding place, but from behind a chair he looked into his room and saw someone or something screaming at someone in his bed. Then it seemed as if he was in his bed and a pair of hands was lunging towards him fast and he was scared. Nobody had that dream often and always thought a werewolf was coming after him.

Nobody thought it was a nice apartment that he lived in. In his room, there was a little door and when you opened it, you could look inside and see the inside of the house. It was a great place to hide, but his mother said not to go in there because she did not want him to get hurt. She constantly reminded him of that as there was one time that he wasn't paying attention and he had cut his knuckle at the base of his little finger on a metal venetian blind and had to get stitches. Because of this *cut* she had to *bring* him to the doctor to stitch his hand. If Nobody had not been careless she wouldn't have to worry about him getting hurt. So she told him to be careful all the time. His scar had an outline of an eye and when the stitches were in, it looked like an eye with eyelashes.

Myth #2 Nobody needs to be careful all the time.

As he got older he also learned that he was different from other kids according to his father. He was told he came from a monkey and when monkeys were on TV, he would hear, "there is your brother!" from his dad. He was joking of course. Nobody was somewhat sensitive and when he was hurt he would cry and then his father would call him a crybaby, fairy, and motor mouth. As he got older, Nobody wasn't sure what to say when called those names, so most of the time, if he was not crying, he would say nothing or be quiet as best as he could. His father also got mad if his hand fell from his wrist in a limp wristed fashion. This happened more when he got a little older, but his father would ask him if he was a homo. Nobody wasn't sure what that phrase meant. Regardless, he was absolutely sure by the way his father said it that it was not good at all, even though his father would say, "he knows I'm joking," when challenged by his mother. Nobody started to realize that there were things about him that his parents did not like.

Myth #3 Nobody thinks being different is bad.

He enjoyed going to the beach, and eating lobsters with his relatives when he went to visit them in New England. Nobody loved it when he was walking to the store with his maternal grandfather hand in hand as well. He felt safe with his grandfather and he knew he loved him too. Even though he had to sleep on a cot in the kitchen at his house it felt like home. Everyone was laughing and playing cards while he was running around with his cousins. He used to get so excited to see all his aunts, uncles and cousins. He loved them and they loved him. Not to mention, the A&W stand was right next door for those wonderful root beer floats. He would see his grandfather praying on his knees, next to their bed before going to sleep. He loved his grandfather and what he really liked was sitting in the front seat of his Chevy Impala between him and his grandmother. She loved him too, but he did not like those big kisses on the cheeks. They went camping, watched hockey and ate popcorn. Nobody also liked to go to William's grocery store and get a piece of pizza for a quarter when he was home in Upstate New York. Seeing that big brown stallion on the top of the grocery store, on its hind legs was really neat. He loved music and he would like to sing and pretend he was on stage in front of a lot of people. He kept his room clean and toys picked up so his mom would not get mad and when he heard his mom sing it was going to be a good day.

Nobody's parents loved him. They told him all the time, but Nobody had a hard time understanding the difference between what he heard his family say and what he felt. Nobody always thought his mother was mad at him even though she said she loved him. He wanted his parents to be proud of him so he would show them all the things he had done to get their approval. If they were happy with him then they would love him. However, he felt like he always had to do one more thing to get their approval. After a while, he somehow got into his head that whatever he did was not good enough and this played out many years later as well.

Myth #4 Nobody needs to make sure his parents love him.

Since he was afraid of getting in trouble, he tried to do what he was told and he spent a lot of time playing by himself in his room or being good in front of the TV. He would always ask if it was OK to do something and get permission first. His mother continued to worry about him getting hurt. As long as he got permission he would not get into trouble. Sometimes he was allowed to do what he asked for and then other times he was not allowed. She told him that maybe he would enjoy doing "this" better instead because he might get hurt if he did the other.

Myth #5 Nobody needs to ask permission every time.

Myth #6 Nobody learns he must be extremely careful not to get hurt.

They moved to a little house and Nobody liked his neighbors. He would always say hi and talk to them as long as he didn't leave the yard. He became friends with a boy across the street and once, while his friend's sister and he were on the swing set, the boy came over and undressed in front of both of them for no reason. That all happened while Nobody was trying to be somebody else in front of the sister. Nobody knew at that moment he wasn't big enough to outshine the brother or anyone else. He was afraid to tell his mother what had happened. He was ashamed and he did not know why. He was sure he would get blamed in some way or get into trouble so he said nothing, because the truth was not good in this case.

How many times had he heard, "Nobody, when you lie you get punished, when you don't lie you don't get punished." So from an early age, Nobody knew it was best to tell the truth. Unfortunately, it seemed that sometimes another rule found its way into the list. Sometimes when you tell the truth you still get in trouble and sometimes hurt, even though he was told he wouldn't. This was another rule he had a hard time figuring out. Without realizing it, he learned that if you think the truth is worse than the lie, and to keep from getting in trouble, stay as close to the truth as possible without speaking the truth or don't say anything at all. There were many times Nobody had to lie just so he would not get in trouble, especially when he was asked what was wrong.

Myth #7 Nobody is afraid to tell the truth.

With all these rules to keep up with, Nobody worked hard to make sure that he was doing the right thing. Because he was so afraid to get into trouble, it would be better to ask first instead of making a decision for himself. Nobody also had to be careful not to be in the wrong place at the wrong time or ask the wrong question when either his mother or father was busy. Nobody did not know what to expect; one time he could get spanked, the next time told to stop it, but more than anything he was really afraid of getting the belt. When the belt came from his father or mother, they would run towards him extremely angry. This certainly was not the way he saw it happen on the TV show, Family Affair, when the dad said, "this will hurt me more than it hurts you." Nobody got hurt more than his parents. He did not like the look on their faces when they were mad. Nobody was trying to make sure not only not to get into trouble but also not get hurt by his parents.

Myth #8 Nobody is hurt by his parents.

Nobody liked to think about what life would be like if he were someone else. He would watch other families and see how they got along and he would wish he could live with them. Nobody wished God would have given him different parents. Nobody wanted people to notice him and like him, but he always heard his mom say, "Nobody loves you, like your mother. You cannot trust anyone." So Nobody tried to listen to everything his mother told him. He was sure that if he did all the things she told him, then all would be well. If he did the right things she would not have to worry about him either.

Nobody heard his parents fight a lot too. This would happen when his father came back from traveling. She always accused his father of things he could not understand. He heard words like tramp, girlfriends and heard his mother say: "you leave me here all alone, I helped put you through school and this is what I get." Nobody also tried to keep his mother happy but she was mad a lot of the time. Nobody heard his mother tell his father she was mad because she had nobody around to talk to and she wanted somebody else to talk to, so his sister was born. Then everyone was happy.

Myth #9 It's Nobody's fault they are not happy.

Episode 2

Moving to the Country

It was nice to have a baby sister around. Nobody helped as best as he could or was allowed to at first. His mother would sing to her, rock her and take care of her. She used to give her a bath in a yellow tub made just for babies. His sister made his mother happy and he was her big brother.

When Nobody was five years old and hadn't started school yet because of when his birthday fell in the calendar year, he was told he was a big boy and that he could take care of himself. So while his mother took care of his sister and as long as he did not get into any trouble, he could do whatever he wanted. It wasn't long before Nobody did not have a lot places to go or anyone to talk to and, because some of his friends were at school, he was by himself more. The more he was by himself, the more he started getting mad at his sister. He was tired of his toys and he did not like his room. One day when his Mother put her in the car seat to go to the store, she left Nobody in the car with her and he placed his hands on her neck and wanted to hurt her. He was very mad, but something inside told him to stop so instead he pushed the cigarette lighter in, saw how it glowed and touched it. When his mother came around the corner he put his hand in his pocket and tried not to make a face. He was more afraid of her reaction than getting a band aid. His finger tip had turned white and it hurt.

A few days later, Nobody was outside playing when they had to pick up his father from work. He had a piece of paper called a pink slip. His parents were talking a lot and Nobody thought he did something wrong. He just stayed out of the way before anything bad happened. After a time, they told him they were going to move to the country. Nobody would go to a school there and ride the bus. His father got a new job and they might even put a pool in the backyard. There was a lot of excitement and they packed up the house and moved away from the city.

The new house was small. Nobody had his own room. There was a farm across the street with cows, chickens and a dog named Ace. The farmer had a pond, and he said Nobody could fish there. Nobody could go into the hayloft and play with the kittens or jump in the hay pile as long as he was careful. The railroad was close by and you could hear the trains at night, in the morning, in the afternoon and at dinner. He could ride his new bicycle in the driveway. There was a tree to climb in the front yard, but the best thing were the woods across the field. He knew he wanted to go into the woods.

There were other neighbors; a Baptist minister lived next door across a short field. Baptists were different his mother and father said.

"You had to be Catholic to get to Heaven and that was a fact!" she would say.

There was a fisherman who lived in a log cabin. He also had a pond that he stocked with fish. As Nobody got older, he would help him with his fishing store and do chores for money. They went to church on Saturday night and everything was good. They would watch hockey, baseball and make popcorn the old fashioned way with oil. Nobody tried to pop it so there were hardly any kernels left when it was finished popping.

Now that Nobody could play outside and had a little more freedom in the country, he visited the barn, rode his bike, played in the fields and had a lot of time by himself. When he was able to talk to someone, he would talk an awful lot. One of his mother's friends would come by with his dog Traveler, an Irish setter, and he took Nobody fishing with him. It was a great time for Nobody. On one trip he had to catch fifteen shiners from the bridge before he could go down to the creek and go after the big ones. This was perfect; he knew exactly what he had to do, and the path was clear to be able to get where he wanted to, down by the creek off the bridge. When he caught the fifteenth fish, his mother's friend kept his word and he went down to the creek. That was a great day and he did not want to be somebody else. He was free he talk to the man and they talked about fishing all day long. He sat with his dog and threw sticks that he could fetch. He had pulled in a couple of big ones. He did not have a care in the world, he was in Heaven.

When he got home, his mother asked how the day went and Nobody told her about their day and he went off into the bathroom that was right off the kitchen and, within earshot, his mother's friend said, "Nobody sure can talk a lot. He didn't stop talking from the time we left until the time we got back." All of a sudden Nobody's gut twisted, he did something wrong again and he was upset with himself. He was just talking; he would have to work on not talking so much in the future. He hoped he did not ruin the opportunity for future fishing trips, but the trips never came again. The friend only visited.

This was just one more time that Nobody thought he was having one of the best days of his life only to find out he had messed it up. Nobody didn't have a care in the world that day. He thought this could go down as one of the best days ever, but he ruined it because, in his excitement, he talked too much. Nobody found out over his short run of years that if he apologized to people they might be less mad at him. So he apologized to the man for talking so much.

Myth #10 Nobody needs to be careful not to say the wrong thing.

Myth #11 Nobody needs to apologize all the time.

When Nobody started school, one of the first things he noticed was that he was smaller than most of the boys his age. He noticed that his clothes were different and he was not as handsome as some of the other boys, even though his mother said he was. As he was starting to get used to his surroundings, Nobody realized that there must be something wrong with him. Since Nobody knew he was small, and felt like he did not belong, he needed to prove he was somebody. Nobody believed that if he made good grades the teachers would be happy with him and so would his parents. This was very important because he also had a hard time getting along with the kids in his class. They picked on him, called him names and were mean to him.

So when he told the teacher what they were doing, he then became a tattle-tale. He could not understand why he didn't have any friends. He was doing what he was told he should do if this happens. It seemed like no one understood him. Since nobody thought highly of him, Nobody told lies to make himself bigger than he was. When his lies were discovered, he became more alone. Nobody tried harder to be liked by the kids in his class. Maybe they did not like Nobody because he would tell everyone what they should do.

Myth #12 Nobody needs friends to make him feel better.

After riding the bus after school and finishing his homework, Nobody spent time outside and visited with the farmer and the fisherman. As he got a little older he would help with chores around their homes, since they were old people. What was really nice about them is that they would listen to Nobody. When he did chores for one of his neighbors he would get paid for a job well done. When he went home for supper, his mother would ask why he would do things for other people and not his own family. Nobody would always say, "I don't know." If he said what the real reason was, he would surely be told why he shouldn't help them. He liked working for them, they liked him and they did not get mad at him. They told him he did a good job. His mother would say many times, "no one loves you like we do and they won't be there for you when you need them." It didn't matter, Nobody enjoyed visiting with them and helping them out.

Myth #13 Nobody believes self-worth is based on accomplishments.

His father started to go to school again so he was studying a lot at night. Nobody played baseball and was in the cub scouts and he soon had other things to keep him occupied. He learned how to ski and roller-skate. He enjoyed skiing and he wanted to be a great skier and keep his knees together. If he was a good skier, people would look at him and say, "that boy is a great skier did you see him go by."
When his father wasn't busy, he would play catch sometimes, but mostly he threw the ball against the cement chimney and practiced fielding the

ball in the summer. Since they were in the country, Nobody needed to have a ride to go anywhere, so most of his time he played by himself or in the winter he went skiing when his parents went. That was OK; he could go ski by himself and see if other people would notice how good he was.

Myth #14 Nobody needs to be noticed all the time.

He did spend a lot of time with his schoolwork and received pretty good grades and got praise for them. He still did not have a lot of friends, but he liked girls, but they did not like it when he touched them. One time a girl told the teacher and she called his mother and they had to meet with her. Nobody was scared that he would get the belt. The funniest thing happened, nothing. He was told not to do it again.

Nobody went to church every Saturday night with his parents. When he was old enough, he had his first communion and confession. He said his Hail Mary's and Our Father's and prayed the rosary, he wore a Scapular because he was told to but did not know why. His mother said it was important and he should listen to her. His father passed the collection basket every week. Nobody's mother was always excited when the priest would acknowledge her as he shook parishioner's hands going down the center aisle. They were always dressed neat and everything was always fine. Once communion was over, they left church. Sometimes they would say hi to people but most of the time they went home.

Nobody had a hard time remembering when it started, but it was becoming a pattern that after church on Saturday nights, his parents started fighting. On those nights there was no popcorn and there was no fun. There was a lot of yelling and his mother screamed at his father. His father would yell for her to stop it but she would keep yelling at him. She kept asking him questions over and over again. This kept on going and when his mother did not get the answer she wanted, the fights escalated. Then they would chase each other around the house. Nobody's sister and he would get out of the way and they would ask them to stop. This is how Nobody learned to yell; eventually they would learn that the person who yelled the loudest would be heard. After the fighting stopped, his parents would usually go their room for the rest of the night. His sister and he would have to go to bed too. Nobody tucked them into their beds after their parents fought.

Truth #1 Nobody has parents that fight all the time.

However, whenever the fighting started, his sister and he had to take cover. It was on one of these occasions during the day while in his room listening to music that his father and mother were fighting, when Nobody happened to leave his room and upon his return, his father ran into his room. For whatever reason, Nobody's father took his Elvis album and bent it in half and threw it on the ground.

Nobody screamed that he was sorry, "Please tell me what I did and I won't do it again."

Nobody liked that album and most of the time the only thing he could do without getting in trouble was listen to the music. That album cover had a blue background with a picture of Elvis in a brown cowboy hat, suede jacket, blue shirt and red tie. Many times, Nobody would look at album covers and try to place himself in the picture and pretend he was looking out from the picture. He desperately wished he could be someone else and somewhere else. It was on one of those occasions he even asked God for help, maybe God was listening and would answer his prayer.

It was hard to watch his parents fighting. He couldn't tell anyone, they were not close to anyone at church. So his sister and he would go to their rooms and lay in their beds. From his room at night, if the light was on in his parent's bedroom, the light would shine on the attic ceiling ladder door in the hall outside his door. The light would reflect off two knots of wood next to each other. From his pillow they looked like two cartoon characters that were face to face. He tried to focus on the faces to make them clearer and pretend they were talking to each other. Nobody would look at those until he fell asleep.

Because Nobody had such a good time playing with the kittens across the street, he wanted one all for his own. He loved watching them chase strings and little balls. He loved the way they purred and when they purred he knew they were happy. He always loved that time petting them on his lap, so relaxed. So he asked for one and kept asking. When he came home one afternoon, his father had gotten him a kitten, who Nobody named Tiger. His mother was afraid of the cat and at night, she would put it between the washer and the dryer with a laundry basket over it. Nobody would sneak out of his bed at night and play with him. He loved that kitten; he would play with it as much as he could. Then one day when he came back from school, his mother told him that the kitten got away and was killed crossing the road. She then called the farmer to confirm her story. He said he found it dead in the road. Nobody believed they were lying. She couldn't stand having the cat out and running around the house. Nobody cried and his stomach hurt so much he just wanted to scream at the top of his lungs at her, but couldn't. He did not believe his mother; he knew she got rid of Tiger!

Truth #2 Nobody's mother lies.

Episode 3

And the Beat Goes On

The fighting continued almost every week after church and then it happened, WWIII erupted in the house. He was not sure what started it, but this time the belts came out. His mother was spitting as she was yelling at his father, running towards him, with the belt held high, like a whip in a western movie. His father would put his arm up, yelling for her to stop but they both kept fighting. Nobody could not tell who was at fault or if they were going to stop. His sister was on the kitchen floor yelling, "Stop it." His mother had a scratch on her chest. Everyone was hysterical; she was yelling and said she was having a nervous breakdown. His father was trying to stop her from swinging wildly. Then all of a sudden an arm flew and caught his father in the head. Nobody saw tears in his eyes as he looked at him and his sister. She wouldn't let his father retreat and continued swinging at him. Her face looked so angry. It was like someone else's face was on her. They called each other names. There they were all in the kitchen, Nobody leaning against the wall next to the phone, his parents on the floor holding each other at bay and his sister on the floor on her knees crying.

Finally Nobody put his hand on the phone, and yelled, "I am going to call the police."

"Nobody please call the police," his mother said.

"Don't you dare call the police," his father said.

His sister was still on the floor crying and yelling. Nobody was paralyzed with fear and was afraid to do the wrong thing. If he called the police, he and his sister could be taken away. Someone would be mad at him; everyone would know it would be his fault. What would people think? All he could do was drop the phone back on the receiver and cry.

Nobody wanted to stop the craziness, but he was too afraid to make a wrong choice. Up to this point he did not make right choices anyway. He didn't want anyone mad at him and that was always the most important thing. He just couldn't move. Nobody wanted to call, but he loved his parents and did not want them to get in trouble and was afraid of what would happen. All alone with no one to help and not strong enough to go through with it, the emotion was let out of the room as the standoff continued and everyone broke apart.

His father had hurt his little finger and left the house. When his father came back home, his parents were calm. They went into their room and shut the door, but he could hear everything they said from his room. His mother told his father that she wanted a divorce. She said that she wanted to move back to Maine and she would take his sister. His father would have to take Nobody and deal with him, since his mother could only handle taking care of his sister. Nobody heard all this and wished they would get divorced, because he did not want to live with his mother either. The following day nothing was said about what had happened the night before and life went on as though nothing had happened. Nobody noticed that his father's finger was not straight. Nobody asked if he would go to the doctor's but his dad refused and it healed broken.

Truth #3 Nobody's mother would abandon her son.

When his father wasn't home, Nobody overheard his mother, on the phone, telling her family how awful his father was. Nobody wanted to talk to people about what happened in the house but he was scared of what might happen if they told his mother. What if they didn't believe him? A new priest was assigned to the parish. He was a bit younger than the last one and seemed nice. Nobody's mother liked him as well. One night, after he was around for awhile his mother brought his sister and him over to the rectory to talk. Nobody heard his mother talk about his father, and it did not feel right in his stomach. She kept crying about how awful it was in the house for her and the kids. Nobody had to say that there were fights, but the way she described his father was not how he had seen the fight happen. That was the last time they talked to the priest about his father.

The Saturday night fights continued with the 'His' and 'Hers' matching belts. One night the minister who lived one house over, knocked on the door to see if everything was alright because he heard yelling from somewhere outside of Nobody's house. Of course his parents said nothing was wrong and that he must have been mistaken. On one other occasion, he also knocked on the door because Nobody was flipping the outside light off and on and as he was driving by he wanted to make sure nothing was wrong. Nobody answered the door and the minister asked if everything was alright. Nobody was so petrified that if he got caught messing with the light and if his parents came to the door it was over. He would surely get the belt and get grounded in his room. So Nobody told the minister he was guiding the ducks home and shut the door in his face. His parents never found out.

Truth #4 There were angels close by.

Belts were not only used on his parents by his parents, they were also used on Nobody as well, but never his sister. He was told that girls were different. When he would get in trouble, his mother, on those special occasions, would charge after him. She was so mad at times that she had spit coming from her mouth as she was yelling at him. The belt came with a full swing and other times she hit him with her fists, coming down on him at the same time. Nobody protected himself as best as he could on his bed, curled in a ball. He tried not to cry. Why was he always getting in trouble?

There were good times. His grandparents would come and visit, as well as some of his aunts and uncles in the summer. Nobody really liked it when his Godparents came with his cousins. They played outside, wrestled, played hide- and- seek and he stole kisses from his cousin. On one visit Nobody wanted show everyone he was tough, he began wrestling with his cousin, and he threw him over his back onto the ground. His cousin started crying and ran into the house. Nobody tried to keep his cousin from going in and telling, saying he was sorry but it was too late. Nobody's father yelled at him in front of his relatives and said he was going to get the belt. His uncle told his father that it was an accident and they were just kids, but that did not stop him. His father charged after Nobody into his room. Nobody screamed, "Don't hit me, it was an accident." The belt came, folded in half, pants down, over his knee. Nobody was as stiff as he could be trying to absorb the pain. After all the excitement died down, his cousin came into the room and said to everyone, "It was an accident" and he was sorry. Too late, all that was needed was an excuse to punish Nobody. However, once his parents thought Nobody had done something wrong, whether true or not, pain was sure to follow. There was no more fun for the rest of the night.

Myth #15 Nobody manages fear of pain.

The next summer another aunt came to visit with his older cousin. She was the aunt that rocked him in the rocking chair when he was younger and made Nobody feel as though he was in Heaven. While they were spending the night in the tent supposedly having fun, Nobody told his cousin what it was like living in the house. Nobody started crying and he could not stop and what started out as a fun night outside turned very grim. After he was done and settled down, his cousin just turned away in his cot. Nobody looked at the stars and asked God for other parents and wished he had not been born.

The next day, while driving in the car, he heard his aunt discuss with his mother her treatment of her son. She needed to stop treating Nobody this way and if she wasn't careful she could end up with a runaway at some point.

Nobody's mother said, "There was nothing to worry about, he was just exaggerating."

Sitting in the car he knew his aunt was right, but why wouldn't his mother acknowledge what was being said and say she was sorry? It was the truth. Why was she lying about this? Nobody was telling the truth, and why wasn't anyone doing anything to help? As with all trips, his cousin finally left and he was back to the way it was.

With all the fighting going on, he tried to ignore it and tried not to get in trouble or in the way. He would tell his parents to stop fighting so he could hear the TV. On one of those days, while he was watching TV in the late afternoon, his parents were fighting in the kitchen. Now the kitchen and living room took up half the house, long ways. There was an arch in between the rooms and it was one step down into the living room. The opening was the size of double doors with half walls on each side that you could see through.

Nobody was on the floor in front of the TV as the fight started to escalate. His mother got mad at his father, picked up a wood chisel, and threw it at him. His father ducked, and the chisel flew straight into the living room. As Nobody looked up, he saw the chisel fly towards him and, in his effort to get out of the way, Nobody was struck on the top of his foot. Nothing was felt at first except the pressure but once the blood started to flow so did the tears. His mother cried out and told him to get in the tub to put water on it. He was yelping in pain as he hopped to the bathroom. With his foot in the tub and his mother right behind him, she kept telling him to stop crying. As this scene was unfolding and he continued to cry, she hit him telling him to be quiet. She kept saying she needed to think.

The cut was too big to just put a band aid on and so they would have to go to the hospital. Nobody was told that he would have to tell the doctor that a chisel fell from a shelf in the cellar. He had better not say what really happened. This was going to be the story, and he had better not contradict what she said. Always worried about getting into trouble, Nobody lied to the doctor. He wished he could have told him the truth, but he didn't, he was too chicken. There was no one to protect or fight for him.

Truth #5 Nobody has to lie to protect himself from others.

Between all the exciting moments at the house, Nobody was active in scouts and played baseball. He was actually a good fielder and played between first base, second base and right field. He wasn't a good hitter, but that was OK as he got noticed for good catches and stopping the ball. This was one sport that his parents liked and he was able to play and not be embarrassed. Nobody was also old enough to become a boy scout. He would go to his troop meetings and earn his merit badges. After one year they were having elections for patrol leader. This was something Nobody desired greatly because if he was a patrol leader his parents would be proud of him and he would be in charge. The scoutmaster asked for every candidate to say a few words on what they would like to accomplish as a patrol leader. This was great. Nobody volunteered to speak first. As Nobody got up, his father was sitting at a table studying; he stopped and looked at him.

Nobody cleared his throat and said, "If I am elected I will make sure we will work well with the other patrols. We will be the best patrol and most disciplined."

He continued to talk about how great they would be. When he listened to the other candidates talk they spoke about having fun. When the elections were over, Nobody had no votes other than his own.

He heard the pack leader say, "One vote for Nobody, just guessing, I bet it was his."

When they got home and his mother asked how the meeting went, he heard his father say to his mother, "I could not believe what he was saying in front of everyone."

Nobody had no clue what he did wrong. He thought he said all the right things.

Truth #6 No one voted for him.

By mid-summer, Nobody was excited about going to Boy Scout camp, but as camp started so did the fun at Nobody's expense. His underwear was stolen; they threw buckets of water on him while in the outhouse through the window and the boys continually teased him. Nobody yelled at them to stop, but they wouldn't. Why did kids always pick on him? He just wanted to be included and be part of the group. He either wasn't big enough, cool enough, spoke funny or had different clothes. He did not know how to stand up for himself and fight. If he did fight he was sure to lose because of his size and he worried he would get hurt. He would get mad enough, but when it came to finally hitting someone he just could not do it. It was like running up to a cliff to jump into the water and then stopping at the edge again and again, saying every time I am going to do it this time. No one was there to protect him and his scout leaders sometime joined in on the fun as well. So when situations became too difficult to deal with, Nobody ventured out of his pack and started visiting other folks around the camp. He met another scout leader, who was more of an adult and they would talk. Nobody told him what was happening in his pack and they discussed how Nobody could respond differently, but nothing changed, or it wasn't changing fast enough. Nobody had no idea that his friend was one of the camp directors with whom he was confiding. Later the following day, there was a big meeting with his pack around the fire and everyone was told to stop playing jokes or pranks on each other. Nobody felt all the eyes on him and the head Eagle Scout was looking at him disgustingly. Nobody knew this was his fault; everyone was getting in trouble because of him. His stomach was turning and he even felt smaller. For the rest of the time at camp he enjoyed arts and crafts, sailed by himself, and selected activities that he could do by himself. He only participated in group activities when he was supposed to. When he tried to do things in a group activity, something would happen to Nobody, so it was best to keep to himself for the rest of the trip. He didn't have to try too hard either, everyone left him alone.

The last night was supposed to be great. That was when all the fathers came out to sleep with their boys. As they were all around the campfire, they decided to play a game where you would have to imitate an animal, person or thing of their choosing. When it was Nobody's turn, they told him to be a fairy and so he flapped his arms and skipped around the fire. Everyone was laughing and holding their stomach but then Nobody looked over at his father; he was shaking his head. All of a sudden Nobody figured out they weren't laughing with him they were laughing at him. He immediately stopped flying and sat down. His father did not say anything to him or anyone else. Nobody was left all alone with no one to defend him.; He did not know how to defend himself anyway. He was not big enough to fight back and he was always scared of getting hurt. After the campfire began to get smaller, a lot of the fathers and kids doubled up in the tents. It just so happened there was no more room with the others so Nobody and his father were in a tent apart from the rest of the group. Not much was said that night and in the morning, they went home.

Truth #7 Nobody's father was ashamed of his son.

A few Boy Scout meetings later, Nobody's father's car got egged while everyone was inside for scout meeting. Nobody happened to be by the window and witnessed the scouts who threw them into the car and smashed them on it as well. Nobody told the scout leader, and the boys were confronted but they denied it and nothing happened as far as Nobody knew. It wasn't long after that, that Nobody's Boy Scout days were over. He did not have any friends in the pack, he was always the last one picked and he wasn't sure his parents were thrilled with the idea of another possible egging incident. He would not end up as an Eagle Scout, like his father was. He was, in a weird way, glad that he did not finish as he was not having fun anymore and he was not liked.

It wasn't a total loss, however, because during camp, Nobody learned a little something about the opposite sex from listening to the head Eagle Scout talking about girls he liked and about how he would like to "plug into them." He heard other various conversations about the difference between boys and girls. He made a couple of comments to his parents and they asked him a bunch of questions.

After many questions and being embarrassed about it, his mother told him to tell her in her ear what he learned.

So, Nobody said in his mother's ear, "It was like a hotdog in a bun."

All his mother could say to his father was, "Yes, he knows," and laughed.

Nobody had no idea what it truly meant and he was not going to ask her. The one thing he did realize was his stomach felt weird, in a bad way, talking to her about it. He felt ashamed about this in front of her and his father was not volunteering any information. Nobody had no idea what the birds and the bees were, but they said he knew. He would find out somehow.

Episode 4

Cat's in the Cradle

As time passed Nobody found a new friend down the road who was a year younger and who needed someone with whom he could play. They played together all the time and were almost inseparable. They went fishing, walked in the woods and walked the cow pastures.

Nobody especially enjoyed the woods. It was here he could go when his parents started fighting and he needed to get out of the way of indirect fire. The woods were peaceful and beautiful. He loved walking amongst the trees and the creeks. He enjoyed looking for animals. One time when he was by himself in the winter, he came upon a rabbit next to the base of a tree, frozen as if in a picture caught in time. In a flash, Nobody lunged forward and grabbed the rabbit by a rear leg. The free leg swiped his hand and cut it open. Nobody knew he had made a mistake going for the rabbit, but the thrill was too much to ignore. He probably was going to get in trouble when he returned home. He could hear it already, he might get rabies, or a bad infection, or why couldn't he be more careful? Then came the speech about why he should leave those animals alone. He seemed to always get in trouble for getting hurt; this he was sure would be no different.

His friend had an 80cc mini-bike and Nobody enjoyed getting rides on it. Since he and his friend were together most of the time this relationship worked well for Nobody. Since there was an age difference, they mostly did what Nobody wanted. His friend had cool things and his parents were alright. His father had Hustler, Penthouse and OUI magazines and whatever Nobody had not learned in scouts he made up his sexual education looking at the pictures and reading the stories about people, who he thought loved each other.

They had a great summer and he finally realized what the fuss was about with girls. Nobody wanted a girlfriend! She needed to be beautiful, slim and if he had a girlfriend like that, other people would think he was special and like him. He was certain on one thing; his girlfriends would have to be pretty. Other boys would want to have what Nobody had. They could not be overweight. His friend said that to be sure, you had to meet the mother to see how any potential girlfriend would turn out. Many times when his parents fought, his mother would yell at his father. She would complain about her weight and when his father did not comment, she would have to get some sort of encouragement from him for the "nagging" to stop as he heard his father exclaim so often.

She would get mad at his father because he liked listening to Anne Murray, a Canadian singer. She would continually ask him if he loved her. Nobody could not understand why his parents stayed married. If they did not love each other they should get a divorce like other people. If they did that, then maybe he and his father could live somewhere else and life would be better. Nobody hated it when his parents fought. It was so ugly, the look in their faces if they happened to spy on him during an argument.

Nobody always wanted to make sure he was evaluating things properly; he wanted to see if the girls he thought were pretty were also pretty to his father. Nobody would ask his father what he thought of a certain girl that he had an interest in. One time in particular he pointed a girl out in a parade and his father said she was homely. So Nobody was no longer interested and started looking out for the pretty girls at school that he could ask to be his girlfriend. It was going to be his mission to make sure he got a girlfriend when he went back to school after summer vacation.

His friend also liked going with him to the farmhouse across from Nobody's house. They spent many hours in the hayloft cleaning pens and running around in the fields with the farmer's dog, Ace. Then one day out of the blue, the farmer gave Nobody's friend a mini-bike he had. This was wrong. Why didn't he give it to Nobody? Nobody helped around the farm too and his friend already had a mini-bike. Nobody was confused about the situation and was at a loss for words. Nobody was mad at the farmer.

He should have gotten the bike. He did all that work and actually did more work than his friend. He would shovel manure without being asked and he had been sure he would get rewarded for all that he had done. So Nobody decided he should not play with his friend. He was mad.

Myth #16 Nobody should be rewarded for doing good work.

It was time for a change. Across from his friend's house was a girl that he was able to talk to. She was nice, but she was not in the habit of playing in the neighborhood. Nobody knew her from school and one day they ended up playing together. They were out exploring and behind their garage there was a part of a structure. It had a blue tarp over it and it was lying on its side. As they got closer and were looking at it, they noticed an opening. Being adventurous, they decided to go into the opening and further investigate. They followed the edge and it felt like a tunnel. When they reached the center, the roof was a blue tarp; it gave a neat bluish glow inside. They were totally separated from the world as they talked. Nobody talked about different things he had read and asked her if he could take a peek at her. So they decided to look at each other underneath their clothes. This was the first time that Nobody saw a real girl close up. They kissed each other but they decided that this was not right and each went home, hurriedly. Nobody was sure he wanted a girlfriend, but he was not going to ask her. She had to be prettier.

Myth #17 Nobody needs to have a girlfriend people think is pretty.

Something else extremely interesting was happening in the neighborhood. New people were moving into vacant lots next to his house. They placed trailers on them instead of houses. One neighbor had two young girls and the other had a boy and a girl. The boy was two years younger than Nobody but he was a new friend that Nobody could play with when his best friend was busy with something else. They did things together but it was different. He did not have a lot of neat toys to play with and because he was a little younger, they were into different things. By this time, Nobody was becoming very possessive of things and he wanted to do things his way and his way only. So it was only a matter of time when those early traits he learned, from the myths that were drilled into his head, would start demonstrating themselves.

Nobody left for a week or so to go on vacation. While he was gone Nobody's friends ended up playing together. Upon his return, Nobody was furious, he did not know why, he just was. He did not want the other boy to play with his original friend. That was his best friend and he wasn't into sharing. This was his true friend and in a roundabout way, Nobody was afraid of losing him. So he asked his best friend to not play with him, and started a fight with the younger boy. This clash over who should play with who went on for a couple weeks. Nobody would not play with his best friend if the other boy was around. He was perfectly content having the boy play by himself with not so much of a head nod to acknowledge his existence. It wasn't long before his best friend's father got all of them together and asked them to work it out. He said that it was a small neighborhood and they should try to get along and play together. It was not kind to treat each other this way. They all agreed to make an attempt. The first project was to build a fort together, and after collecting old doors, plywood and nails the path to building a stronger friendship was waning. After just three days, Nobody wasn't into it anymore and believed, since he was older, he would just pack it in. He told them that he was going to help the other neighbors and earn money. They could play together all they wanted. Nobody, being very sarcastic, exchanged a couple of parting words with the new kid.

Later in the day when the new kid in town was walking by Nobody's house, he threw an apple core in the yard. Nobody saw it thrown from the window. He was intentionally waiting for him to go to his house on his way home looking for trouble. Nobody ran outside and confronted him for littering on his lawn. After a few words, Nobody punched him in the stomach. According to Nobody, he was only protecting his yard. There was no way he'd risk getting in trouble by his parents. Also there was no way this kid could take him so it was a good risk, and worth taking. He would come out on top and that was important. There was no way Nobody could lose. He was justified in hitting him and no one was around to stop him.

Since there were a few days before school started, Nobody stayed around the house and played with his sister a bit. She was getting a little older. They could watch TV together on the little 10-inch black and white in the kitchen. Call it fate, karma or spiritual retribution; Nobody was watching one of his favorite shows, Star Trek. It was during one of those moments in the show when he was asked by his mother, "Who ate the jelly sandwich that was on the counter?"

His sister said, "Nobody did it."

Nobody denied it and said that it was not true, but his mother would not believe him. He started to get mad and continued to say he did not eat it. To which his mother said she did not believe him. This bothered him terribly and he continued to say that his sister was lying. Then he started crying, and his father, from the living room called him a fairy. His mother said that in fact he did do it and he should stop lying before he got into more trouble than he already was. She went on to say the reason she knew he was lying was because he was making such a big deal about it. He continued and continued, just like his mother would do to his father. He would keep trying to convince her that he was telling the truth until she believed him. He yelled that he was not lying and that his sister was but to no avail. Then as this situation escalated, he was sent to his room with no TV.

Myth #18 Nobody tells the truth and gets in trouble.

When school started Nobody was back to studying to make sure he would not feel the wrath of low grades. It was a silent year except that his grandfather died of leukemia at the age of 59. Nobody's mother was devastated when the news came that her father had passed away. He was not allowed to go to the funeral. However, he heard that right before he died, his grandmother asked him what he wanted to do with his watch. He wanted Nobody to have it. From that point forward, Nobody always felt his grandfather was in Heaven looking down at him. Prior to this, Nobody felt alone, but something was different. He heard of angels and he believed his grandfather was one of them. He died on October 18th, 1975.

Nobody was still being picked on and would occasionally get into some scuffles here and there with some kids, but now he was focused on one thing and that was his music teacher. She was beautiful, blonde and thin. All he could do was daydream of her. He would always volunteer and he would always do his best for her. She reminded him of Farrah Fawcett. The highlight of the year was during the last day of school he asked for a goodbye kiss on the cheek and she did. He went absolutely crazy over her and thought of her often throughout the summer.

Truth #8 Nobody feels special because of a kiss.

Myth #19 Nobody knows that to feel special you need someone to love you.

Episode 5

Danger! Danger! Do you Copy?

Nobody was quite an interesting lad. He wanted to be liked, but was small and different. He was smart but as his father would tell him, he had no common sense. Girls were cute but they liked the good-looking boys and he believed he was not good looking enough to get a good-looking girl. He was close to being a teenager so he was too big for the boys in his neighborhood, but not big enough to hang around with the older kids. He did not enjoy being around the house so the only thing left for him to do this summer vacation was to volunteer and help at the church.

Nobody thought he would be blessed if he were to help. In addition, his mother would not question what he was doing if he was to help the priest around the rectory. Nobody's mother liked the priest. Nobody thought he should introduce himself again since he probably did not remember him when he went with his mother to complain about his dad. Therefore, every day, weather permitting, Nobody got on his bicycle and rode about 2 miles to attend daily Mass at the Catholic Church. Who knows, he might even become a priest one day. Then maybe his mother would be proud of him.

After Mass, Nobody would ask the priest what he could do around the house. He helped with the lawn, clearing out the cellar, worked in the garage and a bunch of around the house sort of chores. Nobody felt good. He was doing a good job and the priest liked him. He would talk to the priest and when the priest's mother would visit Nobody spoke with her as well. Nobody was having such a good time he even asked if he could be a lector and read passages out of the bible during church on Saturday night, and he was appointed as a lector.

The first time he read in front of the entire church, everyone said that was the fastest bible verse ever read. It wasn't a big deal, he would practice and learn to slow down and take a breath. It was important that he did this right. Everyone was watching and he wanted to be the best lector, plus this was something he was doing that no other boy in the church was doing. Sure there were the altar boys, but they were not doing this. If Nobody was different then he would make sure he was different for a good reason and not a bad one.

Then one night at church, a new girl showed up for Mass. She was beautiful, blonde and slim, best of all so was her mother. Based on the rules Nobody had organized in his head, she would be OK and he would not be ashamed of having this girl as a girlfriend. He just had to make sure she liked him.

Nobody continued to help around the rectory. He spent a lot of time looking at all the books the priest had. There were a variety of books on sexuality that captured his attention. There was one specifically for teenagers. Since he was twelve, he was close enough. He asked if he could borrow and read it. Nobody wanted to be good for God; he truly wanted to go to Heaven. As Nobody read the book on how someone his age ought to behave to stay in the good graces of God, he felt his chances of reaching Heaven were going to fade. This book was saying things that he was having a hard time understanding. First, the book said that French kissing was a sin. He heard a lot about kissing and from what he saw on TV everyone did it if you loved someone. Except for his mother who said French kissing was disgusting. Nobody thought it was going to be a tough pill to swallow. The book also said that the sin of sex alone was a sin also. Things were not adding up. There must be something wrong with him because all of these things were something he wanted to do or was doing. He needed to pray more, go to confession and hopefully he would get on track. This was a major setback, especially since he looked forward to seeing the new girl in church every Saturday. She sat ahead of him to the left about six pews. He could look at her throughout mass and hoped she would notice him, especially as lector.

Nobody returned the book to the priest and never commented about it but when he came across a book on human sexuality he opened it up. To his great surprise there where pictures of nude men and women, and men's sexual organs ejaculating. This was quite a curious book to be in the house of a priest. When the priest saw the book that no one should be allowed to read, he calmly asked him to place it back on the shelf.

Since Nobody was a trusting sort of person, he, without realizing it, felt people were good and would not do him any harm. The only people he knew who harmed him were his parents and his friend down the road who picked someone else as a friend over him. This would be a theme in his life as he got older, but there is plenty of time for that part of the story. His parents however were the major contributors. All their actions—fighting, getting hurt by them during their fights, lying or keeping silent about what was really going on in the house—all verified that being home was not safe. Nobody found his solace working for other people and getting recognition from them, riding his bike or walking in the woods. He definitely always wanted to be part of something and made to feel special. That was one of his major driving forces in his life. He would do good things to prove his worthiness and then he would be appreciated and liked.

As Nobody's journey through this summer continued, it was not out of character for the priest to bring some of the altar boys to the movies. Nobody had wanted to go from the beginning, but was hesitant to ask. Then one day the priest asked if he wanted to go and Nobody was excited beyond belief. They went to the movies, talked, ate popcorn and had a great time. It was a late afternoon movie and when they got back it was still not dark. The priest was tired and because of some of the work done around the house his back hurt and he needed to lie down. Upstairs outside of the priest's bedroom was a loft of sorts where he had his stereo and sit down area. This was the same area his mother, sister and he sat down with the priest to discuss his father a while back. There was not an actual door which could close; it was more of an extended archway with the bed tucked into the corner. Nobody has always enjoyed music, so he asked if he could turn on the stereo. He put on the music and volunteered to rub the priest's back. The priest said that would be great and he took off his shirt and Nobody rubbed his back as he lay on the bed. It wasn't a big deal to Nobody as he was glad he could help and he liked the priest; however after a while, he realized the sun was starting to set, so he left and went home, not realizing how close he was to an unfortunate incident. This happened close to the beginning of school so, with the excitement of another school year, girls on his mind and another new neighbor with a kid a little older than him, he had plenty of activities to keep him occupied. Nobody's relationship with the priest slowly withered as he was moving into his teenage years.

Truth #9 Nobody wanted to be good in God's eyes.

Truth #10 Nobody should be wary of the Priest.

Myth #20 Nobody believes everyone is trustworthy.

Episode 6

Somebody to Love

S eventh grade, Confirmation classes, his hair, his small stature and his new friend all guided him through the new phase of Nobody's life. To go to school Nobody had to ride bus #82 every morning. While his new neighbors were moving in down the street he never really had time to get to know the older boy. However, they rode the bus together, so it was the perfect opportunity to introduce himself. They sort of hit it off. His new friend was much bigger and in Nobody's eyes a good-looking guy that every girl would like. Nobody felt it would be a good idea to be his friend. They started off playing catch after school and went fishing for Northern Pike in the Little Salmon River. His new friend was pretty cool too. He listened to music that Nobody thought was different and edgy. The days of the Bay City Rollers were over. It was Nazareth, Blue Oyster Cult, Rush and Kiss. This was just the thing he was looking for; this made him cool as well. So he and his new friend played a lot together. He knew that his friend was playing with him more out of default than really liking him, but to Nobody that did not matter. He could tell people at school he was friends with him and since he was cool that would mean, in some sort of way, so was Nobody.

Entering puberty, Nobody became more self-conscious. His hair had to be perfect, and because he had straight hair he needed hair spray to keep it in place. Not just a little hair spray, a lot. He was obsessed with how he looked. There was no way he could look bad. The last thing he wanted to be was ugly, that would be the worst thing. If he was ugly then surely no one would like or love him as a boyfriend. He was still getting picked on a bit and a couple of times he would get into fights. But there was something new and interesting he started doing— he started arranging fights between people. He liked watching other people fight but did not like fighting himself and every time he got into a fight it was because he was jumped or sucker punched and had no choice. He needed people around that he thought would protect him from those things. So he started passing information back and forth between kids until a fight broke out. It was a weird feeling but if people were fighting around him he was not the subject of tyranny against him like in his house. He then associated himself with a fighter and if people knew that, they would be less likely to bother him.

Myth #21 Nobody feels safe if other people are fighting.

After Christmas, it was time for Confirmation classes at the priest's house. It had been a while since Nobody had been over, but what was really a surprise was the girl he had seen at church was going to get confirmed with him. Nobody was able to finally talk to her without his parents around and after a few meetings, she said she would be his girlfriend. They talked on the phone a lot and he wrote her letters, since she went to a different school. During breaks at confirmation class they would go out around the wraparound porch and kiss. He was in Heaven. He felt like he was some-body. He could not stop thinking about her. Since it was winter he really could only see her at Confirmation class or church, but once spring hit he was able to ride his bicycle to her house. Nobody thought to himself that he could even marry this girl. As long as she was his girlfriend all would be fine, he would just have to convince her he was the right choice.

Myth #22 Nobody thinks to be someone you must be liked.

Every day after school, weather permitting, he would ride over and spend time with her. One time they were up in her room and she was sit-ting against the wall as Nobody was kissing her. Nobody pulled away and she spread her legs towards him. She had jeans on, but in a split second,

Nobody was paralyzed. He was not sure what to do and just like when he was trying to call the police, no matter what decision he made he knew it would be wrong. If he did something with her, God would be mad and if he didn't she may not like him anymore. He had an invitation and he did not take it. She looked at him differently when he did not make a move towards her. He was scared and excited all at the same time. He just kissed her and then, as if on cue, her father came home, so Nobody took off and bicycled home.

This went on for a while and after confirmation, he still spent time with her, but he heard that she also had a boyfriend at her school. He asked her about it. She denied it and said that the other boy just liked her but it troubled Nobody. He knew what she said but deep down he did not believe her. He wrote her letters that spoke about his love for her. It was all good stuff, meant to convince her that all she had to do was pick him. To Nobody this was about having a girlfriend, not being in love. If she left him for another, it would be a reflection on him. It didn't matter that she had another, she just had to change her mind and all would be forgiven. Nobody wanted to be in love, AND that was what he thought he should feel if she liked him. He found out the boy's name and ran into him a couple of times and as with everything, Nobody compared himself to him. He was a little bigger and he had buddies with him all the time. During an afternoon visit to her house, they cut Nobody's tire on his bike. It never occurred to him that she invited this to transpire between the two of them. Nobody was angry with the other boyfriend and never her. She was innocent and needed direction to see that Nobody should be picked and she should tell the other guy to get lost. During this whole episode, it never occurred to him to break up with her. He just kept being second fiddle to the other guys while she got what she wanted, which was attention.

Myth #23 Nobody believes you can convince someone to love you.

As time passed, things eventually changed because they were attending different schools. His older buddy was still a factor; they hung out and did a lot of fishing. They did the crazy sort of things boys do. They found a snake near a shed and they started messing with it. There was a big huge tree in the middle of the field next to some junk vehicles. They decided to take the snake throw it on top of the tree and watch it make its way down to the ground. There was an old bus. Nobody teased his friend saying that there was no way he could throw that snake on the top of the tree. Well he started winding that snake up and he threw that snake to the top of that tree. They both laughed at how that snake flew. Then Nobody challenged him to see who could reach the bus first. Off they went. There they were flying through the tall grass at break speed, and as they came up to the bus, Nobody threw his hands out in front of him to brake his full speed run against the bus. He didn't see a screw protruding out and his hand was headed toward it. He never understood who in their right mind would put a screw to hold a license plate from inside of a bus. Nobody's palm met the screw in the meatiest part of his hand below the thumb. When he pulled his hand out, there wasn't just a hole in his hand, but innards came out as well. The first thing Nobody said was that he could not tell his mother. It was such a normal response that he wasn't thinking about what he was saying. His friend said he had no choice but to tell his parents.

"Dude that is awful. You can't hide it from them."

As he proceeded to go home with his hand bleeding and thumping, Nobody knew what was going to happen and it did. As soon as he walked through the door, there is the sudden, "What happened? Complete pandemonium as his mother was rinsing out the wound with water, questioning him on how he could have been so careless. So the normal cycle started. Nobody is hurt, he is wincing in pain and because he cannot keep his feelings to himself, she is upset. Nobody is told repeatedly to hold still and to keep quiet. When her verbal efforts fail, Nobody is hit. As always, she had to think about what to do next.

Myth #24 Nobody gets punished for getting hurt by accident.

Now that Nobody was in the eighth grade he still liked to arrange fights. He was still picked on and invariably got into occasional fights of his own. He still needed a girlfriend and his former girlfriend was still in the shadows. As his taste in music was expanding and his wants and desires were as well, it wasn't long before he tried smoking pot and drank Peppermint Schnapps on a ski trip. Not a lot happened. The pot, he came to figure later, was not that good so there was no real effect, but there was a sense of coolness in the air around him. It was time to ask his Catholic girlfriend to a dance. Nobody was truly looking forward to bringing his on and off again Catholic girlfriend to the dance. If people here at this school saw the type of girl he had from another school, well the effect could be rippling. She was good looking. However, life isn't always that pleasant. His buddy down the road had a chat with his parents like normal kids should. These parents actually sat with their kids and discussed current event topics, things Nobody soon realized were real life. They asked him if he had tried any drugs or drank. What do you suppose he did? He told the truth and said Nobody had as well. Obviously this was one time he got in trouble, for good reason, but he was grounded from the dance. Nobody was a mess, his stomach hurt, and he was crying and felt utterly betrayed by his friend. However, with the dance a day away he had to get on the phone and tell his Confirmation two-timing Catholic girlfriend, that he could not go.

Being emotional he cried through the whole call, not too cool for a tough guy and from that moment on, she was no longer part of his life and it was his buddy's fault.

Truth #11 Nobody is betrayed.

The anger that Nobody felt towards his old friend was astronomical. There were stare downs as they passed each other in school. His old friend acted as though nothing he did was wrong. He did not get into trouble himself. It was not until then that he saw his friend for what the relationship truly was. He could see they were never really friends, just acquaintances who only had each other to play with during the summer months. His friend was much handsomer and people liked him better. He was bigger, girls liked him. Nobody was just someone to do things with in the neighborhood. Why should he think he was someone special?

Nobody lost three things the day his friend was honest with his parents. Nobody lost a friend and didn't understand why, his first two-timing girlfriend, and he was losing himself. All he wanted was for people to like him and think he was great. So back to the books it was; at least with school he did not have to rely on anyone. It was a zero sum gain; he received what he put into it. His grades never let him down and they were there to say he was someone, and the better the grade the better he was.

Episode 7

I've Got Two Tickets to Paradise

S oon he discovered what the teenage book on sexuality had described as the sin of sex alone. With everything going on in his life, which now consisted of reading for hours, schoolwork, playing chess, and riding his bike to nowhere it did not take long for him to realize that what this book had described as a sin wasn't so bad after all. He wasn't hurting anyone. He knew it was bad based on what the book said, but the only thing that really bothered him about this was that his grandfather would see what he was doing from Heaven. He would just go to confession be absolved of his sin and try to do better.

He was totally obsessed about the idea of having a girlfriend. What would all that really feel like once he found someone who loved him? He believed a girlfriend would solve all his problems, forever. Now that he was in the ninth grade, girls were looking better all the time. There was a problem though. Nobody truly was in his own world; he really did not know how to even belong to a group. He had guys he hung with in Chess Club. He tried to hang with the jocks and then the potheads. He had played basketball in seventh grade, but he was too small and did not play with others. He just never knew what to say or do when the topics of conversation stopped. He could only talk about what he did. He got his parents to buy him a weight set so he could make his arms look bigger. That might change the way people looked at him.

He started listening to Van Halen, and a bunch of other bands. He would listen for hours trying to picture himself being on that stage and getting lost in the music. In the winter he still skied with his parents. He did enjoy that. It was him against the slopes. It was one thing that he was truly not embarrassed about and he was very good at. He would talk to girls on the slopes, ride with them up the lift, and have hot coco in the lodge to warm up. He just knew that sooner or later he would have a girlfriend. The problem here was the girls he liked were always not in his school. He wanted a girlfriend in his school that he could kiss in front of her locker so people would see.

There were plenty of issues to keep Nobody occupied in his head. There was still fighting in the house and Nobody kept to himself a lot of the time. His mother would still badger his father until he agreed with her. Nobody could not understand why he stayed with her. His father couldn't even say no to her without voices being raised. If he disagreed with his mother, a fight was soon to erupt. There was always hell to pay when he tried to say no to some of the smallest of things. Once his mother was mad everyone had to take cover.

What is important to note is that Nobody didn't like conflict when it was directed towards him.

He was extremely uncomfortable because he had internalized everything happening around him. He believed in some way that he was the cause of the anger around him. He also believed that if he said the wrong thing, anger would get turned towards him.

With all of the things Nobody could not do or be, the things he had control over was how to be perfect in the site of others if just by glance. Nothing could be out of place, his hair, no pimples, his grades, because if something was, it would mean something was wrong with him. He would hear years later you only have one opportunity for a first impression and Nobody was living it out. He needed to make sure he had the right sneakers, jeans, and jean jacket just so he could fit in. He was so tired of being on the outside and feeling different did not help. He could at least fix the outside so no one would get a glimpse of the inside. He just wanted to be like the other kids in his class who had it all together. The harder he tried, the greater he failed. Nothing was ever good enough. The way he saw himself in the mirror was frightening.

One day in class one of the guys behind him hit him on the side of his head. Now this kid was uglier than Nobody, but everyone was listening to him at that moment and that was all that mattered. The next thing Nobody knows this guy starts telling the whole class that Nobody has a ton of hairspray and his hair is completely stiff and that it felt like a helmet of hair. It was true, Nobody never thought anyone would touch his hair but as fast as he could, Nobody left the room to use the bathroom and messed his hair up so he could say the kid was a liar. There was no way anyone could find out that he had to use hairspray to keep his hair perfect. If they did then they would know he wasn't. When he returned to the class, he acted as though the other boy was lying, and was just harassing him. All he could do was play it out to the bitter end and say that boy was lying.

Truth #12 Nobody lies to protect himself.

As Nobody was becoming more desperate for a girlfriend, he started looking at girls and started trying to figure out which ones he could ask out at an upcoming dance. There were plenty around to ask so one day, he started asking girls if they would go out with him. He would just go up to them and say, "Would you go out with me?" There was no feeling around it; they were cute so he asked one and then another. It should be just as easy as saying yes, make up your mind that you like him and start from there. Then after a series of rejections over the course of a couple of days, one girl said yes. This was great. They would go to the dance; he could kiss her behind the bleachers. The day was starting to look up. She seemed happy too, until two days later. In the hall, she walked up to him and asked why he had asked four other girls to the dance as well. It was more than four but who's counting. Nobody did not have an answer, as usual. All of a sudden he became much smaller and he honestly did not know why. He just knew he wanted to go to the dance with a date and he felt he couldn't go alone. In the end she is the one he wanted and he had hoped she would like him, but it seemed she did not feel the same. Once again Nobody was alone and ashamed for how he had acted. What he needed was a good story to rescue his reputation because, by the way she was talking loudly in the hall, everyone heard what she was saying and Nobody was forever doomed with girls. Now that this girl broke it off, he needed to figure out a way to stop feeling the way he was feeling.

Myth #25 Nobody thinks loves is based on outside appearances only.

Truth #13 When it comes to other people's feelings, Nobody is clueless.

People sometimes do and say things to illicit a response to make themselves feel better. If the feelings of those around them change to something more positive, then all is good for the moment. So it is with Nobody, he had a need for people to like him or at least think highly of him. If they liked him then they would be more inclined to invite him into their group. Just like Rudolph with the Reindeer games, Nobody couldn't stand it when people called him names or were indifferent towards him. He had a need to be validated. This is what fueled some of his lies. This need to be validated was the reason he said and did the things he did. His life that year was moving forward. It still was not going as he'd hoped; he didn't have a girlfriend, school was hard and he had no idea who he was. One thing was for certain: he didn't like who he thought he was. So a new legend about Nobody needed to be launched. He needed people to think he was a tough guy.

Since he went to church in the neighboring town and he did mingle with kids from that school—a rival of his own—he had the makings of a story. The local funeral operator attended the same church with his family. They were well-to-do and Nobody believed they had everything. This made Nobody envious. Nobody had an opportunity to occasionally play hockey in the driveway with the funeral director's son. The son also played basketball for the rival school. It was during gym class one day that some of his former teammates from his short-lived basketball career where standing around, when Nobody attempted to join in the conversation. Ignored and shunned, Nobody asked them if they had remembered the funeral director's boy from the other school. Immediately they said yes. Nobody started describing how he managed to get into an argument and subsequently get into a fight which Nobody won. Eyebrows were raised. Since Nobody had gotten into some fights (even if it was by being sucker punched,) the story did have a bit of truth to it.

Nobody had an internal belief that if you were from another school you would look at those students as rivals with disdain and not socialize with them especially where sports were involved. This was a line of reasoning he was starting to internalize in all his relationships. Just like with his first friend with the mini-bike, he believed his loyalty to the friendship excluded other friends. Likewise, it was easy to bridge that gap here. If Nobody felt he should not like players from other teams, then he assumed the rest of his former team members would feel the same way or have no opportunity to validate the story.

It was an interesting phenomenon; it never occurred to him that someone could be friends with kids on an opposing team. In Nobody's world they were automatically an enemy for living and going to school somewhere else. If you were on a team why would you talk with them, it didn't make sense.

This belief system was so strong it guided him. This is why he spent so much time trying to make people like him. If they liked him, then automatically they would continue without a change of heart. It would be a fact and everyone must believe the facts.

Myth #26 Nobody believes relationships should be absolutes.

Truth #14 Relationships have varying expectations not absolutes.

Things were starting to change rapidly. Nobody was not going around asking girls if they would go out with him anymore. He was not getting into a lot of trouble at his house because his father and mother were focused on trying to move back to Maine. This was actually exciting for Nobody. He wanted a new start, a way to begin again and learn from all his mistakes. He would not have to worry about his own history and try to create new legends that outshined his mistakes (of which people continually reminded him.) He could begin tenth grade at a new school, make new friends and, if he played his cards right, have a girlfriend. However, one item still lingered: the continuing lie about the funeral director's son. Nobody had an odd sense of perception based on how he could connect the dots from his home. He truly believed that the world that was held within the walls of his school would not intersect with the world of the neighboring rival school, even though they were only ten miles apart. Nobody was in the hallway when one of his former teammates came up to him and said something quite interesting.

"Nobody, we were hanging out the other day and we happened to run into the funeral director's son," he said. The blood started rushing to every extremity in his body as well as each and every facial blood repository as the temperature in the room quickly jumped thirty degrees.

"As we were talking to him, we asked him if he in fact fought you and he laughed and said you never got in a fight and you were definitely lying. What do you have to say?" He boldly inquired in front of a lot of people.

Nobody was paralyzed with fear, knowing he could not handle being found out or face anyone, said calmly, "I am telling the truth. Whether he wants to admit it or not is not my fault. No one likes to admit losing a fight."

Nobody held onto his legend. His ex-teammate looked at him with a dull stare and with an unforgiving shake of the head, he walked away. Within a week, Nobody's value had diminished greatly. He walked around the school, afraid to look people in the eye. He knew they knew about the lie and he could not hide from the truth. So when he came home and his parents said they were moving to Maine once school let out, Nobody was more excited than anybody. He could leave this entire scene behind him and start over. No one would miss him.

Preparing to move back to Maine was like sunshine on Nobody's shoulders. It was like the flowers blooming in the spring. You knew the flowers were coming out but you could not quite picture the splendor until they actually appeared. They would captivate your vision once they blossomed. Nobody didn't have a care in the world. He felt great relief because he would never have to face anyone again from this wretched place, especially the kid he said he had beaten up and now knew of his lie. All the kids that picked on him would be history. His new friends would know him only for what he showed them. He would be cool, he would try new things, he would only listen to the best music. He knew he could be the 'somebody' he wasn't. This was exactly what he needed for his life to get back on track. New York was the illness and Maine would be the cure.

Myth #27 Nobody's world would be perfect once they move.

Part II

The ID Factor

Episode 8

New Kid in Town

They moved to a small city which seemed enormous but Nobody knew really wasn't and they got a second floor apartment. What was neat about this place was Nobody's room was way in the back. The buildings here were extremely thin, long and averaged three to four floors. They were all wooden and fifty percent of the buildings seemed like they would sag and give way. In Nobody's apartment you actually had to go through a bathroom to get to his room. There was also a storage room on the floor that had the same unfinished look and feel as the apartment attic of his childhood. This was like the apartment crawl space that he could never go play in. It had the same kind of vertical brown; wooden 2x4's as well as horizontal wooden ones. It was neat but he didn't think about it very long; it just had an appeal to it.

The first thing Nobody did was go down to the community center and find out what activities were there that he could participate in before his sophomore year started. They had tennis. This was perfect! He signed up for lessons, bought a wooden tennis racket and started playing. This was actually a sport he liked. He met a lot of new kids. Nobody still wanted to be noticed. So he decided that he needed to have white shorts and shirt just like the pros wore. He probably needed a backup racket too, just in case. Every day as he left his house on his bike Nobody noticed his neighbor across the street. His neighbor had long hair and was on his porch a lot. Nobody met new girls and he even found out that at the corner store, he could sneak to the magazine rack to view the various articles that displayed the bodies of beautiful women, until the store manager told him to get out of his store or buy something.

Nobody liked this town. It was much better that living in the country. He could steal money from his mother's purse and go down to Luiggi's and have some spaghetti. He listened to music on the radio. He was finally free to be somebody other than who he was and everyone seemed to like him. As the new school year approached, he was starting to play a fair game of tennis. He entered little tournaments and it gave him something to brag about even though he did not win. He even had a short little fling with a girl who was very nice. She was great, but he could never see himself married to her so he broke up with her gently.

School started. New people. College prep courses. This was a big school and it had everything. Most importantly, no one knew him. The first month or so went well. Nobody was able to blend in pretty well with his classmates. Nobody did have a talent to be able to mingle with the jocks, the geeks and potheads. He had to survive and he needed to be liked as those parts of him had not changed. He was slowly making friends.

After school one day a kid from his class asked him if he wanted to go outside and smoke a joint. Nobody thought it would be great to get to know somebody. With a mindset of "off into a new adventure," Nobody walked out of the building. This wasn't the first time Nobody had smoked, but he hadn't smoked since the time he got in trouble. Not understanding what the true effect would be since his first experience was not at all thrilling, he was quite amazed at the feeling he had after the drugs kicked in. After they were done, Nobody and his new friend went back inside and noticed one of the cheerleaders at her locker. Since Nobody needed to be noticed, he spoke in just above a whisper so she could hear what he said as they passed her. As he commented about their adventure, she looked and him with that curly hair and those big brown eyes and said, "I didn't know you smoked pot?" Whether she was shocked, impressed or disgusted it did not matter, one look from her and Nobody knew he was finally noticed and *that* was everything.

Truth #15 Nobody was noticed.

A completely new world opened up to Nobody. All of a sudden he had a new friend who had more friends. He was liked because of his association with the partying crowd and so he was 'off and running.' He would be focused on partying while staying under the radar. He was even proving to himself that he actually did better in school 'high' than when he was not. It slowed his mind down just enough to make a difference. Everything negative he had heard about smoking pot did not apply to him. So with his grades still high and improving, it wasn't hard for him to rationalize building a strong argument for continued drug use based on a platform of a self imposed criteria, which clearly leaned in his favor. All he had to do was keep from getting into trouble and obey curfew. This was not a problem; one thing Nobody was good at was following the rules. He liked to think he was honest amongst thieves.

For the next couple of months, he did different things: skiing, attended high school hockey games, and went to dances. Eventually his family moved into a new house and everything was starting to take form. He also met his soon-to-be best buddy in the whole world who happened to live just down the street from Nobody. His new friend liked to smoke and so did his brother. Their mom was great. She was a very loving and understanding person. Nobody and his best friend were inseparable. After school, they would listen to music and smoke pot. One thing Nobody learned rather quickly was when he bought pot no one was ever mad at him. Nobody wanted to make sure he had the best stuff as well. It was all about the experience.

Nobody got a job and started working in food service at a local hospital, where he was exposed to more kids his age. All of a sudden, he was actually cool. Despite his small size and remaining idiosyncrasies, Nobody was still cool. Since he partied, it seemed like everyone ignored how inadequate he looked- or how he truly felt. If he had pot, he had friends. However, even in this environment, Nobody still felt it was important to do a good job but, just like at home, if he did everything that was required, no one would notice the other things he was doing or care. Nobody's number one goal was to be well received whenever he entered a room. With that comes opportunity. Someone had mentioned at work one night that if you ate a tablespoon of nutmeg you could get high. Reaching another state instead of reality was always a better option than the life he felt, so Nobody endured the discomfort associated with eating plain nutmeg without anything to wash it down in the hope of gaining admiration from those around him. Everyone had a good laugh, and since Nobody was starting to adapt well to peculiar circumstances, he played it off well. It wasn't long after his quest to be a 'cool guy' that the head of the food service department's son let on that he too was a weekend warrior. There was a big company picnic planned, so Nobody and a few others, under the direction of the director's son, skimmed off the food for the picnic. The spoils of their efforts were lobster, clams and corn. That Saturday they would all meet in the neighboring town at the apartment of the department head's son and enjoy the fruits of their heist. The apartment was quite the place. It turned out to be right across the street from Nobody's uncle on his dad's side.

Myth #28 Nobody needs to do things others are doing to be accepted.

His uncle was ten years younger than Nobody's father and he was much different. He seemed to be more in line with the times than his father was. Nobody really had no idea who his uncle was or what he was really like, but he did know that his uncle was currently building his own house with his wife in the mountains. However, one time when he did visit Nobody's family in New York, he brought him his first ten-speed, the same one whose tire was slit by those boys at his first girlfriend's house.

As the party took off, the food was good and Nobody was exposed to a new music group he had never heard of before, the Grateful Dead. As the festivities got under way, Nobody and a girl there were attempting to fit in and so decided that they would try Tequila. After nine shots each and bong hits out of a 3-foot contraption, they both entered into higher altitudes together. Within the hour, they both were 'dry heaving' out on the street. As luck would have it Nobody ended up on his uncle's porch, who inevitably came outside to see what the commotion was about. Upon realizing who was taking the liberty of holding up the porch so it wouldn't fall over, they agreed that it would be their little secret. Finally, someone would not turn on him. So once Nobody was able to operate his bicycle, he went back home in time for curfew, avoiding the possibility of trouble. He had his Visine and potato chips ready before he went in just in case his mother happened to be up and inspected him.

Episode 9

Losing My Religion

Back at school and at work, the topic of conversation was the party. Nobody had a hard time believing how differently people were treating him. He was still small, but now he was on equal footing. The party was a success! People were accepting him! Nobody started to get to know people, he started getting invited to events, and he was still smoking pot. It made him feel good. He didn't really like to drink, but he did to a point. Feeling wobbly and disoriented was not something he liked; he needed to understand everything that was going on around him. As long as he stayed within these parameters, he had a handle on life and, he assured himself, if he kept doing the things he was doing, he was sure to be liked and part of the crowd. The last thing Nobody wanted was to be alone. He would do whatever it took not to be.

Nobody was finally starting to become somebody. His parents were leaving him alone since his grades were good and he was not getting into trouble as much. He was starting to be able to talk to girls now, even though he still did not have a girlfriend. He still wanted to do the right thing and have people like him. To his surprise, life here in Maine was nothing compared to life in New York.

He still felt somewhat ashamed that his grandfather would see the things that Nobody was doing from Heaven. God put pot on the Earth, he justified. If God didn't want people to experience this, why would He put it on the Earth to begin with? Pot had to be a gift from God since it helped Nobody deal with life. In fact, he started believing that maybe a lot of things he heard in church might actually be wrong. What he saw outside of the church did not resemble real life at all. As long as he did not hurt anyone how could this be harmful? God made sex, pot, and all these feelings inside of us, so why not enjoy them? All the church wanted him to do was to keep everything under wraps. The message from God obviously had gotten twisted from the church. Life was here for us to enjoy. All the things he heard from teachers, news and magazines did not add up either. How could everyone be wrong? People just would not lie about these things. Sex before marriage is not a sin, after all. There were many examples of people living together before marriage. Get with the times! Find out if you like someone first before you get married. You definitely do not want to be unhappy like Nobody's parents. There was no way *that* was going to happen to Nobody.

There was, however, something different going on inside of him trying to make sense of these conflicting messages and to what end? Everything up to this point in his life was painful. He should be able to do what he wanted as long as he played by the rules. This was his life and he only had one to live. It seemed that everything he heard his parents say at home was completely opposite from what he saw outside in the real world. This was the battle that raged inside of him: Who should he believe?

His mother was still running the house; it was her way or no way. You had to agree with her opinions. It was always about what she wanted and at times he could not breathe. She would ask questions over and over. When Nobody would say that he answered it already, she would say, "I am your mother and if I want to ask I can. There is nothing wrong with that." If they were still at odds over an opinion and Nobody would not agree with her, she would plead—and even cry until his father relented and told Nobody he was wrong and that his mother was right. This happened repeatedly. If she wasn't happy, no one was. Nobody still could not understand after all these years how his father could stay married to her. They still fought and sometimes after the fights, she suggested that they should go into the bedroom. It was after one of these fights, while Nobody was sitting on the stairs between the living room and family room of their raised ranch with his sister, that Nobody believed he heard his mother tell his father in

French to prove he loved her. Whether he heard it or not, this was not how love should be. It should be spontaneous. Nobody vowed to himself that he would *never* let his life turn into something like this.

They accused Nobody of not spending any time at the house anymore. Why should he? The times that he did stay home and talk, his father would still bring up little comments like he acted like a fairy and a homo or that people who did drugs were stupid and would end up with no job and brain dead. They had no idea that he was proving them wrong. The best thing Nobody could do was keep his mouth shut and stay away as much as possible. So he went skiing, chopped wood outside (which Nobody loved to do,) went roller-skating, and only returned home to eat dinner at 5 PM every night, if he was not working. After that he studied, listened to music and would sneak an occasional toke.

Myth #29 Nobody was proving that drugs are not harmful.

As mentioned earlier, if he did get involved in conversations with his parents, they always ended up in fights. Everyone would yell. It almost seemed like the one who yelled the loudest was right. Many times his mother would say that the problems in their marriage were Nobody's fault. If he would just do as they ask they would not have all these problems. Nothing was ever good enough even when he tried his hardest. Every idea he had was shot down. His father, at times, would say all that Nobody cared about was being the best at everything. That was true, but why was that bad?

Myth #30 Nobody's worldview can't be wrong.

Truth #16 Nobody's mother blames her oldest kid for her marriage problems.

Nobody was following the rules: he kept his grades up, came home on time, kept his room clean, and was preparing for college. No, he would not be a failure. According to them, all of his friends where 'bad influences' and the music he listened to was 'awful.' In his parent's eyes, every path he walked along led nowhere. The only thing that would reap any benefit would be for him to go to college. Eventually, in his mind, all the craziness would end and they would be proud of him for *something*. Nobody was becoming his own man, and he would be somebody, and right now that somebody was a partying college prep high school kid who excelled at partying and his schooling. Nobody started believing that God/church may not be the single most important thing in his life anymore.

Truth #17 Nobody wants to get away from the family.

Episode 10

Crash and Burn

As his sophomore year was weaving its way into spring, the breaks in the cold were always a great reminder that the snow would soon melt. The third quarter was drawing near to an end, which meant that the book reports, essays, and tests were not too far away. Nobody still loved school work or better yet, good grades that he used to validate himself. He now had a mound of work he needed to get started on. It was important for him to always get his work done on time, if not in advance. Even at this age he had a fear of what would happen if he was not prepared. . .a fear he would have throughout his life.

It was customary that on beautiful days like these when the atmosphere in the house was of normal grade and the temperature outside was in the fifties, the family would take car rides to some unknown destination. Do something to unwind and get out of the house they were confined to during the coldest parts of the winter. Nobody's father asked if the family would like to go for one of these rides, to which Nobody said that he would prefer to stay home and work on his projects. So off they went, leaving Nobody home, listening to the latest album of the B'52s.

The weather was extremely beautiful and it was as if it was calling his name. After an hour of work, his best friend's brother called and asked Nobody if he was doing anything. Nobody, torn between working and going on a bike ride, relented and chose the latter. It was a gorgeous day, the temperature was not only perfect for their impromptu activity but for spring skiing as well. How could he say no?

This day would not be complete if they did not enjoy another of God's wonders to absorb the full effect, so they smoke a joint. Riding the bicycle his uncle had given him a few years back, they were on the road, with no particular place to go. As they crossed over the main drag, they decided to go visit another friend that Nobody was not too familiar with since he went to the Catholic school his mother had gone to. It was a cool street that went down a hill and had two right angle turns. Nobody, who was always up for a race, like the day in which his hand was impaled by the license plate screw said, "Race you to the bottom."

Pedaling hard and taking the first left turn on the inside, it was neck and neck. As they both approached the second turn and tried to capture the curve's full support to the right, they were within a whisper's range of each other. As each of them were trying to gain the closest proximity of the curve's inside edge, Nobody who was on the outside, touched his friend and the momentary touch shook Nobody just enough to cause his rear wheel to slide forward, catch the ground and flip Nobody forward. Traveling (or better yet flying) down a steep hill, falling forward at 11 o'clock, Nobody was able to break his fall with only his right hand. His left hand got caught underneath him as he hit chest first. Instead of his clothes absorbing the road, the topside of the left hand took it all. As Nobody stood up he saw his mangled bike. Then he looked at his hand. Most of the skin had been rubbed off, his knuckles were bleeding. There wasn't any blood on his hand, only flesh with rocks imbedded into it. Then the blood started flowing from the edges. In a state of shock, his friend moved his bike to the side of the road, and they started walking to Nobody's Godfather's house, two blocks away.

Noticeably upset upon their arrival, his Godfather called Nobody's parents. Once his parents had returned from their afternoon drive and were reached, Nobody was told they would be right over. Nobody felt the pain and nausea consume him. All they could do was wait for his folks to arrive.

As his father walked in the door, he said, "It serves you right" and then the barrage of accusations started.. "You should have stayed home. You lied to us," his father said. Nobody's uncle, who was standing by and listening, was ready to argue on Nobody's behalf, because he had already witnessed acts his parents had performed in the past. Nobody explained what happened and said that it was an accident and that he was only taking a break. Arguing ensued and Nobody stormed out to the back of the house and went halfway down the steps. His uncle joined in and started trying to reason with Nobody's father and mother, explaining that Nobody was still a kid and it was just an accident, kids are kids and these things happen. Instead of arguing about why it happened, he told Nobody's father he should be on the way to the hospital. At least his Godfather understood and was there trying to protect him.

As they were leaving, Nobody asked if they could get his bike first and so they drove to the spot where the accident occurred. Nobody's father told him to get out of the truck and put the bike in the back of the truck. With hands bleeding and mostly skinless from road rash, Nobody picked up the bicycle. He couldn't help but see the look of disgust on his father's face. Nobody had tears in his eyes. He did not understand what he had done wrong. All he knew was that he hated his family.

Myth #31 Nobody should make sure he never gets hurt.

Truth #18 Nobody wishes he was truly loved by his family.

Truth #19 Nobody's father despises his son.

Episode 11

The Godfather

Life took a desperate turn with stone removal, washing, rinsing, shots, stitches, painkillers, a full hand wrap and absolutely no grace from his immediate family. Nobody didn't want to live in that house anymore. A week later Nobody visited his uncle and talked about all that had happened—how he had to pick up the bike, how his mother had gotten mad at him since the accident and took a swipe at his hand, hitting his hand—and they discussed the future. His Godparents said that if he wanted to, Nobody was more than welcome to move in with them.

It was too good to believe. It was a small house, but they could work it out. He was excited and the future was starting to look better. He had been talking to a new girl, it was looking like he would get away from his parents and maybe he would live somewhere that no one criticized him at every turn. The plan was that his uncle would go speak to his parents, explain the plan and they would take it from there.

So the big night was looming ahead. Nobody was anxious and like many other times while he was waiting for something, Nobody paced in his room and kept looking out of the window. He was always ready and he was always waiting. It was a strange habit he had. When someone said they would come over at a certain time, Nobody would obsessively check the window waiting for them to turn up. If it was his friends, and they would be late he would go completely bezerk in his mind. If someone said they would be there at seven, well they should be there at seven. The problem was that while he was waiting he could not do anything else to keep himself occupied. He was consumed with anticipation and worry, and he would always wonder if they forgot about him. The same was happening here, maybe his uncle had forgotten about him. Maybe he changed his mind about him living with him. Maybe he was really not worth loving. He hated this life, and wished he was never born or at least was somebody else.

Eventually, his uncle arrived. In the lower level of the house, everyone was discussing Nobody's life and where he could live. There was yelling and heated discussions. Nobody's mother was accusatory, claiming his uncle wanted to break apart the family. His uncle explaining that it would be OK for Nobody to live with his family, and it might even be better for all parties. As he was sitting in the background listening, Nobody prayed for this quest to become a reality. What would life be like over at his Godfather's house? He knew they loved him; he would not be a problem. He had his cousins who were close to his age.

His uncle/Godfather had done the unspeakable; he had challenged Nobody's parents. He was like the Baptist minister next door back in New York who tried to find out what was going on but couldn't find the way in. However his Godfather was different, he was family and he was not afraid. Nobody respected him for that. His parents talked about loyalty. But what his uncle was doing was what loyalty was all about. Nobody's parents wanted blind loyalty to them. His uncle was loyal to principle. He was the defender of truth and the truth was that Nobody needed saving.

His parents had always thrown him to the wolves. Whether it was being hit for getting hurt, having to lie to cover for his parent's sins, or overhearing that if they got divorced he was the one they casted lots for and now hearing lately that the reason his parent's marriage was suffering was Nobody's fault.

As the discussions continued, Nobody started paying closer attention. A change occurred in the atmosphere. The emotion had left the house; a decision was made. Oh how he hoped he would be able to leave. Everything would be made right if he had this chance. The waiting immobilized him to a state like suspended animation. As the meeting ended his uncle left without saying goodbye. No one had to tell him anything. In the end, his uncle lost the battle. His parents won and nothing was going right. Nobody was still in 'prison.' Why was God letting this happen?

Nobody continued going to school, listening to music and smoking it up. He felt alone in this world and he felt out of place when he was by himself so listening to music and smoking dope helped him escape reality. He hated being alone and the only thing that made him feel like he belonged somewhere was with his partying buddies.

There is a point to be made here; Nobody only felt he was somebody when he was doing drugs. Alone in a sober state he constantly thought about how he needed to be liked by others, because inside he knew he was unlovable the way he was.

Myth #32 Nobody believes he is unlovable just the way he is.

Truth #20 Nobody's parents do not understand that they have isolated him.

Episode 12

Lucy in the Sky with Diamonds

The summer was a true learning experience. Nobody had tried LSD and mushrooms. He was making a name for himself with his friends and he was not afraid to try anything to find an answer to a puzzling question or reach a pinnacle point in his mindful wonderings. As his junior year was fast approaching, Nobody was invited to a party that his best buddy was going to. He could go, but this was a special place and you had to be on your best behavior if you ever wanted to go back. That was the rule.

They were going over to the brother-in-law's of one of his friend's friend. If you wanted to know what partying was all about; this was the place they all said. Since this guy had kids, everyone had to enjoy themselves, but not get carried away. Nobody was sort of nervous, but he was going to go. As they walked up to the place, somewhat loud music was heard, and they entered. There, standing in front of him, over six feet tall and with a bushy head of long hair, was the man who would place him on a path that would change Nobody forever.

There was free-flowing beer. They were making a mushroom stew. The smell of pot was not just in the air it was the essence of the atmosphere. There were different types of bongs: one was about 3 ft. long, a gas mask with a pipe connected to the hose, a V-shaped one, and a variety of smaller pipes. He had never seen so many party items. This was mind-blowing: the music, the stereo, the sound was so clear. Sitting in the living room and just taking in the music was phenomenal. It wasn't the mind-blowing sound with unbelievable clarity, it was the music itself. It wasn't mainstream it was just on target and it reverberated through his soul.

As Nobody said hello to the host, he was amazed at how tall he was. Nobody was afraid he would not be accepted. Nobody was cordial and at every opportunity thanked his host for his hospitality. Nobody hung out for a while and though he was not a big drinker because he hated the wobbly feeling, smoking was what the doctor ordered. As the night continued, Nobody noticed how his host guided the night with the music, taking care of his albums, putting on the right music at the right time, guiding the atmosphere into a new place of realization. God was nowhere to be seen, and it did not matter. Nobody had found what he was looking for. This guy not only knew how to party, but he also sold pot. Not just any type. He was a connoisseur. His particular favorite was Thai stick. And that was the best of the best.

School finally started. Nobody made it over to the party house a couple more times. He made it past the introductory process and would soon be able to go over without an escort. The Drug Dealer and he spoke a lot about different things and Nobody discussed how his family had lived in town for a while before moving to his current house. He spoke of living on Shawmut Street and his new acquaintance perked up for a minute. This was extremely interesting for his dealer. What Nobody had not realized was that this was his neighbor who sat on his porch nursing beers as Nobody drove off on his bike for tennis his first summer in Maine. Nobody was asked a variety of questions. It was an interesting evening, listening to Doctor Dimento and finding that alternate dimension of reality. As the evening ended, Nobody had a strange feeling something was wrong, but could not put his finger on it. He soon forgot about it and he went on his way with his buddies as they walked home for the evening. The howling of the troop probably woke the dead that night. It was one of the best nights Nobody ever had. The rest of the night was spent frolicking about on their way to their respective homes.

The next day at school, one of the long-standing friends of the dealer took Nobody aside near his locker. Nobody was told that he would not be allowed to go over to the dealer's house anymore. The dealer had realized who he was from his previous neighborhood which made him afraid that

Nobody would tell his parents. Nobody was crushed. Why was this happening to him? He didn't do anything wrong. He could be trusted. He was playing by the rules. He was a good person. He wasn't lying that much. He had good grades. He was even proving that drugs did not affect them like his father had said. In fact, he was getting smarter and his grades were actually getting better. He went home on time. He tried to do things that everyone else wanted to do, regardless of what he wanted to do. He was polite and thoughtful. How could he be turned away from this?

Myth #33 Nobody believes he needs to be accepted by a drug dealer to prove self-worth.

Maybe his father was right after all when he had told Nobody that life was ruled by fate. He'd said that fate was another force that seemed to propel events in someone's life. No one had control over fate. It certainly didn't feel like God was around. Nothing was adding up; life was not fair no matter how hard one tried to do the right thing and Nobody was finally realizing he wasn't trying hard enough to be liked. His academic grades were on the rise and if smoking dope was really a benefit, there was absolutely no reason to stop. With all the proof in his corner, how was it that his situation had not changed? Nobody felt he was on the outside looking in.

Myth #34 Nobody has to try harder to be liked and accepted.

Episode 13

Back in the Saddle

A couple months had passed and the holidays were fast approaching. Besides work and school, Nobody still hung out with his friends here and there. There were many times they would contemplate carrying out truly illegal activities, but Nobody would always slip away at the last moment and not take part in them. He just did not want to get in trouble with the police for stealing or going into buildings they were not supposed to be in. Stealing food here and there from work was one thing, but outright theft was where he drew the line. Except for the times he needed to slip a five spot from the register at work. This had gone on for a couple months, as Nobody was in charge of cleaning the cafeteria area. With the register just sitting there, Nobody would hit no sale and help himself to a small cash advance that would surely not be noticed. Besides he needed it. He wasn't doing what some of his other associates had said they had done. This was harmless; he just needed to be sure he was not caught.

One night as he saw the night supervisor walking from the kitchen through the pots and pans dishwashing area, and as Nobody was moving towards the cafeteria, the place he conducted his secret cash withdrawals, Nobody, in one split second, decided not to take any money that evening since she was walking towards him. However, the phone rang. She was responsible for answering the phone; it was one of her primary duties.

Surely she would not let the phone go unanswered. In this moment of 'brilliance,' the ability to connect all the dots pressed him forward, so he hurried into the cafeteria, and hit the no sale button. As his fingers fell gingerly on a measly twenty dollar bill, there she was standing face-to-face with Nobody.

Nobody's fearless attitude quickly diminished into Jell-O. He had had a rocky relationship with this supervisor. She was very picky about cleanliness and would not let workers leave unless the place was spotless. They had had arguments—or better yet disagreements— and she was definitely not his favorite of the food service supervisors. She had made a lasting impression on him and now, she had him where she wanted him.

Nobody was pleading for forgiveness, and asking her to just not say anything. He could tell she was troubled by the whole affair. She called the Food Service Director in and told Nobody that it was no longer in her hands. She felt badly about it. They would have to wait for the Director to arrive. Once he showed up, they decided to let Nobody resign effective immediately. Since Nobody was truly in a non-combative state and he knew he had committed an unforgivable sin, he was just trying to get out of this with minimal bloodshed. Nobody would have to live a lie, because if the truth got out that he were a thief, people would not trust him. Realizing that this was the official story, he was able to say he quit, period. He hated this supervisor anyway. Nobody had no idea or even understood the concept of what "the grapevine" was. He believed the truth would stay in the director's office, but the truth had hit the rumor mill. Even though he said he had quit, deep down inside, when he spoke to some of his old co-workers, he knew they were briefed on the real reason, so instead of a quitter as he hoped the lie would have been perpetuated, he was a thief in the end. Truth has a way of finding light.

As this crisis passed in his life, he still needed to deal with the issue of the drug dealer. How could he get back into his good graces? His mother had made them always send thank you cards to people who had given them gifts, so Nobody thought it may be a good idea if he sent him something. Nobody decided that he would send him a Christmas card. In the card, Nobody wished them a great Christmas, wrote that he was committed to be a great friend— and given the opportunity, he would prove it— and asked if could be allowed to come back over. His plan worked! Nobody was allowed to go over again. Nobody's life was getting back on track and he had a great Christmas. He had a new job, his dealer allowed him over and he was back partying with the majority of his friends again. Maybe the rest of his junior year would not be so bad after all.

There was one thing that bothered Nobody as he indulged in the foray of drug use with his dealer friend. As they partied on an almost nightly basis, not only did Nobody need a friend, but he needed also a source of illegal contraband. The dealer's wife, though she allowed these nightly musings, would go to bed early and leave her husband to dabble in his after-hour indulgences. Being that this drug dealer was a night owl, it wasn't fair to be up all by himself with nothing to do. So that is where Nobody came in. She would tell them explicitly not to start any smoking until his kids were in bed and to keep their voices and the noise level down. It was an odd apartment. The layout was not a normal design that Nobody had seen before. The bedroom and living room were only separated by an arch and not a door so Nobody would see the wife sleeping on a frameless bed from where he sat in the living room. As they indulged into the night, the music was always low and they had to pay attention not to wake his wife. For whatever reason, this always bothered Nobody. When he asked if he should leave, he would be told it was OK and not to worry about it. However, though he continued to feel ill at ease over this subject, Nobody would push away that thought and continue to be versed about life by his dealer/partying associate and friend. It was during these conversations that he learned about sex, how he needed to lose his virginity as soon as possible, what he should expect out of life for a young man at his age, and get what he deserves. Nobody could not quite piece these little messages into proper perspective. He only understood that according to his dealer, he should have had sex by now, because if he was going to go into the military or college as guys his age contemplate, the one thing he needed to have achieved was experiencing the joy of getting laid. Otherwise, he was bound to be picked on by the other guys.

Myth #35 Nobody must have sex in high school to prove his manhood.

Episode 14

I Want a New Drug

With all this pressure to perform and experience things in life, it was bound to happen; Nobody's subtle obsession with having a girlfriend and not just a hand holding girlfriend intensified. His friends had girlfriends and he felt the pressure that he needed one. The advice he was given from his drug mentor and the details his classmates would share about certain intimate details only further intrigued Nobody. As with most encounters in this area, when you least expect to find what you are looking for, there it is. So it was with Nobody.

Following the Christmas season and start of a new semester at school, it was customary to choose an elective that might help bridge the gap or add a certain skill to one's resume for college. The new semester brought with it a chance for new classes and opportunities to meet new girls. Nobody felt typing class would suit his needs. With mounting pressure from his parents to attend college, Nobody was trying to achieve and add something to his skill set that would hopefully impress them. They mentioned West Point. If he got into West Point or some military school he would be better than his father and the debate would be over. He could finally prove he was somebody. The prestige that came with going to a military college brought with it a certain mystique that would help him attain new heights.

There were processes that had to be completed; congressional letters and the list went on. This was something that he felt might bring a sense of accomplishment to his parents. The drum was still beating that only his parents cared for him and that he needed to show his loyalty to the family by not speaking to his uncle. According to his mother all his uncle wanted to do was break up their family. The biggest grudge in family history had begun and Nobody was stuck right smack in the middle. He loved his Godparents and he knew they loved him, but now he had to sneak around to spend time with them. Thus the big secret had begun. Nobody must never admit to talking to his uncle or aunt in fear of getting in trouble or worse— get shut out from his family all together.

As Nobody was looking into different colleges and military college entrance criteria, he noticed one thing: his scores on the SAT were not high enough. His school grades were exceptional, but when it came to standardized tests, Nobody always had a hard time. He knew he would need special help to be accepted by the military school and he had a never-ending lack of confidence. He was not special enough on his own. Yes, it was going to be a long shot.

He also had one more dilemma: Nobody still had a fear of getting into trouble.

As he sat on the edge of his bed, he realized that his good grades were because of the clarity he received when he slowed down enough to think things through. He also knew that he was caught between a rock and a hard place: the clarity came from smoking pot. Nobody had a hard time sitting still since his earliest memories. He was always into something or talking. This was one of the reasons he had such a hard time with friends. He just kept going and going, like the Energizer Bunny. When he smoked pot he was taken down a notch and finally he was able to slow down enough to be like everyone else. He rationalized that he needed to smoke pot and there was no way he could stop. People liked him more when he smoked. If he could not stop and he needed it to help him deal with life, how would he be able to perform at a military school? He was doomed and his fate was sealed.

What started as a plan to be better than everyone else, to become the person his parents wanted him to be, go to West Point and have the prestige that went with that honor he realized that was not in the picture. Instead, he would now just have to go to a regular college and his parents said they had no money to help. He was on his own.

Truth #21 Nobody believes he cannot cope with life without marijuana.

It was still early in the college application process and he had plenty of time to figure out where he would go to school. Besides, he was getting along pretty well now on the outside. His façade was doing quite well. He still kept a lot of his thoughts to himself and as long as no one knew what he really thought of himself, he could easily blend in with jocks, the partiers and the geek squad. This is what kept him sane; there was always a back-up plan. He needed people around him and he needed to feel accepted. His greatest fear was being alone.

He was looking around the typing classroom at his new classmates and, one particular girl in the back row stood out. Inside the room, chairs and tables were set up in horseshoe formation, with an outer and inner U and everyone facing in. He was sitting in the outer row near the top of the U and had a clear view of her as she was sitting almost opposite of him. This was exceptional since he would be able to see her every time he looked up. First he caught her looking at him. Then there was the smile. Then there was the hello. Then, before he knew what was happening, he had finally met the girl and he was propelled into deep infatuation. After a couple of weeks he was head over heels. What he failed to realize at the time, however— and for many years to come—was that she represented only an answer to the empty pit in Nobody's gut. All he had to do was keep it filled.

That is the problem with the world, what do you fill that empty hole in your gut with? Everywhere you turn someone or something is trying to give you something in the hopes you will be satisfied psychologically in a manner to bring peace to your inner self. However, for two teenagers without a solid foundation of a belief in chastity, it was 'game on.'

They were inseparable. They had similar likes and dislikes. He met new friends; he introduced her to his friends. She met all the criteria he had stowed away in his mind. His dealer approved of her and even gave Nobody the signal of approval—the wink. Nobody was somebody. It was all because of the person he had by his side. He had arrived finally. Life was good. Her parents seemed to like him. She even said she loved him!

Better still, she was willing to take their relationship to the next level only after an extremely long month. His life was nearly complete. The only things left were for her to meet his parents. And have sex, of course.

The big day came when Nobody brought his new girl over to the house. The usual formalities were exchanged and it went well considering the fear Nobody felt inside. Everything came down to approval which seemed conditional, based upon his parent's response, she needed to prove herself to them. He did love her and that meant everything to him. So they continued to spend more and more time together. His grades and work never suffered, but the comments started coming from his parents.

"You spend too much time with her."

"You need to spend more time at home and not with her."

"You do not know what you are doing. You're going to ruin your life if you do not get focused on what is important," his mother would say.

His father— in true form— would tell him to listen to his Mother. It didn't matter; nothing he did was good enough. The relationship was something he wanted. It was not their choice. Her parents liked him, she loved him, and if this is what life was all about why did he get so much grief over this?

As they continued to spend time together the time came when they discussed having sex or experimenting. Nobody described what he thought he liked and she said what she wanted. But they knew they had to be careful, since they did not want to end up pregnant. She professed he would be her first and when they finally consummated their relationship, there wasn't any blood. Nobody was confused, but he did not say anything. Maybe he just wasn't big enough. It did not matter, she loved him and she showed him how much. *You wouldn't have sex with someone without loving them and this is something you wouldn't lie about, either. This was too special.* It was easy for Nobody to bridge the gap between love and sex. He rationalized it by thinking that sex was how you professed your love to someone. Now that he had this feeling inside of him he did not want to let go it. Nothing would come between them. She was his and he spent as much time as he possibly could with her. His mother got angrier everyday that went by. Nobody felt complete for the first time in his life and <u>nothing</u> was going to get in the way of that.

Myth #36 Nobody needs love to feel complete.

Truth #22 Nobody knew what lust was, but not love.

As his love life blossomed and they continued to get closer, the barrage of snide comments from his mother increased. It seemed like not a day went by that he didn't hear more comments like, "Are you going to see *HER* again?" "Don't you spend enough time with *HER*?" "Are her parents getting sick of you yet?"

One afternoon as he returned from work and got cleaned up to go out, his parents asked to speak with him.

His father had something in his hand.

His mother said, pointing to his father "What is this?" Realizing she had gone through his room, Nobody replied, "It is a condom."

His father took a pair of scissors, held up the condom, cut it in half and smiled.

"Well I guess you have experienced everything now, big man" his father said.

His mother just stood there in the lower level of the house, with her hands on her hips, his dad sitting on the couch's edge with half a condom and a pair of scissors. His parents looked at him and asked if he had anything to say for himself. Nobody stood there paralyzed. Whether he was justified or not did not matter. He was just there, standing in the firing line, knowing he was screwed, once again.

"The thought of you having sex with that bitch makes my stomach turn. I can't even picture it. That slut is going to ruin your life," his mother said.

Then the rage started. It quickly rose to a boil. Nobody was feeling isolated and was paralyzed. He couldn't respond or react. All he could do was stand there. Without thinking he reached into his pocket, pulled out a roach clip and handed it over to his mother saying, "This is all I have."

All the while he was thinking, *"What am I doing? Why do I feel guilty for loving someone?"*

He had all these feelings that he was doing something wrong. Not so much for having sex with her, because he knew, the rule was waiting for marriage; but that it was wrong that he loved her. This feeling ran deeper than the one he experienced coming home late or talking back and getting in trouble. It was not his fault he loved her. It wasn't a choice, it just was. According to his parents, she was bad for him, but they couldn't make him turn off his love for someone. He couldn't and wouldn't pretend she didn't exist. This is not his uncle she doesn't want him to talk to; this was his girlfriend whom he loved. He wanted to spend the rest of his life with her, but his mother called her a slut and a bitch.

"This is insane! She is not a bitch. She loves me," he told himself.

Then his mother uttered the words that would change his life forever.

"You have to break up with her if you want us to help you with college."

Whoa! This was a switch. They hadn't talked about college like this before. No, they had said they wouldn't help him with college. Now, it was being held out as a sacred artifact. Nobody started crying and went to his room. He held his aching stomach and wondered why were they doing this to him. He got mad. He picked up the phone, called his true love to tell her what happened and left the house.

"Where are you going?" His mother yelled, but he continued to walk away from his house. This was the dress rehearsal.

Episode 15

Eighteen

Nobody did one thing very well. He was a talker and he couldn't keep things to himself. If there was something bothering him, he was an open book. It wasn't long before he was talking about this situation with everyone. He needed allies, people he could lean on during this time. He stayed out of the house as much as he could. He still followed all the rules, except for one; he would not break up with her. The condom-cutting incident when his mother told him that he had better break up with the girl he loved, drove them closer. It was enough that her parents were supportive of their relationship. His buddies and his dealer said it was unfair to hang college over his head, even his best friend's mom was sympathetic to his cause. He was a teenager, and at the end of the day, his folks needed to deal with it instead of trying to hang his future over his head as a means to control him. Needless to say, he was running out of options. It didn't matter what everyone thought. There was however, a priest that his mother said she had always liked. He thought it was the one that had married his parents and she went to speak with him occasionally. Nobody decided that that he would attempt to lay out the entire story to the priest and see if he could get support. Maybe, just maybe the priest could talk to his parents and work things out. As crazy at it sounded, deep down Nobody wanted to have a relationship with his parents. They just needed to admit that they played a part in the family altercations as well. Maybe that was why he turned over the roach clip. Was it just another way to say to them, 'Here I am. Please love me, all of me.'

As Nobody described the situation to the priest, he was tearful. This was not an act to gain sympathy, it was an honest assessment of the facts. He told the truth about everything: his love, his school grades, friends and family, all the outrageous conditions about going to college, the names his mother called his girlfriend, everything. Everything except the drugs. In his mind, Nobody decided that there was no way this was all on his head. At the end of the conversation, the priest said he would do what he could. The holidays were getting close and Christmas was right around the corner. His mother asked if he could stay at home on Christmas day and Nobody agreed.

He received a nice flannel shirt from his girlfriend on Christmas Eve. This was the first Christmas Eve he had ever spent with anybody else. It was warm and inviting. There was love in the air. Everyone was laughing and talking about nothing in particular (a topic Nobody had a hard time with.) He just never spoke about 'nothing.' It always had to be purpose driven. During the conversation, they spoke about Christmas past and how they kept the tree up through New Year's. This was crazy talk, because in Nobody's house the tree was pulled down soon after the presents were opened. By noon, you had no idea Christmas had even been celebrated. The gifts had to be put away. But here, in his girlfriend's house was what Christmas was supposed to be about. It was a sense of family he desired. Sitting around, looking at everyone, food everywhere, he saw love and being in this room he felt a warm blanket surround him. He felt safe and secure, and as he looked at his girlfriend and felt the warm glow inside of him in this moment, he knew as soon as school was over he would move out of his parents' house. This was the best Christmas Eve EVER. He loved her family and they made him feel welcome. It was priceless.

Truth #23 Nobody's girlfriend had a great family.

Christmas day arrived and Nobody opened his gifts with his family. He was planning to go on a high school skiing trip. He received some new ski boots and other things for the trip that he had wanted. There was no special fanfare. They opened gifts, everyone thanked each other and went and did their own thing within the house. The house was fairly quiet. Later that day, as he was getting ready to hop in the shower, Nobody heard the phone ring. His mother answered it.

"No, Nobody is not here right now," she said.

Nobody knew it was his girlfriend on the phone and asked his mother why she lied about where he was. I guess she thought he wouldn't hear her. It was like she was jealous of this girl and she wanted her son all to herself. He was so angry, he never heard her response to his question or even if she had answered. In his rage he got dressed, putting on the new shirt his sweetheart had given him and he was gone. His mother was yelling at him to stay home because he had promised to stay. All bets were off since she lied. She didn't have to lie. He *was* going to stay home even though that was the last place he wanted to be, but since she'd lied he wasn't. He left and it was her fault. He went to his girlfriend's house and they hung out and a bunch of their friends went out to see a movie together.

When he returned home later that night, he walked in and found his parents waiting for him. They met him down at the bottom of the stairs. He walked past them and his mother tore the shirt off him. There was yelling. Then his father punched him in the chest and Nobody pushed back.

"You are going to break up with that whore," his mother said.

"No, I am not" replied Nobody.

"If you don't break up with her, we're going to return all your Christmas gifts and you will have to move out," proclaimed his mother.

The following morning it was very cold and with no car, Nobody needed a ride to work. It was about three miles, but his father said he would not drive him. So with the temperature below freezing, he walked. He called his mother's favorite priest again, but he said he couldn't do anything. All alone, with only his girlfriend and friends supporting him, Nobody decided to leave. History was repeating itself, just like his father with his father. The deal was done. Two days later, one of his girlfriend's friends came with a truck and helped Nobody pack up his stuff and leave. His mother was pleading for him to stay, but it was too late. They were not going to help him with school. Whatever he did wasn't good enough. Any decision was the wrong one. It did not matter that his grades were good or not.

As he drove away, his mother was on the steps, crying and yelling. It hurt him, but the time had come. He had found a room to rent in a house, near his girlfriend's house. The owner, another dealer, had been arrested for possession of marijuana two weeks earlier and was being represented by the law firm where his mother worked as a receptionist. Nobody didn't plan it that way, but that was a little more aggravation towards his mother. The only thing he needed to do was get his money out of the bank. He had two thousand dollars and one of the last things his mother said was that she would not let him have it.

A few days later he knew his parents were going skiing. This was a time way before cell phones. Nobody went to the bank to see if he could withdraw his money. The bank teller said that since it was an "and" account, he needed his mother to sign for the withdrawal as well. Not willing to give up so easily, he visited the bank an additional three times. He ended up meeting with the bank manager and a relayed a wild story about a stereo he wanted to purchase, needing to get the money before the sale was over and since it was a few days after Christmas it was only for a limited time. His parents were unreachable, as the bank manager tried to call his parents at the house (Nobody provided the number). In the end he allowed Nobody to withdraw the money from the bank. Laughing on how his little plan had worked and reaping in the fruits of his labor, the first thing he did was buy a promise ring for his girlfriend.

On his own, in an apartment and with no one to tell him what to do, Nobody realized that the next thing he had to do once school started back was to get school lunches and get help somehow. He had a job and he needed more money, so taking extra shifts was required. It was on his shoulders. With no one around to help him, he would prove to everyone he could make it on his own *and* graduate.

After spilling his guts to his physics and typing teachers, they helped him with getting school lunches and they changed his college prep physics class to 'regular' physics. This was a big hit to Nobody's ego, but his physics teacher said there was no way he would be able to keep up. Nobody had a hard time and in his mind he could not understand why his parents were acting the way they were. They would rather just let him leave instead of looking at their part in all this. The typing teacher referred him to a psychologist. There was a lot of crying and he went a couple of times. He was not in a place to be able to pay for it so he stopped going. He worked, partied, partied some more, spent time with his girlfriend and went to school.

As his eighteenth birthday was getting closer, his mother got word to him that if he wanted the rest of his things he could get them but he had to meet her at the church of her favorite priest. Without a car, Nobody's grandmother volunteered to drive him. Maybe they could sit and sort this out, but what Nobody didn't realize was that this was an ambush.

As he found his way to the priest's office, his mother, father and priest were all sitting down near his desk facing a lone chair situated in the middle of the room. Next to the chair was a box, which he guessed contained the rest of his stuff. Nobody sat down and looked at the panel. His mother started the conversation and proceeded to give him a piece of her mind. She was shocked when she went to the bank to find out that Nobody had pulled out the majority of the money. She did give him the balance, which was about $250. His father sat there and didn't say a word. The next person to speak was the priest.

"You really had me convinced something was wrong at your house. Your mother has told me everything. You are the big actor, crying to me on the phone, drawing a picture of your parents that was untrue. Your parents are trying very hard with you, but you are the problem. It is very clear to me that you are a liar and will twist the truth to suit your needs. I never want to see your face around here again," the priest exclaimed.

Nobody was dumbfounded and shocked; he looked down at the box. The priest had just described his mother not him. She was twisting the truth. She was lying. Completely befuddled at the course of events that were transpiring in the room, he looked up and said. "I guess we are done here."

Nobody picked up the box with the rest of his stuff and walked out to his grandmother's car. After he retold the story to her, she was in disbelief just as much as he was. As they drove off on this cold and wintery night, with a few flakes falling after this encounter with the priest, Nobody decided who needed God anyway. He believed he was on his own, he knew his grandmother and his girlfriend loved him and that would have to do.

Truth #24 Nobody's mother lies to protect herself.

Truth #25 Nobody turns from God because of the church.

Episode 16

Chained by Love

Nobody had only one possession worth fighting for: his relationship with his girlfriend. He had practically ignored his old friends. He still visited his drug dealer to get his needs met. But the focal point of his life was her. In his mind without her all of this was for nothing. He had to make sure that she loved him through thick and thin. During the 'honeymoon phase' it was wonderful. He never left her side; when he wasn't working he was with her. When he was working, he couldn't wait to get off. He would even fake being sick, just to make sure if she was planning on going to the lake or some special activity with their friends he would be able to join them. As each day passed the noose tightened a little tighter. She wanted a little more space and Nobody freaked out. What would he do if she wasn't around? Worse yet, if she spent time away from him, she might want to be with someone else.

As much as Nobody would not like to admit it or sometimes even fail to realize, he had carried with him a few traits from his parents. The old adage that the nut doesn't fall too far from the tree applies here. One particular behavior he shared with his mother (and they both were very good at doing it) was called 'pushing the envelope.' Simply put, it was when someone gave a constant barrage of questions until the other person relented with a yes. The difference here was this wasn't his family. This was the real world, where other families taught different rules of engagement. With Nobody's fear of being alone and so much riding on him being right, every thought, feeling and motive was a means to an end. In a roundabout way, it was all about Nobody and what he wanted to do. For a long time when you give to someone everything you can, it can be a wonderful experience, but it will get old soon enough. This was a lesson that Nobody never learned. Living in an environment where you had to fight for everything, it was no wonder that Nobody would fight for time with her. This all came at a price and as his noose tightened around the relationship so did the volatility.

They started to have little fights here and there and making up was a great experience. But with two people wanting what they want when they want it and each pushing for the other to give in, the cork finally blew. Once Nobody kept pushing a point and his girlfriend's anger raged so fitfully that she put her fist through the window and the result was a wrist that needed multiple stitches. Nobody also had a rage inside of him that seemed to erupt from the depths of his mid-section. When things subsided there was a lot of sorrow and promises that they would never do this again.

Nevertheless, in this partying environment, with a lot of friends around, there was plenty of opportunity for people to interfere and gossip. What was once a great group of friends had become fragmented. Since Nobody's apartment was the focal point for a lot of the party activities with it came a lot of drama. Couples who needed to borrow rooms. A constant need for a good party spot. Nobody's relationship with her was on display for all to see. Privacy was a limited resource since Nobody was sharing the apartment with the landlord's son; they never had any real alone time.

Every time that Nobody and his girlfriend had a disagreement everyone had to live with it. This made it difficult for Nobody to recover from his behavior and it also placed him in a position to have to apologize just to keep the peace. Since he had no skills on how to properly ask for things or set boundaries, this behavior was his default modus operandi. He may have been right, but his reactions did not match the actual issue. His feelings and his reactions all felt the same to him. He could not differentiate between the problem and the emotional investment he placed in it. It was always easier to admit he was wrong and try to keep that list of things he must remember not to do again. With his internal desire to be liked and not have anyone mad at him, he had no way of working out true disagreements. He tried to steer away from anything that resembled conflict or try a different angle until he got what he wanted. However, Nobody's inner core propelled him to hold on more tightly. He was possessive and jealous. In his mind he would be devastated if she left. So he would always buy things, play the right music to set the mood. While he was doing this the entire time, he was losing himself minute by minute. School was taking its toll and his grades, for the first time, were slipping. English was a total bust. Now that he was 18, he could right his own excuses from class. He bought a 1970 Chevelle Convertible which eased his need to be needed, since people would ask him for rides

As the relationship between Nobody and his girlfriend became rockier and the drugs continued to be used in record fashion, they eventually had a temporary break up. The interesting part of this was their friends were breaking up and the grass was always greener on the other side. So they began doing things to make the other one jealous and there was collateral damage. Nobody's goal was always to get her back and to show her what she was missing. She would see that she made a mistake. About three weeks into their breakup, Nobody had a temporary fling with one of the other girls in their group.

No one can ever understand the motives of the other contributing party, but it was clear to Nobody, that even though she was a nice girl, he was focused on his first love the whole time. Miss Temporary filled the empty hole in his gut and between the shots, he and his ex-girlfriend took at each other and the yearning in his heart for her, his short-term fling was soon a thing in the past. He found his way back into the arms of his first love. They may have been reunited, but it was not rosy. Nobody was extremely cautious, very watchful, and accusatory; the same way his mother was, though he did not know it. From his perspective, his behavior was different.

Still they argued to gain ground on each other. During one of their arguments, Nobody, in an effort to manipulate the situation, started 'pushing the envelope' more and more. Nobody placed ultimatums on the table, just like he learned from his mother in order to get what he wanted in any situation. Nobody had learned his lessons well. Outside of her neighbor's house in their snow-covered yard, going back and forth, they discussed points which would ensure more time with Nobody and no time for herself. Nobody's point, which was subliminal, was to fight from being alone while she was talking about how her father thought it would probably be a good idea for them to do things apart at times.

Myth #37 Nobody believes that absence makes the heart grow cold.

This hit a cord in Nobody's soul. To him this was a total attack on his being. He was sure that her father was trying to get them to break up one little step at a time. If she started listening to him and not what Nobody was expressing, he would convince her to leave him. In complete desperation, coupled with the rage that was growing inside of him, he told her he wished her father was dead.

Nobody had crossed a line and, at that moment, she had to choose between the security, comfort and safety a loving family can provide or him. Family was a term that Nobody did not understand. Families fight through good times and bad times. Parents guide and encourage their children in hopes that they would make the right decisions when moments present themselves. Something Nobody did not know from the context of love he had learned growing up but what he had always yearned for: *a family that would not desert him in times of trouble.*

He had a vision of what true love was but no way of getting to that goal. He never had that feeling or comfort from parents trying to encourage him through those moments, giving him the opportunity to make a decision for himself. It was always his mother's way or no way and he always had to ask first. Nobody never had an opportunity to work through a bad decision or grow through one. There were never any lessons learned, only tasks that needed to be completed and things you needed to do to make sure you did not get in trouble. There were no journeys only waypoints on a map to get to, never mind the distance in between. He had a need and he would fill it, but when he felt it slipping away, he tried to hold on tighter.

Myth #38 Nobody believes if someone says they love you forever, they mean it.

She took his promise ring, threw it into the snow, and walked off. Between scrambling to find the ring and crying out profusely he was sorry, Nobody felt for the first time how his anger could get him into trouble. The rage that he kept bottled up, had been let loose and it scared him. His stomach was hurting. He was dead to his soul. This felt eternal. The walls were closing in and he was paralyzed. He made a mistake that had just cost him this relationship. There was no level of effort that could take this feeling away or erase what he had said to her. This needed time and since he did not believe that God would help him, he did what every rational person would do when hurting; he went to the comfort of his friends. He went to his dealer's house and listened to music.

Music was the other drug, the drug which allowed him to loosen up and quiet the voices in his head. Unfortunately, the God of Noise continued to keep his one true God from him. Lost and wondering aimlessly in spirit, Nobody found comfort with his vices.

Truth #26 Nobody's coping behaviors were learned from his parents.

Episode 17

Changes

As life changes so does the environment. Nobody decided to trade his car for a motorcycle since spring was approaching. The weather lent itself to bike riding. It was also a means to try one more time to get her back. She had been dating another fellow who Nobody got into fights with; however, fighting for her did not win her back. He changed jobs and went back to working for the nursing home managing the food inventory. This was a crazy time for him. Nobody faked being sick to get sympathy from her. He even lied about swallowing glass and brought the lie all the way to the emergency room. Even though they had broken up, they still argued. The rage inside of Nobody was so severe he would peel away on his motorcycle almost wiping out after she rebuffed his advances.

As high school graduation loomed, it was clear that his parents were not going to come, even though they were invited. It still hurt. They had not really spoken since the office visit to her favorite priest, but attending graduation still a meant a lot to him. But that is how it went with his mother; if she felt you hurt her, she hurt you back with a vengeance. So as graduation day was upon him, in the audience were both of his grandmothers, his godparents, and his drug dealer. These were the people in Nobody's life that had cared enough to take the time to see him graduate. As Nobody walked across the stage, it was a weird sensation to know that the people he wanted the most in this life to accept him for who he was were not there. Grateful to the family that did show, Nobody exchanged the normal pleasantries, but no graduation pictures were ever taken.

Nobody decided to move into a new studio apartment. He still did drugs and drove the streets at night hoping to find a girl to hook up with to no avail. He worked, skimmed from the inventory for food and received food stamps. Nobody had parties, cops were called, and he was not a nice tenant for the landlord who had a pregnant wife. However, he needed family. He did not visit his aunts and uncles on a regular basis and had isolated himself from his family once he had moved out. He enlisted in the Army, to get back at his father by not joining the Navy. His aspiration to attend a military academy, if there was any, had died when he moved out of his parent's house. His Christmas tree was decorated with beer cans, drug parapher- nalia, and various weird items involving hallucinogens. He had a couple of girlfriends along the way and those relationships did not last long. They complained that he only wanted to have sex. He could not understand that there was more to a relationship than sex, and when pressed on the issue he just moved on anyway. He was focused on taking the rest of his money and partying until the cows came home. He had until Feb. 7th, 1983, when he would be shipped off to boot camp at Fort Jackson, South Carolina. Eventually he'd become a Microwave Radio System Repairman.

The only event of major consequence, prior to his departure, was when he received news that his first love's father had died of a heart attack. That whole day Nobody stayed home and listened to the radio; thinking about that day when he wished her dad had been dead. His words meant something to her, but to Nobody they were only words when he spoke them. He never understood at the time that words could cut to the bone. He attended the wake. Walking in he knew a lot of eyes were focused on him. He heard little gasps, no louder than a whisper, but he paid his respects. At the coffin, next to her, as he looked at the man who was more of a man than Nobody could ever be, he asked her father to forgive him. A few weeks later, she visited him. They spent time together, the only way they knew how and when she left, that was the last time he would ever see her again.

Truth #27 Nobody repents for the hurtful words spoken.

As the days were winding down, prior to his departure, Nobody moved out of his apartment with holes covered up by psychedelic black-light posters. He sold his motorcycle, stereo and everything else he no longer needed. His told his parents that he was leaving. He decided that he would not stay at his parents' house the few days before he left. They may have wanted him to, but it was better this way. He stayed instead at his best friend's house whose mother had always opened her home to Nobody. She had always listened and had empathy for the trials and tribulations Nobody went through. Years later, she would say that if she wanted to know what was going on, all she had to do was ask Nobody, because he was the honest one out of the crew.

On his final night, with the snow falling, Nobody walked with a small luggage bag along the street. The wind had a good whip to it. Snow blew across his path and his pant legs fluttered like little flags. As he approached the bus station to meet the Army recruiter, he knew he was leaving for good. There was nothing left for him if he stayed. His life in Maine was ending.

Episode 18

You're in the Army Now

"My name is Sergeant Parker. I am your mother, your father, your brother, your sister and your girlfriend." If you need a shoulder to cry on, find mine. You are in the United States Army. My job is to make sure you will not be killed in a combat situation. You may pray to God, but you have to ask me first. What is your name?"

"I am Nobody."

"That is absolutely correct. You are Nobody, a little weakling who needs to toughen up and become a man. That is what you all will be when I am done with you. You will be a soldier first and then a man and then a lover. But, first drop and give me twenty. Private Nobody did not address me properly, so all will pay for his mistake. My name is *Sergeant* Parker. When you talk to me, you address me by my title. Just so we are clear, my platoons always place first in physical training (PT). When you look at the other platoons, just know you will be in the best shape and we will kick their asses during the PT competition. So if you want to quit, quit now and I will send your lazy ass back to the couch watching the Flintstones."

There was no way Nobody would ever quit. He was small and he was around many guys just like him, but he would not quit. If he quit, everyone back home would say he was a failure. He met a couple of guys and did his best blending techniques. He thrived here. He knew what was expected and he did it. Here he could prove he was 'Somebody.' As he watched other guys drop out, he was glad that he was not watching platoons walk by the barracks mopping floors as the dropouts awaited their departure from Uncle Sam's grasp. Nobody got into a couple of skirmishes because some of the black guys stopped exercising when the Sergeant turned his back. This was nothing a little latrine duty wouldn't fix. There were females in a neighboring barracks and if there is a will there is a way to gain access to the forbidden fruit if one tries hard enough. Nobody did eye one girl. They managed to send letters back and forth to each other, professing their undying lust for each other. They would try to use church as an excuse to meet. It seemed odd to try and use God as a means to an end, but it was the only place where the Sergeant wasn't watching. They did synchronize a visit to sick call at the same time once but they weren't able to meet. All in all, it was just nice to have someone interested even though they never were able to get alone to do the one thing they wanted desperately to do.

Nobody excelled in basic training and was doing quite well. By the end of boot camp, he received a 'Superior Performance Certificate' and Sergeant Parker said he had done a good job. No family attended his graduation from boot camp. After a short leave, he was off to the Advanced Individual Training (AIT) in Augusta, Georgia.

It was like a college campus for the Army recruits to learn their trade. It was co-ed and girls were everywhere. The problem for Nobody was that he was a hopeless romantic. He wanted a relationship, but the way he spoke to girls scared them away, and it always left him wanting. He drank a lot and did drugs here and there and kept out of trouble, and still got the highest grades in his class. He was asked to compete for 'Soldier of the Month.' He won! He was striving to be the best at whatever was in front of him. He believed that if he was the best, people would like him and want him to be part of their cliques. However, most of the time he would invite himself. If he did not ask someone to do something with him, he would end up alone which was the most frightening thing of all. To be alone in the barracks with nothing to do would only confirm what he thought of himself. He had to be around people at all times to feel a sense of worth. For someone that needed people around for comfort, he was always outside of everyone's radar. He drank and drank, but he also studied and studied and when this time in Augusta was over, he was left with three things.

One, he was the 'Distinguished Graduate' for his course proving that he was the best. Two, he had won 'Soldier of the Month' for the Battalion and his First Sergeant slapped him on the back for making an excellent showing. Three, one night some of his friends or acquaintances felt sorry for him and bought him a prostitute in a room next to the one they were using at a motel after a night on the town. Nobody did have his true love experiences back in Maine and a couple flings here and there, but he did not have that swagger he wished he had; that swagger that commanded attention in a room when someone walked in. In his mind, he was a loser when it came to women, he couldn't break that barrier of getting any woman he wanted. Now, here he was in a moment in time where he could take what he so desperately wanted, but the pregnant hooker gave him pause. Something deep inside told him that this was wrong. Her pimp or boyfriend was outside the room sitting on the steps waiting for her to finish. He just could not bring it to bear. He could not understand why everything in his body just shut down. This should be special, not bought, and this was certainly not special. After a few minutes of sitting on the edge of the bed, he told her that this was not for him. He asked her not to say anything. He left. Nobody always looked for women to call his own. He could not have sex with someone like this. If he picked someone up at a bar he would have, but this having sex without feelings for someone struck a chord deep in his soul. All he could do was go back to the room, pretend it happened, and wait for the morning.

Truth #28 Nobody has a moral fiber that cannot be denied.

Even as good things were happening that showed the world that there was something special about him, according to Nobody's view, he still yearned for that relationship to make him feel whole and fill that emptiness inside of him. As he left Georgia trekking to Arizona on his next assignment, he had no idea that his path would take him farther from God than he had ever been. He was taking care of Number One. He would show everyone back home that he was somebody, even though he felt like nobody inside.

Episode 19

Living on the Edge

T he first thing Nobody learned was that active duty work at his permanent duty assignment was similar to a regular job. Work all day and party all night was just what the doctor ordered. He was in an Army town and it was a playground for him and his new friends once the duty day was done. As he was getting acclimated, his favorite endeavors were bar-hopping and girl-chasing. At nineteen, he only had one thing on his mind and it was not God and how to live an obedient life.

Within a short period of time Nobody went out on the town almost on a nightly basis. Living in the barracks with nothing to do did not foster a warm comfort level within him. Sure, he could drink but he needed excitement as well, coupled with drinking. He did not enjoy drinking alone or in a room with a bunch of guys. Nobody needed to be around females. He had to be *doing* something that provided a level of entertainment; his love of music brought him to bars featuring cover bands. He had no idea how to be content with himself regardless of what others were doing. In the end, his fear of being alone drove him out of the barracks where he remained until all hours of the night. It wasn't extremely difficult; he only needed to make sure he made first call in the morning and not be late for PT. It did not matter if he was sober, just present and accounted for. As he started branching out into the bar scene, he started finding his way into after-hours parties. Before long, the drugs he was so used to using were now readily available to him. His ability to blend within any crowd was a gift he used to his advantage. Still he always had a fear of getting into trouble; he traded his pot smoking to hallucinogens and stimulants. There were moments that he tested his luck and on those occasions he managed to dodge drug-testing. When he got wind of a test he managed to bypass the test by faking wisdom tooth pain; Army dentists were only too happy to pull the tooth. Nobody used this trick a total of three times with always favorable results.

However, his First Sergeant got wind of his drug escapades and attempted to give Nobody a pop drug test, but since he was temporarily assigned to the Color Guard, Nobody fell under a different reporting structure. Nobody had enough sense to sleep elsewhere for awhile while waiting for his levels of THC to drop and provide a negative result. By the time the commander was legally able to administer the test, the First Sergeant really thought he had Nobody and joked with him about it as he watched Nobody deposit his sample into the cup. In the end, Nobody passed, by probably the narrowest of margins, much to the dismay of the First Sergeant, who said he would be watching him closely. He was certain Nobody would make a mistake and get caught.

Nobody, having successfully angered the First Sergeant, was warned by the 2nd Lieutenant of his assigned squad that he was on the radar. True to the prophecy, upon his first night in the barracks he had a surprise inspection at 4 AM the next day. As a survivor and one always ready for the next shoe to fall from his childhood, they could not find one speck of dust anywhere in his area and everything including his locker was in perfect order and his boots had the look, smoothness and color of obsidian.

It dawned on Nobody that since he was now in the spotlight, the best course of action would be to be there for good behavior instead of a questionable one. He decided to start competing for 'Solider of the Month' and before long Nobody was the darling of the company. Just like Batman had a secret identity, so did Nobody. He was living high in the party scene at night with the local talent and was *super soldier* during the day. The only problem was Nobody had no idea who was the real Nobody. He was in deep cover, but from whom?

Myth #39 Nobody needs to be who he thinks someone wants him to be.

Nobody was still looking for that special relationship and in his quest he started spending the wee hours of the morning attending after-hours parties. In the back of his mind, he would always hear little messages that said looking for a wife in a bar was not a wise choice. The voice was only a whisper. His patience around the matter did not prevail. His need to be around people and in a constant search for *Mrs. Right Now Forever* was a stronger force than good judgment. This drive propelled him. He occasionally got lucky, if that is what you want to call it, but in his mind the morning after was a complete let down. While he had hopes and dreams that one magical night would spawn eternal bliss, in the end, the night turned into what it was supposed to be: a one-night stand.

Since Nobody spent a lot of time making sure he kept his senses about him, it never occurred to him that maybe these women hadn't kept theirs. It never occurred to him that he might have pushed too hard with his hopeless romantic talk. There they were, without the heart connection and, once again, he was let down. Either way, he left unfulfilled with a growing nagging feeling.

It was obvious he needed another feather in his cap, one that would attract that special someone. It did not matter if he loved them; it only mattered if they loved him. The payoff would be that if he could have someone fall in love with him (through the things he did for her) it wouldn't matter if he loved her. He would grow to love her and eventually it would be OK. She would have to meet that certain criteria that he could live with that he had formulated years ago as a young kid: pretty, and not overweight. The people around him would have to approve of her, too. He would be what they wanted him to be, so he bought a Yamaha FJ600 'crotch-rocket' motorcycle to bolster his image even more.

His life continued searching, drinking and doing drugs. For his birthday, a couple of his buddies had rented a motel room and partied the night away. Nobody continued trying to carry on his tradition of 'the cool one.' He found his drugs and offered them around. However, this night was different, his friends in kind, lined up a girl for him. As the night continued and people slipped away, Nobody had a midnight rendezvous with a girl. He had no idea his friends were behind this, so the trigger was pulled: Nobody immediately thought this girl liked him. What was supposed to be a one night fling was only a match to a fire. Like any other couple, who needed each other, they started spending time together. Nobody thought her father was a great guy but he also drank Manhattans (a man's drink.) Nobody was captured by the family environment. Its effect ended up having a stronger pull on him to continue the family relationship and not the actual one he had started with her. When he told his friends about her, they tried telling him that he had been set up and that she had ventured about quite regularly, but it did not matter to Nobody. He would prove that through all the things he did, she loved only him. They continued to spend time together at her father's house. Once the initial infatuation ended, Nobody realized he didn't love her, but he kept pushing the relationship forward and within a very short period of time, he offered a ring-less proposal of marriage.

He had no idea what he had done! Words flew out of his mouth! But, Nobody rationalized his behavior by thinking that, in the dark recesses of his mind, if he was married, all would be fine. Better yet, if someone actually wanted to marry him, he must be OK.

After a few weeks he realized his feelings never matched his words. He just kept the charade going, feeling trapped. His friends were laughing at him. He did not love her. How could he break her heart? So he did what he knew to do and that was to make the best of it. Without knowing it, he distanced himself from her emotionally.

How could he describe how he was feeling when he was around her? In public it was like he placed a wall between them. He was with her, but not with her. He was always two steps ahead or behind, but not side-by- side. He had placed himself in a prison that he felt he had no choice but to live with the situation. She was like him in many ways searching for someone and not knowing how to create boundaries to protect oneself, and putting up with behaviors that, under normal circumstances, would put an end to any relationship.

However, *hurting* people try to fill the holes inside of them with whatever means necessary to lessen the pain. As with many people, sex is confused with love. The world says it is OK to experiment before marriage so you know what you are getting into. The church has it all wrong, it's not keeping up with the times. Those rules were in place to protect the people from themselves in the past, we have evolved. Explore your nature, relent to your desires, you are consenting adults capable of making adult decisions.

In the end, everyone wants the benefits of a committed relationship without putting in the proper guidelines in place. Then when one decides to bring marriage into the picture and it fails at some point in the future everyone wonders why. You can only bake a cake a certain way and with the right ingredients in a certain order. As with committed relationships there is a recipe for a higher success rate that many are too impatient to follow or do not follow at all. When it falls apart everyone wrings their hands and wonders what happened. Whether you believe the book of Genesis or not, one thing no one can deny is that when a man and a woman come together for the first time, no one forgets. Why is that? Could it be how nature or God had meant it to be for us humans, one man for one woman to become one flesh? No, one forgets their first and so when you add more and more people into your trophy room of conquests you have a harder time being satisfied with the one you eventually say you will be committed to. When the chips are down, you will reflect on the one you let slip away or better yet know that there are more fish in the sea to catch, why waste your time with this one and one can easily turn a tragedy into a success story.

In our desires we are blind. We expect blissful results without committing to a life of fidelity to oneself until marriage.

From his earliest sexual beginnings, Nobody had not considered virginity as something sacred. It was to be an appetizer instead of dessert in marriage. Sex has a way of trapping you and if you have a conscience it makes it that more difficult to leave relationships. However this is the trap Nobody was in. Lured by a velvet glove from his adolescence, many factors led him here, some by his own choosing. He would reap his reward for not waiting until he was married to consummate a relationship.

He did not want her father or sister to be mad at him. He did not want to hurt her. He did not want to break his word. How would he get out of the mess he had created? If sex had not been in the picture he could make a clean break. Sex confused everything. Nobody thought he was trapped forever.

Myth #40 Nobody thinks he must keep his word to marry even if he does not love someone.

Truth #29 Nobody made a mistake and somebody is going to get hurt.

So he continued living the lie. Nobody was ordered to a temporary duty assignment in Sacramento to work at the Army Depot to understand in-depth maintenance on a radio van they had in their inventory. Work all day and explore the bar scene in California's capital all night. He went with three other guys and they planned to go out every night. Someone caught his eye after only two days of being out on the town. Once this special someone of the female persuasion was locked in on, within a few minutes, he was at her table. Far away from his Army home, he told his friends to go on without him as the night eclipsed past midnight. He would be fine.

After that his friends only saw him during the workday for the rest of the duty assignment. Nobody passed on the weekend adventure to San Francisco and decided to spend the time with his new Sacramento friend instead. He met her friends. He was infatuated with this girl. She had a son, but what did that matter, it was a teenage pregnancy. She still lived with her folks and they were nice. Her friends told her that she should not get involved with Nobody because he was just like every other GI and soon he would leave her. However, Nobody was not like everybody else. So he said he would come back and take his thirty-day leave with her. He would prove they were wrong about him. As he spoke his words of promise, the future, and his new undying love, the two became one. The only issue he had was what was he going to do about the other girl he was engaged to??!!

His duty assignment ended and they were traveling home. His friends gave him a hard time about his situation. Nobody was too infatuated with the Sacramento girl to care, but in the back of his mind he had moved on. Upon his return to his primary duty assignment in Arizona, he kept his distance from his fiancée. She knew something was wrong and Nobody finally told her that he just wasn't ready to get married. He was sorry, but the trip proved he was not ready for this next step. Thinking he successfully had taken care of this situation and being emotionally connected to the state next door, he actually believed the relationship was over, without understanding the ways of the grapevine. Nobody talked about his trip and this new girl to anyone who would listen. It was all he could think and talk about. Most of all, what he needed to do was get back to the Sacramento girl but he had already used up his leave and he had to wait for his leave to accrue before he could travel again. So they talked on the phone regularly. He wrote love letters. He was proving to her and her friends that he would return.

Then the other call came. Because of Nobody's big mouth, word had gotten back to his former fiancée the real reason for the break up. She was crying and laying it on thick. Nobody was paralyzed. He had hurt her and he knew it. He was in love with Sacramento girl. He was confused. Nobody was sorry he had hurt her, but he did not plan for this to happen it just did. The call ended.

Now that the issue was *really* behind him, Nobody was licking his wounds. His job, he rationalized, was to prove his love to this new girl. To do that, he would keep his word to her and visit her.

Myth #41 Nobody believes love is a feeling and you should follow it.

Truth #30 Nobody hurts another person without remorse.

As he waited patiently to be able to take his thirty-day leave, he continued his nightly adventures in partying. During one of those frequent after hours parties, while playing poker, a GI across from him was acting like a fool and wouldn't keep his mouth shut. One thing Nobody knew to do in a new crowd was to blend in. There was plenty of time to demonstrate who he was later on. Nobody, realizing that one of his favorite waitress' was behind the guy in question, told him that if he did not bow out, he would take all his money in this game. He stayed and with the help of the waitress, they sufficiently cleaned him out. As the house was emptying, one of the guys who lived there pulled him aside and said. "Hey man, I saw what you did with that guy earlier. We particularly do not like GIs, but you handled yourself well here tonight. You are welcome here anytime you like. My name is. . . ."

It was then that Nobody met his new best friend. Together they would travel a path that placed Nobody into a deeper rut than the one in which he'd already found himself. This path would lead to his ultimate demise. He felt as if he had arrived and it felt like a gift from Heaven. However, as with all gifts handed over by the Evil One, what felt like a blessing would soon be a curse. Nobody's desire to belong and be accepted would lead him to places that one day he would regret.

Episode 20

Life in the Fast Lane

Life started moving fast for Nobody. One of his new friend's roommates worked for Miller Distributors so beer was always flowing. Drugs were flying all over the place, whether it was cocaine, acid, mushrooms or methamphetamine (crack) or pot.

Nobody was living high—literally and figuratively. He had a girl in California who was waiting for him. He sold drugs to support his habit. He had an adopted family as well since one of his fellow squad members had opened his house to Nobody. When he needed a place to hang out and rest up, he could just show up. Nobody was actually treated like a family member. Nobody cooked meals for their family and established himself as Uncle Nobody. He had friends, a pseudo family and he was wanted. When his annual leave finally re-set, he took a month off, loaded up his motorcycle, and drove to Sacramento.

Nobody would fulfill his promise and prove he was not an ordinary GI. Leaving at the earliest moment of his leave (12:01 AM), Nobody ventured on his motorcycle from Fort Huachuca, Arizona to Sacramento, California. This was his first serious infatuation since his first love, despite his previous engagement. He was granted permission to sleep in the basement of her parents' house where his girlfriend lived. The adventure had begun! Since he wouldn't be subject to a drug test for thirty days, Nobody smoked pot heavily the first couple of weeks. There were parties, gambling in Reno, Mississippi mud coffee her father made, barbecues, and movies. He was her answer to a prayer, a knight in shining armor or dull camouflage. She was a single mom, living at home, resenting her ex-boyfriend and Nobody proved he was a keeper. Nobody cared for her.

Myth #42 Nobody completed her.

Truth #31 Nobody is surviving by being needed.

As his vacation continued, he heard and saw things that bothered him. Sacramento Girl had a good guy friend she had known for years. On one particular night they were all talking on this guy's huge California king size bed. The topic of crashing after a party was discussed. As Nobody was listening intently, Sacramento Girl described how she would fall asleep (maybe pass out?) on this bed they were all laying on during this conversation. Now looking at her guy friend, Nobody was sure it was how they said it was, but this still threatened him and it continued to bother him. Moving forward, this could not happen. He watched and watched for any secret signals they might pass to one another. As this new jealous behavior was starting to cloud Nobody's vision, he noticed that when she had a few drinks she acted differently. She was not herself; it was as if she was in another place or person. Her body movements seemed unnatural; she was in a different realm with one foot still in the present. She knew who Nobody was while she was in this state and was loving, but Nobody was certain of one thing: he needed to have control of his own facilities since she did not have control of hers. He needed to see everything going on around him and make sure that he could sort of orchestrate the situation to calm his nerves. How would he be able to do this when he went back to Arizona? As his time was dwindling away he knew that he would have to promise himself to her. A promise that would make sure she did not slip away. So he asked her if she would be willing to think about marriage and she said, "Yes." They would have to work out the details later, but as he left California he did not know when he would return because he had used up all his leave for the year, again.

They talked regularly on the phone. He wrote letters and worked very hard to convince her that waiting for him was the best answer for her.

Nobody could continue living knowing that someone thought he was precious enough to wait for. Nobody was now living in the future and focused on something he did not know how he would fulfill. She brought him back into reality when she announced she was pregnant.

With his feet firmly planted on the ground, or better yet his body, completely holding up the inside of a phone booth, he heard her say she was not going to have another child out of wedlock. She still loved him, but he was there and she was in California. So once again paralyzed not knowing what to do, all he could say was, "do what you think is best." He didn't fight it, but inside he knew this was wrong. He heard a voice inside somewhere calling out to do the right thing but he was fighting on three battlefronts: the life he wanted, the life he had, and the life he ought to live.

Nobody felt the pain of not taking a stand either way, which was a decision in and of itself. The world told him she had every right to choose for herself. It was, after all, her body. Somehow, regardless of all those laws and idealistic views, it was, Nobody decided, a way for people to run from their careless decisions. However, Nobody hopped on that train because it was convenient. He knew he would hold to this relationship as long as he could, but everything was different now. He had morals, but he did not stand firm on them when pushed. He also ran from his careless decisions.

Truth #32 Nobody relies on laws to cope with a moral decision.

As his drug use increased, the Army charade continued. He moved out of the barracks and into his friend's house. There were parties everyday now. Girls were everywhere, and he saved himself for Sacramento Girl for a period of time. He eventually won Post Soldier of the Month competition. As he was collecting all the perks that came with this title, Nobody found himself once again with another single mother. This one had two kids and going through a divorce. The perfect person for Nobody to 'help.' He initially was there to help, but his constant desire to be somebody for someone would provide him with the self-worth he needed and desperately wanted. The arrangement moved him into another situation. Between the charades of Post Soldier of the Month, tentatively engaged with the girl in Sacramento, there was now a potential issue in his hometown. He started to see Girl #2 more and kept the calls going to Sacramento Girl. He had a triple life.

The problems mounted. Girl #2's soon-to-be-ex-husband was always floating around and he had a temper. Nobody found out that they shared a same birthday as his. The coincidence gave Nobody pause. He would be there to protect her from her ex if need be. However, there was something wrong, as much time as they spent together, he felt like she was hiding something from him or hiding from her soon to be ex. She repeatedly prevented herself from fully enjoying their intimate times they had together. Nobody could not see past this. He could not see past his paralysis on having to be quiet in the middle of the night when someone knocked on the front door. When he spent the night, sometimes her soon-to-be-ex-husband would show up in the middle of the night. All of these little messages should have warned him. In his gut Nobody knew something was not right, but he chose to ignore these thoughts.

Nobody was too concerned, even though he did not know it, with his need to have someone to hold on to. It wasn't about commitment, it was about survival. He wanted the white picket fence, the kids, and the dog. He wanted to live happily ever after. The problem was he could not see past his own selfish desires. He may have said he cared, but his number one mission was to have someone validate who he was. For him it would be at any cost. The biggest loser in all of this was Nobody. His self-worth was wrapped up in his being able to be the number one soldier, the best partier with the best drugs and someone who women felt was attractive. His life was like a three-legged stool that was very loosely held together. If too much pressure was applied, the stool would break. He had no idea which way was up or down. He was running scared from Army drugs tests, he was lying to the girl in Sacramento and he was sleeping with Girl #2 that had more problems than he realized.

During a conversation with Sacramento Girl he slipped up. While he was talking about his friends and adventures in partying, he mentioned Girl #2 just a bit too often. She immediately knew that Heaven with Nobody had taken a detour. As the questions started over the phone, his stature diminished under the intense questioning. He could not escape. He stuttered and stammered only painting a guiltier picture. Nobody knew that his actions were wrong, but living in a world of partying as the major release valve to the stress one feels, he truly believed his actions could be reasoned away and they could be forgiven. However, once again, words are supposed to mean something and she broke off the pseudo engagement.

When the call ended, Nobody cried uncontrollably at the counter in the kitchen. His buddy's girlfriend was home and she did not know what to do. He was in a perpetual vortex that was spinning out of control. He had created this himself with only his good intentions to blame. He did what any normal addict would do: he tried to forget about it. He did not plead with God to repent for his sins nor did he barter with God, promising he would never do it again. Instead, he tried to hide from his actions and once he put himself together, he went over to Girl #2's house, putting this unfortunate situation behind him by making her Girl #1.

As the saga continued something very interesting was happening with him. He was starting to make sure he was in her field of vision as much as humanly possible. His fear of her leaving, thinking she might find someone who could offer her more had started to swell inside of him. He questioned her all the time, trying to figure out what she was really thinking. She asked for some time apart. She wanted to focus on her kids. This line of thinking only meant that someone was more important to her than him. There was a lot of 'wrong' with this relationship and it was doomed before it ever started, but Nobody tried everything he could to keep it alive. She kept pushing him away, but Nobody persisted. The more she pulled away, the more he pushed the relationship. She told him it was over and she needed to see other people. There was no way this would work. It wasn't about the relationship anymore for Nobody, it was about "hostage" taking. Nobody needed a 'possession.' Something had tripped in his mind. The harder he tried to save the relationship, the more she pushed away to the point where she asked her father to intervene.

Truth #33 Nobody smothers the life out of a relationship.

Throughout all of this, Nobody listened to her father and slowly retreated from her life but only with a few parting shots. He had become obsessed with her in a short amount of time. His behavior was very similar to her soon-to-be ex-husband. Shortly thereafter, without invitation he sat at her table when she was with a date one night. He was pleasant but it did force them to leave. The look in her eye told him that he had pushed to the final point. He was only trying to make it hard for her when he should have just left it alone. He still had a desire not to get in trouble. He knew that if he pushed anymore, serious consequences would certainly follow. Without a relationship in his life, even though he was surrounded by people almost around the clock, Nobody couldn't hide from the fact that he needed someone and it was not going to be Girl#1. He was the last in line.

A soldier friend of his was having a hard time with his marriage (things were not looking good and the wife was very unhappy living on post.) When Nobody was over his house one time getting some drugs from this friend, the wife asked her husband if he was okay with her going out. He was hesitant and asked Nobody if he would bring her out on the town. Always wanting to help, Nobody agreed. What was interesting to Nobody was that he couldn't understand how a husband could just let his very attractive wife out of his sight with another guy, even if it was his friend. They decided that she would meet Nobody at his house and go out from there. He thought for sure all she would do all night was talk about him and have the evening turn into a baby-sitting affair. She asked a thousand questions and wanted to know everything there was about him. They had a good time bar-hopping and listening to music. As the evening was coming to an end they pulled up to Nobody's house where her car was parked, she asked him if he would be interested in some *quality time*.

Totally taken aback, Nobody had a moment of clarity and said, "Your husband is a friend of mine, there is no way I could do this and face him Monday morning."

With this response, Nobody knew he had dodged a significant bullet. Once she had left, he went inside his house and over a few lines of meth he told his best buddy the story of the night. He was ridiculed, poked fun at as the night turned into the wee hours of the following morning. This was the major decision Nobody had made for himself and he felt good about it. He did not second-guess or regret it. As he took the roasting from his friends, he was secure with himself for the first time in his life. The serenity of the moment was one without worry or trepidation. It was a 'shame' that he would soon forget the enormity of this one selfless act.

Truth #34 Nobody experiences the serenity which surrounds a selfless decision.

Episode 21

Frosty the Snowman

The partying continued, the drugs increased, and the search for Mrs. Right Now Forever continued. His never-ending thought was that if he had a relationship with someone then everything would be OK and it remained the driving force in his life. He would be somebody, because that person would pledge herself to him and once this was brought to bear, everything would be OK from then on. Since he was not surrounded by people with a God-centered lifestyle to lead and guide him on a better path, he was left with those who shared a way of life that preached 'if it feels good, do it.' They were all good people, but they were all running from something and to deal with life they all placed as much thrill into it as possible. Feeling good was the best medicine anyone could hope for.

Nobody was moved into his Company's HQ, as the admin clerk, he was close to everyone: the Company Commander, the First Sergeant, and the Training NCO. His new position allowed him to get wind of drug tests. He was living in constant fear of getting caught for doing drugs, so close to everything and everyone of importance. He was a spy behind enemy lines. He looked at everyone from a distance, and had no real connection with anyone. He did his job and served everyone well. He was the Post Soldier of the Month a few months back which gave him the perfect cover. However, the only thing he could do was hurry up, get home and start the process all over again. He started pulling all-nighters a couple times a week. He had another fear: of missing something. If there was a party going on in the house, he had to be there regardless of its effect on him. He was on the verge that his party habits were costing him more than his income, even though he budgeted for drugs. His drug use was at a point that dealing would be the best possible way to continue having fun and maintain his lifestyle.

In Nobody's world, it looked like he had it all together. He cleaned the house and even waxed floors. His room was always neat. He even cooked meals for his three other roommates and girlfriends. He tried to be everyone's friend. If he had drugs to share, he shared them (within reason) and then people would want him to stay around. The holidays were approaching. He had occasionally called his parents, but they were only a memory now. Their relationship was still a distant one. Nobody did try to call once every couple of weeks, but it was always news, sports and weather. His father rarely came to the phone and if he did, it was to say hi and then goodbye. He hardly knew his sister, but she had gotten the cars, help with college and from all indications, she was the child they had always hoped for. It was funny how Nobody remembered that his father used to say that girls were different from boys and should be treated differently. It was interesting how that played out. He kept in contact with his Godparents and his grandmother. When they spoke on the phone, his mother continued to preach that he must be loyal to the family and not speak to his uncle. The fear of getting cut-off from his family—for whatever reason, regardless how that looked, drove Nobody to keep conversations with his uncle a secret. After all these years he still could not stand up for himself and truly face a disagreement. He never saw past the actual confrontation and that it might be a good thing to have if he could only stand for himself.

In the end, he continued to be what he thought everyone wanted him to be. If he wanted something from someone, he would bear gifts, people please and serve as best as he could to maintain a harmony within those relationships.

Nobody had worked hard for all his awards in the Army; he worked hard to try and be the coolest partier out there. The façade he maintained was just a shell. Looking around various rooms, all he saw were people who had their lives together. His was empty on the inside. All the things in the world he had wanted and he worked for did not seem to bring to him

117

the values, peace and the content he had always dreamed of. He knew he would have to work harder. To make it to the next level in his life, and with Christmas and New Year's right around the corner; he needed to be ready to impress those around him.

Truth #35 Nobody judges his insides by other people's outsides.

The drug business was going well and he decided that what he needed to do was ease consumption and save up for the two biggest days of the year. Christmas was just a day that had no feeling attached to it. Christmas was just a party day and New Year's Day was the big shindig. He had not received any Christmas gifts from his parents that year. The wife of a friend gave him a short sleeve shirt because she felt sorry for him. He was a bit disappointed since he never wore buttoned short-sleeve shirts. This gift was ready for file thirteen. Those shirts were for old guys. Still, Nobody made sure he made all the customary calls to his family, old friends, sent Christmas cards and thanked his friend's wife.

These were the rules to let everyone know that you cared. It was interesting that no one ever called him. An abbreviated work schedule during the holidays led to too many stimulant-induced sleepless nights and what was supposed to be two big parties turned out to be one long one. However gearing up for New Year's was still in the plan and he had an eight ball of cocaine for his own use. He and a partner in crime made it to a party where they had peyote stew, a variety of liquors and hidden, illegal desserts. Nobody, who had his own stash as well, was deep into creating a reflection of white powdered residue from a mirror situated on a table. A girl made her way over and conversation ensued. The night moved toward midnight.

His stash was quickly disappearing into thin air. He made additional purchases to keep this new female around. They talked and talked and spoke of life, the good and the not so good. As time slipped by and the sun appeared, they were two people on which the New Year had produced a new resolution. They decided to leave and go up to an overlook on base and the conversation or Nobody's vision was laid out for his new friend. She was a single mom, with a child, the special ingredient that continued to unknowingly feed the hole inside Nobody's gut. It was obvious to Nobody that he could help and he liked her. He did not mind she had a son, Nobody could be a good father. All this ground covered in a matter of hours, sleepless as he was, when he finally when to bed he could think of nothing else.

The night had taken its toll on Nobody. By the time he was able to look at himself in the mirror, his nose was raw to the touch around the nostril. Tracks were visible from the base of his nose down to his upper lip. How was he going to go back to work in the front office next to the Captain's office with a face looking like that? Panic!

The following weekend, after starting to grow a mustache and faking a terrible head cold, with sneezing and nose blowing to cover up his indiscretions, Nobody put on his happy face and with his new girlfriend and her son they went up into the mountains and played in the snow. It was as if all the pieces of the puzzle were falling into place. This was how it was supposed to be. All that had to happen now was for her divorce to be finalized. This was just a minor obstacle; he did not have to worry about her soon-to-be-ex-husband because he was in jail. Apart from that, it was as if pixie dust was sprinkled over them and everything would be wonderful forever. She had become his Mrs. Right Now Forever.

Nobody was beside himself. He had found someone he felt made all the difference in the world. After one month and her divorce final, he asked her to marry him. She accepted. Of course everyone was surprised and happy for them. They partied like rock stars that night, and while the festivities continued at the Iron Blossom with a rock band lighting up the stage, Nobody had an interesting visitor.

It seemed the pot (that was not of very good quality) that he had been selling was stolen. He had traded a portion of his stash for some cocaine and the person who bartered the deal wanted restitution. The barterer wanted to discuss the matter outside so Nobody invited one of his hoodlum buddies to keep everything cordial. It was a tense situation in the front of this guy's old pickup truck but Nobody was able to convince the person that he sold the pot for the money only and since he could not smoke due to being in the Army, he had no idea it was semi-worthless. After speaking for a bit, it was obvious they needed to get inside of the truck because of the subject matter, so not to be overheard. With a sincere apology and little toot everyone was happy. Nobody was safe to enjoy the rest of the evening. He had a price to pay for his endeavors. This was a big night for God's sake and this issue surrounding the pot and cocaine needed to be squelched so he and his future wife could enjoy the night. It was amazing how white powder could extinguish the flame of anger. They stayed up all night and Nobody went straight to work the next morning and kept to himself since he was a mess to look at.

The following day his Captain came in and he asked Nobody to report to his office. This had to be official since Nobody never reported to the Captain in their office setting. When you are asked to report, that means one of two things: something good or bad is going to happen. This is what Nobody trained for: the next shoe to drop and keeping his stories straight. Nobody was an 'awful-izer'. No matter what type of situation was being presented Nobody's first thought would be that something bad or awful was bound to happen. Nobody's job was to always outline the good in front of everyone and make sure they acknowledge what he was doing was right. This was the world he walked in every day, not sure when his time would be up, gripped with the never ending tension, and always wondering when his ship would come in. Living the lie was draining.

"Specialist Nobody reporting, Sir."

"Specialist, yesterday morning I smelled alcohol on your breath. I will not have my administrative assistant conducting himself like this in my office. What do you have to say?"

"Sir, you are absolutely correct. I had too much to drink the previous night, but I had asked my girlfriend to marry me and she said yes. I apologize this will never happen again. We just got caught up in the moment. It's not like we do this every night. I hope you understand, regardless you are right and I am wrong."

For the next hour, the Captain and Nobody talked about marriage and parenting. His Captain was proud of Nobody for taking on a stepchild and filling the shoes of an absent father. Nobody had skated by one more time. Everything was falling into place. This had to be how God wanted it for him, if God was really there. As the week went by, Nobody was given permission to move into her parents' home and maintain a separate room. There were rules that he needed to abide in if he were to stay there and Nobody would obey them. Of course.

Myth #43 Nobody thought he was a smooth operator.

She was his new party buddy. Her parents watched her son. Funny as it may sound; her name was the same as his sister's. They went out all the time, pulled all-nighters and partied as though it was 1999. They had set the date and were going to have a Justice of the Peace perform the ceremony. The wedding would take place at her parents' house, which could support the number of people they were inviting. It was going to be one of those marriages the cops could have had a field day if they had the right information. Everything would be fine. They sent out invitations. Nobody was speaking with his family off and on but due to the lack of notice or some other reason; they would not be able to attend the blessed event. It did not matter. What was important was that this union would be officiated by a Justice of the Peace to fulfill Arizona law, amen. The marriage itself was the solution to all the issues that had plagued Nobody for years. He loved her parents; they treated him like a son. He would work around the house, work on the lawn, and perform other domestic chores. When it came to the feeling in his gut, it was satisfied. The hunger pain of desperation had subsided. There was a completeness that he felt within his soul, He would be a father, a husband, a provider and a soldier; all the things a man should be and the world would know he was a man. Getting married, he rationalized, meant Nobody was also worthy of being loved. He would, in turn, repay her love with his devotion.

Myth #44 Nobody's relationship was made in Heaven.

The wedding day dawned and the final touches were being put together. Nobody felt 6' tall in 5'8" body. The support was tremendous and her family had accepted him. Her sister took care of everything. Finally his plan was coming together. His friend from his bachelor pad was his best man and he even shaved. Of course to get through any event, drugs were required. Snow was falling during spring in the Arizona desert.

Nobody and the entire wedding party were extremely attentive due to the amount of stimulants in their system. Nobody had an extremely hard time standing still waiting for his soon-to-be-wife not because he was anxious but due to the amount methamphetamine in his system. After what seemed to be a long walk down the aisle, she finally made it to his side. Vows were exchanged, the reception party moved into gear. The picture of a perfect life together had begun.

There was the reception, and when the normal activities were completed, the keg got moved to the after-reception party. Mr. and Mrs. Nobody decided to go to the party as well for a while instead of spending time by themselves. When it was all said and done, they finally made it to their honeymoon suite well after midnight; a short night after a long day.

Truth #36 Nobody's marriage was blessed by worldly affirmation and not God.

Episode 22

Love and Marriage

I t was only a week or so after the wedding that she announced her pregnancy. This was a total surprise to Nobody and she immediately proclaimed that she would stop partying. She was doing the right thing and it never occurred to him that it would be a good idea for him to stop as well.

He was the head of the household. He was in charge of discipline and her son would be well behaved. Nobody only had the lessons learned from his childhood for parenting skills. He soon incorporated his learned techniques into child rearing: he yelled, spanked and was overbearing. He had only the best of intentions. Without even the faintest clue, Nobody was nothing more than an authoritarian who spoke of love.

His methods to correct his stepson where not in proportion to the incidents that transpired. Nobody looked for perfection. In Nobody's mind he worked from a framework of 'let's get everything done first, and then we will 'play.' However the times to play were few and far in between or never came. Completely self-absorbed, Nobody worked, came home, partied and did it all over again. He loved his wife, stepson and wanted the best for them and all of this was on his shoulders. He would ensure their happiness. She would stay home and he would provide for them. To accomplish this they must first move out of her parents' house.

Their first house was nothing more than a rented cement box with two bedrooms. It was in the old part of town. When they moved in, the yard was an extension to the driveway. It was filled with beer caps and little pieces of trash.

As his first project, he turned a dirt patch into a lawn. Hours he toiled, conditioning the soil. He went to a local livery and brought in a load of horse manure to place on the lawn and in about a month and a half, after the flies and smells dissipated, he had produced a green lawn. If you drove by this little house in the cul-de-sac you would see one house that stood out among the rest and you would think there was something special about its residents. The inside was kept clean and tidy, and when people came over they would see that even though their furnishings were modest at best, they had what they needed. Couple that with his stereo, the choice music he would have to play to ensure the best party atmosphere, they had the perfect home to entertain. Just because she was pregnant was no reason to stop the after-work activities, the same way he was taught by his first drug dealer who kept the partying going regardless of his wife's intention to sleep. His needs came first over his wife's.

Truth #37 Nobody brought his past into his present.

Army life was progressing well. Nobody achieved second place for 'Soldier of the Year' and shortly thereafter was promoted to Sergeant. He still maintained the perfect cover as daytime soldier. Due to the fact that he was up until the early hours of the morning, he spent that time ironing and polishing his boots. Dress right - dress and boots like glass, Sergeant Nobody had the appearance of a soldier that was always prepared.

Eventually, Nobody was required to go to Primary Leadership and Development Course (PLDC) as part of his training as a new leader. When he arrived and met his new instructor, the first thing he said to everyone was that he would be the 'Distinguished Graduate.' Among the side comments and derogatory remarks from his list of competitors, he just focused on the task at hand. If he could be number one, then he would be respected.

Midway through the course, the soldiers were allowed to have visitors and he was glad his very pregnant wife had come, even if it was for one night. She'd brought a joint for him to smoke. As with most things, time eventually slipped away and she left to go back home after his one-day pass.

When it came to school and classes, these sorts of things were a breeze to Nobody. He picked up things fast and had great retention. As the training continued, his grades proved he had earned the right to compete for 'Distinguished Graduate.' The format for the selection process was similar to the soldier of the month boards. However little did he know that the current Soldier of the Year for his post was attending PLDC as well. This soldier had also earned the right to compete for the cherished honor. As the candidates were milling about, Nobody very arrogantly announced to his nemesis, "Today will be different." Nobody swore to himself he would never again come in second place to this soldier.

It had to be a matter of fate, like his father used say. Fate was believed in and now fate had provided an opportunity. After the boards were finished and the results were announced, Sergeant Nobody was somebody. He was Number One. As he looked to his right and the groups of candidates were starting to disperse, Nobody went to the 'Soldier of the Year,' who was a female, looked her in the eye and said, with all the venom he could deliver in a low and calculating voice, "This is where it counts to be number one. I can't believe you actually thought you would win, especially with how you are wearing your hat tipped back from your forehead. As a sergeant in the Army you should know better."

Nobody looked at people as things and without compassion. He had no feelings of his own and he could not understand others. Nobody truly only thought of himself. People he didn't know, he didn't trust. He was leery and somewhat paranoid. Nobody worked very hard at getting what he wanted and then once he got it, he moved on to the next thing.

Nobody was blind to the fact that the person in front of him was a somebody. She was a wife and a mother, who had had a dream and, as the tears welled up in her eyes, she turned away. Nobody had crushed her spirit and he did not care. To him she was the enemy, someone he could focus on. In reality, he had only met her at the Soldier of the Year board and was around her for one hour. On this day they were together for the same amount of time.

Yes, he had won, but he had lost as well. He was proving to himself and the world, even though the world did not know it, that drugs did not impair your ability. You did not need God. You only needed yourself. People around you did not matter. As he heard growing up, "people are people you say 'hi' to." He never got to know anyone. He never got inside the heads of others to see what made them or himself for that matter *tick*. He only knew one thing and that was to make sure he got what he needed. Today he needed to win, to be able to go back once again to those around him and hear them say he was the best. This was the 'pièce de résistance.'

Myth #45 Nobody believes based on his accomplishments he is the best.

This behavior continued as he played with fire living these two lives. His parenting skills were that of a complete dictator. All his stepson needed to understand was that you need to behave and be good all the time. It seemed reasonable that if he had put a pen mark on his car, that smashing one of his toys would be an appropriate response. Lessons had to be learned and learned quickly. The boy also needed to play in his room when Nobody and his wife had company over. She kept her word and did not party during her pregnancy, but once the baby was born look out.

In such a small house, it was difficult for her not to be around when his friends came over. Nobody definitely wanted order in the house when he was home. He did not want anything to bother him after his day on post. Nobody had developed a very angry tone in his voice and as time continued on it seemed more difficult to control his tone and volume. His wife would say that when he smoked pot, he was much easier to be around. The pot would take the edge off. However, due to the potential for drug testing, Nobody stuck with the stimulants, since they would leave the system faster. Stimulants always increased his anxiety.

One thing always seemed to bother Nobody: playing with his stepson. It wasn't something that he said out loud, but he did not know how to play with the young boy. He provided for his family, he got them a dog named Gonzo and a rabbit named Bonham. He saw other fathers with their kids and it seemed so natural. When he finally had nothing left to do and there was free time to spend with the kid, Nobody just couldn't get on ground level on his knees and look his stepson in the eye. It seemed so foreign, to see a child run up to him and put his arms around him and not know what to do or even know how he should feel. Just to hold the boy to his chest and comfort him was so uncomfortable it was something he had to do for the child instead of him. They played and the boy laughed, but Nobody had to force everything. That was how Nobody's life was evolving. It was a weird way of living because, in his mind, he had to do things for everyone, his superiors, for those going to come over to his house, his squad, and his wife. He needed to make sure all things were on the up and up and ensure that no one was mad at him.

However, there was the tiger in a cage. He needed everything in order around him. The house needed to be kept clean. His squad needed to be, and he wanted it to be, the best squad. However, if one of those things started to get a little out of balance he was sure to voice his opinion and that look would certainly be directed at someone.

Nobody was being consumed by the drugs and alcohol. He thought he was doing the best he could for all those around him, but he was losing his biggest asset, himself. He wanted everything to be perfect on the outside so that people would know who he was and be proud of him. However he had no idea who he was himself. He was walking scared, waiting for something bad to happen and his number one job was to prevent it all from ever happening. It was all about what was happening outside of him and he had no clue what was happening on the inside.

Myth #46 Nobody believed if the outside looked good then the inside would be,

Truth #38 Nobody had nothing to believe in but himself.

The day was approaching for the baby to be born. They choose not to know the sex of the child. Nobody had hoped for a little girl. With false alarms and a few trips to the hospital, the day had finally come. This was the day he'd waited for. Nobody paced from room to room and read a thick book, to pass the time, which was a long twenty-two hours. Nobody, for the most part, was just going through the motions. He had to keep himself occupied because with all the stimulants he had in his system he was quite fidgety. He paced, laid down, paced, laid down, tapped his foot feverishly, read, sat down, listened to his wife cry out for an epidural. It was all he could do to sit still. When it was finally time, they told him to go into the waiting room, since she was going to have a C-section.

He was called back into the recovery room. The excitement he felt was visible by the pep in his step and when he came to his wife's side, the nurse presented him with the baby. His son, a flood of tears burst out of Nobody's eyes. The wave of emotions was too much for Nobody to contain. Nothing around him mattered. It was as if the whole world was shut out from his mind. He wasn't worried about his next line or beer. He was not worried if he would get popped on a drug test. He didn't care if he was the best. He only felt one thing. A feeling he never felt before. Whatever it was, it came from his heart. The pressure was so overwhelming, he had no power to contain it even if he had wanted to. It was a river of uncontrollable tears. He was not crying, Nobody was weeping. This feeling was one that Nobody would feel again. It would let him know God was close by. It would remind him that God had always been near.

"Are you happy?" his wife asked as she noticed the unfamiliar expression on her husband's face.

"Oh yes," he said.

He stood there, looking at his son, small, fragile and perfect in every way. Nobody wanted to stay in the moment forever. Little did he know that it would too quickly become a memory. With the baby cradled in his arms and feeling grateful, Nobody thanked the God he did not know.

Truth #39 Nobody felt love from God.

Episode 23

Taking Care of Business

The celebrations started. He was a real father now, his party buddy was back from a nine month hiatus. Now he had to be even more responsible. The new parents ability to enjoy life to its fullest was strictly impaired due to the needs of the baby. With that being the case, Nobody felt he would re-establish the family business again so that he could enjoy his life while still providing for his family. So the double life began again. They had found new couples they could party with the same fervor as before and not have to stick with the singles. At this level everyone understood the needs that were required to tend to the kids and once they were settled in for the night, then the party favors could be taken out. Frozen screwdrivers made with the finest of Vodkas, mirrors with lines, and the occasional visit with Lucy in the Sky with Diamonds, life was perfect.

In the midst of all the hoopla, they were amazed at how strong the baby was. He would rock back and forth on all fours. As he got older he broke the legs of his playpen. They needed to put cinder blocks around his crib legs so it would not bang against the wall. It was a great story, little did they know it was due to his lack of being held that he was self-stimulating, an action that would trouble Nobody years later.

Nobody came home a few months later and he was met with a flowing river of tears from his wife. His wife described how unhappy she was and how she needed to do more than just sit around the house and tend to the kids. She was lonely and had no purpose. Nobody listened but could not comprehend what was said. He tried to comfort her, but in the back of his mind, he could not let her leave the house to find a job. She might find someone else. This was the first step for her to abandon him. Everything around him was in its proper place. Nobody spent the next few hours consoling his wife while guiding the conversation back to how they could not afford for her to work with the two kids. Once the older boy was ready for school then maybe they could discuss it again. It would be extremely hard for her to work since they only had one car and he needed it. He understood her concern and he would try his best to help more around the house which would give her a break. The only issue with the car was that where she went, he went. He had a fear of her leaving. He needed to keep someone by his side and in her proper place, to fill the hole that was growing bigger and bigger inside of him.

Nobody suggested that she should spend time with the other wives. He bought another dog, this time a Samoyed, named Yukon. Just what they needed in this small house, a cat and two dogs. Yukon was the baby's friend. Yukon waited patiently under his highchair waiting for choice morsels to be dropped. This was how it was supposed to be, come home to his family and entertain his friends who continued to come by for late night parties. The toll was becoming greater and greater on him. With many sleepless nights under his belt, his face started to have a shallow look to it.

His new next door neighbors were nice, but not the sort of folks Nobody usually associated with. No, they were real country. Nobody and his neighbors came from two different worlds. They were a tight knit family with parents, brothers and sisters. A type of situation Nobody could not relate to. He just couldn't understand how his neighbors saw themselves as a family. Nobody would prefer not to be bothered by family and his neighbors wanted to spend as much time as possible with their next of kin. Like his mother, Nobody would prefer short visits and living far away took care of that issue without having to be rude.

Nobody's parents decided to come to visit the baby and everything was, for the most part, on the up and up. It was just a visit. Nobody had made sure that the house was spotless. He steam-cleaned the rugs and took housecleaning to the next level. The house had to be perfect to be able to prove he had finally arrived. Still looking for that affirmation from his parents, he put everything out on display. They came and left. His parents met his wife and children, under the watchful eye of his mother and her little comments. They had survived the inspection.

One of their friend's marriage was on the rocks and to their surprise their friends split. Nobody and his wife were shocked. This was one of his friends from his company in the Army, who worked in the motor pool and was a mechanic. It was sad and made Nobody and his wife grateful to have each other. They did not choose sides and continued to be friends to both of them, however this was Nobody's friend and eventually it was just the husband with whom they kept in touch.

The Army life was a bore and a new field exercise was planned in California. It was to represent a Middle East deployment. At this time Sergeant Nobody had challenged the Company commander to an inspection and said that his team would set the standard for the rest of the company. The commander took the bet and one Saturday with a case of beer and assorted party favors, Sergeant Nobody and his team cleaned their equipment, trucks and radio gear to a dustless state. Nobody was also playing with fire by bringing his squad into his little drug circle. While climbing and building his ladder to success, he was building it with rotten timbers.

It was interesting that night, after a long day, one of his first friends from his early Army days was in his house drinking a few pounders. As they talked about the day, his early Army friend commented on a ceramic devil's head his mother-in-law had made in her pottery shop for Halloween which sat on his TV. The typical red face, black hair and goatee with cat like eyes kept watch over the drugs and people in the room. His buddy looked over to Nobody as all the drugs were laid out on the coffee table and said, "You had better be careful, you could get busted."

It was a weird statement and as Nobody looked up, he saw those eyes from the ceramic head look at him. It was as if they were real and a tingle shot up Nobody's back. Somewhere inside his soul, Nobody knew that it was an idol he had in his house. Even though he felt he wasn't good enough for God, this had crossed a line and it needed to disappear. Within the week the head was removed from the house altogether.

His team had won the challenge, they were rewarded publicly and in fact had set the standard for the company as he had predicted. The dazzling young Sergeant was making a name for himself. His team enjoyed the fruits of their labor and did what they did best when they were not playing soldier.

In his heart of hearts Nobody believed he was on the right track. He knew how to get the attention from authority figures. He knew how to get ahead of his peers. His team always blazed a trail and with his perfect cover, he felt untouchable.

As they deployed to California, Nobody made sure he packed his essentials: girlie magazines and stash. Once there, they quickly erected the radio site and did all the things to make his site the best radio site around, tending to every detail so if there was a spot inspection they would not get in trouble. Their stay was a long one and it turned out that there were two camps within the camp: the normal folks and the drinking folks. The Laundromat on the base was broken and to Nobody's surprise it was received as a gift from Heaven. He found another Laundromat right next to a liquor store. He had one of the trucks and he had a number of people who needed to do laundry on a regular basis and the liquor store profited by it.

The spot inspection did occur, finally. Colonel Somebody showed up and requested entrance into their radio van. Between games of cribbage, they were actually training when this visit occurred. Sergeant Nobody politely informed the Colonel that he was not allowed in the van since he was not on the roster. The Colonel eventually left and one of his team members said, "Holy crap Batman, are we going to get in trouble?"

During the daily platoon meeting, the story was filtered down. The top brass were having their daily meeting and in the middle of it, Colonel Somebody marched into the tent and called out, "Who is in charge of Sergeant Nobody?"

All heads turned to his Captain, who slowly raised his hand. The Colonel went on to say how professional Nobody was and they needed more sergeants like him because he was training his men, had posted all of his signs, and the list went on.

When the field problem was over they all assembled in front of the brigade at which point the Brigade Commander informed the soldiers that only three awards were to be handed out. Sergeant Nobody was awarded the 'Army Achievement Medal.' Nobody didn't pay attention to who had won the other awards. It didn't matter to him. He was at the height of his career. He was proving to the world that he was worth it and even if he was always scared inside, he was the best on the outside. He was climbing the ladder, propelled by his hard work. He was the Captain's boy on this day. He was # 1.

Myth #47 Nobody believes he is untouchable.

Part III

Where is God in all of this?

Episode 24

Shot through the Heart

By the time he made it home and hung out for a while it was obvious to Nobody that something was wrong. With all marital reunions, he thought that as soon as the kids went to bed, his wife and he would rekindle their love for each other and everything would be as it was. As they popped a couple of beers and drew up a few lines, it seemed as though time stood still. Nobody discussed all his accomplishments and recounted his adventures in drinking. He talked and talked, played music and soon drew close to her. The night seemed to be going the way he envisioned. He looked at his wife and saw she was crying and thought he heard her say she was sorry. He wasn't sure so he assumed she was crying tears of joy. He soon forgot about it and they fell asleep.

A few days passed and his neighbor said that he wanted to talk to him about something. So Nobody, went over and they popped a few tops on cans of Milwaukee's Best. The neighbor started telling Nobody that while he was gone, his friend's truck spent a lot of time at his house. This was Nobody's friend that had broken up with his wife. His neighbor had a grievous look on his face and Nobody denied that anything could have happened. But his neighbor persisted, explaining that the visits weren't just for a short period of time but late into the night.

After a couple more beers though, that heavy feeling started to weigh upon his chest. His neighbor was talking but nothing was registering. Nobody heard the man's voice but racing thoughts of abandonment came through louder. Was it true? Had she slept with *him*? How could she do this? He could not sit still and needed clarification. He went back to his house.

Waiting for the right moment was never Nobody's strong suit. No matter how hard he tried to keep his thoughts to himself to process everything, he could never control his desire to know. His impulsive behavior and racing thoughts took command of his mind and mouth. He confronted his wife. She denied any wrong doing. His friend, Mechanic Boy, was just having a hard time and needed someone to talk to. There is no harm in that. Nobody should trust her. Trouble continued to brew inside Nobody. He watched her very closely. She showed her anger towards his neighbor, who, according to her, was ruining everything. This idea put Nobody at ease somewhat. The friend still came by to party, but Nobody was watching and waiting. Since his friend was no longer in the military and working nearby, Mechanic Boy offered to work on his car since it had a problem starting.

While at the garage taking him up on his offer, there was some small talk and Mechanic Boy mentioned to Nobody that he should be grateful for the wife he had. Already suspicious, Nobody did not like the way he spoke. The conversation continued and there were slight hints about how his wife needed more from Nobody. Nobody responded with the appreciative thanks for caring, but we'll work it out. It was none of his friend's freaking business. It was easy for him to just walk in and think he understood what was going on. He was clueless. What he really needs to do is worry about his own family and why his own marriage failed.

Inside, Nobody's gut was sinking fast. Here we go again—another person meddling in his relationship. His wife started acting differently. It used to be that Nobody would venture to bed at a reasonable time to be able to get up in the early morning to get to base on time. However as the suspicion inside of him grew, his need to stay up later until everyone left his house also grew. It was, after all, still a party house.

The fear was slowly gnawing at him. Owning one car also added fuel to the fire because when his wife left, he felt totally isolated and cut off from the world. He would wait by the window peering out endlessly for her return. She would say that she was cooped up and needed to get out.

She needed time with her friends. The kids were being taken care of, but ignored. The anger and fear was building in Nobody.

In the mail he received overdrafts notices for bounced checks. By the time he put all the pieces together he found out that while he was gone she had purchased $325 dollars worth of meth — an eight ball — and overdrew their checking account. When did this happen? Why didn't he know about it? Didn't she know they lived paycheck to paycheck?

The following Sunday morning, Nobody looked out the window and saw that Mechanic Boy's truck was outside of his neighbor's house. The mechanic and neighbor were talking. Nobody couldn't hear what they were saying, but based on faces and gesture, the tension was rising. The conversation got heated and before long both of them were fighting. They moved across the street and they ended up on the ground fighting. Nobody watched from his window. He was paralyzed again. The truth was on display and it still wasn't enough proof to make him act and fight for his own marriage. These two guys had never been introduced. His wife must have said something to Mechanic Boy. In his heart, Nobody knew that he should have gone out there and stood for his own marriage but his cowardice made him believe that he needed more definitive proof.

Here before him stood a man that had nothing to gain by calling out the truth that Nobody still wanted to deny. This man, who owed him nothing, fought for truth and honor and took punches for him in principle. The fight ended and as he watched them split and go their separate ways, Nobody felt nothing but confusion. Nobody pretended he had not seen a thing and his wife pretended nothing happened, too. But Nobody knew she did. The only 'truth' Nobody witnessed was that his neighbor was a simple man with no special talents, who was fighting for Nobody's marriage. Nobody knew he wouldn't have given the shirt off his back for his neighbor and yet his neighbor took a punch for him. A man who knew what honor was and ready to stand for what was right. A man Nobody was so afraid to become had just done what Nobody needed to do in his life. His neighbor with nothing to his name, was wealthier than Nobody hoped to be.

Truth #40 Nobody witnessed what a true man was.

Truth #41 God sent a messenger to Nobody.

She left the house later that day and it was well past midnight and she hadn't returned. Nobody paced the 20' by 15' living room. This proved to be too much to bear. She had managed to get a ride to wherever she was so the car was left behind. He gathered the kids and placed them in the car and went searching.

Without faith in God, Nobody's default survival techniques were used in an attempt to cope with the feelings inside. Nobody only knew drugs and alcohol and he somehow needed to just get through this and it would be OK. The stimulants kept him up into the wee hours of every morning. This night was no different. Placing his children at risk and not even focused on what he was truly doing, Nobody turned the ignition on and began his search. He drove looking for her, stopping at one of their friend's house to see if she was there. His friend met him with an agitated look —coming by late and just knocking on the door—didn't help his friendship. Nobody knew in his heart where she was, but refused to drive by even though he was one block from the mechanic's trailer. No, he preferred to deny everything. After an hour of fruitless searching, Nobody and the kids headed home.

Soon she returned with accusations about a lack of trust. The funny thing was that he felt OK when she was around and could see her. However the moment she was out of his sight panic struck. It felt like the world had ended. The fighting between the couple increased as the days went by. When "he" would show up Nobody would ask him to leave. His paranoia was taking over and at last count, he had been up for four days straight. He must be vigilant. He didn't want to miss a conversation, a secret phone call or a wandering glance. He was hearing and seeing things around him at work. His peers were playing tricks on him and he could not comprehend anything. Did they know he had been up for days? Would he get in trouble? He only knew he had to do one thing: sleep. All he had to do was get through the day. Sadly, no matter how much he wanted to sleep as soon as he got home, but once there, the lines came out. Another sleepless night.

It was Saturday afternoon and she had wanted to go to the Laundromat. While she was gone he was trying to play with his stepson. The baby was safe in his crib. His stepson became chatty, as most three year olds do, and said that his mommy and Mechanic Boy had been wrestling when Nobody had been away.

Panic clutched his heart. He was delirious, he walked in a circle trying to figure out what to do. He couldn't stay in the house a moment longer.

The walls were closing in on him. In a complete panic, he pleaded with his neighbor to watch his kids and could he borrow their car. As he recklessly drove to the Laundromat, another motorist told him to pull over. In a state of complete confusion he pulled over and the driver asked him what was wrong; he almost hit him and other cars. He said Nobody needed to slow down and relax. Nobody was extremely ashamed by what the man had said, and made it to the Laundromat without further incident. Turning into the parking lot, he saw his car and next to it was Mechanic Boy's truck.

Words were exchanged in the parking lot. People were standing near. His so-called friend told Nobody how he was heartless and did not truly care for his wife. He told Nobody that the isolation his wife felt being at home with the kids needed to be understood. According to Mechanic Boy, the couple didn't have fun anymore.

How was it that the Mechanic Boy understood her needs and understood what it meant to be a real father?

Nobody was at a loss for words to say. He could only think of all the words he wanted to say. How this guy was preying on the fears of his wife. How he was taking advantage of the situation for his own needs, since he was recently divorced. Why couldn't he take that rage that was so deep inside of him and just let it out? What were they saying? He worked, he came home, he loved his wife, he did not know what else to do. All Nobody wanted to do was to jump on Mechanic Boy and beat him senseless. He wanted to tear him apart, causing him to feel as much pain as Nobody was feeling at that moment. But he just stood there and took everything they said about him. He quickly started feeling smaller and smaller, Nobody got back in the car and drove home.

When she returned she said she wanted a divorce. Nobody was numb. He walked into the kitchen, opened the freezer, and took a hit of LSD. He drove to the bar and cried all night. What else would an addict do?

Myth #48 Nobody was weak and pitiful.

Truth #42 Nobody's world was shattered and he did not have faith that it would turn out well.

Episode 25

Help

First thing Monday morning, Nobody asked to see his company commander. A shell of a man, Nobody admitted to his Captain that he was a drug addict and an alcoholic. His life was falling apart and he did not know what to do. Within two weeks Nobody went from being on the top of the world to nothing. The Captain listened intently to his 'star' sergeant and for the first time in Nobody's life, he accurately described how he felt and how scared he was. His wife wanted a divorce, she was sleeping with his friend, who the captain knew. Everything Nobody had worked hard for was slipping through his fingers. Not trained in these sorts of things, his captain ordered him to stop taking drugs. Nobody would not have a drug test for thirty days so his system would clean out. He could move into the barracks and everything would be fine. *Little did either of them know that when you stop one addiction something else will need to fill its place.*

Nobody thought this had turned out better than he had imagined considering the circumstances. Someone supported him. He felt a new strength inside and would be able to get on with his life.

Myth #49 Nobody had a chance if he just stopped taking drugs only.

Finding his way back to his old friends again, trying to put this life together, scheming on how to get custody of his son, gaining favor from her parents, he wanted to prove to everyone it was her fault not his, Nobody would revert to his old survival techniques to *prove* he was on the right side of this issue. She would pay for what she had done.

Her family had taken his side and he spent the holidays with them. Nobody felt he had the upper hand in this battle. What the upper hand lacked was the girl, the kids and his dog. But what drove him crazy was the fact that this guy was playing daddy to his kids and was sleeping in his bed. Nobody would drive by the house and try catching them in the act. Nobody had no God to rely on and everywhere he turned he saw people in love and he yearned for that feeling. The emptiness inside was almost too debilitating.

"Can't she see that this guy was feeding her a line to get her in bed with him. Once all this is over, he will dump her and she will wish she had not left him."

Nobody made it through Christmas. By New Year's Eve he met someone else. She was an older lady by about ten years. She was nice and was a good listener. In true 'Nobody' fashion he managed to find a way to see her again. This time, however, although his intensions were not necessarily honorable, she kept him on as a friend.

A couple of weeks passed and Nobody was growing tired of living in the barracks. He felt he needed to find a new place to live. His wife had said that the waterbed had been torn down and he could get it whenever he wanted to. Her new fella, Mechanic Boy, had a regular bed that had been set up in their bedroom. Nobody, disgusted every time he thought about them, made plans to move into the home of an older bachelor friend of his so he could get on with his life. This friend was part of the old party ring but was never inclined to deal drugs and since Nobody was only drinking he felt it would be safe.

Myth #50 Nobody had the best made plans.

The moving day arrived. His roommate understood that he would have his son at times in the home. Nobody had started looking into filing for divorce and was going to petition for custody. He still talked about her all the time and he truly wished she would see that he was the better choice, the more suitable husband for her.

Nobody was filling the bed when he noticed that the carpet under was turning into a pseudo sponge. Angered and upset, Nobody decided his night would be better spent at the bar. Bringing a house guest with him Nobody and he hit the town. After a few drinks and speaking to a few girls, Nobody's night was looking up. Someone was actually interested in Nobody again. His friend wanted to leave but Nobody pleaded his case, encouraging his friend with the idea that they had time for one more Whiskey Sour. Forty-five minutes later his friend mentioned it was time. Nobody was at a point that he was ready to as well and all along thinking his friend would drive and so handed him his keys.

Nobody looked at him and said, "Hey can you drive us home?"

"Sure," he said, but as he was getting into the car, he exclaimed, "I can't drive a stick shift."

In that moment, Nobody pondered the situation and said, "No problem, I am OK to drive."

Traveling down the road at a speed over the legal limit and being only a mile from his house, Nobody noticed the cop on the side of the road. With the grip of fear in his chest, there were numerous thoughts that ran through his mind, one of which was "Oh S*%t!. Nobody saw the squad car pull out behind him. Nobody quickly turned into his new neighborhood, and the blue lights appeared in his rearview mirror. Nobody managed to get to his house just prior to the police arriving. However his tactic did not achieve the desired goal and the police stopped him as he made it to the front of the house. He told his friend to go inside.

Standing in the middle of the very small front yard, his stomach sinking, Nobody felt the strength leave his knees. He knew he was guilty before the police officer opened his car door. Flashes of his company commander and all the warnings they were given about drinking and driving flashed through his mind. Ironically, Nobody thought about the mandatory training for NCOs he recently attended at the police station. There he learned about the process soldiers had to go through if arrested for DUI. He was sure he would be at the same station in mere moments. How would he explain himself? Or justify his behavior? And how could he have been so stupid?

He offered no resistance to the officer. He was cuffed, frisked, and then transported to the local jail where he was processed. As he was walking to his new, temporary home, Nobody noticed two holding cells, one was occupied and the other was not. He asked the officer if he could be in the one by himself, because he wasn't like the people in the other cell. Nobody cried the entire night.

Nobody noticed that his anger increased because of the situation he was in, which he concluded, was all his wife's fault. If she had not done all those things, everything would have been fine. The dominos would have not have fallen this way.

Released from jail the following day and escorted by his Platoon Sergeant back to the company, Nobody's Commander walked by him, shaking his head in utter disappointment, the same way his father had years ago at the boy scout camp. Humiliated and ashamed, Nobody called his wife and explained what had happened. Again, he placed the entire blame firmly on her shoulders.

Truth #43 Nobody's world was spinning out of control.

The second day after his release he called his wife and, by the tone in her voice, Nobody knew she was in terrible shape. She was extremely depressed and felt like she did not have the strength to continue on anymore. Nobody rushed over to the house in an attempt to fix the situation and prove to her that he was the right guy for her. As he stepped in into his old house, the place was a mess. It had not been picked up in a long time. There were kittens in the tub, food in his son's crib and his wife looked like death warmed over. Believing that she had seen how she was wrong in this entire affair and finally needing help, he said he would bring her to the hospital. And so he did. It was determined that she needed to go to another facility where they would be better equipped to care for her. Without realizing it, it seemed as though the medical staff knew the real story— without even asking a single question.

Nobody's wife was headed to a treatment facility that would handle depression. He began blaming himself for turning her into a drug user and the state she was in. It was obvious she could not handle the drugs like he could and this was his fault. Anyone could see that. He started to bear the weight of his actions and would do whatever it took to get her back. When he got her to the facility, he checked her in. The attending nurses asked all the same sort of questions that were asked at the hospital and Nobody did his best to paint the best picture he could, based on the situation. Funny how you can walk into a drug treatment facility and think you need to put your best foot forward. It never dawned on him they were both in trouble.

Nobody saw Mechanic Boy out of the corner of his eye. They met with puffed chests and voices that carried, and they soon were broken up and Mechanic Boy was told to leave. Nobody was told that he should go down the street to a place he thought they called the Serenity Club. His wife would show up in about an hour and he could see her then.

Nobody left. There were a lot of cars and as he approached the building, he soon learned he was tricked. This was a meeting of Alcoholics Anonymous. Looking around everyone was laughing it up. His world was falling apart. Couldn't they see he was in bad shape? Look at them all having to be here at 8 o'clock just so they wouldn't drink. How pathetic they were. He did not belong here, but he needed to stay here because his wife would soon show up.

It wasn't long after everyone started settling into their seats, when a van of people showed up. One of the passengers was his wife. She sat with him and as he looked over at her Nobody was certain he saw tears in her eyes. Nobody truly believed they had a chance now, not because they were in an AA meeting, but because he felt that she knew she was wrong and her tears proved it. How completely blind he was to the fact that you can't turn off feelings and it wasn't all about him.

All his years of dodging and surviving and working so hard to not get into trouble — which was, in reality, his way of running from the uncomfortable feelings he had inside his gut— led to this place. He had learned over time not to *feel* his feelings but work things out from his head not his heart. Think logically and don't feel. Every feeling he experienced was, in his mind, a decision. If you decided you loved someone the feeling would come. If you were mad at someone, you stayed mad. That was what he had learned. And, that was how he lived. There was nothing in between. You fought to win. The goals were to make sure he was as comfortable as possible or comfortably numb.

Episode 26

I Never Promised you a Rose Garden

He heard new expressions like "big book, one day at a time, if you're new just listen, God, higher power, you didn't get here by eating a bowl of cherries, God as you understand Him, the Serenity Prayer." Nobody paused for mere fractions of a second as these new terms were thrown about, but he was too interested in asking his wife if she would leave the other guy. He would be a better husband, he just needed another chance. Nobody apologized for the mess they were in and promised to buy her a washing machine—since this was something she complained about, plus it would keep her home—after finding a new place for all of them to live. Considering where Nobody was a few hours earlier, trying to save his wife from a complete breakdown, he now found himself surrounded by a bunch of alcoholics and drug addicts. Sure he may have admitted to his company commander he was one at one point, but this was different. He found himself in a place where they both could get help, he could only ask her a question to make himself feel better and hoping her answer would make it all better. She could only stare forward with tears filling her eyes.

At the end of the meeting they said the Lord's Prayer and everyone went their separate ways. He had fifteen days before he had to surrender his license to the court and he had a lot to take care of until then. At some point in the next few days while he was packing up his old house ready to move in another, Nobody picked up a Bible from a box and it happened to open to Hosea. There he read in the first chapter where God had asked Hosea to marry a prostitute and bear children with her. Then God asked Hosea to forgive her for being with another man. This must be God telling Nobody to forgive his wife and let her back into his life. He would buy a washing machine, clean up the mess she made of the old house and instead of letting her help with the clean-up, he would move them all into a new place. He had the kids and it would be wonderful all over again.

It would be twenty-five years before Nobody understood what God was showing him that day. God was actually calling Nobody back to Him at that time in his life. Just like God used this example of his love to show Israel that Israel could go back to God even after idolizing other gods. Unfortunately, Nobody could not see that this was about him and not his wife so he thought it was his call to forgive her. Though that is truly what God calls us to do; in this case it was God's call to Nobody which he only took literally and not spiritually.

Truth #44 Nobody had gone astray from God.

He immediately, thought this must be a word from God and then concluded this was his chance to do something different. He would forgive her and by forgiving her would prove he was worth taking back. Looking at this situation only from his perspective, Nobody rationalized that if he would only do this better or that better, the choice would be obvious. It was his fault all this happened. He kept going over this situation a thousand times in his head. He must not be a good lover. He should have quit doing drugs years ago. He should have been a better father. He could have played more with the kids which would have demonstrated to her that he was the best thing for their children and not anyone else. He would put his faith in himself and his love into works. He would show her he *was* worthy of her love and fidelity. He assumed she felt ashamed, so he would remove the shame through forgiveness. Everything would all go back to the way it was. Thank God he saw that Bible passage.

He would put all of this back together again He cleaned up the old house, rented a new trailer to live in and bought a used washer just like he said he would. His in-laws helped with the kids. He confessed to everyone he was a drug addict who wanted to get his act together. He even went to meetings on his own so he could see his wife. It was helping. In one short week Nobody felt as though his life wasn't falling apart after all. He still needed to see the Battalion Sergeant Major, but he would take his punishment and just work through it. He would guide this family back together. All he needed was more determination.

The day came when he needed to report to the Battalion Sergeant Major. He clearly and accurately detailed his story from the time they returned from the field problem and how he went to the Captain and told him of his situation. After a period of time which always seems long to the person telling the story, sitting waiting for the Sergeant Major to say something, Nobody could not see past the poker face across the desk. Then the Sergeant Major adjusted his gazed towards Nobody and said in five words, "This could have been prevented."

Nobody was assigned to a new company within a week. That's all. No further discipline. He was ordered to go to the Drug and Alcohol center. He was still going to be banned from driving on post for a year, but he would figure it all out. Once his wife came back home Nobody would use her to drive him on post. It would be rough and it wouldn't be easy, but together they would be able to make it work.

Truth #45 Somebody finally heard what he was saying.

Nobody actually started to believe that maybe there was a God after all and if he continued to do what he was doing, God would give him his marriage back. The folks in the AA meetings had said that if you stop drinking and doing drugs, a lot of these things would work themselves out. You have to believe that there was a higher power out there. After years of witnessing what the church had done, Nobody began to wonder if he was just listening to the wrong people after all. These people seemed to understand some things, so he stayed sober. He wanted to be the model AA person.

Unfortunately, life doesn't always go the way we would like. Nobody went to pay a surprise visit to his wife. The surprise was on him. He found her roller-skating on a basketball court with Mechanic Boy. It wasn't quite working out as it read in the Bible. Nothing was going the way Nobody hoped it to go. He couldn't handle the thought of not being in a relationship, with a kid and divorced. He hated the thought of being alone. His wife told him it did not matter what he did, she was going to leave him. Not even a washing machine could convince her to stay, the only thing he knew to do was go to a meeting. It was there that people would listen to him. He continued to stay sober because he didn't need to get into any more trouble. Since the divorce was imminent, Nobody found himself a lawyer, who, unbeknownst to Nobody, was in AA as well. Maybe God was there after all.

His anger towards his wife was increasing; she got out of the treatment center and moved in with Mechanic Boy. Why was this happening to him? All he could do was go to meetings. There were plenty of women there who he could meet. He heard some of the old timers tell him that they were just as sick as he was, but Nobody did not comprehend it. He only knew he was in a bind. He needed to figure out a way to get to work. All of these issues swirled around him, adding to his confusion and sense of helplessness. He needed a roommate. A solution! So the search began. He spoke to a few guys in the barracks but they all declined. There was this female sergeant in his company that he had gotten to know. Was she the solution? She had mentioned that she wanted to move out of the barracks and, after a few visits to his place, she decided she would move in, taking the front room.

It took only a short fifty-eight days for his divorce to be final. He was granted custody of his son. He did not want any child support. As he reflected over his recent past, Nobody realized that he had met his wife over an eight ball and got divorced over one. They had effectively met, married had a kid and divorced just shy of twenty-three months. It was time to put his life together and the people in AA seemed like they would be the ones to help guide him. The way he heard it, as long as he prayed to a God of his understanding and at least try, all would turn out well. It was better than the alternative. He was told not to get caught up in expectations because things do not usually turn out the way you want them to. But, in his eyes, Nobody was different. He truly believed his best behavior would be rewarded with a new wife and a new life. All he had to do was not drink, pray and go to meetings.

Myth #51 Nobody thinks good behavior equals an easy life.

His roommate was a huge help. She watched his son while he went to meetings. She was a good person and had a kind heart. Though they were not romantically involved, Nobody was grateful for her in his life during those early months. She helped where she could while his license was suspended and with her in the house, he was not alone. And, she did all this while carrying a baby, conceived during a visit back to her native California.

Truth #46 Nobody felt a level of companionship that filled that hole in his gut.

As with everything during this time period, things were moving fast. Nobody got his license back after ninety days. He could drive (but not on base.) So he came up with a solution. He would get up at 4 a.m., get his son together, and bring him to the babysitter, who left the door open for him to drop his sleeping son on a bed in the house. He would then drive to the gate, park his car, and then ride a bicycle which he chained to a tree outside of the East Gate three miles to get to work by 6 a.m. (just in time for PT). The downside was that the base was situated near foothills of a small thirty mile mountain range in the desert so his morning ride was uphill.

This was his routine. He was no longer the shining star of his company. He was branded. It was hard to concentrate on being a leader with new radio gear to learn. This company sent soldiers to Bahrain for six months' tours of duty and Nobody was concerned that he would be deployed. He was trying to be a squad leader, concentrating on his sobriety, trying to find a new wife, and praying that God would bless him with one. Since the folks in AA said he should pray, Nobody continued with the exercise that had been suggested and it seemed to help.

Nobody talked to a lot of program people. He asked a lot of questions about God. He started working the *Steps*. One of the steps is to write a list of the things you have done wrong and tell them to another human being and God. So Nobody, wrote out the list and decided that it was too personal to tell a person in AA, so he decided to go to a priest.

With sheets of paper in hand and hope in his heart this act would make that huge empty hole go away, he went to confession, face-to-face with the Priest. He started reading it line by line and after a few minutes the priest asked, "What was this crap?"

Nobody explained but it fell on a deaf ear. The priest seemed disinterested. It was no use; he told the priest that he didn't believe the whole Bible. The chapter titled Genesis was just a myth to put abstract thoughts together. He believed there was a God but not like the one described with Jesus Christ. He finally said what he had been thinking all these years: Nobody believed there was a God, but the God of his childhood was dead.

He was going to be a deceased Catholic. God had to be a God of love, who wanted the best for him. He was a forgiving God and as long as he was doing the next right thing, things would work out. There were plenty of people that had talked about God. Nobody spoke to many people about God and everybody had an opinion. After a couple missteps with some sponsors, who Nobody found out were just as sick as he was, Nobody managed to find two different guys that seemed to have their act together and would play an important role in his life.

One guy was a wild man from D.C. that had been sober for a while, had a wife, and drove an AMC Hornet. He was putting his life back together by going to school, however, he was from the streets and extremely streetwise. He could look at a situation and sum it up in the simplest words possible.

When Nobody talked about God and all the things he didn't believe with this man, he received a strange response. The man asked Nobody if *he* believed that he believed in God. Nobody had to say yes. It was at that moment Nobody realized that here—right in front of him—was someone that knew God. That the God this guy knew was putting his life back together. Together, yes, but easily, no.

God did not serve up answers on a platter or a menu. God needed people to walk with Him and rely on him. It was far past religion. It was a walk, no, more like a journey, and would Nobody be willing to let God lead him? This man sat with Nobody, looked him in the eyes, and shared how his life was changed once he let God into it. For the first time in Nobody's life, God was placed in front of him in a man that ran drugs and guns and led a life that could be termed gang-like. Now, here he was, sharing in the most intimate way, how God saved his life.

They spoke about a variety of subjects over the next couple of months. They spoke about money, dating, relationships and the ever-elusive subject of sex. Nobody finally asked someone to tell him about the birds and bees. He had never understood all the different phrases around sex and all the terms that surrounded the sexual climax and the physiology of women.

Nobody believed that his lack of performance in the bedroom caused his wife to leave. His lack of knowledge humbled Nobody. He had always been afraid to ask questions about this subject for fear that people would judge or laugh at him. This time was different. This time, Nobody's sponsor spent the next few hours talking about the subject. He outlined how God had meant sex to be between a man and women.

Truth #47 God had sent another angel.

Episode 27

One Way or Another

The truth be known, the Hounds of Heaven were in pursuit of Nobody. Like seeds thrown down by a sower, God had started to plant seeds. The problem for Nobody was that while his interest was piqued by God, and he believed in God, like most people who have been hurt by religion, Nobody was vulnerable to the false prophets. He was susceptible to half-truths wrapped in a lie, all the while believing his actions were being blessed by God through his experiences. It was so easy to correlate that "Good Orderly Direction" (GOD,) praying, and the results of being a good citizen could be confused with God blessing his endeavors. AA was providing the runway to take off on a new journey and it attracted many people from all walks of life. Like a church, it was a proving ground for people looking for answers and like religion, it provided a means to an end for good living. But, as you are doing good deeds you might miss the entire boat.

Ultimately, everyone is responsible for themselves. Nobody believed that his ideals and search for a union with God, as with everyone, were the same as those of others. He did not trust people without abandon, but he was a bit naïve to the motivations of people. Nobody was befriended by another man in the program who would be a second sponsor. He would become his spiritual mentor, and had long discussions with Nobody about God as well. As with most people recovering from drug and alcohol addiction, the subliminal message that is always present in the psyche is to dull the pain they feel. Once you take away the drugs, that hole needs to be filled with something; meetings, God, sex, exercise, ice cream and the list goes on.

Nobody now had two ideas that he believed would be the magic bullet to solve the way he was feeling, regardless of the warnings he heard from the more experienced people in AA. One was to find that special relationship, fall in love, get married again and live happily ever after. The other was to get good with God so He would bless him with that new soul mate. It didn't matter in which order either. This would be Nobody's battle for years to come. He would still confuse sex for love and if any good incident happened he would believe God was blessing him. *The funny thing about blessings is that unless they are formal, you never realize that what you are going through at the time is actually a blessing.* One must go through experiences on faith and once the emotion has subsided, one must reflect and determine whether or not it was a blessing. However, it would take trial and error to finally understand that, because it feels good doesn't mean it is good. The major problem with people in early recovery is they confuse feeling good with recovery when it might only be temporary relief.

With the free flow of spiritual ideas and the lack of maturity Nobody had in spiritual matters, he found that his new mentor was involved in a new age cult called the Rosicrucian Fellowship. Christian Mysticism was how it was described. It provided the answers to those tough theological questions. There is no hell because hell is all in your mind. Focus your thoughts and tap into the power God has placed in your path as you try to attain a higher spiritual plane. The group had books on meditation, spoke of out-of-body experiences, and the use of Astrology to help guide through this phase of your spiritual journey. It gave an individual actual purpose for oneself. As Nobody was being introduced to these things he never heard of before, there was a certain word that his brain latched onto, but was never brought into the forefront of his mind. That word was POWER.

As he started reading and participating, they called what they were doing "white magic". There was a fine line between the two forms of major magic and it took a strong soul to stay away from the dark side. Nobody was ready. For the first time he believed he *"understood"* the nature of God. '*We were only on a temporal plane and our spirit was more important that the physical.*' This thought empowered Nobody for he knew with this new knowledge and understanding he might attain a new level in spiritual understanding and it might impress the new women he was meeting. This could be how he would find his new soul mate. Besides, astrology surely was not bad; his mother read the horoscopes almost every day out of the paper growing up.

Myth #52 Knowledge, meditation and good intentions through spiritual means would help Nobody.

With an early morning dose of meditation to get his day started, working very hard to keep his emotions in check and trying to reach this higher spiritual plane, he would one day be able, through meditation, to reach the spirit world or the ether. Nobody was well on his way to spiritual enlightenment. As he was feeling empowered and understood that as long as he continued to work towards his goal of spiritual utopia, blessings would befall him. Through his good intentions, Nobody was obtaining spiritual pride in a tall order. Being accountable to only himself and his situational ethics, Nobody could rationalize any behavior. God was Spirit not the God of the Bible. Jesus was a good teacher that had reached the highest spiritual plane in history. Jesus spoke of many things that could only be understood with the application of metaphysics.

Truth #48 Nobody replaced the God of Abraham with mumbo-jumbo.

Nobody was guided by his new spiritual mentor and his wife despite the fact that he was still a rookie with the learnings before him. He had faith that all that he was learning was true. The women he met through these prayer or chart reading meetings could be options for his future wife. During his first chart reading, his mentor's wife said, that after reviewing everything, it looked to her that Nobody's problem was not drugs and alcohol but relationships. As he heard these words inside, this was truth that Nobody could not deny.

However, Nobody had a gift from his youth in which he could look at people and sum up people's pain or anger in their lives. It was a great gift and it kept him out of a lot of scraps. However when he looked upon these women, they seemed to be damaged goods. Now that he was empowered, he felt this was God's way of giving him a reprieve with this insight.

Nobody could take his time while waiting for God to present his gift to him which would be his soul mate. And, since he was a spirit being in physical body he would be able to indulge the yearnings of the flesh— without repercussion. His spirit was a higher form anyway. It was truly a spiritual path that Nobody felt would bring to him all that he wanted out of life and love. Just like they said, Nobody would possess a sane mind, soft heart and sound body. The problem with his relationships before was that he invested too much into the physical and not enough in the spiritual. So when he looked upon these women, he believed he saw their spirit and he now knew who he should avoid. He finally had it all together only after a few short months.

Nobody met with his DC sponsor a few times and shared his new spiritual path. His sponsor did not seem to be thrilled about it, but he was gracious. Nobody did not truly follow the suggestions of those in AA. They said that he should entertain one sponsor and not go around asking the same question of many people until you heard the answer you wanted. Nobody was now soliciting the advice from two sponsors and stayed with the one whose choice words reflected well inside of Nobody. This is what many have called the 'softer, easier path'. His DC sponsor would later tell Nobody that when he left Nobody's house that day, that he had puked outside due to the darkness he felt surround him while he was there.

Nobody was praying to a god, working to find a better understanding, staying sober, and providing for his son (and using his son to show how good a father he was for all to see.) He decided that if women were praying like he was, that had to be a good sign. He was sure they wanted a clean and sober life just as much as he did and that they had to be just as spiritual as he was since they were in the program. He just needed to prove to them that he was the best option out there for the taking. The confidence he felt growing in him was fragile at best.

Back on base, he was getting along in his new company and was assigned a team. Instead of trying to be the best solider he could, he was focused on getting his life put back together. So while he should have been learning as much as he could about his radio vans, he spent every waking moment living in the world he called recovery. He had an opportunity to go to Basic NCO School which would prepare him for the middle tier of the NCO ranks. It truly was a next step for career soldiers, however Nobody had other plans. Using the best persuasive skills he could possibly muster, he made a request of the Army to send him to the Army treatment center. At roughly six months sober, he wanted to go there instead of the school. The Army granted his wish; he was set to go in a few weeks time.

As his meditation abilities grew, he was able to have the force of his heartbeat rock his entire body. The focus and concentration were paying off. One morning—much to his surprise—he entered a new dimension. During this time of meditating, he stepped into a multicolored mist-filled area, similar in appearance to the Orion Nebula. He was experiencing and witnessing something he had never before seen in his life. His body was aroused which did not seem Godly, but placed Nobody in a conundrum.

He went to his spiritual mentor and described what had happened mentally and physically. He was assured that he had entered the Ether World he had read about. He needed to continue and hopefully he would meet his spirit guide. As interesting and intriguing as this was, Nobody felt he had crossed a line that he should not have crossed. Everything made sense but nothing added up.

Reflecting back on that morning, Nobody caught a glimpse of this spirit world and right before he had pulled himself out he had felt scared. This wasn't the anxiety you feel looking over the edge of a cliff or roof. No, this was a sense of terror that had seized his heart. A feeling that told him he should not be here. He had opened himself to something that was not meant for him. This had to be the forbidden fruit from the tree of knowledge. Nobody had been lured as Adam was, by good intentions and a promise of knowledge. Oh, how beautiful knowledge is when one cannot seemingly endure the ebbs and flow of life! How easy it is to latch onto something that seems secure, only to find out it gives way once you place all your faith into it leaving you victim to the consequences. Like peeking through a hole at scenes not meant for your eyes, Nobody had realized that if he were to continue down this path with what he knew in his heart, he would be participating in the occult. There was no fine line between white and black magic. There was good and evil, and as of this day, Nobody was able to distinguish between the two.

Truth #49 There are forces out there keeping Nobody from the one true God.

Episode 27

All You Need is Love

Nobody's empowerment seemed to fade. He'd gone back to basic praying techniques passed down through ages. After all these years of trying to make that feeling inside of him go away, he had only found temporal relief. In his mind he was looking for that one sentence or phrase that would make everything better. Now that he was sober and trying to do the next right thing he was sure he was only a moment away from the answer. Deep inside he felt that he was a failure with women and he did not have what it took to be a man's man even though he was obsessed with them. He was still afraid of confrontation. He had all these crazy thoughts swirling around in his head. He just couldn't make sense of it all. He hoped that during his month long stay at the army treatment center he would find the answers he was looking for.

For Nobody it was all about positioning. Since he had seven months of sobriety he felt like he was an old timer around a bunch of newbies. But, just like the day he was in the treatment center with his wife trying to put on an appearance, he was not in the treatment center because his life was perfect. Regardless of how he got there, he was going to be there.

'Terminally Unique' was a term someone had once used to describe him. In a way it was true; he just could not see that he was really just an alcoholic addict trying to get his act together. He thought his life was just a tad bit different than anybody else's. The funny thing about the mixed messages he was giving himself was that they were confusing. For someone like Nobody who was trying to make sense out of nonsense, he ended up exposing himself to a world of contradictions. Anyone that is in survival mode cannot see past the trees in a forest. His life was still ruled by his emotions. He was still looking for a new drug to take all the pain away. Maybe if he prayed more, maybe if he worked the 'steps' harder, maybe if he found a girl at church, maybe if he wasn't a single parent. . .it was the noise of the peanut gallery in his head that would not shut down long enough for him to see the big picture. He wanted it his way. Based on how he felt at this moment, he could rationalize hot chocolate as the cure. It was all for this moment or being left alone for the next. He just could not be content with the life he had. Something had to change to give him a sense of progress. His DC sponsor once told him that when his life got boring, that would be the sign that he was starting to live a normal life. The thought *terrified* Nobody.

Upon his arrival, he was assigned his bunk and had to go through the intake process. They asked the normal questions.

"Do you smoke?"

"Yes."

"What brand?"

"The cheapest."

"What were the most drugs you did in one night?"

That night. It was the night he'd met his wife. So he spoke about the eight ball of cocaine, peyote stew, the quarter grams of methamphetamine and the booze. After relating the tale of the tape, the intake physician said he felt Nobody's big party night was ranked number two. He was astonished that Nobody was even alive to tell his tale. According to the ranking scale, Nobody would have had to have been a step away from an overdose to be designated a number one. Ironically, in the mind of an alcoholic and drug addict, being number two was impressive, but any of them would have liked to be number one. Nobody's competitive side was showing, even under the most deadly circumstances. A number one classification would be something to hold his hat on in the future. Nobody told him that, in the course of that night, he had felt his heart give a couple of weird beats in his chest. The doctor had a point, but this time Nobody was proud for being number two. In his eyes a near brush with death was impressive.

Nobody, always looking for something to prop himself up, now had more information to do so. So he became a self-proclaimed "Pontificator of Sobriety" standing on his soap box. He still needed to work on his ego. Just because you are sober doesn't mean that all the old behaviors go away right away - or at all. Ever. Nobody still had to be the best at something, and today it was going to be sobriety.

Myth #53 Nobody looks sober.

During his stay at treatment Nobody had made a commitment to himself to really give this a try. God would not have brought him this far if He did not want him to get better. Besides the groups were intense. As he started sharing parts of his past there were times when he started to cry. Not just a small tear here or there. He felt deep swelling from the recesses of his chest. Once, this feeling turned into a flood of emotion which seemed to pour out from his chest. The question he continually raised was, "Why?" Why did his wife cheat on him? Why did his family behave the way they did? Why?? Why would my parents do those things as I was growing up? Why did they make him choose who he should talk to? Why give him ultimatums about love and college? Why was he subjected to sneak around to speak with his relatives just to keep peace? Why was God intent on punishing him? Why was he not a good enough lover? Why couldn't he find a relationship where they live 'happily ever after'? Why did it hurt so much? Why, why, why?

The pain just ripped his soul apart with each time he shared at group. The other guys had different issues. What it came down to was that, in his mind, Nobody felt that if only he had a relationship, all of this pain would subside. If only. During one of his group meetings he talked about his sister. He felt tremendous guilt for having left his sister. When all that stuff happened with his parents and his girlfriend at the time, he just walked out. He never kept in touch with her and he had just barely finished high school and partying until he left for the Army. How could he have been so callous? He left her there with them, all alone and he did not defend her or even show her he cared. Torn with guilt and shame, he was dumbfounded by his actions. She had lived there right alongside of him. She had witnessed the same things he did and when he was able to leave he did it without looking back. He had abandoned her. And for that he felt deep remorse.

He immediately sat down and wrote her a letter in which he expressed his sorrow for leaving her there in that environment. As he wrote, a solemn tear hit the page. He loved his sister, but they never really talked after he left. Consumed with his own world for these past few years, whatever it was that drew his attention, he had left her behind. He was kept abreast of the latest family news, but it was all news, sports and weather. As he placed the stamp on the envelope, put it in the mail, he thought for sure she would understand the place where he was as he looked over the past. He had explained how he was sorry for leaving her with them all alone.

When he was finally able to make phone calls, he called his sister in hopes of rekindling their relationship. He finally reached her. He heard her voice and his mind was filled with expectations. As they were talking his heart was starting to fall from his chest to the floor. She said none of the things that he had written about had happened. She did not understand where he was coming from. She was fine and the parents he described were not the ones she knew. She loved him, but she did not understand what he was talking about. Nobody heard his sister tell him one thing very clearly: he shouldn't lie about this sort of thing.

Completely at a loss of words, Nobody's world shattered further. He needed someone to validate his past. He hoped his sister would be the one person he thought would help him put his memories in perspective. But, what she just told him was that he was messed up in the head and what he believed did not happen. He was the reason there were problems in the family and their parents' marriage. She was just fine.

Myth #54 Again, it's Nobody's fault they were not happy.

When he started to look at everything from her perspective, it did seem to happen that way. She had been able to get a car, something his parents said he could not get. She had help getting into college, something he was being manipulated to attend. Now that he remembered, it was always his sister this and his sister that. His Dad would say that girls are different than boys and should be treated differently. It was true. They *had* treated her differently. She had survived the best way she could. She played by the rules to get what she needed. Nobody had made a decision that he would not live in a lie and he was paying the price for that choice. As the years would pass Nobody would look upon the relationship between his sister and his parents and see how she would ignore the behaviors of their mother that he'd pointed out as he grew up. He would hear the excuses to justify her behavior and how the rest of the family was out to get his mother. His sister even gave him the loyalty speech. She would accuse him of meddling into affairs that did not concern him. The hurdle that Nobody could not overcome was that when he tried to point out behaviors that were not appropriate, he was always chastised. In their world there was only one truth and it was not his—it was theirs. He would spend years wanting them to just admit that *something* he said was true. That they, too, should acknowledge that there were specific incidents that happened that were wrong. That they also have a role in the way a relationship blossoms or withers.

Nobody's hopes and dreams, unknowingly, would revolve around his immediate family's acknowledgment of the truth about their past. Peer into it and instead of generalizing and saying they did the best they could, listen to him and acknowledge that Nobody was somebody who didn't have to always apologize to get back into their good graces. Unfortunately, they would continue to look outside of themselves. Any hint at becoming whole would require a two way dialogue into the past. To attempt reconciliation would be met with disdain and accusation. Nobody would go back time and time again hoping it would be different, each time only to be pushed aside and always blamed as the real problem.

The truth that would elude Nobody until he was much older was the fact that his family would willingly sacrifice their son and call him the liar before looking at themselves.

His sister, the one ally he thought he would be able to count on to validate who he was and proclaim, "Yes, you are right about what had happened!" had just let go of his hand. Just like in the movies, someone risks their life to save a person from the edge of the cliff, holding on with one hand, grasping another person's arm and pulls them up from ultimate doom. The embrace that told you everything would be alright once you were pulled to safety. At that moment Nobody saw himself falling over the cliff, his hands reaching out screaming for someone to save him, to love him, to tell him everything would be alright. If only he could go back to that day he was rocked by his aunt on the rocker.

Love was validation and Nobody had found it, through a new family: his 'family' in treatment. He met people who would share their hurts and desires, people willing to admit their part and work to find the answer. Nobody was still a 'Babe in Toyland.' He heard that he truly needed to trust in God as he understood Him. Nobody wanted to believe but did not know what to believe. He was told to just pray to God and don't try to figure it out. Just hit down on your knees and pray.

At one point Nobody sat under a large tree, overlooking the city. It was after dinner and the sky was dark and clear. Nobody dropped to his knees and with his arms stretched wide, wanting a gust of wind to be the sign that God was listening, he prayed a prayer to turn his life over to God. He asked God to remove the pain and fill the whole inside. Telling God he did not want to be a statistic. He just didn't want to pass treatment, like his counselor said he was trying to do. No, Nobody wanted to live a life devoted to God and recovery.

"God take it all away, so I can live outside this pain. Please God, help me. I want to give all of me to You" Nobody proclaimed.

There was no great wind or burning bush. Just a moment of solitude. A slight, gentle breeze felt cool across a tear on his cheek. For a brief moment, it wasn't God that was listening, it was Nobody, and he felt peace.

Truth #50 Nobody was on a hill with God.

When it was time to leave treatment there were the ceremonious 'good-byes'. Nobody had met a lot of people in the community that he had considered friends. As he was saying good-bye to a hardened biker who had years of recovery, Nobody said, "I will come back to visit in a couple of months."

The response was quick and to the point from the biker. It would be a statement that Nobody would carry with him throughout his life and would mold how he would approach any situation or conversation. It was a truism that hit Nobody in the chest, a truth that made him take a giant step in how he would relate to others in the future.

The Biker said, "Don't make promises you cannot keep."

Taken aback by the authority in which the words were spoken, Nobody acknowledged the statement and bade him farewell without any future commitments, never to return to El Paso, Texas.

Episode 28

The Age of Aquarius

I t is funny how when you are in treatment or in church all the rules and conditions for a clean and pure life make all the sense in the world. There is an understanding that certain measures must be taken to allow the person a chance at a normal life. The clarity is so sharp and everyone gives agreement with the proverbial 'amen' or head nod. However, being the humans that we are, when you are out there all by yourself, left to your own desires and needs, how quickly one can revert to old ways to compensate for the feelings one has. How all the rules that one knows must be followed, be adhered to even if it doesn't feel right following them. By running from his feelings for many years, and after only a few months of sobriety, Nobody had begun unlearning his old ways of living, but those habits that cannot be undone overnight.

Feeling empowered by his new sobriety-induced confidence, Nobody embraced the need for recovery. With his roommate watching his son half of the time, Nobody was able to go to meetings nightly, meet more people and brought his son when the live-in sitter wasn't available. While he was showing up and speaking words of wisdom, that did not fool the old timers in the room. They would smile and listen and nod their heads. In private conversations he had with them, they would mention that maybe his way of thinking was at odds with the tried and true methods of AA. However, in the back of his mind he was still looking for Mrs. Right Now Forever, an idea that was not easily shaken from his mind. He had heard what they said about relationships in the first year: that you should stay clear of them. Some of these rules were not meant for him, he was in a way still just a bit different than everyone else. He was terminally unique after all.

The pressure that he placed on himself for a relationship was mounting. Nobody was painfully aware that his roommate was going to leave the military and go back home to have her baby. In a few short weeks he would be an 'alone' parent. History was repeating itself, it wouldn't be long when Nobody would be alone with only his son, just as his mother had been alone with him. He would also have no one to talk to if he did not find answers to his upcoming loneliness.

Nobody went on dates and spent time fixing dinners, hopefully to 'bait the hook' (where he would dazzle his guest with the great and wonderful things he could do.) There was no doubt, he could not have anything out of place in his home. The lines in the carpet would show that his house was clean and well kept. The food would be presented in the most desirable fashion, demonstrating attention to detail and great care. It was all in the presentation. He was a single dad who had his act together on the outside but inside just a man screaming for someone to love him.

Nobody couldn't understand how guys around him could act as though they did not care about the relationships they were in. He would hear them talk about football games, going out with the fellas and so on. These terms were so foreign to him. If you were in a relationship with someone, shouldn't you spend as much time as possible with that person? Doing things with friends you could do as a couple, but once you were with that someone special that was where you should remain. That someone special that God has out there for you should provide the yin for your yang.

Myth #55 Relationships are meant to satisfy all needs for Nobody.

It just so happened that on a weekend that his son was with his mother, Nobody and a bunch of folks from the program decided to go to a treatment center AA meeting, some seventy miles away. He went over to his friend's house to pick everyone up. The Arizona night sky was riddled with thunderstorms. It was those on-again off-again heavy rains, during the tail end of the monsoon season. The sun was just getting ready to set.

Multiple mushroom storm clouds were sweeping their way across the plains between the mountain ranges. It was not uncommon to be swept away if you ventured into washes during a storm. All that water has to go somewhere and during storms, washes were temporary rapids that moved the water to the valleys. So when the monsoon season hit and it rained, water is in abundance for a very short period of time and its one goal is to move to lower levels as fast as it can.

As they were leaving and trying to get to the highway from a dirt road, with the windshield wipers on high, he could barely see the road and Nobody's car slid into the ditch. With the rain coming down in torrents and water up to the door of his car, the ditch had turned into a small wash. They felt for a brief moment that they would have to wait for the rain to stop before attempting to get out of the car.

Only one front wheel was still on the road. It was the rear of the car that had slid, the ditch had an undefined end and it emptied into a flat ahead of them. If Nobody could just ride the ditch to the end they might just make it out. The challenge was on and with front wheel drive, Nobody thought he could get them out of the situation. If he has was not able to keep that one wheel on the road their hopes for the evening would be dashed. So the challenge ensued, they were chanting in the car, "Go, Go, Go." Nobody very gingerly began the journey through an easy application of the clutch. The car slowly started its procession toward the flat. The car was gaining momentum and after five minutes, Nobody managed to get the car out of the ditch and back on the road. The night was saved and off they went laughing and joking about the strange turn of events.

When they arrived at their destination and got settled in, Nobody noticed a girl with a red bandana over her head. He was drawn to her and could not stop looking at her through the course of the AA meeting. He was sure that she was also sneaking glances back to him. When what felt like the longest hour in history had past, Nobody walked over with the intent to introduce himself to her. With only five months of sobriety and still failing to understand that a woman in treatment is not necessarily there on vacation, he went over and said, "Hello." And, with a simple word, his life would be changed forever.

She looked at him and he was mesmerized by her mysterious appearance. "Hello"

And then she posed the age-old pickup line "What's your sign?"

Memories of astrology charts flashed in his head. So did the near miss in the ditch. What if they had not managed to get out, they would not have made it here. He was connecting dots and they formed a heart. Nobody believed that Divine Providence had led him here, to this moment in time. This was the clue he was looking for, seeking with never-ending passion. Finally, after all this time, his perseverance had paid off. There is *no way* this could be a mistake. Under no uncertain terms should they have gotten out of that ditch without it being a miracle. There needed to be a sign that told Nobody, "Hey look over here for your one true love."

Of all the questions in the world to ask, this was the one question that made the world stop. It triggered something. His head turned. He stopped. He looked at her and then, he listened.

His mind raced. His thoughts were blurred. In his mind, he was still confusing so-called 'answered prayers' with God. Picking from a menu of spiritual options he had been exposed to, Nobody didn't understand that astrology and horoscopes were forms of Divination. These are expressly forbidden by the God of Abraham. Nobody believed in God, but a mosaic version, pieces of abstraction that, when placed together, provided a larger picture someone could identify but, if you looked close enough, the small pieces did not resemble the whole. Nobody had pieced together a picture of the future that he desperately wanted to be true for him. In a split second, he saw a match made in Heaven instead of one made in his mind. If he had learned anything from the Rosicrucians, this would have been a warning to run.

"Aquarius," he said.

"Cancer," she said with a sultry smile. She was the same sign as his mother.

Episode 29

Look What the Cat Dragged In

M any men before Nobody have been drawn in by the physical prowess of a woman who upon further review should have not even spoken to, women like Delilah and Bathsheba to name two. However, Nobody's need for companionship and his continuous belief in some of the astrology jargon along with his subliminal desire to save someone would soon propel him into a dark abyss.

He visited Red Bandana Woman and telephoned her against the advice of those around him. Nobody was attempting to jump into a relationship at about six months of sobriety when he should have been steering clear from it. Not to mention it is not a good idea to start a relationship with someone in treatment. Men and women in treatment are not there for eating too much ice cream. Patients, by their true name, are usually there for a major problem in their lives, drugs and alcohol in this case, but as with most people it is only the symptom not the cause. People go into treatment with plenty of baggage just below the surface. When the vice that was used to squelch the emotional pain is taken away, those feelings must be dealt with. Meaningful ways to handle those emotions are meetings, service work, treatment, food, and exercise. However, many turn to sex as a means to alleviate the emotional pain or to take the focus off their real problems. Sex. Nobody saw an attractive sexy female who, by asking only one question and giving him 'the look' suddenly became the object of his desire. She gave new meaning to 'love is blind'. He only saw what was directly in front of him. He knew she would solve all his problems.

He got to know her in a mere short month, but unlike Nobody, her child was in the custody of the state because she had drawn a knife on her soon-to-be-ex-husband. According to her, the guy was a bit crazy and she really needed to get away from him. She said he was unpredictable and was known to be violent at times. She pulled the knife like any other protective mother would do. She said she was protecting her son from one of his outbursts. Nobody didn't understand why she was in treatment, but she was. She liked him, and isn't that what truly matters? He soon believed the idea that they were meant to be with each other. She said she wanted to stay sober and to Nobody this all sounded reasonable. These little issues with the state were temporary and *he* could help *her* get *her* life back together. All she had to do was love him and Nobody believed she did. The magical afternoon together during her day pass proved it. He continued to pray to God for His will but in truth, Nobody was praying for *his* will. It was obvious to those around him that Nobody saw only what he wanted. But Nobody truly believed this was what God had planned for him and as long as you were patient all things were possible. Nobody had been patient for six months.

Her treatment facility allowed everyone to go to Sierra Vista for an AA Halloween party, and Red Bandana Woman was able to attend and said she would meet him there. Nobody had his opportunity to show everyone the prize he had caught. He would be able show everyone he was worth something. Yes, he'd show them that his ex-wife had made a mistake. What's more, he would, in an indirect way, prove to her the same thing. Nobody was somebody after all. You had to be somebody of value to have a woman like this on your arm.

While Nobody awaited the arrival of Red Bandana Woman, he was talking to folks but always looking to the door for her. He had no idea what her costume was going to be and she had said she would surprise him. As he mingled with the crowd he was able to talk with his DC sponsor. The van arrived, when she walked through the door, the look on his sponsor's face was priceless. Nobody was in total awe himself. Nobody had told her that he would wear an Indian costume and she showed up as his squaw! It was a jaw-dropping costume. Just ask Nobody and every guy in the room. All his DC sponsor said was, "Here comes trouble."

Nobody looked at him and said, "That's **my** girl.

His DC sponsor looked at him and chuckled and said, "Oh boy."

He said he had seen this type many times over the course of his life and Nobody should be wary. In a word, he said she was trouble. Nobody saw a tigress he could tame because she loved him and he would be able to provide everything she needed. She would not venture away. Yes, she was a prize and many guys wanted her, but she wanted Nobody most of all.

Ignoring the flashing billboard signs that said turn back—the sign that said don't place your hand in the cage because you might get bit, the advice from his sponsor and the little voice inside that said this was dangerous—Nobody decided he should follow his heart. Because it was connected to his loins, Nobody's heart was a powerful ruler. Her vacation at the treatment center was going to be over soon and she mentioned that she did not feel safe in her hometown and she specifically did not want to stay in the house all alone without her son. She didn't have a job. She was collecting government assistance. Nobody came up with a wonderful idea. Since his roommate was moving out to have her baby in California, Red Bandana Woman should move in with him. His roommate was moving out a week before her release from treatment. They could live together and he would help her get her son back from the state, finish up the divorce she was going through and for all this she would love him. She would help him watch his son during the day. This *had* to be a God given relationship. The timing was impeccable. All the pieces where falling into place and the square pegs were being easily jammed into the round hole with a sixteen pound sledgehammer. If someone tells you they love you, backs it up physically and commits to the relationship with you and your son, just like turning on a light switch, everyone can live happily ever after. This was too good to be true. God had answered his prayers. Red Bandana Women was now going to be his *Hometown Hottie*.

Myth #56 Nobody sees sex as a commitment.

Nobody believed he was right and everyone else was wrong. He was on a mission and he would see it through. His roommate was packing up her things and moving back to Los Angeles. Nobody planned for the delivery of his new hottie to his house and was even able to get one of his previous flings to drive to the treatment center and bring his *Hometown Hottie* to his house while he was working. Once she arrived, she could instantaneously be his wife, mother to his son, lover, friend, and satisfy all his needs to make him feel complete. Two different people with different needs, each trying to get satisfaction from the other.

Blinded by the events unfolding, Nobody lived in a world and exposed his son to dangers he never thought of. They were attempting to establish and present a stable home environment to the State. They attended meetings together. Nobody kept her in his sight and watched who she talked to constantly. After a little while his *Hometown Hottie* started demonstrating a weird sort of behavior, one minute she could be sweet and the next extremely angry. In one weird moment it felt like the days he was growing up. She said she had been diagnosed as being Bipolar and with the proper meds she was fine. It was just the stress of not having her son with her. She was sorry for the occasional outbursts. She promised she would make it up to him later. As long as she said and showed him that she loved him, that was all he needed.

Nobody watched and, as she continued to gather attention from the guys around her, his insecurities intensified. He had to constantly say he loved her and then wait for her to say it. All he needed was to hear those words and the anxiety would subside until the next thought of losing her set in. This behavior did not take long to become engrained into his mind. He would come home every day for lunch and watch her favorite soap opera during this time with her. He needed to know what she was doing, but, with only one car, she stayed at the house with him hoping that she would remain happy shut up in the trailer with their love to feed her happiness.

What really drove him crazy was when they took turns going to meetings because his son had to be watched. She would go out for coffee after and he would sit in the trailer waiting impatiently. He would interrogate her when she came home. Without her by his side, he was an empty shell. He could not concentrate.

While he loved his son, the time he spent with him was more about taking care of his basic needs while waiting for her to return. Nobody had created enough stress inside of him wondering what she was doing apart from him, that he tried to make sure his son behaved. Nobody constantly reminded his son not to spill his milk during dinner, but he could never see past the event. If his son did spill his milk, clean was only a couple of paper towels away. These moments Nobody would see one day as precious were lost forever. While he was waiting for her to come back, he put his son in the playpen as he sat on the couch, counting the minutes. These were moments where he could have rocked his son. However, Nobody's mind raced so fast about things that he could not control that he couldn't concentrate on what was directly in front of him. He tried to focus on other things, but all he could do was to wait for his *Hometown Hottie* to walk through the door. Once she did, it was like a drug and the anxiety subsided. He would pretend he had been doing his own thing the whole time and those past hours of fear and insecurity had never occurred. She was in his sights and she was his. This would be a character trait that would plague Nobody for years, but in varying degrees as time passed.

Drifting away from the principles that had kept him sober and the spirituality he had gained, Nobody's new item of worship was a relationship. If they were puzzle pieces, no matter how hard they tried would not fit perfectly together. The two lovebirds had moments of searing intensity and other times her anger or rage ruled the day. Nobody worked hard to make sure she would not get angry. Nobody always seemed to fight this 'push and pull' of affection from her. They were like magnets. When two similar ends of the magnet were close you could not force them together. However, the moment her anger subsided, Nobody was unable to pull himself from her. Nobody, in a very short period of time, had gone from providing everything she needed to make her happy, to the one being dominated. He was being played like a fiddle and manipulated by her. *'Hometown Hottie'* surely had Delilah in her family tree.

Truth #51 Nobody was lost in a relationship illusion.

Episode 30

Spellbound

As Nobody was realizing what was going on around him it occurred to him that this relationship he was in seemed to be very similar to how he behaved growing up reacting to his mother. How he tried to watch his every move and word for fear his mother would get mad at him. Now he was watching everything he did to make sure this primary figure in his life did not leave. He kept his son close for fear of her temper. No matter how the ledger looked as you compared the numbers, it told him he was in a bad situation. He was caught in a vicious circle he could not get out of by rational thinking. His irrational thinking prevented him from making the right choice. Everything about this relationship was baked with ingredients to make a bomb, however with his blinders on he would only reach out to taste the icing and he refused to take a bite and acknowledge the truth of the matter. That the cake may look good on the outside but it was the insides that really mattered. He still attended meetings and started sharing with his DC sponsor.

Nobody ran down the list of things she had said or done. Like her belief in a subterranean culture that you could get to by flying over the North Pole, which some Admiral had discovered. How there was a secret society that truly ruled the world from this subterranean culture and advised all governments. How one day she and her ex-husband would make it there because, in essence they were actual soul mates. The issue was they could not live in this world together. How, at Denny's, she'd said that if Nobody continued to be jealous, she would give him something to be jealous about. If he did not stop, she would go to bed with someone else and rest his fears. She had said it with such venom it made his skin crawl. It was true, Nobody was jealous. He had to know her every move, had to try and keep this tigress in the cage. But the look in her eyes when she said that made her seem as if she was possessed. Those 'cat like' eyes piercing him through the chest with an intensity of a hot iron. He was put in his place in front of everyone. Her statement even made a few people fidget in their seat and the look he got was as if they could not believe what she had said.

He shared this with his DC sponsor and added that she liked to get coffee at Denny's near the trailer park in the mornings while he was at work. Befuddled as Nobody spoke, "Who would she talk to, and why does she need to do that anyway?"

Nobody told him how he questioned her because guys would call the house asking for her or the phantom wrongs numbers when he answered the phone and her Bipolar diagnosis.

Sitting in his sponsor's car, his DC sponsor had reached a point he wouldn't hear it any longer. Enough was enough. He looked at Nobody squarely in the eyes and using the simplest of words, told Nobody the truth.

"Nobody she is crazy. She is not good for you or your son, can't you see? Nobody, I didn't want to tell you this, but it's something you need to know. She is also performing oral sex on some guys after the meetings. You need to get rid of her now or you'll end up drinking and drugging over this woman. She is screwing everyone but you."

This pushed him over the edge. He was bawling almost uncontrollably. Suddenly he felt angry, "How do you know that?"

"Nobody, why would I lie to you? Do you think I find pleasure telling a guy his girlfriend is going down on guys in a parking lot after a meeting? I told you before, I have been on the streets. I have seen this before. You are being used. She may love you, but the person she is will never afford you a healthy relationship with her. Sadly, I don't believe she can help herself."

Nobody tried to rationalize his DC sponsor's comments and chose not to believe them. His sponsor had to be wrong. Staring into the dashboard, Nobody's mind began racing faster and faster. There were so many words that wanted to come out, that were spoken within his mind, but he couldn't move them from his throat to his lips. They were right there; all he had to do was say them aloud. She needed to leave. *IF* only he could just say them. His heart could not go through with it.

Truth #52 Nobody failed to listen to God's messenger.

When he got home he confronted her. She said his sponsor was lying and he did not care for her anyway. Yes, she was mad, but she would not ruin what they had. She was sorry for some of the things she said. She moved closer to him in a sultry fashion. She agreed that she needed to see the doctor to change her meds. Upset but calm because she was next to him, Nobody said he would not leave. Her touch said that it was OK and all insecurities he had felt driving to the house subsided when he was within her sight and reach. As long as he could see her and was within arm's reach of her essence, he was OK. It was when she was out of his sight that the cycle of crazy thinking began.

He could not leave her under his own power. It was as if he'd taken a hostage and through his pain and insecurities the roles had reversed. She had power over him. He could not break free and was too afraid to try. The God he had surrendered to on that hill in El Paso was nowhere to be seen. He was slipping farther from the program. The truth of the matter was he was running from his inability to take a stand for himself. The tigress he thought he could tame had him cornered in her cage and she blocked the way out. His only choice, he believed, was to appease her and not get eaten.

In the back of his mind he knew he could not trust her. He'd held out hope that she would stay and not leave him. With no backbone to speak of, Nobody was trapped. His only job was to keep her in his sight and away from any situation that would lead her away. He heard what his DC sponsor said, but he tried to block the truth from resonating in his mind.

In the presence of other men, Nobody was a mouse - in his mind. From a sexual perspective, everyone around him had what it took to satisfy her hunger. All he saw were men that, if given the opportunity, would take her from him and then laugh at him behind closed doors. He could hear them telling her that they were big enough and manly enough to keep her satisfied. He also heard her passionate affirmations of what they'd said.

This was the battle that played over and over in Nobody's mind. He did not have what it took to truly keep women happy. Nobody had to perform and behave in a manner that would convince her to stay. If she stayed then all the subliminal messages about his worthiness over the years would validate who he was. He was in this yo-yo like relationship and his goal was to convince her to stay.

These straw men that Nobody was battling in his mind and, in reality, only had to be in the presence of a woman. All these straw men had to do was slowly walk over, say a couple of words, and lead her away. Nobody had to manufacture who he was to be able to be in a position to do the same. It wasn't about who he loved - it was about who loved him.

Myth #57 Nobody was inadequate as a man.

Truth #53 Nobody wanted HER to love him.

Myth #58 Nobody's unlovable.

Though he was afraid to confront the situation head-on, he watched who she was looking at and tried to capture any hidden conversation or an unsuspecting wink of an eye. He felt threatened anywhere he went and around men in the program. Were any of these guys someone she was with? His actions undoubtedly smothered her, but there was no other way Nobody knew to squelch the anxiety that would rise inside of him when he was alone, at work, or outside of earshot from her. The safest place he felt was at home with her. He would do whatever he could to make her happy. He had no voice. Even if he said what he truly felt, there was no volume to it. If he tried to express his suspicions, he knew she would leave because of his false accusation. He could not say anything until he had visible concrete evidence. He tried to make sure she didn't get mad at him with the questions he asked. They were always simple questions wrapped in a statement spoken as a truth, then he would gauge his feelings by her response.

There was a song on the radio that Nobody loved to listen to. The lyrics painted a picture that he could almost see in his life which rang deep in his soul that called out his name. It spoke of chasing dreams, kisses like poison, with green lights actually red. He was being lured into a Black Widow's lair without heeding the warning signs. Captured by the melody, the words never found a true home in his heart.

Episode 31

Reefer Headed Women

S ome time had passed since the night he confronted her about what his DC sponsor told him and a lot of the noise he was hearing grinded to a halt. He came home one day to find his son standing in the doorway to his room. He had a black eye. She was in the kitchen. Instead of being a responsible parent protecting the child at any cost, Nobody was paralyzed. Instead of running to his son and grabbing him up, Nobody went to her to find out what had happened. Of course she was sorry and apologetic, and Nobody heard the proverbial 'it will never happen again' speech. She had been angry at Nobody since all she has to do is sit around the house and she had nobody to talk to.

His son had come up behind her and was in the wrong place at the wrong time. This whole thing with her child, watching his and not having hers, propelled her into depression she said. Nobody was trapped and did not know what to do and he was actually afraid of her. He had set this scenario up again, just like his mother when she was alone and his first wife when she was also alone. He was playing the same chess pieces again. With quick mood swings he never knew what to expect or what she was capable of. He was speechless and felt powerless. Words were racing again in his head, but nothing of substance came out. He only tried to make the current situation better by soothing everyone and 'make it better.' There was stillness in the house for the rest of the night. He loved and hated her in the same breath. His sponsor had told him before that this was lust not love, but those were only words. He wanted to believe her and he told her she needed to go to the doctor and she agreed.

Nobody was grateful that the black eye healed before his ex-wife had his son for a weekend. He just couldn't face the questions. He did not know what to do and was too afraid to act on his true thoughts about the situation. He lived in his secrets.

They planned a trip to visit *Hometown Hottie's* parents, who were recovering alcoholics as well, but far removed from program. They lived on a farm seventy miles away. She was able to visit her son who was in foster care in the same town. She was on track to regain custody of her son soon. They spent the night in the house she used to live in with her husband.. There was a strange eeriness being in that house. Nobody felt as if he was treading on unholy ground and need not be there. All in all, her parents seemed to enjoy him and he caught a few glances from her mother, giving her daughter approving glances. Nobody knew how to turn it on and when.

The discussions about her anger came up a couple of times during their stay and on their way home (they were headed to an AA meeting before going home,) she looked at him and said that she had been really struggling with her mood swings. She was scared of her anger. She went on to say that she loved Nobody and the last thing she wanted was for his son to get hurt again. Nobody asked what she thought the solution was. She looked at him and said that she should smoke pot because it was truly the only thing that calmed her nerves. It sounded crazy. Her experience said that when she smoked dope, bad things did not happen.

The irrationality of the statement never pierced the skull that encased his brain. He connected those dots from his own experience. He remembered how everyone had thought he was nicer when he smoked pot. So, naturally this was a reasonable request and a solution to a problem for which he hadn't found an answer.

Truth #54 Nobody plays Russian Roulette.

Nobody said, "OK." He also completely ignored every red flag he saw and felt, the tell-tale signs his sponsor had laid out for him in his car, and ignored his gut feelings about her fidelity and her anger. Dismissing his need to maintain his sobriety, forgetting about his son's best interest, and neglecting his overall sanity, instead, he focused on his need to be loved by her and how he wanted her. Most of all he focused on his belief that this would work out.

It was as if a switch went off in his head and nine months of sobriety were forgotten. Nobody made the choice to visit the drive-thru of a nearby liquor store instead of driving to the AA meeting. When he got home he called his old roommate, the one he met playing cards. Nobody asked him to bring over some pot. Within one hour Nobody had stepped off a cliff. She was happy and repaid him for his actions once everyone left for the evening.

He went to work the next day and he got wind of an upcoming urinal-ysis. Fear and panic began to creep into Nobody's thoughts. Would he get popped to take the test? Would a lapse in sanity cause him to put everything at risk with the Army? He was right back where he was before, living a lie. He could not let anyone know he was drinking and doing drugs again. His life was still an illusion. He spent a sleepless night drinking soda after soda trying to flush his system. Fear, panic and anger ruled him. This was her fault. He held on to this belief.

Similar to Samson and Delilah, Nobody went back time and time again only to be betrayed. His love or lust for this woman drove him to do things others only shake their heads at. The insanity of drug and alcohol addiction and no God only led to more chaos. His name did not get called for the piss test. With his desire to continue his charade, he petitioned the company commander and became the Drug and Alcohol NCO. Additionally, he asked also to be reassigned as the Nuclear, Biological, and Chemical NCO. He rationalized that his ineffectiveness as a field Sergeant leading a satellite team, knowing that the person who had the position was transferring out, this would work out well for him because it allowed Nobody to stay close to her and be home every night and weekend.

He managed to get his act together at work and soon started demon-strating excellence again. He passed inspections by the Inspector General. He was beating other NCOs who went to school for this. Six months passed then he became the Re-Enlistment NCO. He was still the Drug and Alcohol NCO and he set up all the drug tests in the company. He would supposedly put the numbers zero thru nine in a hat for the company commander to pick the 'winning number.' Soldiers whose last digit of their SSN number corresponded with the number drawn were 'winners.' The number nine was miraculously never picked.

The custody issue of his *Hometown Hottie* was drawing near to an end. She needed to borrow Nobody's car to finish up some of the administrative issues. She would be gone for a couple of days, staying with her parents. Separation was a killer for Nobody. No matter what was said to calm his nerves, life was completely put on hold while she was away. He had no life without her, no matter how crazy it was. She called a couple of times and said all was well and that she was going to hang out with some old friends, one of which was a previously mentioned guy that she had fooled around with but nothing ever came of it. Nobody objected, but to no avail, she was going to do something for herself and he would have to get over it. He did not hear from her until the next day.

Pacing the trailer, he found she never made it back to her parents. Where is she? She had his car, now he was trapped. It was a sleepless night similar to the one with his ex-wife, and Nobody was a basket case. He was angry and vowed to get rid of this woman once and for all. He just needed to lure her back so he could get his car back. When she finally called, she apologized and Nobody, furious wanted her back immediately. She said that she had in fact gone to bed with that guy and that she would not come back if she were going to be kicked to the curb. She said there was no room for her to breathe in the relationship.

The pressure she felt from him was crushing, she got high and one thing led to another. She did not understand how this could have happened. The meds the doctor had given that she thought was working obviously weren't. She loved him but all the pressure with her son being in foster care, helping raise Nobody's son, and Nobody's jealousy was just too much to bear. Could he forgive her?

"All he could say was would you please come home so we can talk about it?"

As he waited for her all he could think about was how he would gallantly throw her out of the house. He imagined her with that guy. She would pay for hurting him after all he was doing to help her get her son back. Decisions have consequences and she had one coming. Two hours had passed and when she arrived he was ready to grab his keys and shove her back out of the door.

Sitting at the kitchen table, the first time he sat for almost a day, she came through the door. He could not help but want her. The moment she walked through the door it was as if an angel came through. She ran to him, hugged him and said she was sorry. He had melted again and he asked her if she would show him how much she loved him. Her response was, "After what I have done, you still want me?"

Nobody had nothing inside of him. He had been stripped of his manhood. No God to run to and no program to lean on. He was a shell of a man. He only knew that he needed to feel differently from what he was now feeling. Sex would validate him and she would stay.

The Father of Lies had perverted sex for Nobody over the years, by luring him to the wrong conclusions about this subject. The beauty God had intended sex to be between a man and women was brought to a level of shame, guilt and foreboding. Sex was the only way Nobody could register if someone loved him. He somehow connected dots from his childhood memories. His parents went to their room after fights. He saw how people made up on television. So it was with him. When they had sex he would feel that she loved him. Nobody was ashamed of himself and wanted to die. Someone had said in a meeting one time that if you did not like the way you were feeling you needed to stop doing what you were doing. However, Nobody went to the wrong place to feel better and he sank deeper into despair.

The problem was what he witnessed earlier in life - whether right or wrong - was completely perverse here. They weren't making up, he was taking a drug to make himself better.

Myth #59 Nobody felt sex healed all ills in a relationship.

His sponsor was right. It *was* about lust but the desire was so strong and the thought of losing what he had with her forced him to make irrational decisions. He was in a prison, and because of his fear of the unknown and no faith in anything, he just held on and kept her close. None of what he thought actually worked; she was still slipping from his finger tips.

A couple of program people reached out to him since his disappearance. One person was his DC sponsor, who Nobody said he did not want to talk to again (not because Nobody hated his DC Sponsor but, because he knew the truth and until Nobody faced it, he did not want to be reminded.)

Another person who Nobody respected also called. He was retired Air Force and currently working for a defense contractor. Nobody had been home thinking about how his life had taken a turn for the worse and hoping that it would change. The phone rang. The guy asked how he was doing and said he had missed him. He'd been wondering if Nobody was OK. God had sent another messenger, a path to be taken, a possible way out, someone he could trust to lay it on the table, but all Nobody could say was that he appreciated the call and he would reach out if he needed anything.

Truth #55 Nobody decides not to listen to another one of God's messengers.

All of this worrying and wondering what to do and, at the same time just wanting her to be totally in love with him, Nobody was still sitting there after the call when his *Hometown Hottie* came home and talked about how she was pulled over by a cop. She talked about that all the while he was interested in only looking at her ass as she bent over while he was pointing out something on the back of their car in her short shorts. Was she trying to make Nobody jealous? Did she oblige the cop?

All these things that popped up were isolated incidents which she would mention. He already felt small, as it was, and he had no response to these little narratives she came up with. They didn't add up, because she loved him. In his world he had to see it logically and not feel it in his gut. What if he is wrong? This was always the question that held him bound up inside. The evidence had not reached, as the phrase went, beyond reasonable doubt. She kept challenging him to trust her and he did with a heavy sigh. There were times when they were partying that he could not even cope with her speaking with someone else, just out of earshot, behind a closed door. He always thought she was scheming against him, but could never prove it for sure.

By this time methamphetamine was back in his life. Drugs were flowing at the same rate as the booze if not more. They had gone over to a friend's house (some folks they had met on a chartered bus on their way to a concert.) His *Hometown Hottie* and the husband wanted to go talk about something in another room. Even with the guy's wife talking to Nobody directly in front of him in the living room, he sat there fidgety and panicky and wondered, in his mind, why this guy's wife was so calm. This is not right and he could only count the minutes until her return. It took every ounce of strength to sit in the chair and act as calm as he could without going and knocking on the door and interrupt them.

His emotions ran very high and reached fever pitch, he felt like screaming out, *"What the @#$% are you doing in there?"*

When she came back into the living room, it was like the air got punctured out of a balloon. If what he sensed equated to no harm, then no foul. His fears were unsubstantiated and he was wrong again. They had met another couple and the wife had asked his *Hometown Hottie* if she wanted to take a bath with her. Where did these people come from? What was it about her that attracted this type of behavior from others? The crazy part was this girl's husband knew and was OK with it. His *Hometown Hottie* had said that although she was flattered, she declined. How was it that he kept finding himself in these situations where people were openly out to take her away from him?

He was living in a world ruled by lack of faith. The flesh, as the Bible would describe it, was completely in charge. In his mind, he was getting to the point that this obviously would be his lot in life. He'd given up on changing his life or himself. This was the life he deserved. This was his punishment. This was hell on Earth. Nobody also had gotten sick many times and he had bouts of severe asthma after he had smoked methamphetamine and other chemicals. The breathing issues necessitated trips to the emergency room. He regularly developed bronchitis and it seemed every couple of months he couldn't breathe properly.

Nobody's time in the military was almost over. He had landed a job in South Carolina. Maybe they just needed a change. Now that she had her son and her divorce was final, she was free to leave the state. Nobody was able to take his son with him wherever he was planning to go, too.

So on February 5, 1990, leaving behind all the people that could possible take her away from him, Nobody and his family set out to drive across the country. With two kids, a cat, the love of his life, and another bout of bronchitis, Nobody set out on a new adventure, hoping a geographical change would fix everything.

Myth #60 Nobody felt a new beginning would change everything for the better.

Episode 32

The Gambler

There were a lot things told to Nobody when he was in the program. Many seasoned members offered these suggestions which could be seen as a gateway to emotional bliss, per se. These have proven to be helpful for those that truly wanted a better life and remain sober. Nobody obviously ignored them.

1) Whatever you put in front of your sobriety, you will lose.
2) No major changes in the first year.
3) No relationships in the first year.
4) No matter how bad you feel, go to meetings.
5) If it hurts worse when someone is around then when absent, the choice is clear.
6) If you hate the way you're feeling, stop doing what you doing.
7) Pray to God for His will in your life, not yours.
8) Love is not a feeling.

He had rolled the dice. Nobody wanted the beautiful relationship that the Bible described in the Song of Solomon, two becoming one, both providing for the other. He envisioned life with the proverbial house with the white picket fence, a dog and everyone living happily ever after. Like the atheist who claims that all the natural ingredients were there from the beginning to promote life without the presence of God to create life, but by some magical moment when all the particles joined at the precise moment which created something from nothing by some force other than God. Maybe if Nobody wished long enough, like the atheist hoping science would find another answer besides the God particle, the relationship of his dreams would be produced. He just needed to be in the right place at the right time, since all the pieces where there. In other words, the 'rules' did not apply to Nobody, because his situation was different.

Unfortunately, this is not how it works. So many people want a relationship of never ending love, a vow of fidelity, love and respect. Once they realize they have found their soul mate, all their dreams will come true. However, many want the benefits of a Godly relationship but few work through the steps needed to produce it. Even then, that is not a guarantee. But one thing is certain: an individual cannot hope for a beautiful cake if they do not put the time, effort, patience and the correct ingredients in the proper order. What they end up with is something totally different. What may look like a cake certainly does not taste like one.

They pulled in town three days later. The excitement they shared was high as they found a place to live. They bought furniture for their new home. Nobody met his new boss. The future was looking great. When the moving van arrived it, it felt like Nobody had made the right choice. She needed him now and that made him feel much better even though there were moments when she voiced her displeasure over the move in public and in private. South Carolina *was* different and it *was* a culture shock. He tried to calm her as best as he could and convince her they would be OK.

Funny thing about major changes: if there isn't a solid foundation or maturity with which to handle change, there will be struggles. Most couples pray and look to each other for the support, but for Nobody and his *Hometown Hottie*, old survival techniques ruled the day. Neither was respected or loved.

With the delivery truck arriving out front and both excited to get their new bed, especially after a few nights on the floor, a rough looking guy with shoulder-length hair jumped out of the cab. Nobody's fears jumped to the front of his mind as well. For five days, Nobody had felt peace in his soul and within seconds of seeing this guy, all his hopes were dashed. The next thing he knew his wife and the delivery guy were engaged in conversation complete with laughter and smiles. The drug deal went down within ten minutes of meeting one another. Some things never change, and Nobody realized it was Déjà Vu all over again and he was powerless.

He would have to see how this played out, they had just arrived and he did not want his imagination to run away from him again. He did not want to give her any reason to leave him or his son, but now - *once again* - he would have to worry about what was going on when he was gone.

The new job was different, working for a cell phone company produced challenges. He found out quickly that this job had normal and abnormal hours. He would work during the day and then have to be on call at night. He would also have to work nights to perform monthly maintenance on his assigned cell sites. This meant long days and nights, she was home alone more often than he would like her to be. The good thing was that if he had to work at night it was in the middle of the night when people were not using their car phones and she was already in bed. He kept very close tabs on her to make sure she was where she was supposed to be. His boss called him into the office one day to go over his cell phone bill, which he did not have to pay, but it illustrated something. There, in front of him, was page after page of call detail, all to the same number and with frequency of ten to twelve times a day. His boss told him he needed to monitor the condition of the cell sites as he was driving the coverage area and not talk to his girlfriend around the clock.

Truth #56 Nobody made sure everything was where it was supposed to be, ALL THE TIME.

They had met new friends and the furniture guy did turn out to be a dealer of sorts. Nobody kept a watchful eye, but nothing could be seen or derived from the interactions he witnessed. It seemed as though everything was OK on the outside, except for one thing: his gut knew something was not right, it was almost too perfect, but without proof, his conspiracy theories were without merit.

He had nice neighbors in their townhouse community—a couple of single, urban professional types on one side and a military family with teenage girls who would babysit for them on the other. One day, about three months into this adventure, the father, who was a Sergeant First Class in the Army, came over as Nobody was washing the car and started a casual conversation. At one point he asked Nobody if he was married.

"No why?" he asked.

To which the neighbor responded and looked towards Nobody's house, "I was just wondering."

Funny thing about denial is that you know the truth but, in recesses of the mind you don't want to believe it. You push away the truth so you won't have to deal with it. You hope that it is a dream and that it will go away so you never have to do anything. Like magic it will resolve itself on its own. If it is relational maybe you can love more, try more and hope more, but in the end do more. Acknowledgment of the truth means you have a couple of options:

1) Acknowledge what you see, accept it for what it is, but no longer hide from it and take responsibility for your own actions or lack thereof.
2) Acknowledge it and make changes in your life, the way you behave and respond.

In the depths of his mind, Nobody knew what this guy was saying. He knew the neighbor was trying to tell him she had guys over. Nobody believed he wasn't good enough for the relationship of his dreams and was being punished by God for all he had done. When you believe that, you tend to take your lumps in life and continue on without striving for the future. Drawn only by outside appearances and using that as a gauge for success Nobody lived by two words that perpetuated him forward; *if only*. If only everything around him would get in order then so would his life. If only she would see how much he loves her. If only she would get her meds right then she would be fine.

However, that is not what life brings. For those who believe in a world without God, a low self-esteem coupled with years of failed relationships from his youth to now, had produced this unfolding tragedy. A victim who will eventually need help, poor Nobody. If only, the system had been there to help him. If only he had called the police that night when he was a young boy standing by the telephone as his parents were fighting. If only he would have done what his parents had said. If only he would have told the truth. If only he never did drugs and the list went on and on in Nobody's head. If only Nobody could hear God's voice through all the noise.

To God this is a lost soul that God loves deeply, that loves him so much that will also allow him to feel the pain of his actions. There had been messengers God sent that were ignored. Nobody was so caught up in his addictions, whether drugs or relationships, that he was too blind to see that he continued to bring this pain on himself. His fear of the unknown held him captive. He had many confusing messages in his mind about life including is there a God or isn't there one? He lacked conviction to finally say what he believed to be the truth. He would need help to undo the patterns, through counselors and the program, but he needed God too. God is the catalyst for all things and Nobody needed God to give him the strength when called upon through prayer. Nobody needed to rely on Him and only Him when faced with life, not just the bad times but the good times as well, to build up interest in grace. But what would it take to reach that point?

Nobody had just rolled craps. He immediately believed that Furniture Guy was coming over to the house when he was gone, but his neighbor would not elaborate. Survival is a strong force to combat, in a new town, no one to rely on but her, weird work hours, Nobody chose denial and never brought it up again.

Work was tough and he had to provide for his family, but his total attention was on his private life and that left a lot to be desired in his professional life. The love of his life was receiving federal assistance and was under psychiatric care, and she was trying different meds to balance her moods. Not sure how the doctors would have felt about the illegal drugs she was ingesting, but this is what they would do until the right prescribed med was found. It was always an experiment with the meds. A tweak here and a tweak there, Nobody hoping and wishing that soon the roller coaster ride would end. Nobody was looking for her to change so he wouldn't have to. Pain is a motivator.. For some, it takes a lot of pain before any changes are made. God loves His children and with that love He will allow us to find Him through the pain of our decisions. Nobody now had moved to the roulette table hoping his luck would change - yet again. He was still gambling, however.

When Nobody came home from work, she had a habit of wanting to leave the house, run some errands, maybe buy some drugs or what have you. That also meant that Nobody was left in the house with the two kids and that's when Nobody's imagination would run amuck. Where there is smoke there is fire and with this particular female who was smoking, sometimes the fire was somewhere else.

One afternoon sitting and waiting for her to return, the pressure and anxiety he felt became too great. She said she had to go out for a couple of things, but it did not seem right and she was gone just a tad too long. Trying to resist the urge to leave the house, but failing, Nobody gathered the kids, placed them in his work truck and headed out. He knew where he was going and that was to drive by Furniture Guy's trailer, which you could see from the main road. As he was driving by, there she was in the driveway, standing in front of him looking like she was about ready to lean in for the kiss, but this was a snapshot of a moment, not the following second, he never saw if she kissed him goodbye, because he was driving by. The anger boiled inside of him. He was filled with rage. This was not where she was supposed to be. The feelings he felt were like the day he drove off on his motorcycle, recklessly, after arguing with his first love, or the day he borrowed his neighbor's car on that day he caught his first wife with Mechanic Boy.

"Why was this always happening?" Nobody asked himself.

His mind was racing at the speed of sound, with many words sprinting through his mind and the truth he needed to espouse could never reach his lips. He drove back home. When she arrived, he could tell she knew something was up. As calmly as he could, he asked where she had gone. She said just out and that she also drove by the Furniture Guy's house to see if he had anything. This was always the trap, she told the truth but not all of it. She was a pro and too much of one for Nobody. He could not outsmart her. If she had lied he could have caught her, but not this time. He would forever wonder if she had kissed him goodbye, but in the depths of his soul, he knew the answer was yes and he stayed at the roulette wheel, putting his money on black.

With the neighbor's kid watching theirs, Nobody and *Hometown Hottie* decided to go to a local bar and have some fun. It was close by and it catered to people of his age group, very similar environment he was used to in Arizona. The clientele were not your local college kids, but more of the seasoned partiers, which meant people, came in, went outside and came back in. They chatted and, after about an hour, Furniture Guy showed up with some of his friends.

Much to Nobody's dismay, he felt he had to struggle for face time with her and soon thereafter someone at the table made a request for some pot. Furniture Guy said he would go, she wanted some too and so, of course, volunteered to go with him. Powerless to stop the unfolding events and consumed with fear of looking like a fool by running interference, Nobody did what he always did: nothing. She left with Furniture Guy and he was left alone, nursing a beer.

"Why was he here again? What did he have to do to be number one in her eyes?"

He was a fool. It wasn't normal for your girl to leave with someone else. Yet how could he make this statement out loud, he would only be chastised for not trusting her. The fact of the matter was that he did not trust her and he was powerless to do or say anything.

One of Furniture Guy's buddies came over to keep him company. After few minutes, they went outside to partake of a joint, hoping to lighten his mood. Back in the bar, they talked about news, sports and weather. The time was ticking away; he felt the joint may have been laced with something. He kept asking what was taking so long and his table mate said that they must have been held up. It was almost surreal. For a minute, Nobody believed that this guy knew the real story between Furniture Guy and her. The way he said, "I bet they had to wait for the guy to show up" seemed like a spoof. As usual, Nobody was afraid to ask the real question that needed to be asked.

Lost in his mind and trying to keep his game face on, Nobody hated the way he was feeling. He hated his life. He hated her. He was trapped in his own circumstances. After almost an hour and half, she finally returned, Her clothes were different. She was wearing a black T-shirt of Furniture Guy's. Nobody sat there, looking at his girl, perplexed to the point of absolute rage. Something inside him took over his mind and he was able to at least ask one right question, "Where is your blouse?"

She had been drinking a beer and spilled the beer on it. Since they were driving by his house as they were driving back to the bar, Furniture Guy gave her one of his T-shirts. A reasonable answer. Since Nobody's rage, in these sorts of matters, could never find its way into his fists to beat a guy to a pulp for fear of getting hurt, losing, or in trouble, he sat. These people - what were they doing here? What was he was doing here? This is not how it was supposed to turn out. Again, everyone was having fun except Nobody.

Nobody felt the whole world was looking at him seated alone at the table, saying how much of an idiot he was in their eyes. How Furniture Guy was banging his girl right in front of his eyes and he was oblivious to it? This wasn't working out. The drugs, his life, how could God let this sort of thing happen? He was a good guy with a good heart. He just wanted to be loved and in return he would love back. What was wrong with that? Some days he felt as though being dead would be the best answer, but he had his son to think about. His son was the only reason Nobody had not tried anything foolish outside of doing drugs, having a Bipolar emotionally unstable female in his house who had a propensity for rage and liked to screw everyone else but him..

What an awful father he was! How could he have gotten to this point? He needed relief. The only truth he knew was the program. God had abandoned him and at least the folks in AA would understand. Sitting at the table, zoning out to his current circumstances, he heard a voice from his past. A voice so clear there was no mistaking it. A voice of a guy who always said things the way they were and never pulled any punches. The voice said, "If you don't like the way you are feeling, stop doing what you are doing."

How true! After a night like this, Nobody knew he would go to a meeting after work the next day. He'd get his life back together. He was ready to step away from the roulette table, hopefully once and for all.

There was no denying Nobody's pain. He did go to the meeting the following day and spilled his guts as he shared. Personal experiences coupled with suggestions have proven to provide better direction than direct advice from people in the rooms of recovery. After Nobody explained the status of his life, since going back out, many personal experiences and the solutions used by others were offered up during the course of the meeting. He even decided to pick up a white chip. What wasn't different, unfortunately, was Nobody's willingness to change. It is one thing to identify problems in life but, after time, willingness to do something about it is necessary. Nobody saw all the markers along the way, but still refused to pursue the inevitable that everyone pointed out. There is a saying in AA that *half measures availed us nothing*. So instead of looking to himself for the solution, he did the one thing that was not offered as a suggestion, he told her that he wanted to stop all ties with the Furniture Guy and use other people they had met for future drug purchases. He did not like Furniture Guy and he knew that the result of this ultimatum would prove significant. If she was resistant, then there was more to the 'friendship.' After a quick conversation, it was settled, and he was feeling comfortable within his situation.

Myth #61 Nobody thinks tweaking instead of all out change will solve an ongoing problem.

Nobody had smoked methamphetamine in the past, an action which aggravated his asthma to a point of incapacitation when an asthma attack hit. He used over-the-counter medication and whatever he could to ride out episodes as best he could without a doctor's care. Seasonal changes were triggers for asthmatic episodes. So when the early fall of 1990 brought a quick cold snap, Nobody's asthma problems weren't a surprise. This one, however, was extreme. Nobody complained to her that this attack was severe. He was having extreme difficulty in breathing that scared him. He told her he needed to go the hospital. She had other plans: they were out of dope and she needed to restock - right then. At that particular moment, she said upon her return he could go to the emergency room.

The clocked ticked, his lungs tightened. He was battling dizziness and the room was shrinking around him. Nobody began crying out to God for help. Nobody prayed. He was sorry for all that he had done. He was sorry for not taking care of his son as he had intended. He did not want to die. Oh, how he hated her! How could she leave him here? Truly alone and his breathing extremely shallow, his kids were asking him what was wrong as he laid on the floor. He cried, "God, *please* help me!"

After another breathless fifteen minutes had passed before she returned, he could not even get words out of his mouth, he just slowly picked himself up and crawled to the door. Closer to the car, she helped him in and said she was sorry for not believing him. His head felt clouded as he pushed on. By the time he got to the hospital, he could only move a step every minute. It was an eternity from the car to the emergency room door. He was using all his energy to push air into his lungs. The air didn't seem to reach even his throat. He felt as though he was suffocating. Nobody held on to anything he could. He leaned against walls for support. He finally reached the emergency room door where a nurse immediately grabbed a wheel chair and ushered him into the ER. Lifted onto the table and given a shot of what he thought they said was adrenaline, Nobody had finally found help.

The hospital staff got his lungs opened up and after a few hours he was able to breathe. He left the hospital and drove home. When he got home, he sat her down and said their life was a shame and it needed to change. He needed someone who would choose him over anything else. He had almost died and he had never been more scared in his life. She needed to get counseling. If she did not do this, there would be drastic changes which no one would enjoy, especially her.

Sensing his seriousness and honesty, she went to the see her doctor the next day and they referred her to a counseling center for high risk families. Their family interview was schedule for October twenty-third, a month away.

Now moving to the black jack table he asked the dealer to hit him one last time and wanting a better quality of life with the so-called benefits of the party atmosphere. They just kept drinking for the most part and tried to find that elusive balance between the two. Nobody loved concerts and since his tickets for Fleetwood Mac were refunded due to a canceled show, they decided to buy tickets for The Black Crowes and Robert Plant. Her new medicine should not be mixed with alcohol, so she would be the designated driver through mutual agreement.

Nobody could put aside his rules if it suited his needs. He decided to go the hotel across the street where he easily drank as much as he wanted to prior to the show. She would be driving them home and he could throw a bit of 'caution to the wind' and enjoy himself. Drinking a flurry of gin and tonics very quickly got Nobody's night off to quite a start.

Myth #62 Nobody believed everything would go according to plan.

The opening act of the concert was a bit boring, providing no entertainment value for Nobody, who soon became restless. They got up and walked around a bit, making it back to their seats just as the lights started to go down. Their seats allowed them to see the entire arena in front of them. It was about two rows down, that Nobody noticed a couple of people smoking a joint and it was slowly making its way towards him. Needing a boost for an already slow evening, Nobody asked for a hit and was granted his request. Wanting another hit, he got up from his seat and followed the joint. He found it close by and sat in the aisle gesturing for the current owner to pass it to him. As he was taking a hit and looking down, there in front of him running up the steps, was an undercover cop, pointing at and yelling to Nobody. Trying to drop the joint from his hand and kick it away, Nobody was grabbed by the officer. His girlfriend saw the entire incident, and came forward to where Nobody stood. He was able to give her his keys before being escorted by the police as the song *Good Times Bad Times* was heard as Nobody was leaving the arena.

In the elevator, Nobody looked at the officer and said, "They told me if I went back out that I would either die, I'd be institutionalized or go to jail."

"Who said that?"

"The folks in AA."

"Well, they were right about one thing. You are going to jail."

Truth #57 Nobody crapped out.

Back in a place where no one belongs: a drunk tank. The exposed toilet seemed like a throne in the middle of the cell. There was no way he would take a crap with forty guys around him. There wasn't even a seat. Trying to find comfortable real estate in a cell with only bolted down benches and a floor with patches of vomit and whatever else on the floor was becoming a Petri dish experiment, Nobody sat, watched and waited. It could have been worse. Nobody was charged with simple possession. This was a minor offense, considering all the different types of drugs that had passed through his hands. He made his one phone call to his boss. Nobody was not a good liar so he shared the truth: that he was arrested at the concert and would get into work once he was released the next morning.

Once the shock of his arrest subsided, he couldn't understand why he had even called his boss. while sitting in the cell. All he needed to do was to have her call him in sick, but it was over, his days were numbered and he was a dufus.

After twelve hours he was released and had a date to appear in court. His family was only five days away from going to the Family Care Center. Now he was the bad guy. After all the crap he had put up with her, he was the one that got arrested. When he arrived at work, his boss called him in the office. There were no pleasantries. Nobody was informed that the company's policy had no opinion on what happened to him outside of his normal work hours.

Nobody apologized for his actions and said, "I am going to start attending meetings."

His boss rebuffed him, "I don't believe you."

Nobody hardly believed it himself. If found guilty, he would lose his license for a year. His job required him to drive everywhere. If his license was revoked, he wouldn't be able to perform his job. He would then be let go. All of this was of his doing. There was no one else to blame but himself.

He sat down with his neighbor after work that afternoon. His neighbor offered him a Natural Light over which Nobody recapped his evening. He took a swig and contemplated the can he had sitting on his knee. He wondered why the can sat there looking at him. He raised the can, took a final swig, and placed it on the end table. A picture forever etched in his mind was that beer can sitting on a square cream colored tile coaster. The can stood in front of an oversized, oval-shaped olive-colored table lamp which had a brass colored ring for a base and a white pleated shade, half the height of the lamp itself. He left the can there, got up, said goodbye not only to his neighbor but also to his old friend addiction and he never picked up a drink or drug again.

Truth #58 Nobody had met his match.

Episode 33

Running on Empty

With his job on the rocks, the upcoming meeting with the Family Center, a pending court date, an emotionally unstable woman living in his house, two kids and a cat, Nobody had only one recourse: an AA meeting. Nobody got the address of a church with a Saturday night meeting and childcare, so he packed up his family and they all went. It was a big meeting which broke into smaller groups so more people could share. Nobody followed some people into a smaller room.

He spent two days fighting with himself. Defeated, emotionally bankrupt, and going over everything in his mind, wondering how could he have been so stupid. This would be the room that God would eventually challenge him into a decision, through His many servants in the room.

Nobody shared, but was not completely honest. His words didn't fool anyone. He picked up another white chip and committed his life to sobriety. She did as well and it was the start of many decisions they would make.

They'd made the decision to not mention his arrest during their intake interview with the Family Care Center. Nobody was afraid that mentioning it could hurt her monthly welfare check, which, in turn, could create additional, bigger problems. On the day of their appointment, they walked through the door and Nobody was pleasantly surprised. The Family Care Center wasn't what he had expected: sterile offices in a medical building.

However, this was a three story old house with a warm feel. Everyone looked 'normal.' He saw mothers with kids but no men. The welcoming staff person directed them into a room where they would eventually meet the intake team.

The room was a bit dark, but there were a lot of toys for the kids. It must have been a finished basement for a home at one time, Nobody speculated. The chairs were living room style and not like the kind you'd find in a doctor's waiting room. He chose one with high armrests that were shoulder high, one that once you sit in, you just sank. He sat and waited.

The very quiet environment gave him a feeling of peace. More peace than he had felt in a long time. The director and her assistant entered the room as Nobody watched from his chair. They were warm and welcoming as they shared how the center could help families put their lives back together and at no cost to the family. They explained that they believed Nobody, his *Hometown Hottie*, and kids were considered a 'high-risk' family. The director pointed out that if the family wanted to get better, honesty about the state of their affairs was important. It was suggested that they participate in group and individual workshops which would help them better deal with the sometimes overwhelming pressures families deal with at times. More than anything else their goal, the director said, was to help families keep their children safe in a nurturing loving environment.

Nobody looked over to his son, who was playing with some toys. It was peaceful here and the kids could sense it. A tear formed in his eye as thoughts were going through his head. The thoughts weren't racing around like before, but slowly and clearly, one at a time which Nobody could comprehend in their entirety. The director was talking and Nobody was in his own thoughts. He heard a different voice—that of his girlfriend now. She was doing the counseling tap dance. As these thoughts seemed to penetrate his psyche, he realized that he had not been a good father. He had paraded too many women in front of his son and they had left. There was no continuity in his life and he was setting a bad example. Not to mention he was an alcohol and drug addict five days removed.

They were asking her questions about her past and why she was referred to the center. As he heard her answer, he felt a nagging urge to move forward. He felt an urge to do something, open his mouth. Then to himself he said, *"What do you want me to do?"* The pressure behind the tear could open a floodgate of emotion in his chest if he said a word. It was a risk he was, at this moment in time, willing to take. Nobody, aware of the tranquility within his being and from the quiet recess of his mind, heard, "Tell them the truth.The truth. What was the truth? The truth was all he had been thinking and holding in for so long. He was afraid of the unknown. If he told the truth everything he had could be taken away. What was that worth anyway? He had played it over in his mind a thousand times, and the result always came out the same. If he told the truth, people would leave. They would see him for the fraud he really is. But for some reason - maybe the peace he felt in the room - he knew he could speak the truth. Nobody looked at his girlfriend and the director and compared the two. He saw pain and love sitting in front of him.

His girlfriend was a good looking jewel, who possessed the illusion of love, but he had taken it on the chin with her for a long time. Then there was this lady, who he had just met, and there was no doubt her words matched the look in her eyes. He had trusted so many people in the past; girlfriends, a wife, army buddies, and family, just to be let down and hurt repeatedly. He truly felt like a hopeless romantic. He just did not have what it took to have lasting relationships. All he wanted to do was rest and go back to that rocking chair of long ago, where he felt safe, and just have someone hug him.

Sitting in this room, looking over to this lady in front of him, how easy it was to see the love in her eyes. Yes, he *had* felt a lot of pain in his life, but he did not want to hide anymore. Yes, pain hurt, but sitting here and listening even half-heartedly when love presented itself there was no mistaking it. Love can shatter all fear. Nobody always connected sex with love, but here in this room there was definitely love and it was powerful. There wasn't any sex.

Nobody wanted a 'do over.' Then heard the encouraging voice again, "Tell them the truth."

He blurted out, "I was arrested last week, I'm about to lose my job and I do not know what to do. I am an alcohol, drug addict and we need help."

The tears came, his chest was heaving and the old tired balloon of a chest had let out all the air. There he said it, the truth as he knew it. Stunned, his girlfriend's mouth dropped open. The assistant stopped writing. All eyes were on him. For about ten seconds, silence.

The director shifted her chair to face Nobody.

"We can help you and your family. This is what we do here. You are in the right place and I can assure you that you are safe. It will take a lot of hard work, and if you try and are honest, I can promise your life will change."

So many times he had wanted to say what was really going on in his head and so many times he had altered the truth to survive. It would be a long time before Nobody knew what the real truth was, but at this stage he would do the best he could. He would let out the pain he had bottled up for so long.

Up to this point, Nobody did not have any hope in his life. He knew God was there, but he was a failure and he needed to get his act together before he would feel God's love and this was a start. What Nobody did not realize was that this was God's love being played out right in front of him. This was a miracle, a spot in time where all points were converging to create a situation that one day Nobody would see how God's love was being orchestrated.

Truth #59 God's love was being orchestrated for Nobody.

They had set up individual and family sessions. Nobody started going to meetings daily and did the things he was told. He prayed every morning, saying 'please' and 'thank you' to God at night. He didn't drink and they cleared the house of everything. He and his *Hometown Hottie* started going to NA meetings as well where there were more people of their age group. There were also plenty of women and the way some of them dressed made it hard for Nobody to be there. Before long they had a routine going. The Saturday night AA meeting was, by far, his favorite. He loved going into the back room with these folks that had a lot of time in the program plus it had childcare.

Things were starting to have some manageability. Work was hard. His boss would page him daily during his noon meeting, but he kept going. As he was sharing in meeting, the pain that was inside of him usually came out in tears. He kept going back to things growing up, as the topics were brought up. But he was tired of running, if it came out in tears, it did not matter. He was not told to leave and, more importantly, he felt like he belonged.

They took turns watching the kids for meetings on days other than Saturday. It was customary to go out for coffee after meetings, but Nobody only did that with her on Saturday nights. She however went on those other nights and Nobody stayed home with the kids that he wasn't on-call at work, which would require him to leave at a drop of a hat.

His much-dreaded court date had finally arrived. The cleaning crew (police officer's by day) at his office had tried to get the arresting officer to drop the charge but it didn't work. Nobody went to court and he was on the lookout for the arresting officer. As he saw the officer make his way across the parking lot, Nobody prayed a phrase his old DC sponsor had taught him, "God your words, not mine" and with that, he dashed towards the officer and said, "Hello."

Nobody asked if he could speak to him for a moment. The officer nodded.

"Sir, I know what I did was wrong and I know that I am about to lose my license. When that happens I will lose my job and I deserve it. However, I want you to know the only thing I can show you today is proof that I am trying to put my life back together. This is my thirty-day chip. I picked it up the other night and this letter."

"What's the letter say?"

"It is my pledge to a Family Care Center that if I drink or do drugs again, I authorize them to take my son from me and place him in foster care."

The chip was something that demonstrated Nobody's true state of affairs. His life was on the rocks, but the past thirty days had been the best days in a long time, because Nobody was telling and living in the truth.

He knew there was a price to pay for his actions and was willing to pay the price to get it all behind him. Today hung in the balance. It was sort of interesting how standing there in front of this man, who had probably seen guys like him a thousand times and heard the same old excuses, had given him the time of day.

The officer asked for the letter, read it and looked at the chip in Nobody's hand. He looked up again at Nobody and back to the letter.

"OK, Nobody this is what I am going to do. I am going to recommended that you go through pre-trial intervention. You will have to go through some classes and community service. Once you successfully finish all the requirements, this charge will be expunged from your record. Also, you will not lose your license."

Truth #60 Nobody learned what mercy was.

Once all the formalities were done with the court, he was able to leave. As he sat in his truck, he gave the key a turn. He paused. He wept. He thanked God. Nobody knew that God loved him and he did not have to prove anything to anyone.

Episode 34

Shattered

C hanging your life is hard work whether you are just angry, or angry at someone all the time, an uninterested father, a workaholic, fitness junkie, a person obsessed with sex, a couch potato or a regular church goer going through the motions. It takes a reasonable amount of effort to change old habits you think are good for you and the rationalization that goes with it to keep the dream alive. It is only after you recognize that something is out of kilter in your life that the hard work begins, which many never attempt. Many go on for years living a perpetual cycle where nothing changes and we become so comfortable, that we become numb to how our behaviors actually affect us or others.

Without pain there can be no love, without love there is always pain and love through pain can show what love really is. It is a strange state of affairs when many claim there can be no God because of all the evil in the world but, if everyone loved God with abandon and truly loved their neighbor and did not succumb to their own desires as a first priority before loving others, evil would not be present. Unfortunately, love for God is replaced with good behavior. Pain can make a man fall to his knees and reach out for help. Happiness doesn't drive a man to his knees, over time happiness drives man away from God. A man who can have anything in the world he wants, eventually can't find anything to make him happy and won't reach out for help for his ultimate condition until he feels the pain. Pain is the dinner bell for God's love. How can God reach his people if his people will not reach for Him? He wants a relationship with his people and he has given everyone free will to choose him for the object of their love, but we all want something first. We want our own plans to materialize first.

Regardless of how hardened a heart, at some point, someone has at one time yearned for something from the deepest recesses of their soul that nothing around them could satisfy. They have hurt or have been hurt and come to believe that there is nothing really out there for them. They want to believe in something to relieve the emptiness that faces them at some point in their lives but never can seem to find it.

They try going to church, sex, drugs, rock roll, and lessen their standards for that someone special to get rid of the emptiness quicker. They spend money hoping the next purchase will finally make the difference. Many live in seclusion just so they can protect themselves from pain. Professors and great thinkers try new ideas and reach conclusions trying to deal with pain and leave everyone doomed to an earthly grave and/or raise their fist toward God saying, "I will show you by proving you don't exist." Funny isn't it how people work so hard to try and not believe and rely on God when it is easier work to believe when the evidence is right in front of you. We are a microwave society, we all want the answers now and when it doesn't go according to our own plan we blame God or say it is the proof we were looking for a way to say there isn't one.

That is similar to a computer saying that because a virus was allowed to get inside its circuitry that proves it wasn't built by man. If the man really loved the computer he would not let that happen in the first place. However, it still doesn't mean the man did not create the computer to begin with. It only means that something else wants to destroy the computer with a virus. The man who created the computer allowed everyone to create programs that could be used by the computer and since man left the choice to everyone to build the programs, this is what you are left with; some who are true to the original intent of the computer and some who are not.

Furthermore, before people are willing to change, many want to see how their behavior is affecting others first. If they don't see anything, they then justify their actions as a response to the others. What a strange way of looking at life. We have been conditioned this way by the world. There have been many people whose goal in life is to try and get out alive and they have forgotten how to live or have never started.

When faced with pain and love, you can see how truly alive one is and this life has been given to us by God. Life is not an end result it is a journey and a path. The argument isn't, where is God in all of this, the question is, where are we in all of this?

Some believe if they mind their own business and keep to themselves, life's reward is tranquility. If they go to church every week and keep out of the line of fire they can go and live their life in peace. If there were just the right amount of laws, then everyone would behave properly and the world would be a better place for it and we would all live in peace.

This list goes on, and every sentence always begins with "if only," "I would like," "I just want," "I have done all of this" and "if you would only." However this is how we were made and no matter how many reasons there are, there is still only one truth, but everyone wants something to make them feel better. Whether they deny it or not, when felt threatened that something will be taken away or feel they need something to remove the pain, their behaviors go with it and it can be perverted in every imaginable way.

The only way out of our current dilemma is not with what can be done for me or what can be done to someone else to make me feel better; it starts with one's self to change. That change must always begin with what is the object of my focus. The world wants to deal with the collective and hope that once rules are put in place everyone will follow and Utopia will be achieved. However, God wants to deal with the individual so he can work with the collective. Like the rich man in the Bible, he asked Jesus what he needed to do. He was told to leave it all behind and he went away disappointed, because he could not let go of the life he had for the one he wanted.

Nobody had thought this way, substituting God for Good Orderly Direction and tried to live by the rules in some strange sense. He believed if he showed love, the automatic response would be love in return, but the world is not like that since no one can force someone to love them back. Nobody had a picture of what life should be for him and he wanted what everyone around him had. He did not realize that he had always been judging his insides by other people's outsides. Why was he different from anyone else? His goal in life, along with his actions up to this point, was to try to protect himself from the pain he felt inside. He made attempts to soothe it or simply make it go away. If he just played by the rule book of never ending rules in the hope that it would work out, he would be rewarded. The reward he wanted was a long lasting relationship. He wanted to grow up and be happy just like everyone else.

Myth #63 Nobody believes pain can somehow be removed from his life with Good Orderly Direction.

The good news for Nobody was that a path had been laid out for him. Between counseling, meetings, praying to God, and his good orderly direction, Nobody saw areas where his life was changing and improving. However, he still placed more value in the earthly relationships within his life to provide comfort instead of a heavenly one.

As time went on, he started sensing something was wrong again. He was not the focus of her love and Nobody was suspecting there might be someone else who was. The hints were starting to surface, that nagging feeling again like a stage hook pulling at him in his gut to get him off stage. The time she spent out after meetings was becoming longer. He shared his concerns with people and they confirmed his suspicions. However, the truth was not presented in a manner that Nobody wanted. He wanted the distinctive truth, with all the facts. He wanted an account that outlined the entire affair so he could say, "See this is why I am asking you to leave." There would be no debate; the facts would speak for themselves.

Truth #61 Nobody wanted a God on his terms.

Nobody shared the clues with the Director at the counseling center and his friends in AA, and everyone seemed to stand back and wait for Nobody to make a decision. Here he was again trapped in confusion of his own making, hoping that if only he'd do the right thing, it would all work out. Unfortunately, Nobody was afraid to do the one right thing for himself. He was afraid of the pain and the unknown.

As his pain was mounting, he made it to the regular Saturday night meeting and as he was listening to his little group of regulars, the little voice inside him told him that, when it was his turn to share, he should place his hurts on the table.

Nobody spoke of the affairs, the black eyes, the little teddy bear bag filled with prescriptions, her diagnosis, the night of his asthma attack, the Family Care Center, and the tears flowed. Nobody's life on full display to be squashed by all those around him. He had been a fool trapped in the world of 'if only' that never materialized. He was placing his happiness in the hands and moods of others around him.

The next person started talking about how tough of a day he had at work. Then the mood shifted, a lady across the table, interrupted the man and said that they needed to stop the meeting for the moment.

She looked over to Nobody, with a love in her eyes that only God could produce, she said. "She has to leave tonight, if you want any chance of a normal life. You are going to have to believe it before you see it. You are going to have to trust that God loves you and the strength of God will lead you through this before you understand the way out."

A man sitting next to him pushed his card with his telephone number to Nobody and placed his hand on Nobody's back. The truth had been presented. The key to change was a willingness to remove that which is bad from one's life. It was his choice now. He either had to believe or continue on the path he was on. The people in the room were living proof that it was possible to live again or start for the first time. The world's sarcasm of God was not present in this room, God was there and He had pierced Nobody's heart and the truth had been placed conveniently at his feet. If he did not listen to what this complete stranger said, which was the truth, he would only have himself to blame. God in the most loving manner and probably the easiest way he could to get his attention, had knocked him up against the side of his head with his own 2x4 of truth, from which he could not run. *Hometown Hottie* had to leave tonight, without knowing what was on the other side.

Truth #62 Nobody had to believe in something other than fear.

Up to this point in his life, it could be said that Nobody was starting to believe that God, of some sort, was there. He saw God work in the lives of other people, but always felt that there would always be that one place in his life God would leave him hanging there out to dry. He just wasn't special enough. He always had to fight for love. Still, after all these years, he was afraid of being alone. He placed his value on how much another person needed him and his pride had kept him in situations. It could be said he did not give up or walk away.

By the time he got home that night, she was still out and so he sent the babysitter away. His son was asleep, but her child was still awake. He took him out of bed and they both went downstairs and they played with the Nintendo. Being three years old, he really did not have the aptitude to play, but for two hours on the couch, Nobody played and her son watched as he sat on his lap totally relaxed and safe. They had never, had the real bond as father and son, but were as close as they could get. The feeling of that boy on his chest, knowing he was safe would never leave Nobody. It was sad that this would be the last night he would ever see *Hometown Hottie's* child again.

Her son was more collateral damage from a damaged relationship that impatience brings about. How quickly can someone put the blinders on to only see what they can get out of something instead of being able to pull back and truly weigh out the situation. Nobody had been living in a dream world where everything would eventually work out in his favor. Tonight, however the truth was skillfully placed directly in front of him.

As one o'clock hit, the door opened, she did not readily look over at him on the couch. Her hair was disheveled on the back of her head, which look like it had been slept on. Nobody saw truth through his previous denial. He believed she loved him, but she had her own demons to contend with. Her physical behavior toward him that night in bed was one riddled with guilt that he could once again clearly see.

He was a different man at this moment. He had heard repeatedly - both in the program and in churches - that the truth will set you free. This night through all the tears he waded through in the presence of loving people who spoke with him after the meeting over coffee, he got to the essence of his situation. No words could adequately explain the resolve that had been unveiled within him. There would be no arguing, only action on his part. He was the solution. He couldn't wait for someone else to leave, couldn't play victim anymore, he just had to do it and have the faith that a power greater than himself would lead him out of Egypt.

Truth #63 Nobody saw the pain that denial brings how it is soothed with the truth

Later that morning, with a quiet reserve, a gentle voice, and a confidence that could not be countered, Nobody with words that pierced through all the emotion said, "I cannot live like this. You need to leave immediately."

And she believed him!

It had only been two days since she was asked to leave. Nobody knew he had to call his old DC sponsor and apologize for how he had treated him and to thank him for not being afraid to speak the truth. His sponsor was a true man of courage who was not afraid to risk a friendship to save a person.

"She's gone," he said to the man with whom there hadn't been any contact for two silence and anger-filled years.

"Congratulations and how do you feel?"

"Like a free man, without the world of indecision resting on my shoulders."

Nobody didn't have any idea how he would manage his work schedule without her to watch his son. How he would manage the late night trouble calls? Inside of him, Nobody sensed it would be OK. He needed to walk through things without knowing the future. This was going to be an adventure. He was going to have to rely on people around him. He would have to ask for help. He was going to have to live with the fact he had no answers. Nobody would have to face the real world, one issue at a time, and with all its uncertainty. He would have to walk in faith and use prayer as the healing process for him to soothe the emptiness of regret. He would have to walk this walk with God and God alone. Nobody knew that, together with God, they would turn a life of regret into one of promise.

Part IV

The Road

Episode 35

Fly Me Courageous

Walking in faith under any pretense is not an easy task. Journeys are challenging because the traveler may have to traverse across the landscape and have valleys, meadows, hills, overlooks, waterfalls, rivers, and mountains to climb or cross. Like any situation many want to see what they are getting into before they try something new or put themselves at risk. The wonderful part of having the reality of your life revealed is that whatever circumstances it shows, once the truth of the situation is presented, there are choices.

Years of doubt can harden someone to a point that subconsciously they live and breathe an attitude which denies any essence of hope. You are in a world seemingly filled with disappointment after disappointment, which leads to future doubt. You look around and start believing all the negativity and live in a world of terminal hopelessness where your pain is so unparalleled that no one could possibly understand the root of your dilemma. Even you do not understand it because your vision is so clouded that you can't see beyond it. You start buying into the notion that maybe God isn't out there after all and no one can help you.

A hurtful past, coupled with the thought that God has left someone fending for themselves, can be a driving force in someone's life. The festering anger that comes with this can also produce the same hopelessness just projected in an entirely different manner. You live in emotional isolation, and when you interact with the world, you lash out and try to protect yourself from those you believe are out there trying to hurt you. Still no one understands your pain and you will not let your guard down for whatever reason because, in your mind, you can't be hurt anymore and if you do you will surely die.

Then one day hope arrives and you do not even recognize it or you believe it is for someone else but never you. This is the path many take in the life they live. They hold out hope as an object that is always just out of reach and meant for someone else. We all have a yearning that we quite can't put our finger on, but it is there. However, the gift of life with the variety of emotions and the frailty of it can extinguish the glow it once had that we were born with. When hope arrives, we don't even recognize it because our senses have been dulled.

For comparison purposes, the Appalachian Trail has an eight mile approach trail, which is the precursor to the actual expedition. Many start the 1,800 mile journey from the exact beginning. Some at the start of the approach trail and still some only hike sections at a time and hope that one day they will complete the entire journey in a patchwork of expeditions. Let it be said that Nobody's approach trail was twenty-six years to the actual trailhead. He had finally brought all necessary gear (willingness,) had investigated the trail (the history of his situation) and knew in his heart that he needed to embark on this journey. He packed what he thought he needed. With only part of the truth revealed to him, he no longer used his fear of the unknown or his need to get it right first as an excuse to prevent moving forward. Like many backpackers on their first hike, Nobody had some painful realizations. Within the first few miles, hikers realize their pack is too heavy, how physically challenging it is to hike, and more importantly, they realize that what they thought was important to bring, turned out to be unwanted baggage.

Truth #64 Nobody walks in faith.

The next few months of Nobody's life was all about new routines. He spoke to people on a regular basis, went to counseling, worked the program, and lived one day at a time. He wept a lot in meetings and, even though the emotion was intense, he continued walking through the fire. He asked for help and he let it all hang out. The pride that had driven him to work it out for himself was diminished to one singular item. He still held on to his need for a relationship, but God had protected him from chance encounters and for a time he did not push it.

One thing Nobody was learning, no matter how much of a cliché it was, a lot of his issues were rooted in his childhood. The fractured relationships with his parents - especially that with his mother - had taken a toll on him. Nobody started seeing that the need to have a female relationship was a continuing driving force in his life. Being without a significant other, moved him into a depressed state. Looking back on his life, he always tried to save women and give them a reason to pick him over others. Nobody picked soon-to-be divorcees with a child that seemed to always need someone to save them. It wasn't an issue if he loved them, it was only important that they loved him. He had a need to know that someone loved him at any cost and that love had to be shown, not spoken. While he was volunteering at the AA club working off his community service, Nobody came into contact with many new people in recovery. Just like a hospital, many AAs are, in varying degrees, healthy. It is usually the healthy folks that can differentiate between the healthy and the unhealthy ones in a group.

One day a girl showed up at the club—with a story and luggage—and she was in need of a temporary place to stay. A woman in need is a beacon that Nobody can spot 500 hundred miles away. Since it had been a month or so since his *Hometown Hottie* had moved out, there was room in the inn. In the back of his mind, Nobody thought he just might benefit from helping this girl out and offered to let her to stay at his house. The adrenaline was flowing and he had purpose. However in the back of the club an older lady who was a bit wiser than Nobody was slowly making her way to Nobody. She had taken a liking to Nobody's son, whom she'd gotten to know as Nobody brought his son with him when he performed service work at the clubhouse (cleaning toilets, mopping floors and making coffee.) It was obvious that this new bit of unfolding drama - the girl who had arrived with luggage - was relaying to anyone who would listen, had reached this older lady's ears and she was making a beeline towards Nobody. She tapped his shoulder and asked if she could talk to him, he obliged her. Nobody had a propensity to do as he was told by women (this was similar to being a good boy.)

The older lady looked at Nobody and said that she knew this girl happened to be in jail the night before. Yes, she needed help, but based on the events that led to her arrest, it would be wise for Nobody to go and tell the girl he needed to withdraw his offer. She looked at Nobody's son and plainly said, "he's been exposed to enough already."

Nobody, having a better understanding of his life history and his need to be needed, realized this lady had been prompted by a force greater than him to reveal the truth.

Truth #65 Nobody saw God's messenger intercede for him.

Nobody tried to fight the truth, but he knew in his heart that she was right. His life had been very routine as of late and what else would a human do when everything is going well but ignore the methods that got him there and live for his needs first. Just like David and Bathsheba. Nobody went up to the girl and told her he had *No Vacancy* after all.

One of the men - an 'Old Timer' as they referred to those who had many years of recovery - came over and told Nobody that he needed to be involved in a men's group where he would be guided by strong men to teach him how to live independently. Nobody knew the man was right. He realized that he'd been needing to fill his emptiness with something. He was a man with a mission, and, for once in his life, he had some hope. He was seeing God's love around him and life wasn't as bleak for him as he had thought.

His *Hometown Hottie,* who had been getting help from the Family Care Center, had been discharged from the program. She had an episode with the counselors and they felt that she needed to find help elsewhere. In some twist of fate, Nobody happened to be the only single male parent receiving help from the Center. It had dawned on him that if it hadn't been for his ex, he would have never found the place that was providing for him - a safety blanket of sorts for him and his son. He had heard that God could turn something seemingly bad into good, and because he was willing to surrender to God's will as best as he could, he was starting to see God's love around him.

The men's group consisted of about ten men all from different walks of life who met regularly. It did not take long for the boys to tell him he was a crisis and relationship junkie. He needed something or someone to fix and it wouldn't be until he came to grips with that reality that the next part of his journey would unfold.

Going through recovery from drugs and alcohol is a process in itself. The first year is about physical withdrawals, second a mental change and the third a spiritual one. However, Nobody was fighting bouts of undiagnosed depression. Prior to a men's meeting at dinner, Nobody was extremely down and negative to his situation. His constant belly aching was reaching a fever pitch. They told him to shut up and sit in it.

The guys told him that it had taken him twenty-six some years to get to this point and he wouldn't be better overnight. No matter what, they said they were sitting right there with him and they would still love him, even if he was or was not a prude. They'd been meeting at the home of one of the members when the host mentioned he thought he had a leak around the chimney, so Nobody, needing something to do climbed up on the roof, joined the construction worker who had been sober for over twenty-six years. This guy had been sober about as long as Nobody was alive. As they talked and Nobody continued his pity pot story about how bad it was. The old-timer stood up and looked at Nobody and said.

"What were the last words Jesus spoke?"

Coming from his pain, Nobody said. "Father, why have you forsaken me?"

"No," the old-timer said, "forgive them for they do not know better."

He continued, "and you don't know crap."

That night he was told that he was breaking out of a shell and it was supposed to hurt, and if he did not fight he would surely die, not unlike a butterfly that must break through a hardened cocoon to straighten its wings as it pushes through so the wings strengthen and the butterfly doesn't die. He learned from this sage that his spirit had been broken as a child and only God could restore it. His attempts to fill the emptiness through women would only delay the process. He still felt the pain of his growth, but he was at least seeing that there was a chance if he just kept moving forward. Looking at himself was hard work.

Truth #66 Nobody saw the truth being presented.

The next step in his journey required what they called a fourth step. Nobody knew that this would be a challenge unlike any other. This was a major step in the process of his recovery. Even in the Bible it says that before you attempt to tell an individual about a speck in someone's eye be sure to take the plank out of yours. It was time to put it down on paper. It was time to work on identifying his behavior over the years. It was time to not be afraid of what he would learn about himself. With a composition notebook and pen in hand, Nobody wrote it all down. He wrote down how he hurt people, lied, stole money, his part regarding issues within his marriage, how he treated his stepsons and his own son and he spoke about his parents. The writing continued.

The next step was to share what he'd written down with God and another human being. However, even though he needed to share this, he was still afraid of what others might think.

There could be consequences if he shared this with just anybody, so Nobody chose carefully. Nobody had his sponsor. He was a good man, who had the ability to speak volumes through his silence even on the phone. He was patient, loving and had experience living. Not a religious man, but he knew the business world and was the type of person who would let Nobody get all his hurts out of his system and then ask questions to get Nobody to look at himself.

Nobody grew up in world where he was indirectly taught that the way you were feeling was caused by a situation or events around you. If you were mad it was because of some injustice or that someone had treated you badly. Most of the time when he was mad, people were not behaving the way he thought they should act. Nobody was a person who felt his feelings and tried to run from the painful ones. Now that he did not have drugs or alcohol to squelch the pain, he felt that whenever he was by himself or quiet, he would keep trying to find the cause for the way he was feeling. The target he had was his mother and father.

While in counseling he would relive all the events, the shouting, the fights, and how he pleaded for someone to validate him. After all these years he just wanted them to admit their part in the family situation.

His relationship with his parents was still rocky. They continued to fight over family philosophies and who should love who. While his parents crafted responses around blood ties and loyalty, Nobody always reverted to those who had been there for him. It looked as if they'd never come to a resolution.

Faith is like this. Stepping out, not looking down, with a belief that there is something there to step on, and worth walking toward. Take all the recent experiences with God and tell yourself that God would not have brought you this far just to leave you. God loves you and wants a relationship with you, but at times there is something a person must do to bridge the gap with God as well. It is about being willing do things that go against what you thought was the best way to live. Sometimes that means waiting. Many times that comes down to just moving forward and not holding on to things that hurt too much. You have to do things that you would not normally do on the faith that taking risks is not bad.

The promise of a 12-Step program is that if you work these steps to the best of your ability you will have a spiritual awakening. It wasn't about the drugs or the alcohol anymore; it was Nobody's problem of living. He was tired of living the way he had been and now that he was able to see his past in a different light, Nobody needed to share it and finally unburden himself.

God has a sense of humor. He just doesn't put people in your life for happenstance. Like the saying goes when the student is ready the teacher appears. So for the two weeks after his writing was complete, Nobody tried to set up meetings with other men to share his writing. Every time they said yes, something happened at the last minute to thwart the meeting. Nobody needed to get this out of his system and into the air and not hold on to it any longer. After many failed attempts to find a softer and easier way, Nobody called his actual sponsor and said he was ready. They scheduled the meeting for the following day.

Truth #67 Nobody could run from the past no longer.

Episode 36

Break on Through
To the Other Side

His sponsor led Nobody out into the shallow backyard with a chain linked fence overgrown with vines as the bees were busy bustling about from one honeysuckle to the next. The afternoon sun beat down directly on them as they sat side by side on the elevated cement slab of a patio. It was that lazy time in the afternoon for a good siesta when all was quiet except for the insects and the light rustling of leaves. His sponsor opened with a prayer and asked that God comfort Nobody and allow the healing to begin, that he would find peace and know in his heart of hearts that God loved him before, during, and after the events listed on the papers in Nobody's hand. Even though Nobody still had a lot of work ahead of him, he would still continue to make mistakes. Nobody hoped he would find forgiveness and acceptance. Nobody knew that it takes time to undo the wreckage of the past. He still felt emotionally small around other men and less deserving but he would follow this through. Even Paul the Apostle went away for three years after his conversion to get his act together before being a leader of the early church. If he can be a champion of God, chosen by God, with his pedigree, then there was hope for Nobody.

With a wavering voice and in slow halting phrases, Nobody started reading. He exposed to his sponsor the good, the bad, and the ugly about himself. He didn't leave anything out. If he remembered it, he had written it and spoke it out loud. As he read what he considered his deadliest sin, the tears and emotion poured out of his chest like a tsunami. He could only get one word out every ten seconds as his chest heaved repeatedly. Acknowledging his worst sin out loud took every ounce of energy he had. He was fighting his fears, his hurts, his lost loves, and childhood and the wall around his heart was breaking apart. It was as if each word was a crumbling, disintegrating stone or brick that had been once added with every hurt Nobody experienced. His sponsor placed his hand on his back and told him it was OK and the outpouring continued. The fighting had stopped. He was releasing the pain that had been bottled up for so long. It did not matter if it was right or wrong, it was his truth and he was giving all to God.

So many people believe they have to figure out the solution for their life before actually surrendering and reaching for help. This only prolongs the healing process. It doesn't, as one would hope, shorten it. Surrendering to God without an answer is where the strength lies.

When Nobody was finished, his sponsor gave him a hug and said he did a good job. Now that he identified all his ills, Nobody felt relieved as though a hundred pounds have been lifted off his back. But now he needed to start doing something about them. So he faced them fearlessly. He saw the patterns he had with women. He saw how he used his anger to lash out at people. He saw what kind of father he was. More importantly, he saw that he had a hard time being by himself and that had caused him to make bad decisions.

As he discussed these topics over the next hour it was clear that God was present and he had the right person in front of him to find his way through the muck and mire. Feelings aren't facts, but the fact remains that, after what had just happened, he felt lighter than he had for years. He felt loved and he was no longer ashamed of who he was.

Truth #68 Nobody comes to terms with his life.

For the first few months of his new life without the drugs and girl, Nobody had been spewing his pain and made a few changes to find relief, but today he made this first step towards God. This is what he accomplished; he told God and another human being the exact nature of his condition without earning favor. He was naked as he had ever been and loved like never before.

Nobody worked and focused on the way he behaved. He found people who helped with his son, so if he was called out in the middle of the night he could carry his son into a friend's house and fetch him later. He continued with his counseling and found a new church to attend. It was a Unity Church, something from the New Age movement. By all appearances it seemed nice. It had a choir and the message was geared toward some of the language he heard in meetings. Their message said that if you placed and managed your thoughts in a certain manner, the help you are looking for would arrive. He never got into specifics of the church, the tenants of faith. There were some single women attending and it was a far cry from the church of his youth and the Rosicrucian's. The people from the Unity Church were nice, very helpful and understanding.

Still working on getting parts of his life put back together, his relationship with his parents seemed to improve. After speaking with his sponsor, they felt that Nobody could call his mother and offer amends for his part of the relationship. She accepted and because she had wanted to watch his son for a while, Nobody agreed and put together the money so he could fly his son to Maine for an extended stay.

Ever since his arrest, things at work were not rosy. Nobody's complete focus was just collecting a paycheck. Concentrating on career advancement, though important, took the back seat. He had tried to find other work but nothing seemed to fall into place. The job was a hard one as a single parent, he could see that God was taking care of him and he had a support system. However, he had fractured the relationship with his boss; he was not an ideal employee and was not attempting to learn new things to advance his career. He had made a couple of official complaints about his boss and since Nobody was totally self-consumed, Nobody hadn't realized that he was setting himself up to be let go.

Nobody felt the world should be fair and his behavior and attitude demonstrated it. When you live in a world that is self-consumed with what is in it for me, many people lose focus on what truly is important. It isn't always being right.

Working late one Friday night performing quarterly maintenance, his boss brought in beers for everyone. This meant that Nobody could not make his meeting nor meet his friends. Nobody was pissed. As a response to a joking criticism from his boss, Nobody reported him about having alcohol available during their late night maintenance window.

Nobody got his son off to Maine. About a week later, Nobody was called into his boss' office and was terminated. They said he did not have the required skills to be an effective employee. This was a hard one, and he could not hold back his tears in the office. He turned over all his tools. It was like leaving a family (the only one he had, in a weird sort of way.) There was always tension and conflict growing up, why should this be any different? He spent the rest of his day at his house grieving the loss and trying to figure out what to do next. Nobody was thankful that his boss waited until his son was out of town to end his employment. Could it be that God was setting the stage to have Nobody isolated so He could work on himself? He told his friends what had happened. A few people clapped and commented that God did for Nobody what he could not do for himself. They had been tired of hearing Nobody complain about his job. A week later, people said he actually looked better and the rings under his eyes were fading. So while he was looking for work, Nobody volunteered at the prison, doubled up on his meetings, and worked on himself.

He met with his Unity pastor a few times and they worked on how he could get his mind thinking in the right direction which would help him see that help was on the way. He only needed to be in the right frame of mind when help arrived. Nobody needed enough patience to allow God, a spiritual consciousness that he needed to tap into, to guide him. He just needed to think positive so health and prosperity would follow. This was a wonderful message that Nobody translated into *if he did the right things, life would turn out fine*. There is truth in that idea, but it wasn't the whole truth. And, it doesn't take into account that the world is a dangerous place no matter how you think.

Myth #64 Nobody is told that right thinking produces a positive life.

He spent time at the lake with some friends from the program and he'd worked it out that his son would stay in Maine until he found a job.

It was 1991 and there was a recession. Nobody, like a lot of people, was out of work. It was a time when the familiar chant was "It's the economy, stupid." One day out on the lake, one fellow mentioned that he had moved to Charlotte and while he was there found a job based in Columbia, which he had wanted all along. It was a strange statement, with a weird spiritual context that actually stuck in the recess of Nobody's mind.

Nobody was about two and a half months into joblessness when one of his friends got him an interview at her company. This was an industrial parts store. The interview went well and Nobody was offered a job. The problem was the salary: this job paid $6.35 an hour compared to his previous $11. Nobody went home devastated. He was doing all the right things, he was praying, meditating, going to meetings, counseling and trying to find Mrs. Right Now Forever, the one God had meant him to find. There were some minor setbacks but his intentions were good. How could this be? Desperate for answers, Nobody called his DC sponsor who was in Arizona and laid everything out to him. His DC sponsor's belief in God varied greatly from Nobody's in that he was not a religious man, but he believed in the God of Abraham and Jesus Christ of the bible. These were the biblical roots that Nobody was familiar with, but because Nobody was still trying to find his own way, he subjected himself to other 'off the beaten path' teachings and religious beliefs that would keep him from the God of Abraham as was actually written in the Bible.

He asked Nobody if he felt maybe God did not want him in South Carolina. The comment was a jolt to his system; its suggestion took a moment to sink in. Then the excuses started, what about his furniture, his support system, money etc. He was told that he could sell it all, it was yard sale stuff anyway, and eventually he'd get it all back. They were just things. As the conversation continued Nobody realized that of all the places in the world he could go, two stood out: Maine and Arizona. A sudden a peace fell upon Nobody. The truth, when presented, cuts through all the emotion. As he hung up the phone, he made the decision to place two phone calls, one to his mother and one to his ex-wife to see if they would help him out.

His first call was to Maine, and it soon became obvious Maine was not in the cards. He called his ex-wife and she said she'd allow him to sleep on the couch until he got a place to stay and, in exchange, she would be able to spend time with her son.

Nobody had found an answer in his pain. In one hour a path had been laid out. There were no obstacles. He would have an "estate" sale, pack his bags, go to Maine, retrieve his son and head out to the *desert* one more time.

He had only one destination. He also had two months of unemployment remaining, a somewhat dependable car and a small U-Haul. The future was uncertain, but Nobody knew in his heart this is what he needed to do. He had faith that it would work out. Having unloaded his mental and physical baggage, Nobody had a much lighter load to tow. He was a single parent, without work, and without a plan. God was whittling him down to the right size, while Nobody was putting one foot in front of the other. His faith in God and himself was growing. He had everything he needed and he did not care what others thought of him.

Truth #69 Nobody's faith was building a bridge to God.

Nobody had one task left before the drive across the country was to begin: he needed to fly to Maine and retrieve his son. Just like the first trip when he dropped his son off, Nobody wanted to visit people he had not seen in a while in addition to his parents. His mother was upset that he would go see his relatives, when according to her, they did not care about him. This caused another outbreak of emotion in the house, just like old times. With no car at his disposal and not enough money to rent one, Nobody asked if his parents would drive him to his aunt's house. They refused. His mother started crying and yelling. The loyalty speech was dusted off and the rundown of how horrible a son he had been picked up from where his mother had left off. It didn't matter that he hadn't seen his aunt in over nine years. His mother, however, wanted complete devotion from Nobody regardless of her behavior towards him. Nobody, however, wanted to spread his wings and make the most of his trip. This particular aunt was his mother's sister so he thought it would not cause a stir.

They went out to eat instead and while driving to the restaurant, his mother was yelling at his father pleading with him to take her side on this issue. Her point was that Nobody should only see them and not see other relatives. Once his father agreed with her, she turned her focus on Nobody. She told him he should think of his parents first, belaboring the point crying and pleading with Nobody to change his mind on the subject. Nobody tried to bring balance to the conversation as best he could and attempted to set some sort of boundary. Without raising his voice, he explained that love is also given not only received. He simply said that it did not matter if their lives had been busy and they hadn't been able to reach out to him; he wanted to see his relatives because he loved them.

This was a topic that was always too much for his mother to bear: the fact that someone could love more than one or two people outside of the nuclear family. She had expectations and if someone did not meet them, his mother's love was withheld until they changed. She could not see that her effort to gain love was actually pushing Nobody away.

His mother also believed that if she was not getting along with a sibling, then she assumed that her husband and children should also be mad at them. This seemed to be the case; she was mad once again at her sister and so, she believed, should Nobody. She kept yelling at him, saying he did not honor his parents. She was trying to convince Nobody that he should only care about them. His mother continued her tirade. Out of the blue Nobody's three year old son, hit Nobody's mother saying, "don't talk to my daddy like that."

A hush enveloped the car. It was as if all the air was let out of a balloon. The tension and the emotion that had been held in by the car had been pierced, and Nobody's son curled up in his lap.

Episode 37

Arizona

A three day drive across the country landed Nobody and his son in Sierra Vista, Arizona, a town he'd once believed he had left behind for good. He quickly rekindled his old AA relationships, transferred his unemployment and began looking for work. He slept on the couch of his ex-wife's and while he was there everyone was on their best behavior. After about a week, through many discussions with different people, he ran across a Mormon family that invited Nobody and his son into their home. They had a converted garage and ran a child care center from the house during the day. They watched his son while he went about to do his errands. The arrangement was simple: help around the house and he could stay. Unfortunately, Nobody was still a bit self absorbed and the help he provided was limited. They had two girls and a boy all in their teens. They were all trying to do the right thing, but Nobody could tell they had issues of their own that would soon bleed into his affairs.

Nobody was introduced to Mormonism, an interesting family-oriented religion that practiced good works. However it did not jive with Nobody's view. He learned that you could attain, with adequate faith, coupled with good works, a level of god-likeness once you die. Once he heard the Mormon beliefs, he knew this is not something he could hang his hat on. The worldly message was proper: family, community, services and a place he could belong, but the underlying message was not his. It was just a bit too much for him to handle, and although he needed a place to stay, Nobody knew that once he let out of the bag he did not believe what he heard, his days were numbered in this home.

From his earliest childhood days, Nobody had wanted to be a police officer and not knowing what God wanted for him he made a wager with God. Nobody said that he would apply for law enforcement and telecom jobs and the industry that offered a job first would be where he believed God wanted him. He would tell the truth and not hide even one fact about his past. He took entrance tests and interviewed with surrounding police departments. When asked about his arrests he said that a police officer saved his life from drugs and to this day he calls him to let him know he is still sober and that he wanted to be part of an organization that brought the truth of a person's circumstance into view. He additionally sent out a flurry of telecommunication resumes.

The Lunch Bunch Group had a cake and a one year chip to present him for his one year sobriety. It was a tradition for all AA birthdays. It was sort of a weird day since these were the people he turned his back on in 1986 and now it was Oct 18th, 1991 and he was celebrating with his original crew. To his surprise many people showed up and more than one birthday chip did as well. Nobody had a way to make an impression and on this day, he was surrounded by people that cared for his well being. At the end of the meeting, one of the old timers, lovingly, told the crowd that the cake was not for Nobody, but for everyone else in the room since they had to put up with Nobody's antics during his initial tour of duty in the town. It was the least they could do for themselves. The room exploded with laughter and everyone agreed that Nobody was a wild one and they were glad he made it back into the rooms.

Two payments were left in his unemployment benefits. He attended a Tuesday night meeting. The feeling of despair was sweeping over him now due to his lack of employment. As he was sharing, he started crying and he expressed how he did not understand that, of all the places in the world, why God would put him back in the town he had left. It was as if he just woke up and here he was. Contemplating what he would do next, he heard a voice deep in his mind that told him he needed to make amends to the people he had hurt while he was here. Struck with revelation, he chimed in again as animated he could get with his hands and said he got the answer. He needed to work steps eight and nine with someone and make amends. After the meeting an old timer told him to call him in the morning with the list of people he needed to contact and they would go over how he would make those amends. A man on a mission, Nobody wrote the list and made the call.

They discussed that he would write letters to husbands of old flames since it was probably not a good idea to go up to them. He would find his old fiancée he broke up with and apologize. There was money that needed to be re-paid, but the important thing was that he had a list he could work through and while he was in this town he would take care of everyone on the list.

After a week of convincing his ex-fiancée's father that his intentions were pure, he was able to speak to the girl he broke off the engagement with and made amends to her. He managed to speak with his ex-wife's father and though he was not thrilled to see him again, he entertained the conversation and at the end asked him if this meant he had to like him. Nobody laughed and said, "No." Her father winked at Nobody and invited him in for coffee.

He dropped off letters, paid back some old loans and even returned an old library book he had kept. The librarian did not know what to do when she saw the book. She forgave the late fees since they quadrupled the actual value of the book.

When he had run through all the people that he could get in touch with, he continued looking for work with a load that was lighter that he had experienced in a long time. It was just freeing to know that he had cleaned up some of the wreckage of his past.

Nobody found a Unity church in the town and he began attending with his son. He made an appointment to meet with the minister at his house to try and figure out what else he could do while he was trying to do the next right thing in God's eyes. At the minister's house, Nobody was struck by the obvious inconsistencies between the man's behavior (smoking) and the manner in which the household was presented. The situation did not resemble what Nobody's inner core told him it should be. It felt as though a cloud hung over the building and Nobody did not feel that it was a spirit-filled home. He heard the same sort of ideas that he heard in South Carolina, but they did not have any appeal to him.

Nobody made a few follow-up phone calls to potential places of employment. During one call in particular, he asked the gentleman if he had received his resume. He said he had but it was 'somewhere on his desk'. Nobody volunteered to drive by and drop off another copy. The gentleman agreed, so Nobody got dressed and drove three hours to drop off a resume in person. It was late in the afternoon when Nobody arrived. He introduced himself and shared that he had driven three hours. The gentleman, who was looking down, raised his eyes and said, "If you drove three hours just to make sure I had a copy of your resume, I certainly can hire you." They arranged another trip so Nobody could meet the senior VP of Operations the following week. Nobody felt that everything he was doing was paying off. He thanked God for giving him the strength to walk on a path he had no idea where he was headed.

He was hired and needed to start work in a week and half. A place to stay was next on his "To Do" list. He needed to find a place to stay temporarily while he searched for something more permanent. Having only one more unemployment check coming, Nobody began to wonder *what was he going to do with his son? Would the Mormons watch him or would his son's mother?* All these questions and issues needed to be dealt with. He made a few phones calls and found a halfway house for men in early recovery in Phoenix. They said he could take a room for one week while he looked for something more permanent. Being sober for a year was no problem with the halfway house and he would have a place to lay his head at night. He was grateful. Driving down the road reviewing the list of all the preparations that had to be made and the excitement of knowing there was direction in his life, gave Nobody more strength.

He started to develop a deeper love for God. Even though he started experiencing God in AA and not in a church, he was grateful that he had found Him where he did. Though he did not understand at the time, God's grace was being placed upon his life.

Truth #70 God met him where he was and Nobody was listening.

The sun had since moved past the horizon and the moon was shining brightly in a cloudless sky. The stars were little giant sparkles shouting

230

there is more to the sky than just the moon, when somewhere between there and nowhere in the Arizona desert, Nobody heard a clunk. Then he felt a jolt. Another clunk. A shutter. The car very quickly ground to a halt. He could only get it into first gear and made it to the side of the road. As he got out of the car, everything was flashing before him. *Now what was he going to do?* Car troubles meant he needed money he did not have. He also didn't have credit since he had filed bankruptcy after his divorce. He saw a mom and pop service station on the other side of the highway that was near an exit. He walked to the garage and there was someone still in there even though it was after hours. Nobody made arrangements to get his car towed. Nobody was two and a half hours away from what he called home. Left to fend for himself outside (the garage attendant said they would look at it in the morning and departed for the evening,) he made a phone call to the Mormons for a ride. Alone in the desert he was truly a man with only his thoughts. His car had stopped near a lone monolith called Picacho Peak a place where the most western skirmish between Union and Confederate soldiers during the Civil War took place. It was a majestic sight to behold, with the moon above its peak.

Nobody thought, prayed and looked up and said, "God I know you are there, you can send the boils if you would like to test me, but I know you will lead me out of here. I will do whatever it takes. I know you love me just give me the strength to endure."

As he gazed at the peak in wonder until his ride arrived, he thought to himself that this would be his Mount Sinai. The spot where Nobody knew God had met him and Nobody would walk with God out of the desert.

A day later he got the quote of $450 dollars. His transmission would be fixed so he could drive it for a while but it still needed work. Ideally the transmission should be replaced. Nobody was in a bind so he approved the fix. He still needed the money.

"God please help," he said as he sat at the table trying to figure out a way to come up with the money. Then he heard the small voice inside of him say, "Borrow small amounts of money."

Off he went to visit old friends, the Unity Church and people in the program. He asked if he could borrow twenty dollars which he said he was not sure if he could pay them back. He called his old counselor from the Family Care Center and she said she would send $600 by Western Union. He managed to get another $350 from an accumulation of minor donations.

As for his son, he still did not know what to do. His mother said she could not watch him and he had not found a daycare center in Phoenix yet. At an AA meeting he asked if anyone knew who could help him. A girl spoke up and volunteered her sister. Nobody said he would entertain the idea but then asked multiple questions about her sister. The girl said she understood where Nobody was coming from and, with a wink in her eye, she said her sister was nothing like her and was always the good one.

The next day, he brought his son over, he checked out the place and immediately felt warmth about the home. The sister said she would love to watch his child for a week while he was in Phoenix getting his affairs in order and that he did not have to pay her anything. She knew he was trying to get his act together. Her sister had said that she had admired the strength he demonstrated in meetings to set his life right and it would be her gift to him. She had two other kids his son's age and her husband had agreed to help as well. Two strangers God had placed in his path and he might be taking a risk with his son, but he prayed a silent prayer and took a moment to hear God. He had felt nothing but peace about this person after he prayed. He took her up on the offer.

When he got back to his place, he had received a phone call from a nearby police department. Nobody had passed all the tests and interviews and they wanted him to join the force. As interesting an opportunity as this was, Nobody had made a deal with God and telecom is where he would stay.

He went to the Unity church for what would be his final time. The people had been gracious to him and he needed to thank them for their help. After the service, they gathered around him and presented him with a check for $300 dollars and told him that they felt he was a worthy investment. He did not have to pay it back. They believed God had something big planned for him and they wanted to make sure they did not get in God's way.

After a week of asking for mini loans, he gathered $1275 and only had to pay back half. As Nobody was driving to Phoenix, it had occurred to him that two weeks earlier he had no idea why he was in Sierra Vista. He had only known that he had to make amends to the people he had hurt. Once that task had been completed, he had been catapulted into the next part of his journey.

Nobody had found a studio apartment with a pseudo futon for a bed and a large closet he converted to a room for his son. The apartment building was a converted extended stay two-story motel. Daycare was lined up and he managed to find people in the program he could call on. He had just enough money for all his deposits and rent. He was amazed that God had provided the exact the amount of money he needed. His sponsor from South Carolina would always tell him that God would help move mountains as long as Nobody wasn't afraid to bring a shovel.

Truth #71 Nobody received what was needed.

After the end of his first week, he went to pick up his son. He was fine and he had had a good week. The woman who watched his son said he behaved well, and only had a couple of issues of extended crying when he had wanted to speak to his Daddy. He could tell his son had been well taken care of and he was grateful to her for what she had done for him. That evening he ran into the babysitter's sister and thanked her repeatedly for offering up her sister to watch his son. She went on to say that her sister, who watched his son, just found out she had a brain tumor. Nobody was completely caught off guard and soon realized what a selfless act she had performed. Nobody also knew that if it had been him, he would not have done what she had done.

Truth #72 Nobody saw another one of God's angels.

He loaded up all their belongings in the company van and they left the town of Sierra Vista exactly three weeks after Nobody made the last possible amends he could make. God had placed him there long enough to tie up loose ends before moving forward.

Truth #73 Nobody had left no baggage behind.

Episode 38

By the Time I Get to Phoenix

For the next few months, life was normal. He met a lot of new people including his new boss, a Christian man who was about eight years older than Nobody. His co-worker was a humanist who was also a nudist on the weekend and it was interesting listening to the different views they both had on life. The humanist lived for himself and believed we were just beings on this earth to enjoy it. He did not hurt anyone so as long as he left people alone, what concern was it of anyone's what he did or how he did it? As time went on, Nobody could see the guy wasn't happy by his remarks about the world. Nobody was a man who was currently looking inside of himself for the answers to life. Pleasure used to be the gauge for happiness. Nobody was sure of one thing: he could not go back to that place where living for himself was the only goal. The way we live may look different on the outside, but on the inside if you are chasing a feeling the let down is the same. Nobody didn't have all the answers to his life that was for sure, but listening to this nudist showed Nobody that this man didn't have a clue, either.

Nobody had lived like that before and hearing this line of reasoning from his co-worker only solidified his current quest to understand God. One thing Nobody knew for certain: living a life thinking that way missed the point of hope. His boss believed in Jesus Christ and lived his life as best he could with what God had provided. He called himself a 'Bible Believing Christian,' a term that was new to Nobody. He always looked at people as Catholics, Baptists, Unitarians, Mormons, etc.

While in the office, Nobody mentioned to his boss that he had a hard time with churches and religion and that throughout his whole life he had been let down repeatedly by either priests, churches, New Age movements, etc. He had tried a life of chasing pleasure with no fruitful outcome. He had never found any relief spiritually until he made it into AA. After about fifteen minutes of Nobody's comments, his boss said that he could hear in Nobody's voice a yearning for a deeper understanding and a relationship with God. The problem was that he felt Nobody was judging Christ by the failings of people around him. Nobody should not judge Christ on what he saw people do but to judge Christ on what he did and has done for Nobody. He cautioned Nobody that people, even himself, would let him down if all he did was base his beliefs on what others do in the name of Christ. Churches were filled with people trying to find the same thing and everyone needs the help Christ had to offer. While he was happy that Nobody believed in God, was Nobody ready to place his faith in Christ and take the next step?

His boss continued saying that the problem with the worldview was that while many were preaching that Christian principles were good to live by, the spiritual implications are impractical and the church is out of touch with real life. Why believe in Christ and live by those moral standards when, by all practical purposes, they go against human nature? There may be a god, but not one based in Christ. Why would you waste your life on hope and prayer? Living a Christian life will provide you with good orderly direction and make you a great neighbor, but deep down, you're a loony tune to believe in the resurrection of Jesus Christ. His boss said he had struggled with this for a long time and once he started taking the behavior of the church out of the equation, he was able to see the love of Christ in his life more clearly. These were the competing positions he felt Nobody was wrestling with.

Truth #74 Nobody agreed he lived by most of the teachings of Christ but not the faith in Christ.

His boss told him of a non-denominational church that he should visit. The following Sunday he went and found himself among a congregation of over 2500. Nobody enjoyed the service but he was just one fish in a sea of people. He wanted what the pastor said he could attain if he placed his faith in Christ. Still a man with his thoughts, he still wanted a wife and his life in Phoenix was a lonely one. Nobody was grateful for his boss and he prayed to God, always hoping that right around the corner the answer to everything would be in his grasp, an answer he could be happy with and add purpose to his life instead of just staying sober. He just hated the waiting. It always felt as though he was waiting and his walk was a series of baby steps.

But life progressed slowly with chicken pox, occasional dates, car troubles and meetings. After about six months in Phoenix, a rumor was floating throughout the company that they were going to be bought by a larger company. At the time of mergers and acquisitions that could only mean one thing: layoffs.

Episode 39

Take the Long Way Home

The new owners of the company were due to arrive. They had set up a series of meetings in which they could meet with people individually. The rumor mill was in full force and Nobody was concerned. He was in a town he was not familiar with, he had no money and he was a single parent. Additionally, he was still looking for the answers in his life. He found a local sponsor and challenged him because Nobody had a habit of trying a bunch of different solutions at once to solve one problem and never allowed one thing to simmer long enough to show results. The local sponsor suggested he try one remedy. Nobody accepted his offer and decided that he would only attend church and go to AA meetings instead of a set of different types of meetings around the area, like Narcotics Anonymous, Emotions Anonymous, Co-Dependents Anonymous etc.

Nobody was a person who always had to have something to do, a plan, a list or a direction. Idle time made him most uncomfortable. With all the work he was doing to improve his life, he still traded one way of living for another. Previously, he had questionable behavior now he had good orderly direction. His life was still based on feelings derived from results of his efforts. If he felt he was doing the right things then all was well, if he felt badly, then he questioned that what he was doing was the right thing after all.

He had grown up in a home where everything had to be understood and everyone knew what was happening. All actions and decisions were questioned. If he was able to keep his parents happy by making the right decision or adjusting an erroneous course, all was well. This translated into a man that needed constant validation. It would only be natural for this sort of thinking to be expanded upon as Nobody grew up. He had to have vision towards the future or his world would seemingly look as though nothing of value was happening. He needed to check with everyone to make sure he was doing the right thing. He had not realized that time was sometimes the best teacher. He also had not realized that time, coupled with location and following his heart, could be the key ingredients for God's will to materialize. Some days one must walk forward to find what has been prepared for him. The Bible and many other inspirational books are littered with examples of struggling people who ventured forward on faith only to discover God's hand in all aspects of the journey.

This was why his sponsor said to do just one thing. He needed to bake one cake and not try a thousand different recipes for pies, tarts and muffins if the end goal was to just have a cake. If you put too many ideas together or formulas together you end up with a system error. It just doesn't compute. Nobody had to simplify his thoughts and walk on one set of steps instead of trying to straddle multiple ladders all moving toward better living. Apart from that, he wanted a better relationship with God more than anything else, Nobody still wanted to prove to God that he was worth loving. Going back to his old belief system, Nobody still worked hard for people or God to love him. If he let up, then they would forget about him and he would be alone.

The time leading up to these dreaded reorganizational meetings kept Nobody pacing. As was his norm, he was unable to keep still; when he had nothing to do he always was on the move. Whether switching channels on the TV, running, cleaning the apartment, walking in the mall, going for a ride in the car, visiting different people at work during the day, Nobody was always moving. Unfortunately seldom was his son more than a peripheral part of his activity. He tried to figure things out by reasoning through a thousand scenarios. The possibility of being laid off placed his mind into overdrive.

He prayed to God to not let him down, because Nobody was scared that he had made the wrong decision by moving out to Phoenix. He was scared that he would lose his job and have nothing. What would they do? He had a million scenarios with only one outcome: something awful would happen for sure.

He had years of hearing and assuming he had never done anything right, always questioned, made to feel as though his opinion or thought process was not to be trusted. He was a broken spirit of a man that was now on the right path but seemingly had not come to grips that he was smart, intelligent and loved by God. He was unsure of himself. Nobody could provide the lip service on his life and his thoughts to convince you he had his act together. He could cite examples of where God orchestrated events. Nobody never truly walked in faith he just stumbled forward and God happened to be there. He had been taught to worry. In adulthood it was his fear of making a wrong decision that prevented him from so many opportunities and if he did make a wrong choice, Nobody believed his life would be forever ruined.

Being OK was always in the future and never at that moment. This could only mean one thing, fear had never moved out of his mind. At every opportunity his old friend would whisper in his ear and remind him that he should be afraid. Because when it really mattered and Nobody needed God, He will desert Nobody. When he is the most vulnerable and at his weakest point he would be crushed and made to pay for all he had ever done.

Myth #65 Nobody was unworthy of God's true love for him

As Nobody continued working the Steps, he started seeing how his childhood had affected the way he thought about himself and how he reacted to things. He was, by all accounts, still very afraid of making a mistake. When he grew up he was always challenged. Nobody was afraid that he would be labeled a failure or stupid for taking a risk that might not pan out. Going back to the day he tore the flesh off his hand from the fall, the message that had always kept resonating in his mind, *"It serves you right, if you had done what we said none of this would have happened!!!"*

If he could hear God and follow God then all would fine. This life he had would work out. Nobody's relationship with God was in his head and resembled his relationship with his mother and father. It had to be based on merit. Success in this world wasn't about if his life worked out and if he received everything he dreamed of. It was about the faith he had to walk it out with God. No one had never taught this message to Nobody, so for him the message he lived by was clear, be careful or you might choose poorly.

Myth #66 Nobody believed deep inside God would eventually punish him.

He was called into an office with two people: a very attractive women and an HR rep. Pleasantries were exchanged and the woman explained how they were going to combine staff with their main office in downtown Phoenix. She said she would have to see how his position would fit into their current business structure. There it was. The kiss of death for his employment. The great mumbo jumbo of business. The trite *we care, it isn't personal it is just business, blah, blah, blah*. Nobody understood what they were saying.

Listening intently and assuming the worse, Nobody looked at her and very calmly said, "I understand all that you have just said. I am a single parent and I was unemployed for about four months this year. I live in a studio apartment and have no family in the area. I rent my TV and my car is on its last leg unless I get a new transmission. I need a job and will do anything to stay employed. Can you help me?" This would be what he would call his first seat belt moment.

The HR person in the back stopped writing and looked up. Nobody had thrown all care to the side and as naked as a man could be, he had pleaded for mercy in his deepest moment of need to a person he did not know and it was a woman.

All experiences in Nobody's past with women only left a bad taste in his mouth because they couldn't be trusted. Nobody, whether foolish or otherwise, had heard right before he spoke those words in his mind's eye, "Lay out the facts." She looked down at her notes, jotted something down and looked back up and said. "If you don't mind moving to South Carolina, I have a position for you there."

The sheer force of her words as she spoke them leveled Nobody. All the tears, borrowing of money, stranded in the desert, living in temporary places, trusting families with his son and the sacrifices he had made. But how could he have doubted God only one minute before, between his question and the answer. God had guided Nobody from South Carolina to Arizona to be in the proper place at the proper time, in the proper office, with no windows, with a woman who was known to rip apart companies and throw people away in the name of business.

He was just offered a job in a state he had left eight months earlier. Considering how large the world is and that Nobody was at the right spot to find the job in South Carolina sitting almost 2,000 miles away in Arizona, was unbelievable.

God had answered his request in his darkest hour when he was in the most need, even when he failed to have faith. Nobody had proceeded toward the Red Sea, always wondering if it might not have been better in Egypt after all, like the Israelites' thought in the Old Testament, only to find that this path was filled with God's blessing.

He jumped from his chair and exclaimed, "Yes!!"

He told her he had left South Carolina eight months earlier in hopes of finding his fortune here in the desert and instead he found the path back to his chosen family. He told her she was a gift from God to an answered prayer.

When he left the office, he ran down the hall to his office and placed a phone call to his sponsor in South Carolina. He dialed the phone with immense joy in his heart, and heard the ring at the other end and then the familiar, "Hello." The response came with a slight pause between the two l's.

"You will *not* believe what just happened! God just answered my prayer in the wildest way! I found a job in South Carolina via 'Phoenix. I'm coming home."

Truth #75 God had never deserted Nobody.

Episode 40

Home Sweet Home

Four months later Nobody was traveling every morning to Charlotte while the Columbia office was being set up. He had been provided a company truck, moved into a one bedroom apartment where his son had a mattress in one corner and Nobody had his in the other. He was reunited with old friends and his adventures retold. He was a new man. His faith in God had increased and he was ready for whatever God had in store for him. From Charlotte, Nobody was able to get home every night to go out for a run before it was time to pick up his son from the daycare. A year ago he was a chain smoker and in the back of his mind he had always wanted to quit.

About a year prior, Nobody read, by chance, something in the Bible. The verse talked about how salt was good but if it loses its flavor, what was it good for. That verse resonated with him. Numerous times he attempted to stop, but after reading that verse, he went down to a half pack a day from two and then to none for an extended period of time. On New Year's Eve, after about a two week break, he thought he would smoke one just for good old time's sake. For whatever reason he got sick to his stomach, fell asleep, missed the turn of the clock and never smoked again. From that point on he replaced smoking with running.

That is how one must look at their relationship with God. God must replace something that keeps you held back. That is why he said not to have other gods or idols before Him. There might be a deeper meaning to this. Unfortunately many have a hard time removing one bad thing and replace it with a new thing to deepen their relationship with God. For many it can be their faith in God, that to have faith in God one must set aside their lack of faith in God. If there are some that don't believe in God, maybe they need to see Him at work. If the lack of prayer is providing the results that are not desired, maybe praying without expectations is a better course of action.

Nobody had discovered how he relied on cigarettes for relief instead of going directly to God. Answers to prayer on many occasions are not instantaneous; it is a process that everyone must go through if they are serious about their relationship with God.

This is how Nobody saw his prayer life in regards to timing. There was his timing, what he thought God's timing was, and then God's actual timing in answering prayers. These three philosophies do not line up well for an impatient person. It doesn't mean that God is not listening, it only means that the answers are not delivered when we want them and usually not in the desired form either.

It has to do with expectations. Many have turned away from God, because unlike a store, if you pay enough you can get what you want. Many feel they have been faithful and what have they gotten for it? They look around and may not see the white picket fence, a white house, kids or a faithful spouse. Instead they see tragedy and unfulfilled desires. They have been fed by a world that says you deserve to be happy. You should and you ought to be. . . (fill in the blank.) Many have stood on a pulpit and said good acts will receive good rewards. It is always the perception of the word *'rewards'* that confuse many. They personalize everything and say that since nothing is changing maybe God isn't there after all. This argument has stretched from here to the sun, without considering how magnificent the sun actually is in its never ending light.

Nobody had yet to learn that just because you believe a granted wish or desire is a gift from God, it might just be your imagination in disguise. Just because you desire something doesn't mean that if you are faithful to God it will be delivered. God doesn't always reward someone for good behavior, he blesses due to obedience.

The flip side is, as Nobody's heart is in the right place, but his feelings will drive him over the edge, because he is fighting two wills: God's and his. It follows that age old adage, 'be careful what you pray for, you just might get it.'

For Nobody, unfulfilled prayer was a wife, it would only make sense. The hunt continued and with a few failed attempts at having the icing before actually baking the cake, he was left with nothing. This was his weakness and was extremely overt in this area. Nobody was more focused on the outcome than building a relationship. That did not stop him from trying. He had heard many times that if you wanted change in your life you needed to change yourself. This method of wife searching that he was utilizing wasn't working. Something different needed to be tried. So with his sponsor he made a vow to only date for the next year in the hope that if he changed during this process then he would attract a different sort of woman.

Two months into his vow and sitting alone one Saturday afternoon, in the depths of extreme thought, focused on what he did not have as opposed to what he did have, he knew something was still missing. During this time of dating, Nobody was brought face-to-face with himself. It forced him to start relating to life differently. He knew that the time was now to bring something new into his life. As he looked at his son playing, he knew he had to bring to him something more worthwhile than a mother. In great despair and feeling at a loss, Nobody opened up the yellow pages under churches. He started calling, one by one hoping someone would answer. Answering machine after answering machine, giving church service times or asking him to call back during church hours; he hit the S's and someone answered.

"Hello, S Baptist Church." The person on the other side answered.

Nobody surprised, started talking, and said he was searching for something and did not know what. He had a good life but there was a hole inside that no amount of music, exercise, meetings or mayhem could fill. He was concerned about his son and wanted something different for him. The voice belonged to the worship director, he had only stepped into the church to get something and usually did not answer the phone but was compelled to when he heard the ring. Nobody, who had already seen God at work, knew this was his next stop on the journey.

Truth #76 Nobody finds comfort at God's house.

Episode 41

Holy Water

Now a Baptist Church was not what Nobody was looking for. Growing up his mother would make comments about the Baptist preacher who lived next door and how silly it was to get fully immersed for baptism. Nobody remembered how, when they used to drive by and see people wearing their Sunday best when leaving the building, he always thought they were different in a weird way. These thoughts were derived from the little comments he heard over time and had formed an opinion even as a child.

As he and his son were walking up to the church, he couldn't help thinking that they - the Baptists, those different people - had answered the phone. They were actually greeting him at the door and showing him where he could bring his son for Sunday School. There were a lot of attractive women, too. The sermon was actually good and Nobody was able to see the words jump right out of the Bible. Why, this wasn't that bad at all. They had a singles ministry and that had totally perked his ears. They had Wednesday night dinner and after, if you chose to, you could go knock on doors to people who had visited the church the week earlier. Being a person who was brought back from his own personal hell, Nobody thought this would be a valiant effort.

So Nobody immersed himself. He was going to Bible study with a group of his peers. His son had activities he could participate in. It was also the perfect place for Nobody to work out his vow about dating. If these girls were here, they had to be strict in that regard anyway. They must be or why would they be here? Just like him they surely wanted what God wanted for them!

Being the extrovert he was, it was not long before he and the single's minister went out knocking on doors together. Nobody felt they were the 'yin and the yang.' Nobody brought the understanding of real life pain and recovery and the singles minister brought the Book. They spoke about a lot of things and Nobody started what would soon be a wonderful passion of his which was discussing faith from a realist's perspective. In time this would be termed the study of the apologetics, but for now it was enough to engage in the conversations. With his heart bearing in the right direction, Nobody still loved his heavy metal, which raised a few eyebrows in some of his singles gathering. He continued to defend his choice of music.

This is what he was learning - that he had a choice and all he had to do was make it. He just needed to turn from his past and choose Jesus. He needed to go to church regularly and get into the Word. He started spending time in the morning with his son reading him excerpts from a children's Bible. His son was a very active child and when separated from his father, he would act out. Many would say that his son was a bit too much to handle when Nobody was away but what could he do? He was doing the best that he could. His son needed a mother but for now they stuck close to church activities and Nobody continued to read to his son.

Nobody went on dates and started learning how to appreciate a woman for who she was. He saw a lot of people who were in the same boat as he was. Some were older and it looked to him like they had been single for a long time. This was something Nobody could not envision, being single forever. However, the formula was working. Between his meetings and church, things were picking up. He was practicing a lot of new behaviors that were more productive and his mental health was improving.

One night, during home visitations, the singles minister asked him if he would commit to the church. This was something that he saw many people do at the end of the services. They would, through a transfer letter, change churches and would be baptized in the immersion pool behind the altar. Nobody's life was getting better, his son was settling down, and he felt a deeper bond forming with his son.

As he drove home that night he started thinking about how he had kept away from Jesus all this time. He heard the Roman Road scripture and how he only needed to make a verbal commitment to Christ as his Lord and Savior. It was true he had done this during his confirmation years ago, but there was something different doing it again and really meaning it this time. In the Catholic Church, there were a lot of ceremonies to run through - the Sacraments as the church called them. For the most part he had just gone through the motions not really understanding what he was confirming. If he was going to commit to this church, he would need to be baptized. From his point of view it was plain and simple. He would be part of this church and everything would be fine and hopefully all aspects of his life would continue to get better.

As with most people, Nobody concluded in the back of his mind, that there should be a payoff of some sort for giving his life to Him. Not really grasping the fact that a relationship was a two-way street and not a one-way street. With pure intentions, he still hoped that he would be blessed for his Baptism. Nobody would be blessed in many ways - beyond his imagination - but the main reason for his baptism was to get something beneficial out of it. It certainly would be a start but not the finish. He still felt like an outsider when he was in groups or participating in activities. This probably would help him with that, and once baptized, he would be more readily accepted. He believed he was a 'good sort of fella' and he was ready to give up a lot of things, but not everything. A lot of the things they said were harmful to his soul, he did not believe, but they were nice and he respected their opinion. He still loved his heavy metal music, his language was still a bit crass, he still enjoyed horror flicks and although he would not say it out loud, once he met someone he liked he wouldn't let a few church rules get in the way. However, he had made his decision, and on the next Sunday during the altar call, he moved to the front. The team was ready for him and he expressed his desire to join the church.

His AA three year anniversary was approaching and Nobody was excited about his upcoming baptism. His aunt, who was a born-again Catholic, was the only person he felt he could talk to about God at this level. She had been a part of the charismatic movement in the seventies and had found a heart for Christ. This was not something he could talk about with his parents, but they were supportive of his efforts. He wanted to call his aunt and talk about the church he had joined, the baptism and what was really going on in his life. He loved this aunt, she always told him she loved him and accepted him for who he was. Nobody had always longed for a love he felt from his relatives to come from his parents, but the more he wished the more his parents pulled away.

Nobody was an emotional man. He played out his rough exterior, but deep down he was still someone searching for answers. He was not afraid to talk to anyone and share what was going on. Still, with all this time under his belt, it was still all about him. He would listen to people just enough to give everyone time to get what they wanted to say, before he picked up where he left off in a conversation. He was an open book from that prospective willing to talk with anyone about any topic as long as it was his.

Over the years, he called his relatives to keep in touch. He had called his aunt, the youngest of all the sisters to share the Good News. It occurred to Nobody that his grandfather had given him a watch years ago when he had died. Surely, not his last words but, nonetheless, close to the last and he mentioned casually to his aunt that he would like to get it back into his possession. Nobody had petitioned his mother for it and it was on its way. His aunt mentioned that she also had another old pocket watch of his grandfather's that she would send to him.

The conversation continued and Nobody, also excited about his upcoming AA anniversary, mentioned that he would be three years sober on Oct. 18th. Then there was silence.

"Hello, are you there?

"Yes, can you repeat what you just said?" she said with an air of curiosity.

"I just said that I would be three years sober coming up."

"I heard that, but what was the date you mentioned?" now with a more determined tone.

"I said, I would be three years sober on Oct 18th."

"Nobody that was the day your grandfather died."

All a sudden a mosaic of pictures flashed through Nobody's mind. How he had always felt his grandfather watching him while he was dealing drugs. How Nobody had pushed those feelings of shame aside. How a couple of times he had wanted to commit suicide, but the thought of his grandfather watching and not wanting to disappoint him, even in death. How his behaviors sexually always brought upon feelings of guilt and shame, as if his grandfather was there in the room, hoping Nobody would have more love for himself than to put himself through these situations. How many times had he laid in bed and thought of his 'Pepere' in Heaven looking down at him, knowing this would not be the life his 'Pepere' would have wanted for him.

The visual picture of his grandfather telling his grandmother to give his watch to Nobody, when she asked what she should do with it after he died and could this have actually been a 'prayer of covering' over Nobody? Nobody, over many years, felt he had to prove to people to love and accept him. This was different; this was a thought beyond all thoughts. His grandfather, as he was dying, thought of him. He was in Maine while Nobody was in New York, and saw the other grandchildren all the time, but his 'Pepere' remembered him. He knew all along what was going on in the home he grew up in. Could it have been a prayer that his grandfather asked God to watch over him?

He remembered waiting for his grandparents out in the front yard all day as a child, looking for that Chevy Impala to come down the road. It was an eight-hour drive from Maine, but Nobody had waited in eager anticipation as soon as he got up from bed. Time would stop until their arrival. He always felt safe in their presence. He remembered the time he walked hand-in-hand with his grandfather, back in Maine, to a store down the street from where they lived on Sabattus St., next to an A&W Root Beer drive-in, and the canned onion mix he made that could be placed in soups and roasts. He remembered seeing his grandfather pray beside his bed with his white T-shirt, boxers and those socks. He had truly loved this man without reservation. He remembered the day the phone call came. How his mother had fallen into his father's arms crying. All these thoughts moving from left to right in a matter of seconds; all converging on one major point that could be easily seen by Nobody.

God loved him and his grandfather loved him. Whatever prayer was spoken that day - directly or indirectly - had been fulfilled. God and his 'Pepere' had been watching over him all those years. To drive the point home, like only God can, Nobody had been brought to his knees on that night of October 18th, 1990 as he surrendered his old life to God. It was the fifteenth anniversary of his grandfather's death. Though love can be misinterpreted by the pain of circumstances, the desired result was accomplished; the focus of his own desires had been severely removed on that day and the convergence of this information had been hidden from him all these years. When the student is ready the teacher appears. This had certainly rung true. Since the day of his arrest, Nobody had made the commitment to change and from that day forward Nobody had started down the path from death into life.

As one generation was dying back in the early seventies, prayer had been fueling the younger generation blossoming by a simple act. The facts could not be ignored, there were too many road signs along the way that told Nobody that he had been special in his grandfather's eyes and in God's. So much so that he continued to watch over him and no one would ever convince him otherwise.

As he stepped into the immersion pool two weeks later, waist high in water, he thought of his grandfather's love as he renewed his vow with God and accepted Jesus Christ as his savior. As he fell backwards into the warm water, it slowly engulfed his body as it went under the water baptized by his own choice.

Hallelujah, Amen.

Episode 42

Blinded by the Light

There is a major misconception out there that once someone is saved all should be well. One had only look around a church to see all the smiling faces to see that. The baptism of a person usually yields a period of intense joy and evangelism. The realization that life will still continue to have ups and downs no matter your relationship with God was taught to Nobody in AA; he would have been sure to fall off the wagon soon after his baptism without that lesson learned. Nobody, still holding to his vow of chastity, connected whatever dots there were in his head that a reward for good behavior was due. He was holy in this regard. If Nobody had been paying attention to the lessons in the Bible, he would have seen how many characters had suffered greatly after pledging their lives to God. A life of obedience did not always offer comfort. It offered comfort of the spirit in spite of the circumstances.

Living around men who also have been given free will is where things get tricky. The issue is that life in the flesh, presents an experience that can be termed as a gift. Those who are on the quest of 'enlightenment' want to remove themselves from the essence of life itself and rise to a higher plane. Depending on what flavor, this could be good or bad. Those who question God's existence claim there could not possibly be a God due to all the evil in the world. These critics see around them certain life circumstances that, in their eyes, proves one of three things—there is no God, or He exists but has entirely removed himself from the day to day interaction of men and doesn't care at all, or He exists and it requires recompense to deliver good graces. Even today, many worship so-called gods/idols in many various ideals; sex, money, ambition, power, and religious beliefs, etc. Many have prayed to these items without realizing what they were doing or what they were forming allegiances with. They anticipate rewards from these things, believing, if they lean this way that, praying to God while not changing certain aspects of their life, will bring forth grace from God. The rewards they experience may not have been godly to begin with. Even Satan hands out blessings; one of his favorites is 'delusion.'

When the God of Abraham gave man free will he meant it. It wasn't fifty percent of the time, and then when men behaved badly enough God would step in, fix it and make wrongs right. He isn't going to scare us into behaving or show miracle after miracle and continue to reason with us to have Him as the object of our love. Many a man has tried to scare men into behaving by their prescription so that you might fear their actions while ignoring the eternal ramifications many seem unwilling to grasp. Free will is free will. It is the ultimate choice and the ultimate gift of love. In the absence of love, evil exists in whatever form it may present itself.

Choosing God doesn't mean that bad things won't happen, but you will have the strength to move through it when they present themselves. God is not a 'sugar daddy' in which, if you perform x, y, z, then a, b, c will occur with a direct result and then be tapped on the head and pronounced "good." If, by performing these so-called religious tasks perfectly, one may believe to have reached some pinnacle point of revelation. Then upon that epiphany one may expect to have it manifest itself into a fleshly reward and have all adversity removed. Those are lofty ambitions of men who still want to separate themselves from the masses pointing out they have found a way to remove themselves from the horrors of the world. But, they are themselves men who foster good deeds only to have their reward dispensed on Earth. There are many organizations that believe this and profess to have a major secret that can only be revealed to members after you have gone through many stages of progression.

Nobody had, to some degree, been exposed to this in his life, but he still battled God just like some of the heroes in the Bible did when they walked with God. However, he viewed that his work at the church and the

252

things he did in the service of the church were the bridge to rewards from his Heavenly Father. These actions would be translated into an approval from the people around him. He still had a blind spot that God needed to work on.

Unknowingly Nobody still wanted a hybrid God that loved him and gave permission to have what Nobody wanted when he wanted it. This is the rub. Nobody believed that what he wanted and did was good thinking and behavior. Never once did he think maybe God disapproved. Nobody still had that one wish he could hold on to that would fill in the gap. A force above all forces he could tap into and that force was marital love. Marriage was however a gift from God. Though he was on a more righteous path, his ambitions still clouded the desire of his Maker to perform even greater things in his life.

Being alone was Nobody's nemesis and this was an 'evil' Nobody fought constantly. He paid so much attention to his loneliness, he was actually worshiping it. This one thing reminded him that his life was unfulfilled. With all the wonderful things happening in his life, this one box was currently unchecked and the holidays seem to heighten the awareness in this area.

Nobody's job provided him with a lot of windshield time to converse with God. Like a child in a store wanting candy which is just out of its reach in the shopping cart, Nobody was still trying to cut deals with God to answer his never ending plea. Nobody was using, as the basis of his plea, parts in the Bible where all you have to do is ask God and all will be provided.

Truth #77 Nobody tries to bargain with God.

Proof texting is a way of finding Biblical text to support your argument based on your thoughts. Usually the words are taken out of context to support a claim instead of reading the text as it was meant to see the essence of the Word. Nobody was trying this method to have God grant his wish. He was persistent. He knew God was there and he boldly brought it to Him. Nobody couldn't figure out why God was silent on this matter. He had received revelation on countless things but in this area there was nothing to be heard. The emotion was so extreme, Nobody even entertained suicide, because of the emptiness that wrought throughout him. Thankfully, he was a coward and did not have the courage to follow through. If it had it not been for his son, Nobody's world may have been different. He couldn't desert his son.

Myth #67 Good Christian behavior always equals earthly rewards.

Pain is relative. To see a child go through a temper tantrum because they were denied candy, one would think that significant trauma had occurred. However to that child, it was the end of the world. The child's father, his maker, may have already given his child too much candy and didn't want the child to get sick. The father knew what was best for his child even though the child did not. In many cases the father doesn't have to give an explanation. It is just better not to give it to the child and continue with trying to pay the cashier. To the child the father has forgotten about him. The grief and emotional pain is overwhelming and the belief that the candy will make all the pain go away and not being able to have it is traumatic. When the father is not looking, the craftiness of the child might shine forth as the child secretly finds a way to get what he desires, even against the wishes of the father, who loves the child dearly.

When people hold the cards, they feel empowered to do what is in their best interest even if it is selfish and not in the spirit of good will for all men. The majority of people will always make sure their needs are taken care of. This is not a general statement; it is a truth that describes the nature of man and everything changes when a person says, "I want" or "I don't want to." Both mean exactly the same thing and all bets are off when a person has the resolve to attain his desires.

People do not like to be told what to do. Free will, given to us by God, must be played out in its entirety or the gift is lost. Without pain one could not understand love. Pain is immediate and love is usually seen in hindsight. Lust is immediate. Like a father watching his teenage son make a series of bad decisions, even though the father gave him good direction at some point, he can only stand by. Just like our Father in Heaven, he gave us life, he holds all the cards and sees our desires and wants and hopes that you will one day turn to Him instead as one lives out his gift of life. That is why we need God - to provide the direction we need to find our way home to Him.

Nobody, being the good Baptist, was still holding on to some of his old beliefs or bad boy ways and was not terminally unique. It's just that needs have manifested itself in other areas of his life. It hasn't been all converted, just the areas he wanted. His relationship with his son was blossoming. The time that he has spent with him had actually improved his behavior during their separations. Reading to him had strengthened the tie between them and brought healing into the spirit of his son. Nobody's focused attention on his son was working.

Although he had not been given his soon-to-be-wife, Nobody was acting properly to ensure that he would not be punished if he stepped out of line with God. Nobody had not reached the understanding yet of what obedience meant. However, this should not take away the fact that good things were happening. Garbage in, garbage out; conversely, good things in, good things out. The progression in his life was apparent but the laws of the world were still making their presence known to an agreeable degree. Obey the rules and you will be accepted - it just works well in a church environment.

Some of the people he hung around with still questioned the music and movies he entertained, however, Nobody defended his choices. What could possibly be wrong with Black Sabbath, Metallica, Gun and Roses and a variety of others that could affect his relationship with God? He was smart enough to filter out the differences, plus the music itself was good. The same could be said for poison, it has been added to many flavors and to the unsuspecting recipient while it tasted good going down, the poison was still in the mix wreaking havoc to the ignorance of the consumer. The same with movies, his friends were just prudes when it came to this stuff. Within a few hours Nobody would wonder why he still felt separated from God, never understanding that watching questionable content could contribute to his relationship with God and actually foster a feeling of separation.

Attending the singles Bible study group regularly, Nobody was an active participant. He kept up with his assignments and offered input. He was doing everything he was supposed to do. With the knowledge he had learned from AA, he could easily grasp concepts laid out in the Bible. He had an ability to cross that divide between real life and Scripture, so he thought, always bringing to the forefront the human element that made living up to the 'auspicious' of the Bible difficult. This was well received by those in his group, but he was only laying down the reasons why he could not fully commit all things in his life to Christ. This is not uncommon for just about everyone on the Earth. No one is excluded from being human with the natural wants and desires.

With all the positives, the clock was ticking inside his head. Over this period, while he had this vow about chastity, his silent expectation would be that he would still be rewarded and he would find a 'nice' girl. He was starting to doubt his marketability, and then, it all happened. Like David's first glimpse of Bathsheba, in through the gymnasium door, where the single's Bible studies took place, she walked in, with her small boy in tow. Nobody happened to be standing next to the singles minister when everyone seemed to perk up upon her entrance. Nobody looked towards the single's minister who said very plainly, "I would keep away from her." To anyone else those words may have been adhered to but to Nobody this was a challenge. In a split second, just like the day his DC sponsor voiced a similar warning when he saw *Hometown Hottie* walk through the door of the Halloween party, all restraint was thrown out the window. Nobody had a new focus of attention and her name was *Church Girl*.

By morning's end he had introduced himself. He used every means necessary to gain access. They had so much in common (both being single parents, for example) and in Nobody's mind this was going to be different. Funny how the mind works when a certain button is pushed and how all caution is set aside. Over the next two weeks, he was able to speak with her a few times. He found out that *Church Girl* was dating someone in the single's ministry, separated from her husband who had cheated on her, gainfully employed ☺, had a car ☺, and he had met her at church ☺. Nobody learned that she was twenty and being thirty years old, Nobody felt this was insignificant. *Church Girl* had graduated from high school in her junior year ahead of schedule and had been in the work force ever since; she was obviously very smart for her age.

Nobody looked at all the facts, saw the pattern and said to himself, *"This is different."* The eleven months he had been working on himself had paid off. He only had one thing left to do and that was prove to her that Nobody was the best choice. *Church Girl* was beautiful, heads turned when she walked into a room and if he was able to land this one, everyone would think he had the *'it'* factor.

Myth #68 Nobody believed that this might be the woman sent from God.

Episode 43

It's a Miracle

With many men interested in *Church Girl*, Nobody used the kid factor to gain premium quality time. After about a month and finding his way into her circle of friends, he managed to get *Church Girl* to come over and watch a movie. The boys would be able to play together so on and so forth. They started talking regularly and there seemed to be some attraction present but not at the level which would convince her to jump. Nobody was determined. Believing he was lacking physically, he needed to reach past his own natural failings to compensate. He started helping her out around her house, took care of car needs, and cooked dinners.

Now for a single female parent, who had a self-absorbed cheating husband and the understanding that many men wanted one thing from her, Nobody's persistence in others areas provided for an alternate avenue of approach. Her current boyfriend, who came around off and on seemed to have a singular purpose as well. While he understood that it wasn't serious, there were occasions when Nobody drove by and her boyfriend's car was there and the lights were off. This did not deter him, it only propelled him further. His need for a relationship was so strong that in a short period of time, he had gone from being focused on God and Nobody's son, to her.

The morning time that was set aside reading to his son slowly diminished. All free time he had was trying to find things to do with her and when she couldn't or was with someone else he placed his life on hold until she was available. He maintained as cool a profile as he could, but, while he may have been praying to God for her to notice him, he was in total "gotta have it" mode. *Church Girl's* hubby was off doing his own thing and attending college. He was creating a lot of static through his lapse in temporary child support. The court proceedings were in disarray, due to lack of funds, a variety of delay tactics, and non-appearances in court by her husband. Inevitably, her life was put on hold.

As Nobody started to get a feel for the situation, he failed to see how he'd ended up deep in a pattern of rescuing. After all this time working on himself, making serious improvements in many areas, he was catapulted back in time. When fear of any kind is present and timing is not in one's favor, it tends to make men and women do things they would otherwise not do out of desperation.

In the book of Genesis, God promised Abraham that he would be the father of nations, but Sarah had been barren and she was getting too old to have a child. In their impatience, Sarah begged Abraham to sleep with Hagar, a maidservant, to produce a son, later named Ishmael. When God fulfilled his promise and Sarah finally had Isaac, there was strife between Sarah and Hagar. It was why Hagar was sent away to be on her own. Ishmael is considered the father of Islam. Sarah's impatience with God in His promise for Sarah to bare a son continues to breed angst within this world. Nobody, like Sarah, was impatient and did not allow events to unfold in God's timing and circumvented God's providence in his life.

Church Girl's circle of friends was tightly knit and so were the conversations. Most of the members were part of the singles ministry and this was the common bond, since the on-again-off-again boyfriend was part of this group. Nobody, who was now an active part of this group, was not however part of its Wednesday night escapades to a local tavern. Nobody befriended a single father who was also part of this group. Since he needed to find out information about *Church Girl's* boyfriend, gossip was a key ingredient to understanding the dynamics of Nobody's new foe.

The spiritual aspect of learning what God's intent for Nobody was cast aside. Hoping this was God's will for his life, Nobody found himself as her confidant. Providing assurances in his new role, the topic of her boyfriend finally came up. Her indecision towards this was now a discussion point that could not be ignored. Nobody thanked God for allowing him to be the sounding board. Whether by design or by Divine Providence, he was able to offer suggestions. The door had been opened and Nobody eagerly walked through.

His conversations with the single father friend did not leave any doubt about Nobody's desire to have this woman one day. He was able to find out what the other guy was up to and use that information to his benefit. Nobody was truly infatuated with this woman, but was oblivious to all the 'red flags' that were popping up around her. He saw them as obstacles that needed to be overcome and not reasons for concern. He learned more about the pending divorce that had been in the works for over a year but was going nowhere. By the end of the third month they were very close, she was nearly ready to cut and run from the other guy. Nobody had offered a viable alternative out of necessity instead of love. One evening after he had prepared dinner for her, he made a proposition to choose him and let the other guy go. She accepted. Nobody had won.

The following day, in his joy, he shared his triumph with the single father and a few other points which Nobody should have kept to himself. Nobody's enthusiasm and excitement led him to be careless in the information department. He inevitably shared something he wasn't supposed to and it got back to her a couple of weeks later. What he considered to be the start of a new life - happy, joyous and free - turned out to be a disaster. He'd received a phone call from her and *Church Girl* was extremely angry at him. Nobody was once again paralyzed. She was furious and did not want to see him again. Completely devastated, Nobody withdrew from everyone. He had made a mistake; this one had cost him terribly. He couldn't concentrate at work and he only performed the minimum needed at home. On that following Saturday, he laid curled in his bed holding his stomach.

Truth #78 Loose lips sinks ships.

At about 2 PM, from his bed, he could see people walk to his front door, he thought he saw her coming through the blind. With excitement he waited for the knock, but none was heard and then he saw her leave. He opened the door and found the book he'd lent her. Back to bed he went shoulders slouched, when his phone rang. A friend from AA called and asked if he would go for a walk. With nothing better to do, and his son at a sleepover, Nobody went. They walked five miles along the Broad River Walk and in that time Nobody explained the entire scenario and his current feelings. It had helped and he was able to get rid of a majority of the pain. He just did not realize how absorbed he was with her. He came to grips with the fact that he needed to move on and remember how this felt and learn from it.

How could he have been so stupid? Everything was riding on being with her. Nobody had placed so much faith in her to justify his self-worth. Had he kept his mouth shut, none of this would have happened. He went to church the following day and saw her from a distance. The pain in his stomach was wrenching. Oh, how he longed to be with her. She saw him, but provided no assurance or glimpse of hope from her actions. He was doomed. His only chance and he blew it.

Nobody spent the following week getting back into the normal grind, with Bible studies and meetings. He wanted to call her badly. The effort it took to move forward instead of backwards was overwhelming. In his boredom, the apartment became spotless. Nothing else could be cleaned unless he wanted to remove the enamel from the tub and toilet. There were lines in the carpet and it smelled good. If anyone showed up they would think he had his act together. That was just on the surface, deep down he had placed his reason for existence into the acceptance of one woman in his life and this time it wasn't his mother. Sitting on the couch, numb to the world, the phone rang. His phone never rang. Nobody was always in the habit of calling out.

"Hello,"

"Hey it is me, do you have a minute?"

"Yes, but before you say anything, I just want you to know that I am sorry and I never meant to hurt you. I messed up and I haven't been able to forgive myself. I can't believe how much you meant to me and now that you are gone, I have been lost without you."

"I know and I think we jumped the gun too quick. I have been praying to God asking if you are the one for me and I keep hearing that you are."

It's a miracle. God not only answered *his* prayer but *hers* as well.

Myth #69 Another match made in Heaven for Nobody.

Episode 44

Into the Fire

With a new burst of energy and his prayers answered, Nobody was in love again. There were only a few obstacles to overcome. They spent a lot of time together. They went to church. It was a ready-made family. She had her son and Nobody had his. Priorities changed and so did his life. He felt three feet taller, and when he pulled that picture of her out of his wallet, nothing else mattered. About four months into their relationship, he asked for her hand in marriage. She accepted and a date was set.

Truth #79 Nobody was afraid of losing what he wanted.

He was determined not to let this one get away; his entire self-worth was riding on her being with him. In the past, that empty feeling was filled with drugs, alcohol, music and sex. In recovery, that empty hole in the stomach should be filled with meetings, prayer and meditation. These were all good honest behaviors but had just been a pacifier for Nobody. He had never turned this part of his life over to God and allow Him to bring forth a partner that would help bring out the best in him. Yes, he had stopped destructive physical behaviors, but in the end, he trusted his own judgment in these matters.

When someone makes the decision to make a play for what they want or can accomplish, unless that person is truly grounded in faith in God and truly listens to the sound advice from others, more than likely the human will can consume that person. Decisions are rationalized and, depending on the circumstances, people even try to convince everyone around them that their decision is sound, work to gain affirmation or make it a private personal decision while no one is looking. Freud may have said that the 'ID Factor' was the prominent behavioral trait during the early years but, without a strong moral compass and the support of other strong moral compasses around you, a person's 'ID Factor' will tend to rule the roost no matter what age you are. Seeking guidance is not a show of weakness. It takes an act of self will and understanding to do the right thing even when it doesn't feel like the right thing to do. Nobody had not gotten to the place where he could distinguish the differences yet. He never ran any of these decisions by anyone. Those who are not bound by a governing morality or understand the importance of one will, in varying degrees, allow their own self will to take precedence. Inherently, Nobody knew that if he had run some of his plans by someone and asked for an opinion, he would have not liked the answer. So he just told everyone what he was doing, exactly like he did with God.

Thus far, it has not been alluded to some of the other behaviors Nobody demonstrated which he viewed as reactionary conundrums. These were behaviors that, if someone were to find out about them, would immediately leave and abandon him - in his opinion. One of these was his anger and sudden outbursts when confused. He yelled if he felt he was not heard and that could take the form of rage, which scared his son. At work, he was not always the nicest person and the term grumpy, temperamental and hyper-sensitive could be used to describe him when he was not feeling well. Nobody was obsessive about the look of his home. If the apartment was in order, then his life would be in order. What would people think if the house was even just a little messy? If there was a to-do list, that list needed to be completed or life could cease as he knew it.

These were the same behaviors he saw on display by his family growing up. He vowed he would never be like that once he got older. When the realization hits that the nut did not fall too far from the tree, people are faced with a choice, continue in the same manner or change. All of these traits, in their worst form, Nobody had been working on in an effort to change but now, since his focus was to ensure that he and *Church Girl* live happily ever after, he would work hard to make sure these character traits were under control. Nobody would hear years later that you can keep a beach ball under water for only so long and it will eventually pop out somewhere. Nobody tried to keep these under control. He would attempt to recognize the triggers as best as he could. Nobody had his work cut out for him. He had all these behaviors to work on and keep track of. He opted to hide all those hated behaviors instead of resolving them. A lot of them may have worked to protect him in the past, but now he chose romance instead and was willing to venture down that path before the inside job was complete.

Oblivious to this and to the legal consequences, they moved in together, combined families, finances, hid their decision from the church and prayed to God to bless their decision. God would not have put them together if He did not want them together. There was still the issue of her divorce that needed to be rectified. Her soon-to-be-ex-husband was behind on child support, which made life difficult for her. No worries, Nobody would be there guiding her all the way. He would stick by her and prove that she had made the right choice as she walked through this difficult time in her life.

When Nobody returned to South Carolina, he continued to see his original counselor from the Family Care Center and it took little time to have this as a topic of discussion. Due to the circumstances and the needs of his girlfriend, Nobody was able to secure counseling for her as well. His counselor was a child advocate in the court system and had many legal tools at her disposal. So if anyone would be able to help Nobody get his girlfriend's divorce finalized, she was the one.

The whole story was told. His counselor met with *Church Girl* individually and provided the name of an attorney that could gain a little traction in this area. As with all divorces there are two sides to every story, but *Church Girl's* was compelling. The attorney said that it would require a bit of time but could be worked out. There were a few things that needed to be adjusted to be able to ensure that none of her actions would be construed as damaging to her case. One was her living arrangements. South Carolina has a law that says that unless there is provable abuse of some sort, couples must be separated for a year prior to a divorce being granted. It is during this year that many shenanigans occur that are used to prove one's case against the other. The year was up but now they had to file for divorce and since there was custody on the line, the game had changed. If she was going to prove that her husband's lifestyle was not proper for joint custody then the cards must be stacked a certain way.

To make matters worse, the ex-husband started initiating more delay tactics. Her appointed lawyer said she needed to establish an alternate living location that looked like she lived someplace other than with Nobody when her son's father picked him up for visitation. They were also going to have to get a private investigator to watch her husband's actions and get proof to solidify their case that full custody belonged to *Church Girl.* This was pretty interesting, since they hired a female private detective and the investigator managed to get *Church Girl's* ex-husband to ask her out on a date.

A pseudo home was donated to them from his counselor, at no cost, near her farm that was once used to house the property handyman. The charade was in place, on nights that he was to pick up or drop off his son, she would be there. There is no way this was against the will of God, because all the pieces were falling into place. There was only one problem, as these events were taking place, time was slowly disappearing, the time to have a final divorce decree executed and the time before wedding date they planned. They spent more time wondering if they would have a wedding instead of planning and enjoying the thought of one. Their happiness was based on the lack of speed in the court system and an ex-husband who did not care if he was divorced or not. He was going to do his own thing regardless of her wishes. If he was divorced, the child support order would be more than he was paying at that time.

Since these things were out of his control, Nobody's anger escalated and he had a hard time keeping it under wraps. To add more complexity to this situation, Nobody removed himself from a leadership role in Bible study group because of his living arrangements. He still wanted to obey the rules even though he wasn't obeying them. This was his compromise to himself in an effort to stay true to the Baptist Church and its code of conduct. Nobody told God what he was doing and never waited for an answer and just continued moving forward. He believed because he told God what his plans were, he felt he had done his part in that relationship.

Not learning from the lessons of his past and believing in his heart this relationship would be the answer for all that ailed him emotionally,

Nobody worked diligently to line up all the support he could to keep this house of cards standing but it was starting to get windy.

Truth #80 Nobody was living a lie.

Trying to juggle all these events he hoped that, if he worked hard enough, his reward would be a fruitful marriage. His goals were admirable, but his methods were lacking. Thirty days out from their wedding date it was obvious that nothing would work out in time to be able to be legally married. As they reviewed the reality of the situation, it could easily be seen that this weeding would not be able to take place for a while. After a long conversation, they decided that they would cancel the wedding and wait until all legal proceedings were complete before even setting a date. They informed all the interested parties. Two weeks later, after dinner one night there was a knock on the door. Nobody answered it and to his surprise the Singles Minister was at the door and asked if he could come in. There was no denying the fact, according to the church he was living in sin and the Singles Minister was going to call Nobody on it.

Episode 45

Shot Down in Flames

Nobody was surprised to see the minister at his door step. No one spoke until everyone was seated in the small tension-filled living room. *Church Girl* asked the kids to move into their room and she stayed in the kitchen as the conversation started. Nobody sat at full attention on the edge of his seat as the Singles Minister confronted Nobody about his current living arrangements. Nobody felt like flint was being struck by steel and the spark of emotion was created by those words. Nobody, who had always been an extrovert, had positioned himself within the church and was an assistant table leader. He was told that their actions were considered 'ungodly' and the church would have to discipline them, if they did not change their current circumstance.

Nobody had been sitting there initially paralyzed. He did not know what to say or how to respond and the anger was building inside of him. Someone else was going to try and take something away from him that he loved. The outburst which had been brewing and growing beneath his diaphragm finally tore loose. He, very directly and with a tone that could chill the blood in someone's veins, told the minister that there are times when the church was wrong and only accounted for strict rules and never took into account 'real life', a term which was appropriate since the minister was as out of touch with 'real life' as it was. Nobody and *Church*

Girl had no choice but to combine resources and he believed the reason the minister was there was because they were worried more about reputation than people.

It was so simple, so obvious to Nobody. The church did not understand what they were going through. The Senior and Singles Ministers never understood how a person like Nobody, who had been to Hell and back, could ever have found grace with God. Even though he was an active participant in the church, Nobody still felt like he was not part of the group. There were circumstances outside of his control and, with God's help, he would go it alone without the church. He shared this with the minister. The minister suggested an alternative plan: Nobody and *Church Girl* could get married in a private ceremony in the Senior Pastor's office. A public ceremony, with all the hoopla and festivities could be arranged at a later date. This was a great idea. Except. . . .they hadn't mentioned that her divorce wasn't final. They could not legally get married. In Nobody's eyes, God was providing the means to get through this issue with his counselor, the attorney, and the temporary house. The only thing standing in the way was the court.

The real sadness in this whole affair was that Nobody had enjoyed his time with the Singles Minister those many nights that they went and visited people to share the Gospel. He had performed his baptism and today that relationship, that Nobody had cherished, was now at odds. Two days later a letter came in the mail stating that the church no longer considered Nobody part of the church body. Accordingly, they were free to attend services, but would not be listed in the church registry. The letter spoke of the Greek root word pornea and how their actions reflect the meaning of the word. They were still offered the private ceremony, if they chose to. If not, then the ruling would stand.

With pen in hand, Nobody composed his response. He addressed it to both the Senior and Singles Ministers.

I received your letter the other day and was shocked how so easily one can turn a back on a fellow Christian. Your use of the word "pornea" is inappropriate for this example. We are not living together to just have sex, satisfy an immoral hunger and swing from a chandelier. We are living together due to the circumstances the world has presented us and as two people who love each other from the heart and not the body. We made this decision.

We are faithful to God and many times in the past I have seen where the church cares only for the church and not the will of God. And, I believe this is one of those instances.

In Luke Chapter 2, Joseph is ordered by the Caesar to Bethlehem, where his family of origin resides for a general census. The Bible continues to say upon their arrival there was no place to stay, which means his family had no room as well. Could it be that his family did not approve of Joseph's situation with his betrothed and who was with child? That due to his family's view on the matter, it seems they did not even entertain a room for Joseph and family. In this case, it could be assumed they were cast aside, by a family everyone so desperately needs, without understanding the true Will of God in this story.

Likewise, we feel we are in God's Will, which I believe you are unable to see or will even try to understand, so we will find a room elsewhere.

Nobody in Particular

The letter was sent; Nobody found another reason to hate the church. He had never disclosed the crucial aspect of the story where the ministers might have helped them. Not understanding the true Wisdom of God and how his miraculous wonder may have intervened will never be known.

The Bible is littered with examples of what many would call ungodly behavior by today's standards, but these biblical heroes were used by God to promote or carry His message. Nobody was not a hero of biblical proportions, but he never truly allowed God to work in his life. Nobody held on to the one thing he felt he would surely die from, loneliness.

On their own, with no church and just the support from the people in the program, they continued waiting for the divorce proceedings to be finalized. After what seemed like an eternity but was, in reality, a mere month, she was finally granted a divorce. No more depositions, two households, private detectives, orders of child support and awaiting the winning verdict against her now ex-husband. A lot of tears had been shed and a lot of sleepless nights led up to this point. It has been said that if it is God's will, He will pay for it and if it is our will, we will pay for it. There was no denying who paid for this relationship.

Truth #81 Nobody was granted his wish.

Episode 46

White Wedding

F ree to get on with their lives without the fear of retaliation, they purchased a house, set a wedding date, bought two German Shepherds and started living happily ever after. Since there was no crisis to overcome which had consumed many previous idle hours, some of those behaviors that had been under wraps started to find their way to the surface. A little at first but they were poking out from under the covers. One of those was yelling at the kids.

Church Girl would tell Nobody about his yelling and, after some thought, he'd apologize knowing there was a monster inside of him. No matter how hard he tried to temper his anger, it would flare up. Sudden verbal jabs and that expression of anger on his face scared not only the children, but also her. He would blame his behavior on too much sugar, the pressures of work, etc., but deep down he knew he needed to work harder at *concealing* it instead of *healing* it. He did not know how to break the habit. He took the advice of one of his program buddies and started practicing speaking more softly when he was trying to convey a point. In the program, Step Seven asks that we are to humbly ask God to remove these character defects and this one was rightly considered.

Growing up, Nobody remembered how yelling was used as a tool to increase leverage in discussions; the person who yelled the loudest and for the longest time was the victor. So when it came to the kids, Nobody was strict and demanded obedience. His soon-to-be wife looked on hesitantly but did not say much. Nobody knew he had to work in this area and some days were better than others.

The wedding date was set. Nobody chose his best man. A friend of hers, who was an ordained minister from some New Age religion, would facilitate the ceremony. This was a plus since they didn't belong to a formal church. It was better than a Justice of the Peace. The location would be Charleston, SC on the beach; his parents were going to come to this wedding. By all accounts, this was going to have the main ingredients of a real wedding: wedding portraits, flowers, bridal shower, invitations, bridesmaid and food. His parents would have an opportunity to meet his bride and watch the kids during their short two-day honeymoon. There was plenty of excitement about the nuptials. Life was, for the most part, without incident. She would be a good wife. She loved his son and treated him as her own and saw to all the things that a loving mother should do. Nobody had finally gotten it right. She was pretty. They had kids, dogs, house and a job; all the things the world would say made him a *success*. The only thing that never dawned on him was he was checking off all the items on a list, he had never listed the main ingredient for any marriage: Love.

Truth #82 Nobody loved the thought of marriage.

Life was about going through the motions. Nobody assumed he was loved for the things he had done. He believed others would work equally as hard so they, too, could be loved.

On their wedding day they exchanged gifts. She gave him a watch with an inscription on the back signifying the date and her never-ending love for him. Everyone was happy. The routine of life settled in rather quickly since the honeymoon had really been over months prior to the wedding. Those character defects kept popping up all over the place at the most inappropriate times. *Church Girl* must have spoken to someone because after about six months, he was taken aside by an old hat in AA. It was brought to his attention in a loving way, that by this time in Nobody's sobriety, some of his erratic behaviors should have subsided and that it would probably be a good idea to see if he might have a medical condition.

Reluctant at first, Nobody consented with hope that some of the angry outbursts would subside. Nobody wanted to make sure that there were no reasons that his wife could use to leave him. The meds it seemed would get him out of hot water and since life was about not getting *into* trouble, he did what he could to stay out of it. The meds would be the answer. Nobody visited a doctor and was diagnosed as mildly manic depressive. It was common for addicts and alcoholics to suffer chemical imbalances in the mind. The doctor was in the program himself. He understood, from the person who had referred him, that Nobody truly had been working a strong program to better himself. The meds would help his mood swings. However, it was not a sign of weakness and chemical imbalances were not to be ashamed of, they just needed to be treated. This would bring a balance in the course of Nobody's day.

It wasn't just anger that popped out of nowhere, but other emotions as well. Nobody received a phone call from one of his old AA friends in Arizona (the one he told one day *'don't call me I will call you'* while waiting for his *Hometown Hottie* to come home.) Once sober, Nobody called his friend and thanked him for his call that day. Nobody would always remember and call that man for years to come - all because of one simple act.

His old AA friend said, "I was calling to let you know that DC sponsor's wife passed away in her sleep after calling in sick to work, yesterday."

This threw Nobody for a curve. He had really enjoyed being around her and his DC sponsor and she was only in her mid thirties. He felt bad for his DC sponsor and Nobody cried. He couldn't explain why. His entire life Nobody was able to turn his feelings on and off like a water faucet but this triggered something inside of him that he just could not turn off. He was not close to her, but he was sad for his DC sponsor. The last time he saw her was at the Phoenix airport with his DC sponsor. Nobody had found out that they had connecting flights. Since he had lived in Phoenix, he went to the airport to see them, if only for thirty minutes.

Whatever her death triggered in Nobody didn't need to be understood. It was just grief. It was the first time he had actually grieved a loss in his life.

Church Girl had gone to Al-Anon meetings for a while but eventually stopped. Nobody was active in the program and would not change that part in his life for anything, and while we was starting to come to grips with his emotions, the comments started to come out.

271

"Do you always have to go to the meetings?"

"Can you skip one meeting?"

"I would be happier if we got a bigger house."

Nobody was also starting to become more self conscious. Genetics were starting to kick in, the big weight gain. He did not like the way he was starting to look and was sure she didn't as well. Nobody had always felt he was less attractive compared to most of the competition, so his deeds needed to compensate for what he was lacking physically. When Nobody's beloved recounted how she came to her decision to be with Nobody it always made him cringe. She always mentioned that one day she asked God if being with Nobody was what God wanted for her. The way she said it was like in the back of her mind she was really saying, *"I am not attracted to Nobody, but I will settle for him if that is what You want."*

Nobody was ten years older and had seen some of the guys she had gone out with and according to Nobody's measuring stick he was not as handsome. Nobody felt his looks would be a reason for her to leave, once she really saw what she was married too. Either way, he needed to keep the pressure on himself to offset his physical failings. It was only a matter of time when she would stop listening to God.

Truth #83 Nobody thought love was physical attraction, even in marriage.

They found a new house - a beautiful colonial home in Lexington County on a wooded cul-de-sac lot. It was picture perfect. He built a kennel for the dogs, installed his own irrigation system for watering the lawn, and skillfully sculpted the landscape. The kids were safe to run around the neighborhood on their bikes. When anyone would look upon it, the house had perfection written all over it.

He found a new job that paid $30,000 more a year but would require some travel; would she be OK with that? Her answer was yes.

Everyone has their secrets and Nobody was no exception. The facade of his life, similar to his childhood, had a certain look about it. Nobody wanted to be upright in the eyes of everyone around him but he had a couple issues that were kept under wraps. When it came to sex, Nobody was all in and he thought about it consistently. One part of him understood his vows and the other side of him was locked into fantasy. *Church Girl,* being a little progressive, had said that she had no problem with Nobody going to strip clubs with the boys occasionally. At one point she even purchased a subscription to Playboy for him. They even had ordered the Playboy channel on the cable network. This was Nobody's chance to watch this material at his leisure without retaliation. If that was true; *why did Nobody feel compelled to view in secret? If Church Girl knew how attracted he was to this, she would think he was a pervert.* He would secretly flip through the channels while his wife was doing something with the boys in another room. He would gaze at the magazines when alone in the house. He acted as though it was no big deal in front of her, but when alone, he was consumed. When he traveled, he would go to the clubs with the boys, but call from outside the club and never mention where he was.

These are exactly the sort of destructive behaviors the Father of Lies will use to exploit a person later at the most opportune time. Pornography is as addictive as any drug out there. It is a drug of secrets. The secular society has put such an emphasis on sex, open relationships, sex before marriage and as long as everyone is a consenting adult, *what* could possibly be wrong with that?

God intended sex as the strongest bond between a man and a woman. A bond to the spirit of a woman will propel a man to lose his life in order to save her and his family. When you share the strongest bond with more than one person in your life, its strength is diminished. What used to be sacred is now a commodity. The problem is twofold, a man is a visual being and unless properly trained and grounded, it is very hard in today's world to live pure. The strength of sexual addiction's power is unimaginable to a female. One side of society works on a males desires and when they fall, they are categorized unfavorably more times than not. These behaviors contradict the true nature of men, men must work hard to understand women, and the same should go for women as well.

Movies are released that romanticize a women's right to find true love outside of a loveless marriage. The movies depict a heartless husband and a new opportunity to bring fulfillment into the wife's life. This is dressed up to give the wife permission to experience, *Looovvve*. Now on the other hand, if a husband commits adultery he is a vile creature who has left his wife to raise the kids. What if the husband's adulteress is the other wife, noted previously? Then we are stuck, it only works if the other guy is single.

The husbands are characterized in some movies as unfeeling to the wants and needs of their wives who have no choice but to submit their bodies to a man she loathes. What do the husbands know about their wives, they are too busy tending the fields. The women are portrayed as victims of marriage and missing out on what destiny had in store for them as well. The movies of the day were: "The English Patient," "The Bridges of Madison County," and "Horse Whisperer." And, Nobody and *Church Girl* were avid movie goers.

Bible verses are taken out of context to prove that the Bible is wrong on the subject of marriage when, in fact, it does outline equality in the differences of the roles. The continuing social view on the Bible is that it is dated and the main message about men and women are not applicable in today's society.

However, let us not lose sight that if people want to believe in something, *'they will find it'* and live accordingly. If they want to prove their theories in spite of the evidence, they will prove it. A life without a true relationship with God will not provide the joy and fulfillment over the long term. Society has and will try every means necessary to short-circuit the process to try and gain long term results while using short term desires. What happens in the end is that if one person feels they are not getting all their desires met in the relationship or get what they feel they deserve, green pastures are just around the bend.

Now that Nobody and *Church Girl* had been married for a short while, an important need was brought up in the marriage. *Church Girl* wanted to have another child. Nobody had informed his wife, prior to getting married, that he had had a vasectomy. She had a son and they had agreed this would be suitable. Mature for her age, extremely intelligent and a professional, it never occurred to Nobody that she was still 'a girl at heart' when they met.

Nobody couldn't understand why this subject was such a driving force for her, but it was. He was in the market of keeping her happy. *Church Girl* decided they would approach this subject using a fertility clinic and choose from a menu of sperm donors. In his heart of hearts, this was not a desire he had, but he went along for the ride. Slowly, he started feeling that he did not have the total package to keep her happy, especially when they reviewed the types of donors to choose from. They ranged from athletes, doctors, lawyers, engineers, tall, dark and handsome. As Church Girl was determining which donor would bring the best child she wanted, not one of the descriptions matched him. Nobody was not tall, moderately handsome, and pleasantly plump and, as we said before, he was fighting genetics. How could he compare to these men? He was fighting an unknown enemy. As they would go through the checklist of donors, it was like she was imagining being with someone else who could give her what she wanted. *Church Girl* was stuck in a marriage with someone who was only half a man. Yes, he saved her from her past, but Nobody's only recourse was to go along with the process to keep her happy. This kept her focused on the future instead of the present.

Myth #70 Nobody was less than a man.

The doctor appointments, the sperm screening, temperature taking, the money and the emergency runs to the doctor to get impregnated by a syringe. For *Church Girl*, it was all about the *'baby'*. Nobody was not able to express his true feelings on the subject; he went along because he felt he had no choice. If he said what he truly felt, abandonment would soon follow.

Nobody's son was also suffering. Nobody had been the only consistent force in his son's life. Nobody's son was strangely calm when in Nobody's presence, but once Nobody left, his son's foundations erupted. When on the road, Nobody would receive calls from his wife informing him that his son was in his room crying and howling uncontrollably. Nothing would sooth his pain. Nobody had not witnessed this before and was shocked. His only recourse was to try and convince her that he would try to figure it out somehow.

There were other behaviors at school that took the form of anxiety. He could not concentrate or sit still. Nobody felt he had to do something.

Hoping it would go away wasn't an option, but Nobody needed to listen to the advice of trained professionals.

They consulted other behavioral professionals in hopes that a solution could be found. He spoke to his ex-wife about it and she had the same struggles with her first son as well and that they had to monitor his behavior and understood what Nobody was going through and offered suggestions. One doctor had suggested committing his son into a controlled environment, but there was no way that would happen.

The answer was out there and Nobody needed to find it to satisfy his wife and son since the pressure was mounting. Conversation was always centered on his son's behavior. Nobody was being pulled in two directions. He loved his son and he loved his wife. He had internal struggles and he was afraid because a wave was coming and he wasn't sure how he would ride it out. His son was referred to another behavioral therapist who said she could work with them. It would take time, but their prognosis is good based on the two visits they thought.

With all the different issues in the house to deal with and his new job, the last thing Nobody needed was a visit from his in-laws. That's exactly what he got. His father in-law was an atheist and a very smart engineer. He was a person who had a multitude of opinions, all of which were logical, of course. His mother-in-law was a God-fearing woman who had a servant's heart. It could easily be determined that his wife, though she believed in God, took after her father. Throughout their stay, there were many conversations which ranged from his wife's desire to have a baby to his son's behavior and how best to deal with it to Nobody's new job and his laptop (he'd received it the day before their arrival.) Everyone was just having a grand ole' time and since the topic of one particular day was the baby, this is what everyone had to look forward to. Nobody was floating in and out of the conversations, but Nobody heard hushed tones and his ears prickled with heightened sensitivity. Nobody, like many other folks, had the ability to hear even the slightest whisper in the largest auditorium when it concerned him.

Nobody had overheard her father tell *Church Girl* that Nobody was *'just'* a phone guy during a conversation in the kitchen as he sat in the living room fiddling with his new computer. It was easy to stay focused on it and set it up, his job *'required'* it. *To be clear he was so focused the world*

276

could have easily exploded and Nobody would have looked up for a second to see what the commotion was all about.

However, this was just a small side conversation, the real concern *Church Girl's* parent had were the issues with Nobody's son, his job (which did not meet her father's expectations) and this baby. It felt as though, they thought, the *Church Girl* was in over her head. Though years earlier, Nobody had made the active decision to have a vasectomy, it was obviously the wrong choice since their daughter, *Church Girl*, had to go to the clinic for a baby.

It was just another reason why Nobody was certain that he did not measure up. His anger was boiling and his thoughts raced. He did not know how to deal with his son, she wanted a baby, her father thought he was a glorified phone tech instead of a true professional.

After a couple of days of this, Nobody was in his own world. He could not get his computer to operate the way he wanted it, his wife was watching her temperature, and her family was excited that maybe she would need to go to the clinic and they could go along. What a joyous occasion this would be, as Nobody isolated more and more into his laptop.

Church Girl announced her need to visit the clinic Saturday afternoon. A preoccupied Nobody sat in front of his computer, his butt squarely planted on the couch, and told his wife he needed to get his work done. He added that, since her parents were willing to go with her, Nobody would stay home with the kids.

As he looked out the window watched them leave for the clinic, he had a sick feeling in his stomach. She wanted a baby and her parents were supporting her in that quest. Nobody secretly did not want one but was afraid to say it. Regardless of his feelings, he watched them drive away.

At that moment, in his silence, Nobody broadcasted to everyone his true feelings about the baby. He never spoke a word about it after that either and would never admit that he hoped the fertilization would fail. Regardless of his inner thoughts, he realized that something monumental had just occurred as they drove away to her appointment to gather another guy's sperm. He had just witnessed the beginning of the end and nothing in the world he could do would ever reverse it.

Episode 47

Crumblin' Down

S imilar to every action there is an equal and opposite reaction and for every plus there is a minus. With no luck on the fertility path, the next something new would be for his wife to start her own business. *Church Girl* was very talented and decided to start a transcription business. Computers were supposed to make your life easier, be more productive. This meant she needed a new computer to facilitate her duties. The internet was just starting to hit the big time and the ability to get online was important. Online chatting was starting to emerge. Email was great but if you wanted to talk with someone and you saw that they were online, why not just ping them. It was a wonderful way to communicate. Since it was somewhat new, everyone was doing it. Everyone had someone they could instantly connect with. Nobody was no different. When his wife got in on it, they even bought a camera to be able to see each other when traveling. Like HAM radio operators you could find new people to talk to. If someone had a camera icon, you could connect with people anywhere in the world.

In the midst of all the chaos with his son and the baby planning, Nobody was pinging people, too. This was a way to make a computer phone call when you knew someone was in front of their computer. He'd ping coworkers and an office admin from work off-and-on after business hours, harmless of course; nothing dangerous. His wife was in on the game but, if Nobody was doing it, it was different and she would get mad at him when he was on his laptop.

Church Girl altered her work schedule and decided to work a bit at night. Being in the transcriptions business allowed her to type whenever she wanted to. It seemed to Nobody that she should keep *his* schedule but he didn't push it with the kids and all. All married couples get into routines with each other, some are healthy and some are not. Unhealthy routines were sometimes called a merry-go-round. Nobody and his wife would get on their merry-go-round nightly and you could set your watch by it. Nobody would lay in bed wondering when his wife would come up. As long as she was downstairs working, online and talking to someone, he could not go to sleep. He always wondered exactly what she was doing.

One night as he heard her typing away furiously, he silently moved down the stairs. When he reached the bottom, he had a clear shot of the computer screen. As Nobody used the best stealth approach possible and made that initial turn that would have made a CIA operative proud, he saw his nemesis: another man. Was it some guy his wife had befriended or a work-related contact? It didn't matter. She was in her nightgown and was sitting away from the camera.

"When are you coming up?" he said - taking her totally off guard.

Nobody will never forget the picture of that guy on the screen when he surprised her. She immediately sat straight, told the guy she had to go and turned it off. Of course Nobody had questions and she had answers and they met in the middle with anger. It was starting all over again, he felt the relationship slipping. Two nights later when Nobody was home, his son started crying in his room uncontrollably. Nobody was able to finally witness one of his son's moments and the look on his wife's face said it all. She was reaching her limit.

At the therapist's office they went over everything and she started seeing his son regularly. Nobody and his wife were also seeing his original counselor. To Nobody it felt like they were both ganging up on him when they got together. It seemed like everyone needed him to do something and he had to get everything right. The problem was he was just trying to get through the day, looking for relief. He had to keep work in check and perform. He was working towards winning a trip at work (his company chose one Technical Consultant every year and he wanted to give his wife the trip they never had for their honeymoon.) It was all building up, trying to soothe his wife and keep her happy, and hope that his son was OK. Then there were the customers he had to tend to, sales reps he had to answer questions for, traveling for work, and staying on top of his recovery.

One Saturday, by chance, Nobody looked in the garage where he saw his son messing around with a chain. Recently, his son had placed nails under all the tires of the van and now with this chain, he could damage something or hurt himself in the process. Startled, Nobody ran out and stopped him from what he was doing. He called the therapist and she said that it was clear to her that he might need more in-house therapy. This was going in the wrong direction fast. That was not what Nobody had wanted; he wanted a little parental guidance. The therapist said they would perform a couple of tests and make a decision the following week.

Scrambling for an answer, Nobody called his ex-wife. He told her everything. She was remarried and had a great husband by all accounts. They were set up at her house to deal with these sorts of issues that kept her other son safe and a set of routines to help with the behaviors. They all decided to get his son out of town before the therapist placed him in a home. Within a week, Nobody placed his son on a plane and he was whisked away to Arizona.

Crushed could hardly explain how Nobody was feeling. Believing he was a bad father and choosing his wife over his son it seemed, but he didn't know what else to do. The pressure from his wife and now the therapist to do *something*. Logically, it was the best thing considering the situation, but the pain in his stomach would not go away.

Myth #71 Nobody had abandoned his son.

Truth #84 Nobody made an informed decision.

Nobody was speaking with his sponsor and they were discussing the topic of his son, the sponsor suggested that maybe it would be a good idea for Nobody to attend some Al-Anon meetings for a while. He was so focused on his son and what his wife was doing, that he was losing himself and Al-Anon helped people who got caught up in the behaviors of others. With no place else to turn, Nobody agreed. So, the next Saturday night instead of going upstairs in the church to his normal AA meeting, he ventured downstairs. As he walked through the door, thinking he came in by accident, his buddy's wife said out loud, "Oh brother, look who just walked in."

Not quite the warm welcome for a guy whose insides were in disarray, but he did have it coming, Nobody used to sell used stereo gear to her husband to her chagrin. Nobody seated himself next to her and said, "I am here for real."

Silence at times can be so awkward, and in a split second he saw her demeanor change. They started the meeting. There was no doubt Nobody was irritable and unreasonable at times and he definitely tried to force solutions. Nobody was also completely obsessed with trying to find out the answer to problems and situations over which he had no control. After listening to a few readings and some people sharing, he understood that he was finally home. He had looked downwards most of the meeting but when he looked to his friend's wife, the look in his eye told his whole story, and she knew it, too.

Now that he was going to Al-Anon meetings did not mean he was automatically a saint. He liked to get his way, but that made him who he was. By all accounts he was doing the next best thing. Al-Anon helped him to curb his reactions to situations and learn how to respond instead.

He learned that he looked at the world through his colored glasses and that his wife was looking at life through hers. Al-Anon was teaching him how live his life even though the world around him wasn't tracking with his thoughts on how life should be. That is, if someone disagreed with you, that was OK. It did not mean you had to hate them or not talk to them. This was in stark contrast to what he was exposed to in his life growing up. It was hard work to undo the behaviors he had been used to for so many years but he was tired and wanted a better way of thinking and living. AA had kept him out of jail but, in the few short weeks, it looked like he had finally found a true home in recovery.

It would not be long before he would be able to try out these new behaviors. In the program, it is strongly suggested that men work with men and women work with women. When people are hurting and the opposite sex is available, it leaves too much room for trouble and inappropriate emotional bonds to happen. Likewise, when couples start sharing their marriage woes with someone from the other sex, opinions can be cast into the conversation and the vision can be skewed.

As his wife was conversing with people on the Internet, her attitude about marriage was starting to change. She would make comments about their marriage issues and talk about what people online told her.

Similar to unfulfilled love every woman seems to have as was described earlier about those movies of the day, Nobody started getting a feeling this was how his wife viewed their marriage.

God made men a certain way and women a certain way. The balance between the two provides all that is needed for a fruitful life as God intended. From Nobody's viewpoint, he could go down the checklist and say he was doing all the things a husband should do. He was a provider, he had taken a new job that paid better but he did have to travel about 35% of the time. They were a young family; he didn't need commentary from others on how their marriage should or should not be.

New requests started coming from his wife. She wished they could sip wine together by candlelight. She started describing scenes of a love she yearned for; a maiden taken down by her lover. Nobody again was fighting an enemy he could not control: someone else's desires. She was describing a loveless marriage and now she was talking to people he did not know offering insight to her that would take her away from him. Nobody couldn't grasp what he was hearing, but he could tell what he was feeling and she was drifting away. The baby issue was always in the background. They were four years into their marriage. There was no way he could be Prince Charming every night. He certainly could not sip wine. What else could he do, then? He discussed it with a couple of his program friends and sponsor. Nobody was told that one-on-one time was crucial for every marriage but that love was not a feeling. It was the commitment that made any marriage last.

He heard about how his job was keeping him away from her and her son. With her job at home she was lonely. Then when he was home he would go to meetings and that was an issue. The list was getting longer and his Al-Anon sponsor kept telling him to try and do the next best thing, whatever that was. Nobody tried to keep her in his sights as much as possible. He watched her every move trying to see if there was anything going on. He was fearful and was right back where he was a few years back: trying to hold a relationship together that was untying itself.

She had befriended people over the Internet from Australia, who would be traveling to the States and wanted to visit. It was interesting to meet foreigners. They were slightly older and had kids the same age. They had always wanted to visit America and they thought it would be a good idea to swing by and say hello. Nobody, unknowingly, would compete against his wife by his accomplishments. The Australian family stayed at their house. They had brought over a didgeridoo, an Aborigine tube-like instrument that fascinated their host. Nobody was consumed with fear while they were there. In his gut, he knew his wife was tolerating him by this point. He noticed the glances they shared back and forth between his wife after some of his comments or conversation topics. He tried too hard to impress them and he just felt as though they were tolerating him as well. Nobody hanging from a limb, was trying to hang on for dear life!

Even with the people in his house, he felt his world falling apart inside of him and felt alone in the middle of a crowd. He could not say or do anything right while they were there and his wife behaved as though she was embarrassed by him. While they were just hanging around talking he would go off and try to play the didgeridoo.

It wasn't uncommon for Nobody to be reminded of the things he had done wrong while company was around and this was no exception. As much as he wanted to reply with how he felt, he just sat and listened. She assumed he didn't care. The contrary was true. Whenever he was in these sorts of situations his thoughts would spin in his mind extremely fast. He could see the truth and want to speak the truth but either a conciliatory phrase would be uttered or nothing at all because he just couldn't grasp the essence of what he wanted to say. Silence was the next best choice if words could not be found.

The Australians eventually left and two weeks after that, *Church Girl* said she needed time alone. She wanted to go to Atlanta for the weekend by herself to "shop" and sort out her thoughts. Their counselor tried explaining to Nobody that she needed to decompress. Nothing could make Nobody believe this was not the kiss of death. As he discussed this with his counselor during a one-on-one session, his face contorted in the counselor's presence. She mentioned that the look he had made her feel uncomfortable. If he could see himself in the mirror, she said he might see the anger for himself, the anger that his wife saw. This was the monster inside of him he wanted no one to see. It was *his* anger that he was demonstrating in front of his counselor. No matter how hard he tried to make everyone happy, this is what he got. Whatever happened to just being happy in each other's presence. Isn't anyone hearing him? There has to be something wrong when your wife says she is going to Atlanta by herself for the weekend. No one does that.

After sitting there in the counselor's office, completely dumbfounded, Nobody left. Even his counselor seemed to be in on it. Nobody had no choices. He had to work, he had to pay the majority of the bills, he couldn't drink, he couldn't produce kids anymore, his son was with his mother because he couldn't handle it, he needed to stay in recovery and now his wife needed space. Was she going to meet someone? Was it that guy she was chatting with? The pressure cooker was building.

She wouldn't reconsider and left for the weekend once her ex-husband picked up her son for the weekend. Nobody was once again enmeshed in a relationship. If he felt that everything was fine within the confines of the relationship and all was well, he could function but, if he sensed it wasn't well, then the world around him collapsed. He couldn't see anything passed his field of vision.

Day one was not too bad, he could barely get the yard the work done. He had gone to a morning meeting and evening one, there was no hiding his anxiety. He had to stay occupied. The folks in Al-Anon said he needed to detach from her but how was he supposed to do that? He was sure he was being punished by God for his thoughts and for looking at those magazines to ease the stress. The emptiness inside of him was just unbearable. He could hardly move from one moment to the next. He had not heard from her, he said the Serenity Prayer a million times, but no relief. Where was God in this? He was trying to do the right thing, but it seemed as though nothing he did took away the feelings.

Day two started the way day one did. He went to a meeting but could not concentrate. He had not heard from her and he was getting worried. He did not know which hotel she was staying at so he couldn't call her. As the afternoon wore on, he called his counselor and asked if she had heard from *Church Girl*. He just needed to hear *Church Girl's* voice and know that she was OK. He needed this knot to move out of his stomach. He called her parents to say hello, and casually ask if they had heard from their daughter. He was sure he sounded like a loser, but he was desperate.

Nobody lived in a colonial type house where you could walk in a circle from the kitchen to the dining room, foyer, living room, laundry hall, and back to the kitchen. Nobody circled that area for over an hour, looking out the window every few minutes to see if she was coming. He called her folks again, he just couldn't help it, he needed someone to reassure him. He called his counselor and she told him to let it go.

Nobody yelled, "How can I let it go? I am feeling this right now!"

He couldn't even sit anymore. Who had she been with? Why hadn't she called? It was eight o'clock Sunday night, well past the time someone should come home from a weekend away. That should be about six. Now she never told him what time she would be back, but the world, according to Nobody, he assumed it should be about six. So this meant she was two hours late.

He called his sponsor and was told that whatever he did, when she got home not to jump down her throat. His sponsor sensed he was pretty volatile.

"Just take a deep breath, she is her own person and you cannot control her. Yes, this is tough situation but you need to behave with dignity and grace during this time. The way you respond will have repercussions. Just pray that God will give you the words. Tell her you missed her. Calmly tell her you were worried and because she didn't call or even say what hotel she was at, it left you on edge all weekend," said his sponsor.

"These are not unreasonable comments, but the manner in which you present them will make all the difference in the world. If she did in fact meet someone, there is nothing you can do to change that. The only thing you can do is pray and learn how to keep your wits about yourself as you start understanding how to create boundaries to protect yourself in the future," he added.

This was good stuff, it all made sense. Just like learning new plays on a football team as a rookie. Your coach was a visionary and you could see the play develop on the board and you could see your part on how to make it all come together. However, that is why they are called rookie mistakes; the excitement of it all was enough to lose focus for a moment.

Half past eight. The garage door was opening. He told himself to practice the things as his sponsor said. Keep your mouth shut. Be calm. Don't react. You had a bad weekend but don't let her know it was bad. He could do this. She was home and safe. The emptiness was suddenly filled with relief. He could breathe now. He sat on the couch in front of the TV as though he had been there sacked out for hours. She came through the door, his angel. Oh, how he missed her and loved her. She was so beautiful, he could not lose her. He would change. All this flashed in his mind as he saw her.

She said hello, he got up from the chair and all this emotion was welling up inside of him. The only thing he could say was. "Where the $%^& have you been?"

Episode 48

Slip Sliding Away

The mood in the house was cold. *Church Girl* kept talking about these lost feelings of love in the house. She described this vision of what she thought love was supposed to be. It sounded like she wanted to be a fair maiden who needed a knight in shining armor to wisp her away every night. He wasn't against it, since this was his modus operandi to begin with but Nobody was getting tired of not being good enough. From his vantage point he was trying to keep the whole ship afloat. Now on top of everything else he needed to perform every night. How come the maiden never came to him? And, the drum beat sounded about his traveling. A job she agreed that he should take, but it didn't matter. By this time she had stopped trying to get pregnant at the clinic. It was obvious she was yearning for something that Nobody was not able to provide.

Al-Anon was starting to play a major role now. He was learning how to handle himself better little by little. He began to understand that his perceptions were somewhat skewed. Even though he had a controlling personality, his attempts to control his environment were futile. He was going to have to start accepting the world around him and adjust to it instead of working to change everything to his desire. That also meant Nobody would have to start accepting himself the way God made him. These were things he had heard in AA, but here the message was loud and clear. His happiness had been based on those around him. In his mind he thought he was to run interference for someone's feelings. It had been his job, he told himself, to try and keep those you love happy.

However, Al-Anon had a lot of good literature and one in particular was very helpful: the Al-Anon bookmark, called *"One Day at a Time."* It was a daily guide on how to behave. This was in stark contrast to so many of his habits he had in his life. One of the biggest hurdles to overcome, and this may be hard to understand, was Nobody's inability to actually say 'no.' Nobody could go around and try to manipulate a situation to get things the way he wanted them. However, when his truest thoughts were challenged and he had only an ounce of doubt and sensed that you were upset at him, he would relent to that person's wishes instead of saying, no. Keeping the peace was important. At work, he would always think of new things to improve processes. He had to be the best at all things. This had not changed, he still wanted you to say, "Wow, look at Nobody - he is somebody." In the end, he couldn't stand it if someone was upset with him so he was the perfect go-getter.

His wife wanted to be noticed for her accomplishments as well. Being in the house all day working from home was a bore. She was a violinist and started playing at a church they started attending. Nobody was certainly not opposed to this and his attitude was that if she wanted to play in the church that was fine. There was one caveat though: as long as it didn't interfere with *his* plans. He never said it out loud, but sometimes nothing needs to be said. She had asked a few times if he would go with her to practice and he went. Nobody was not into the whole scene of sitting and watching her practice. He was disinterested. His body may have been there, but his mind was elsewhere. Nobody couldn't sit still for long periods of time. He always had something to work on or get done. It wasn't bad, just different. He was happy for her but that was the extent of it. So when she questioned him on his lack of support or interest, even he couldn't explain it to her. It was difficult for him to even say that he didn't share the same enthusiasm she had. He wasn't used to expressing his true feelings. Nothing changed here. He kept the real truth to himself. Instead, he said she was right and he would try to support her. This type of behavior was a common occurrence in his life and one that resonated in his mind. So when he looked or heard how other husbands dealt with issues with their wives, he assumed he had no backbone or as usual did not measure up as a man. The way he heard it from them seemed like they had no issues in their marriages. Everyone seemed to have their own interests and met up at night to consummate their marriage.

It never occurred to him that it wasn't complicated. He just didn't want to be part of her practices, just the performances. However, Nobody confused the point and was hyper-sensitive to her feelings and felt he should feel differently than the way he was. The fear of speaking the truth and have her think he did not care about her was too much to bear. It was in this conundrum that Nobody was always trapped. If the truth was actually spoken, it would mean he did not love her and she would then leave.

All in all, if he had been a seasoned Al-Anon, he could have easily said, *"I am glad that you enjoy playing the violin, I support you, but since I am not musically inclined it is hard for me to sit there and listen during practices. I will go to any special event and will attend church."*

These are the types of responses it would take years for Nobody to express. He would watch and hear people speak like this and it would baffle him to a point of discouragement. The hope was in the Al-Anon literature he read from and the meetings. Learning from the experience of others and how they struggled and learned to communicate gave them a better sense of self worth. This inspired Nobody to continue trying.

He knew from all of his dealings with God that this was where God wanted him to be. It was a crazy world inside of his mind, one side he wanted his way and another he would do whatever it took to keep the peace. These were all the things he was learning to unwind by taking the suggestions and through prayer. He had always felt he was crazy and he had to work hard to keep it all in check, so no one would find out. He was starting to see that he did have a lot of work ahead of him, but he did not feel hopeless. After all these years, he finally found the answer and he was now living in the solution. It would be a long road, but he finally had a project and it wasn't trying to keep everyone else happy at the sacrifice of himself.

Truth #85 Nobody realized he was somebody.

Throughout life every person can look back and relate to someone that made a lasting impression. Nobody had such a person; it was his next door neighbor. When they first moved into their current home, the new neighbor, one lot over, was a biologist and worked for the Department of Natural Resources. Never in his life had Nobody seen a person so committed to the land and property. His neighbor worked all day and worked late into the night on a new workshop, pool and landscaping. His neighbor attended the church Nobody's wife ended up playing the violin at and was a small group leader there. However, from all the different people Nobody had met over the years, this was one of the first Christians that Nobody knew who walked the walk. His neighbor was not pretentious and always had time to talk, even when he was busy.

At one point when Nobody and his family did not attend that church, his neighbor asked if they would like to attend and even offered to carry his son to church. As Nobody watched this man, he saw the love he had for his family, community, and the way he took pride in his work. Nobody trusted him. His neighbor loved God and was not afraid to say it but never force-fed anyone. He was just a man who loved God and knew who he was. It was Nobody's nearest outlet to talk about things he did not have experience with. Nobody was amazed how gifted his neighbor was and how he saw God's blessing over this man. Nobody would look out from his closet window at times and watch what he was doing and wish that he had what he had

It was obvious his neighbor's wife looked up and respected her husband, as did his daughter and his son as well, even though the son was a bit wild. That balanced way of life seemed so foreign to Nobody. He had been warned by his sponsor not to judge his insides by other people's outsides, but the truth was very apparent. This guy used the gifts that God gave him and it was evident in all that he did and said. He was a man Nobody hoped one day he would become if he kept doing what he was doing. Nobody dreamed he would be respected by his wife, to have her look up to him and admire the man he was. However, on the inside of Nobody's persona, he was afraid and felt small among men and lacked experience in that crowd. Nobody's whole life had been chasing skirts instead of hanging with the fellas. The guys he did hang out with were only acquaintances and deep friendships were never established. He had never been blessed into manhood and now he was feeling the repercussions of it. His father had not taken him from boy to a man.

While his home life was falling apart, Nobody never mentioned any of this to his neighbor, even though every ounce in Nobody wanted to spill his guts. He was afraid his neighbor wouldn't understand, it was complicated even from Nobody's viewpoint. Still not totally grounded with God in his heart, the marriage, in his opinion, had to be worked out by Nobody. There was no way God would be able to help. It would be years before he understood that for a marriage to grow and survive, God needed to remain in the marriage and not cast out after the vows had been spoken.

Church Girl had mentioned that she needed a new car. After the little fiasco upon her arrival from Atlanta, Nobody was only too anxious to do something worthwhile for her to mend that fence. Plus, as a provider, he must provide and he was geared to provide as a means of proving himself worthy. His hope was that if he purchased the car, there might be a chance she would love him more for it. So, Nobody bought a car from another neighbor who worked at a local dealership. The mood had lightened somewhat and Nobody felt that this might be the break he was looking for to save his marriage, but that was a fleeting moment in the time space continuum.

After what he believed was a few weeks of heavy contemplation on her part, *Church Girl* mentioned she wanted to talk to Nobody. Her son was in bed and she asked for the TV to be turned off to ensure full attention was paid to her. She reiterated her need for space. Nobody was smothering her, she said. The baby issue was brought up, the travel his job required, his unbearable controlling personality, and his time spent in recovery were some of her concerns. He immediately knew why she wanted a new car, her other one was old and repairs were always needed and she wanted something more sound when she walked out the door. Completely numb to the feelings around the conversation, he did what he did best, out of his bag of survival techniques: try and convince her otherwise.

Love was a commitment not a feeling. Lust was a feeling. Marriage solidified the commitment. Marriage is about a life together that had ingredients. It is to have romance, sickness, good times and bad times. It is where they are to grow as individuals within the bonds of matrimony. It is unrealistic to think that when she talked of her visions of love and never ending romantic scenes out of a movie, that they were to be lived out. Her wish to capture that feeling again, was as though she wanted something other than what they had. They were just going through a period; his outbursts were getting less severe. He loved her but they needed to get focused on the marriage while attending to their needs together. They both were on their second marriage and they needed to buckle down and work through it. True the honeymoon was over, but this is where the hard work needed to start. He had his faults and so did she.

The counseling they had been attending seemed to be biased against him. Ever since she started seeing his counselor, it felt that the women had developed a closer relationship than the one he had previously with his counselor. He could only imagine that she was describing him as some over-bearing 'ogre' and if you lived with him, you'd feel unloved too. He asked if they could try another counselor, to no avail. Her attitude during the conversation grew more hardened. She was trying to say something as though it was on the tip of her tongue. She then took out the 'B' list of reasons to leave and went through all the items she was unhappy about. Nobody continued defending and tried to reason things out. Then, in what seemed to be in one complete breath, she said she had a hard time with all the time he spent in Al-Anon and he needed to choose between her or Al-Anon. The final ultimatum had been tossed into the middle of the ring. The one item in his life that she knew he would not yield.

Nobody's current life was a direct result of his eight years in the program. The quality of his problems had improved; he wasn't healed, but his life was on the upswing. At this moment in time all was not lost. Life was dealing a series of hard choices. In the past this would have put him over the edge of the abyss, but inside his hearts of hearts, he believed what they said in Al-Anon and no matter what happened around him, he would be OK. He would survive.

Without reservation, Nobody looked up and said, "Well that was easy, I choose Al-Anon."

Whether it was a carefully laid trap with only one outcome she was looking for or a misspoken threat, the die had been cast. The switch in Nobody's brain had been thrown. The marriage was over. His feelings had turned off. She could not be trusted; she had brought him to this point and was tossing him to the side. He had stood by her through her lengthy divorce; put up with all the shenanigans of her ex-husband, had sent his son to Arizona for multiple reasons, but he was gone. Cast off by the Baptist church, the search for the worthy sperm donor and now, after all that he had invested, it would yield nothing. Another lost book of dreams or would it be? What she was asking him to do was sacrifice his life for hers in so many words. This was a price he would not pay.

Truth #86 Nobody had repeated history at a different level.

Episode 49

The Big Chill

It was decided that they would move into separate bedrooms until they figured out what to do and how to proceed. There had been a couple conversations of reconciliation that Nobody initiated. This way of living was difficult; being in the same house with her and her son was hard on Nobody. *Church Girl* said she was still unhappy in the marriage and nothing he could do would change it. By this time, the first car payment came in and he finally understood the depth of this decision in trying to make her happy a month previously. He just knew at some point he would be responsible for this car. She had played on his weakness to secure a new vehicle on her way out the door.

Rejection was a major button in Nobody's life which had caused much pain in his efforts to deal with it. Instead of the easy mechanisms of drugs, alcohol, and readily available unhealthy relationships, Nobody now relied on Al-Anon and his sponsor for a place to share his hurts. The views around this situation with his wife seemed to be in his favor. They say that there are always two sides to a story, but even when he admitted his part in the whole situation, his AA buddy's' wife, who originally voiced her disdain upon his Al-Anon arrival, looked upon him with compassion and understanding. She said he was fighting a losing battle from a women's point of view and how the dialogue had evolved over the past few months, it was obvious to her, his wife was gone and wanted it that way.

Being self-employed and the ability to work from home which afforded her some flexibility in her schedule, his wife decided she needed to visit her parents. For the second time in a matter of a couple of months, Nobody was alone in the house. He did not have to worry about his son. His wife was gone and she wanted a divorce. It was also hard to have a bond with her son knowing that he would soon be removed from him sometime in the future. His feelings were walled off from those closest to him. Nobody loved her son but he knew that it would soon end and he did not know he would continue a relationship that was not bound by blood. The house felt truly barren. He was going to have to go it alone again, but this time it would be different.

Not being able to sit still, with no yard work to complete and no new projects on his horizon, Nobody did what he always did on Saturday night: he went to a meeting. He mingled with friends before and after the meeting. A customary tradition after every meeting would be groups of people to either go out for coffee and dessert, a movie or back home. Being an avid movie fan, Nobody started asking around if anyone wanted to go to one. Nobody had been talking to an acquaintance from his early days in AA. At the time this friend had been married, but now she was divorced. They talked a bit and he mentioned the movie and had thought it was a great idea. She tried to get more people to join them, but no one took them up on the offer.

A chill ran up his spine when he realized that he would be going to the movies alone with her. The red flag rose, but Nobody still had not learned his lessons well, and did not bother to change his mind even though this was not a good idea. They drove separately to the movies and met inside. Standing in line, it had to be the most uncomfortable position he had been in a while. Nobody did not want to stand too close to her and kept his distance as far away as possible. He spoke to her from a short distance. Two people could have stood comfortably between them if someone had tried. Every nerve in Nobody's body said this was not a wise choice and with every move she made towards him there was a counter move away from her. Nobody would look away and speak to her fifty percent of the time and try to act as though he was there by himself. A thought he wished he had acted on. It wasn't fair to his friend *Movie Girl* either. He was acting as though he was ashamed to be around her, when the fact was he was afraid someone would see him and tell his wife.

Then he saw his neighbors, the cat breeder and the car dealer, and his heart fell to his knees as lightning struck him. He said hello quickly and disappeared into the dark auditorium. When he and *Movie Girl* moved into the theater, he hung low in his seat to remain incognito. Once the neighbors passed, he took special note of where they were sitting. Nobody, keeping a watchful eye, dipped deep into his seat when the car dealer left the theater temporarily. The movie was good, but for a person who is sitting on pins and needles the movie took forever to finish. At the first sign of the credits, Nobody excused himself, thanked *Movie Girl* for going to the movie, apologized for being a bit moody and hightailed it home. It dawned on him that if he arrived home before his neighbors did, they could vouch for the fact that he was home after the movie.

Why had he done that? Why did he care? She said she was leaving, but it wasn't right. He just hoped he got away with it - in the end. One thing was certain, whatever feelings of sadness he had were now replaced with worry and trepidation.

Nobody left the stub of the movie ticket out so his wife would see it. This was an act to further cement his story of being at the movies, running into the neighbors, and home before midnight. The next day upon his wife's arrival, it was still a cool reception and her feelings had not changed. For the next week, it was as if two ships passed in the night going to different ports. These ships who passed along each other's port side never signaled each other to ensure safe passage through the common waterways of the house.

Early Saturday morning out on the deck, Nobody decided to join his wonderful bride with a cup of coffee. She had an interesting look on her face.

"Who were you with last Saturday night at the movies?"

Nobody was never a good liar when asked direct questions, exclaimed that some folks wanted to go to the movies after the meeting and went to see *Lethal Weapon 3*.

"Who were they?" she continued.

"Well a couple of us. There was this guy, you might remember and this girl you don't know and a couple others that are new to the program that I did not know went as well."

'Well someone told me they saw you there and you were with *someone*."

"That was a perfect visual and I would say they were right. Hey what is all the fuss about? I went to the movies, came right home after, I even saw our neighbors and beat them home."

"Oh, is that why you left the ticket out to show that you went to the movie and so could show in advance there was nothing to hide? That's funny because you are notorious for picking up everything out of place and placing it in the trash. My friend, who used to work with me at the doctor's office, called me and said she saw you with a girl and no one else. If what you say is true, I would like to call the guy that was with you and that will be the end of it."

Church Girl was ready to crucify Nobody, "I actually know the guy you mentioned."

As uneasiness gripped his stomach as she continued speaking, "I think I will call him to verify your story, because I know you are lying."

The bantering for position continued for a couple of minutes, she had what she wanted and Nobody had easily given her the keys. Nobody relented and said he did end up going with only one person. The reason he lied was that he knew it would end up looking bad and it would not matter what he said, she would not understand nor want to. With a devilish smirk, she was sitting with her arms crossed and legs crossed as well. Her top leg had the swing of a pendulum swinging forward and back in an overly determined manner, Nobody's tail between his legs, she had crushed him. She was finally justified. She could now say she was leaving because of Nobody. He had been with someone else. She could start her story from the middle chapters and blame him.

Truth #87 Nobody was painted into a corner.

She had continued going to the local church where she played the violin and Nobody stopped attending because he was discouraged from recent events and ashamed of the direction his marriage had been headed. As he looked upon her, he did love her, but he could see she did not love him. Nobody was an obstacle. Whether right or wrong, Nobody's inability to deal with pain effectively had brought him to this place. Whatever lure there was to continue ahead and go to the movie had been far stronger than going home alone and having to think about the divorce in an empty house that night.

Prior to this, Nobody still held out hope that there might be a chance to find a way back into the bedroom together, but now the light didn't even flicker. The fuse had been pulled. His sponsor confirmed to Nobody that *Church Girl's* plan had always been afoot and if it wasn't this, it would have been something else she would have used to push the relationship pass the point of no return. From her previous divorce, she had stacks and stacks of legal paperwork. Now that she had the upper hand, she said if they could equally divide everything they could spare a lawyer and cost. She would just draw up divorce papers from her archives and submit them to the Clerk of the Court.

In South Carolina, you have to be legally separated for one year before the state will grant a divorce. Drawn from the experience of others, Nobody requested that a clause be placed in the document that said both parties "could act as if unmarried" this would ensure the removal of any foul play one might assert on the other during the year separation. She was reluctant at first but then acquiesced. They had agreed to the items that they would split, and of course he needed to pay for the car. He would stay in the house and she would eventually move out.

Nobody was clearly not a hero of the Bible but a normal human being who, at this time, did not always think of God first when those feelings he dreaded took residence in his gut. He had been accused of doing something he did not do even though what he did was wrong. This place was very uncomfortable and Nobody needed to do something. Sitting in these feelings, he wondered what would happen in the future - would God leave him and punish him?

In one of those moments of quiet desperation, he called her folks to tell them he would miss them. Always with a sensitive spirit, Nobody had cried on the phone while talking with them. He thanked them for everything and wished it would be different. His wife, having found out about the conversation, was angry at him for calling. The same way his folks reacted when they found out Nobody spoke to his aunts and uncles. *Church Girl* looked at him from the archway into the living room. She asked him why he even called her parents to cry a sad story to them. She looked at him with disgust that reminded him of the day his mother said it made her 'sick to her stomach' and how she wanted to 'throw up' to think he had sex with his first love.

His wife had rolled her eyes and said, "Act like a man!"

It was another critical blow to his spirit. He had pictured himself *less than* again, and now it was confirmed. He wasn't strong enough or man enough. What was it about him that was so poisonous to women after a time? He thought he was a good provider and husband. He tried to lead the household. Why couldn't he put his foot down and be the man of the house? Why was he always weak? He had always cried throughout his years, his pain was real and it pushed through. He wasn't trying to gain sympathy. He hurt and when he felt the hurt, tears would follow. Why had God made him this way?

Myth #72 Nobody wasn't man enough to keep a woman happy.

After a few weeks, Nobody began getting involved with *Movie Girl* to a point. They spent time together at her house, a couple times a week, and went home at a reasonable time to his frightfully empty master bed. He kept his coming and goings to himself and asked his new friend to keep the details of their involvement to themselves, until the separation was legal and *Church Girl* was out of the house.

To shield the hurt as he had done so many times before, he decided that if she was leaving anyway, why should he keep trying to hold out for any possibility of reconciliation? Having to stay in the house seeing her every day, knowing she was so far out of his reach was unbearable. Knowing that someone else would eventually touch her killed him. It was obvious she had no respect for him. He could not relive those feelings again. He had been there so many times before, watching old girlfriends move on to other guys. His first wife's affair, his live-in who slept with multiple bros under his nose and now this plagued his thoughts. The only remedy he had was to change focus. He decided he might just start talking to *Movie Girl* and before long *Movie Girl*, after their many conversations, couldn't understand why *Church Girl* would kick him to the curb.

His wife was suspicious, but could not really say anything. Nobody never prayed about this or asked for a second opinion from his sponsor. In fact, since his wife would be leaving soon and the documents signed, it was time to buy a Harley. Isn't that what guys do when these sorts of things happen in their lives? It was time to branch out and be somebody. The Harley was something he had always wanted and since he was going to be single again, he might as well buy one and prop his persona up a bit. It was just one more thing to take the focus off of him and on something new. However, before he could put that wheel into motion, his wife needed to get out of the house. The final night together in the house was upon them. It was about five in the afternoon and he had just gotten home from work. The phone rang and his VP of Sales called and said that he and the President of the Company were in Charleston. They had an important meeting at eight the next morning with a client and they needed his expertise in that meeting. They apologized for the short notice but they needed him to attend if he could. That meant he would have to drive down that evening.

As Nobody sat in the living room with his stepson and his nearly departed wife and looked between them, it was a tale of two feelings. If he stayed, it would be uncomfortable for him, if he left he would have a better shot of gaining something from this situation than staying in the house dreading her departure. Why would he want to put himself through that and then have to sit there in the room wondering what to say or do. He would end up going to bed early anyway. With a final glance at his wife across the room, knowing she was wondering what was going on, he told the VP of Sales that he would drive down. His wife very solemnly said, "Do you have to go, this will be our last night as a family?"

"What are you talking about?" he exclaimed.

"Does she want me or not?" he thought to himself.

He had a final tug on his heart as he looked to his wife and his stepson. What would Nobody ultimately gain by staying? So many times he asked her to change her mind. So many times he said he would change and those conversations always ended the same way. He had tried before and *now* she wanted a sentimental moment to end this whole relationship? He asked if it would change anything and she said, "No."

He walked out.

Episode 50

Born To Be Wild

The following morning the President of the company said he was surprised and extremely grateful that Nobody showed up and congratulated him on making the tough choice since leaving your family on such short notice was difficult. The President was sure his wife understood and Nobody would be rewarded for his dedication to the company. The warmth of the President's words did nothing to sooth the knot Nobody had in his stomach, he only turned on his work switch and acted as though nothing was amiss. By the time Nobody got home that day, the movers had arrived to pick up her stuff. To his surprise it was the worship leader and someone else from the music team. The picture was clear after reading the expressions on their faces when he welcomed them. She had convinced them that he had committed adultery to gain their sympathy. It hurt that he was described that way from how they responded to him but there was nothing he could do, nothing to change it. Even though he was talking with *Movie Girl*, it only solidified her story, but not the chain of events that led to it. They were however amenable.

The real issue was Nobody was tired of fighting a battle he could not win. He believed his life had something new for him and he was ready to grapple it. Nobody would not let this bring him down again. He would be stronger this time and one thing was abundantly clear: Al-Anon was at least teaching him that he could stand on his own two feet in the midst of turmoil. It did not mean the end of the world was near as he used to think. He just hadn't captured the total essence of his relationship with God yet. From a good orderly direction viewpoint, he was taking care of himself to some degree and that gave him some semblance of sanity.

A week after she moved out, his company announced the annual trip winners for the past year and he was one of the winners. He had worked very hard to win this trip to make up for their short honeymoon, he had to chuckle when he heard the news.

Truth #88 Nobody felt vindicated.

Between wining the trip and sporting a new sinister blue Harley, Nobody was a new man. People looked at him differently as he rode his Superglide to and fro. He would bring *Movie Girl* out on the town for rides. He would ride to meetings. It opened his world to new people outside of the program. The Harley shop loved him because whenever he showed up, he bought something else to accessorize his ride.

The folks at the meetings said that even though it had hurt, overall he was doing the right thing. They believed his estranged wife was the one that had the issues at the end as some of her comments did not reflect a person who was willing to do what was needed to make a marriage work. It was true that there is an A side and B side to every record but in this case, it was workable. It gave him some peace that he was believed by his elders. From the chaos at work and what the world had to offer, he still felt safe when he attended Al-Anon. For so many years he had been upstairs in AA, he wished he had found this place sooner. It was like all the comments described him to a "T." Yes, he had issues with addiction, but that was still just a symptom to the real problem.

A person showed up during his meetings that he said hello to a couple of times. However, this time as she entered, something different caught his attention. She wore camo pants and a white short-sleeved shirt that gave a slight hint of an armband tattoo. A feather peeked out below the cuff. She sat across the room but she did not notice him. He was a mess anyway and in these meetings Nobody shared the way he was feeling and what was happening in his life. Nobody shared how he struggled just to keep his mouth shut and not say everything that happened to pass between his ears. He was now learning how to act in public appropriately by responding to situations and not reacting to them. It was like he had entered charm school. He still felt crazy with the clutter of thoughts but less people were acknowledging.

As the relationship with the *Movie Girl* progressed, she made it clear that they would not consummate their relationship. She debated whether or not she should go on the cruise as well. She did, however, keep talking about her biological clock and her desire for them to align goals if the relationship was to continue. Nobody entertained her thoughts and spoke clearly about his goals as well (working, riding his Harley wherever and finding that someone special in his life,) but refused to comment on her biological clock. He clearly articulated his love for Al-Anon. They did go on motorcycle rides, but he could tell she was going along just to please him and, as time went on, she would find something else to do instead. She complained that it hurt sitting on the bike. The *Girl with the Armband Tattoo* had a liking for his Harley, and it didn't go over too well when Nobody mentioned to *Movie Girl* that he had given her a ride after a meeting. What did he care, they weren't serious anyway - just singularly committed. This other person was a casual friend in the program and she had a boyfriend anyway.

The pressure was building from *Movie Girl* to bring their relationship into sharper focus. *Movie Girl* wanted to introduce Nobody to her counselor and kept asking if he would go with her. It felt like a chore, but those old tapes to keep a relationship alive under any circumstances still played and after a few promptings, Nobody went along.

He wasn't sure what to expect but, after a few minutes it was clear, there was a hidden agenda and that was the topic of *children*. Sitting in the room, hearing words fly back and forth, it was obvious she needed affirmation that if the relationship was to move forward children needed to be there. This is a funny conversation with a guy who has gotten clipped years ago so he won't have any more children. What was even more interesting is that he had just gone through this *'issue'* with his estranged wife. Of all the women in the world to get hooked up with, Nobody was sitting in a room with another woman who wants a kid and is looking at him to provide it.

How in God's name had he found his way back to the exact same place he was a year ago? If there was even a reason to thank God for something, it would be getting a vasectomy. There is no doubt, based on Nobody's track record, that more kids would have complicated his life even further. He was reminded of something his father had once told him: "Keep your pecker in your pants." Hindsight is twenty-twenty.

At a loss for words, he left the session with a thousand thoughts. He felt this overbearing pressure to produce something he could not. Also, what was *Movie Girl* thinking? The comment was made to see if a 'reversal' was possible. Nobody still remembered the pulling sensations during the procedure and didn't want to relive any of it - ever. He drove away laughing to himself, realizing that he could see how this relationship would play out if he went down this road again.

"Thank you God for revealing the truth," he yelled under the thunderous roar of his Harley.

Truth #89 Nobody saw the truth, a possible repeat of history.

Movie Girl decided that she did not want to go on a Poker Run with him the following Saturday. Learning from Al-Anon to always have a plan B, he asked the *Girl with the Armband Tattoo* if she would go as friends. She said yes. Her boyfriend had other plans with his child and it did not include her. They met at the rally point and when he saw her show up in a black leather vest, he couldn't help but keep his initial reaction to himself. He had once said jokingly in a Bible study when asked about what people should look for in a spouse, he said, "Animal magnetism first, then ask if they believe in God." He certainly asked about her views about God during the course of the day and found that she was a little older than him, had two teenage girls, had been divorced for a time and was trying to get her act together as well in Al-Anon. From that day forward, and one of the first times in Nobody's life, he had found a female friend close to his age. This was not the biggest take away, while he did admire her beauty his fondness towards her was not like his previous snatch and grab campaigns. There was a certain level playing field they had both ventured onto and he actually saw her eye to eye.

She was unsure if the relationship she was in was good for her. Her boyfriend had a five year old boy and she wasn't sure she wanted to go through that again. The *Girl with the Armband Tattoo* did not like to deal with the child's mother, who still had a very active role in both father and son's life. She had sensed that if that relationship continued, trouble might brew and her opinions might always play second to her boyfriend's former wife.

Truth #90 Nobody saw a person weighing out facts instead of feelings to make a proper decision.

Not wanting to create another crisis in his life, Nobody decided not take anyone on the cruise he had won. It was his first vacation ever like this and he wanted to do this by himself. It was a first of sorts. He had learned to go to the movies by himself, not wondering what people thought if they saw someone by themselves. This time he would go by himself and claim his independence and not let his being single represent a bad mark against who he was as a person. He just wanted to have fun and he did. He watched people, smoked Cuban cigars, bought gifts for his buddies at the Harley shop, gambled in the casino and didn't worry about finding a girl. In the path to independence he had tackled a looming fear he had always had. He spent time with the other trip winners and participated in company events, and never once thought he was less than the people around him. He stuck to his daily routine of prayer and meditation. He was pleasantly surprised to have found a 'meeting' on board and was grateful for the life he had.

During his trip it had occurred to him that the relationship with *Movie Girl* would not go anywhere. *Movie Girl* had started asking poignant questions about the future and he was not ready to commit to anything. He had prayed about it and every time he envisioned himself with her, his gut went sour. Not because she was not attractive, but because their life goals did not match his. He knew if he wanted to find joy in his life, no breath was certainly better that bad breath. A term his boss had repeated to him when it came to recruiting employees. He had to call it off, and this would be another first.

In Nobody's life, everyone usually left him. He was the pursuer to everyone, even his guy friends. He always had to bring something or asked to be involved. Nobody's personality wasn't necessarily warm and he had a sarcastic tone to everything. He was on the right path, but still self-absorbed. He heard his folks say that you always need to look out for number one, because no one else cared. These were harsh words for someone trying to connect with people throughout his entire life. He wanted to believe that it was different; however because of the path he had been on and the situations he had placed himself in, it seemed to have always played out that way. It was a self-fulfilling prophecy that not only extended over himself but his parents as well. Think about it, if someone continues to speak a lie over and over, eventually it becomes the truth, because the lie overshadows the reality. Another term used repeatedly by his parents to make Nobody turn to them for support was trust. This too played out in his life.

When Nobody looked at the world and saw himself, it was always in a diminutive view. How many times he had been let down; he had been angry with God so many times, but how could he turn his back on Him? Deep down he knew it was only God he could rely on. The reason he couldn't trust anyone around him was because Nobody couldn't trust himself. Only God would love him fully. The problem was there were certain things Nobody wanted in his life and he hoped and prayed God wanted the same things for him. He loved God, but was unsure if God wanted him *single*. It was a weird place to be wanting God to give you something and knowing that it might not be in your destiny as a true follower of God's will.

One thing was certain though; he needed to end the final scene with *Movie Girl*. She was a nice person, but she would not be in his future. Not wanting to drag it out and use her, he called her and said he needed to call the relationship off. There was not a lot of fanfare, he had spoken to his sponsor to go over the things he needed to say and made notes to keep track of his thoughts. When it was done, she was mad and had said that this had never happened to her before. Nobody standing firm, said, this was also a first for him and he hoped she would respect his position. He said goodbye, hung up and took a ceremonial step into the future by himself with God as his guide.

Two nights later he attended a Christmas party for the area Al-Anon group. The *Girl with the Armband Tattoo* was there with her boyfriend, who, by the way, was the speaker. Nobody was sitting amongst many of his friends from the program. Listening partially to the forty-five minute long oration, Nobody stole glances to and from her as often as he could. It was just his luck that someone who was a nice person, who he admired, and who he had an interest towards was taken. As friends, he had told the *Girl with the Armband Tattoo* that he had broken it off with *Movie Girl*. He was doing OK, but knew he wasn't going to be in a relationship where there was pressure to bring children in. Sitting in this room, looking at the guy she was with, he couldn't help but feel let down. This guy happened to be the guy he said he was with the night he went to the movies while *Church Girl* visited her folks. He was sort of a program 'icon' who had a very smooth demeanor of someone 'learned.' It drove Nobody mad, because while he spoke of his feelings, this guy would utter wisdom. When he had finally finished his story and he walked back to his seat, the *Girl with the Armband Tattoo*, who he had been eyeing the whole night, gave the speaker a hug and kiss. Even though he had seen them together before, this moment felt like a sword going through his heart. Nobody knew she was weighing out her options, but it still pained him to see it.

Thinking to himself, *"Why is this so difficult?"*

Episode 51

Bridge over Troubled Water

Life is a series of ups and downs. For those who struggle with addictions, anger, depression, self righteousness, and control, life at times can be overwhelming especially when life never seems to go your way. Religious organizations and utopians will, through perfectly good intentions, want to convince or enforce new modes of behavior on those around them because they believe they know what is best for an individual. Some want, what has been termed in the halls of recovery, the easier softer path. We seek a life of tranquility where the highs are extreme heights of wonderment and the lows are just north of adequate. It is the swing between the two points on the S-curve of life that many are trying to solve.

Nobody wanted God's will in his life. He wanted many other things as well, but the life God has given us, at times, can seem cruel and unusual. What could be a difficult situation could be a point where God is actually strengthening you for greater things. Then at other times life can be tough, just because it is life.

Her girls were with their father and Nobody asked the *Girl with the Armband Tattoo* if she wanted to go to the movies. She accepted and they went and shared a nice late lunch at Shoney's. Always being a talker, Nobody wasn't afraid to share his thoughts. By the way he spoke you might think he was extremely honest and insightful about his feelings, his threshold was always deeper than others but he still carried fears just like everyone else. He listened to her lovingly describe her girls and describe her hopes and dreams for them. She brought up the fact that she had broken off the relationship with the guy she had been seeing. She did not see herself raising a young child again. Her girls were in their teens, about the same age his son, and she didn't want to be in a relationship for the wrong reasons. They talked about the past, the struggles and victories they had encountered.

Isn't it funny that after all the broken relationships and those that hardly have any life in them deep down, the ember is never quite extinguished? Everyone wants something bigger in their life and we still have hope that one day, by some certain act of fate or miracle, it will all come together. After listening to her share part of her story with him, he couldn't help but notice that the ember inside of his heart was glowing a bit brighter. Nobody was spending time with someone who was talking his language. He remembered, as she was talking, how cute she was when she had asked him to return a movie for him on his way home a couple of nights earlier. As small of a favor as this was, it can be a blip on the radar or a single beat of the heart. Nobody had never trusted anyone to return his movies for him to the movie rental store, but she was entrusting him with something. A little point to ponder in a world filled with a higher order of ideas to contend with, but this was special to him. It meant he had to do something he did not necessarily want to do, but at the same time he would for no particular reason.

In a world where ideology rises above the individual, the individual is counted but never truly dealt with. The system is conditioned to believe that if they make a valiant attempt to account for everyone's needs then it will all work out for everyone. Everyone will be happy. In Jesus' teachings, He clearly stated many times that it is the individual that needs to be addressed. If the individual will take ownership of his relationship and work within the confines of God's love and will, then it will not matter what happens around him. He clearly states that handling of the little things is a gauge on how you will handle the bigger things. This is a first step in serving others with no significant impact on the immediate future, only a clear indication of things to come.

Christmas was just around the corner. His son was in Arizona and he would stay there for the holidays. Nobody had ventured through

Thanksgiving without incident but Christmas always brought up his first divorce, the confrontation with his father on Christmas night and the move out of his parents' house. He loved giving gifts to others, even though many times none came back to him. Over the years he called people (friends, bosses, company commanders and family) on Christmas morning to wish them a Merry Christmas. As rough around the edges as he was a lot of time, he loved reaching out to people and when he slowed down long enough his heart was on display in many different ways.

When it comes right down to it, everyone wants to be special and believe that someone cares for them. It doesn't matter how strong-willed you are or how popular you are. When you go to bed at night and no one is around but just your thoughts, we all want assurance that we are thought of and cared for.

Nobody went to his Saturday night meeting like he always did. It was a week before Christmas. Nobody had spent his time engaged in the program, actually putting into practice many of the things he had heard. He talked about his thoughts about being alone in the house and how he tried not to force solutions though it still plagued him at work. He finally was able to sleep in his bed again; he had to buy a new mattress just to have something fresh to sleep on and a symbolic act to settle his memories. He worked hard at living life on life's term and it was obvious to those around him that he was at home in these rooms. All of these things he shared openly in meetings, describing how he was putting his life together again, he received encouragement to continue pushing forward; he was trying not to live in the confines of his mind. Someone had mentioned that the mind was a dangerous place and it was a good idea not to go there alone.

The *Girl with the Armband Tattoo* showed up and waved as she entered the room and had a smile on her face as she looked directly at him. She carried with her a small decorative holiday bag and walked straight over to him. They exchanged pleasantries and she then held out the bag for him. 'Shocked' could not accurately describe his reaction. He always was the first to do something nice for someone. He didn't have anything for her and he immediately was mad at himself for not getting her anything. It always seemed like it was his responsibility to inflate the tires of a relationship. Tonight, minding his P&Q's, someone came to him with the air pump. He took the bag, as she sat down in the chair next to him, and with her palms on her knees she leaned forward to face him. She had a little smirk on her face, she was enjoying this. She turned her knees so they were almost touching his as he reached into the bag. The tissue paper revealed nothing in the upper region of the bag, he had to dig deep and at the bottom his fingers found a small something lying flat against the bottom. There held between his fingers was a tree ornament. As he looked at the figurine, a part of his heart was touched that never had been touched before. It was a pleasingly plump smiling angel that had a cabbage patch kid-like face, its clothing was a humble beige dress to its ankles and a white apron and appeared to be flying from right to left, with a crop of golden brown hair and a head band with a gold star. The shoes and clothing seemed colonial in nature and on the bend of one elbow held a red bird. But that was not what touched his heart, it was the banner the angel held with the other hand flying over its head. The word "Hope" was written on it.

No one in his life had every given him 'Hope.' This small little gift, probably found on the counter at a Santa's village store, had touched his heart. Speechless and awestruck, Nobody felt again that God was speaking directly to him through her. The emptiness in his gut was instantly gone, it hadn't been filled with sex, gluttony, pride, drugs or obsessive behavior, it was filled with 'Hope.' It took a few seconds for all this to register, but words could not describe the warmth that erupted from deep within the confines of his heart. The gift of a lifetime had just been given to him and it was 'Hope.' It wasn't a night to remember, a surprise party, a trip to an exotic land, it was 'Hope.' Once again God had taken his message to Nobody in a single word, given to him in a way that had stripped away all the hype around Christmas. Hope had been proclaimed again, but this time it wasn't by the birth of Christ like so many years ago. This small herald angel was singing again, he knew that he needed to continue on the path he was on and that God once again had come to him in the simplest of terms to deliver a message and he received it. He looked up to the *Girl with the Armband Tattoo,* thanked her for giving him the best gift ever, with a passion and sincerity that could not be mistaken. Safe and secure, like the day when he lay in his aunt's arms so many years ago on that rocking chair, Nobody felt the love of God in his heart. He felt the warmth from the woman who sat next to him. No longer would he look at her as the *Girl with the Armband Tattoo,* but the *Friend with the Armband Tattoo.*

Everyone wants their life affirmed and this night his path had been confirmed once again. He did not know where he was going, but he was sure that 'Hope' bridged the gap over the troubled waters of his life and that would be all he needed.

Truth #91 For the first time ever, Nobody had hope.

Soon Spring was in the air, flowers were blooming, the great annual pollen drop was over and the *Friend with the Armband Tattoo* had become his *Girlfriend with Armband Tattoo*. At the turn of the year he had been promoted at work to cover the region and he had many offices to support and a team of technical consultants he was responsible for. Passionately engaged in his work and always a customer advocate, he could easily see how to transition customers from one telecom carrier to the next. When it came to his line of work, he was exceptional. The problem was that those around him could not see technology or the process as clearly and precise as he did. This always led to frustration on his part. Not sure if he was using the right words, he found that many times it felt as though he was repeating himself. Patience was not a virtue with which he was comfortable.

When Nobody was told that he needed to perhaps be under a doctor's care for his edgy and sometime depressive attitude, he took it in stride. Counseling should not be abandoned. The combination of the two helped him learn new behaviors with the meds taking the edge off. Up to this point, it had not dawned on Nobody that the principles of Al-Anon must also be applied to the work environment as well. In addition to the medical remedy, Nobody still prayed regularly, read his daily readings and always asked God to give him the strength to live out His Will. It isn't supposed to be a formula; that if you do these things, then everything will fall into place and you will be blessed by the Almighty One and your life will flourish and everyone will know you are a man of God. No, that is not quite how it works though many wish that it would. A walk with God will tend to bring a series of personality adjustments that can be painful at times but in the end, if you are willing, a better person will be produced. A walk with God does not start with one act of good behavior or a pat on the back and then one can walk with the confidence that they are forever blessed. No, a walk with God is a journey, similar to a walk through a mountain range. There are peaks and valleys, easy and difficult stretches that will test your resolve. Sometimes you must push forward and move up the mountain, even though your body says stop and give up. If you want to be happy with the world around you and be part of society in that regard, Good Orderly Direction is the prescription for you. However, Nobody had prayed many times for God to help him be a better person not just to those around him but for God himself. His walk wasn't perfect, but in his heart he wanted to be better than he was and God most certainly provided the opportunity for Nobody to make that choice.

One day while visiting the office in Charleston, they had had a good month of sales for the previous two months. When the telecom business has good sales, and it is time for the new customer to be switched over, there are many balls in the air and a lot of coordination and scheduling must take place, especially when they all seem to be cutting over to their service all at the same time. Nobody was guiding the service coordinator through the process to minimize the time the customer was temporarily without phone or internet service. The coordinator asked if he could record what he was saying to refer to later. Nobody obliged and continued to assist where he could. Another part of his job was to offer technical assistance in bringing proposals to maturity and provide technical solutions for potential customers with their products. In the chaos of answering questions from what seemed every direction, Nobody's frustration reached a crescendo and to those watching may have looked like a wild man frantically waving his arms trying to make everyone understand moving from room to room, trying to juggle all the balls in the air at the same time, trying to help as best as he could and all the while being recorded at the same time.

Two days later, he decided to drive his Harley up to Charlotte and work in that office. The Regional Sales Manager called him into his office and said that an HR complaint had been raised against Nobody. The shot to his heart was instantaneous. If he would have been standing, he would have fallen to the ground. He could not offer any insight, but he needed to be ready for a call from the VP of Sales. Time stops when things like this happen. Movements are all captured in slow motion as the world moves past you. You see the world carrying on, oblivious to what is transpiring within the soul of a man. When the phone call finally came, Nobody listened intently.

"Nobody, when you were in Charleston the other day. Your behavior was absolutely out of bounds. You were swearing, talking in a loud voice, visibly angry, and storming around the office. You were demeaning to the staff. It wasn't just one complaint. The Customer Service Rep said you were swearing and it made her uncomfortable. Your attitude towards the service Coordinator was awful. To make matters even worse, you were recorded!" his VP had said.

Nobody had no idea he had behaved like this. He knew he was rough around the edges, but he never thought it was like this. As he was listening slumped in the chair, anyone walking by would think that it was a life-less corpse being propped up. The VP had very succinctly described his behavior. He had, over the years, characterized his mother this way, and Nobody hadn't a clue on how close to the tree this nut had fallen.

"Nobody you are one of the smartest guys I know and you are valuable to this company, but if you ever do this again you will be fired!"

Nobody could only say, "I am sorry and I had no idea I was such an ass."

They continued to talk and the conversation turned towards getting his attitude adjusted. The VP suggested a couple of books to read that might help him with the way he dealt with people. He said it was important for Nobody to apologize to those he had upset. This would soon blow over but he had a part to play in that. Emerging from the office, Nobody had come face to face with himself. Like the night he was arrested there was no denying what he had done. His heart hurt as he saw himself. He had not even realized how he had behaved in that office that day. He had hurt people without knowing it. It was one thing when you are mad at someone and you intentionally hurt them and you walk away with justified anger, if that can be called justified anger, but it is totally different when you do not have a clue and the mirror is put in your face. The words he had heard in Al-Anon rang so true, that he was dumfounded. He was irritable. He had been angry and obviously unreasonable without knowing it. He made a couple of phones calls and truly expressed his apology to the two people he had hurt.

The once brash and overly confident man who had a talent in front of customers and who seemingly thought he had the world by the balls, had been cut down to his right size. Driving down the Interstate seventy-seven miles from home under the thunderous sound of his Harley, Nobody wept, prayed and pleaded with his Maker. This day put a stamp on Nobody's life. Within six months, people at work would jokingly call him the new and improved Nobody. This would not have been possible if it hadn't been for His miraculous way of presenting the truth that one could not deny. However, it doesn't always require knowledge but truth and that night as he went to a meeting he embraced the Al-Anon program fully, he prayed to God to give him the strength to change and he took another step away from the person Nobody used to be.

Episode 52

Love Her Madly

The relationship he had with the *Girlfriend with the Armband Tattoo* was moving along very well. They were well past the casual stage in their friendship. He had always been the one to make the first moves to make sure he did not lose an opportunity. He chuckled to himself when he thought back to the first night he had kissed her. They were on his couch watching TV and talking about nothing in particular. They were not at the 'sweet nothing' stage but still with no actual direction in the conversation.

Nobody had wanted to ask if he could kiss her so many times before, but he did not want to ruin what he had with her. So many times he had rushed into relationships going for the big bang. That emotion of an intertwined relationship so soon upon meeting diminished the need to find out who he was trying to get to know. Only to find out later that what looked good on the outside did not match what was on the inside. He never allowed someone to make a first move. So he was shocked and equally amazed when he looked over to her and she asked him if he would like to kiss her. He would never forget the twinkle in her eye as he moved closer to her that night with only a kiss.

A few months past, they were an official couple and were making future plans. Even though his divorce was not yet final, with only a couple of months left on the year-long wait, it did not stop their intentions to live together. He had financial issues due to two mortgages. With only one income, he was living pay check to pay check and one major issue would put him in dire straits. She thought that she could put her house on the market to rent.

They prayed to God about it, but heard no response. Not understanding the ways of God in their fullest, they continued to move down this track but doing things differently than before. Nobody decided it would be a better idea to talk it over with someone prior to making a final decision. He called his sponsor who had been by his side over the years. Nobody needed to run this idea by him to get some feedback. Obviously, Nobody had learned a thing or two from his past snake bites.

When it came to relationships, he acted first then wondered if it had been the right decision. This time Nobody remembered the pain and would go into this with his eyes wide open. His sponsor knew all that had transpired with his soon to be ex-wife and over time even his neighbors had said that they felt she had lied about things to them. He had made a recovery from that marriage and even the man next door, who was the epitome of a man walking with Christ, soon acknowledged that life might be better off for Nobody but still believed that they should have had tried to work through those tough periods Nobody and *Church Girl* had encountered. It is the give and take that makes a marriage work.

With the thought of marriage in the back of his mind, he told his sponsor of their intention to move in together. He explained that he wasn't driven by lust as he had been in the past. He respected and cared for her and she was not only beautiful to him but she was his friend. He also trusted her. Nobody knew she only had eyes for him. He knew that she was tired of failed relationships as much as he was. He described how they would present it to the girls. They were planning on renting her old house and she would move into his. This went on for about thirty minutes while sitting in his closet which had a window that overlooked the neighborhood as he discussed it.

When Nobody finished, his sponsor, who had always been a man of few words but when he spoke carried a silent strength beneath them said, "It seems to me that you know how to make a good decision."

Another first! It did not matter what the subject matter was, he had not tried to sell his idea and present it in a way to make someone agree with it. He had just laid out the facts, did not try to hide anything and let the cards fall where they may. Nobody also spoke with his sponsor's wife, who he attended meetings with, and she also felt that he was going through the process the right way. This does not mean they approved or disapproved of what he was doing. This only meant that they heard it; Nobody wasn't fooling himself and was at least making an informed decision.

Yet, how long had he waited to hear someone say, "I think you are making a good decision."

Years of trying to gain permission to live from his family and always second-guessing his own decisions. Running around gathering opinions and hoping not to make a wrong choice and making sure the consensus favored his decision. This time he just expressed his feelings, the facts and obviously since he was confident, it must have been the difference. However, a positive reception to a presentation doesn't always mean it is blessed, by God.

Nobody was starting to live for the journey and not the destination. His world was starting to improve. He was no longer riding on the waves of his emotions, never knowing if he was on God's true path for him. Nobody knew he was moving in the right direction.

Perception is a term best defined by what one believes is seen and drawing a conclusion. Symbolism can be seen as items that represent a meaning. For example a wedding ring is a symbol of a person's commitment to a relationship and an engagement ring is a promise to a commitment. If everyone were to think about how they perceived Nobody's relationship with his soon-to-be ex wife, they would say that he had moved on and they were sure to perceive that his true love was the *Girlfriend with the Armband Tattoo*.

However, every day when Nobody removed his watch - a wedding gift from his second wife - she was there on his wrist, calling out to him, ever reminding him that they were still linked. Truth or fiction she was still there. When *Church Girl* called about some item still needing discussing, they would have to come to an agreement for the final divorce proceedings. Ultimately, Nobody relented because he needed her to agree and eventually sign off on the Quit Claim Deed for the house so he could be the sole owner.

There was still a bond there that he acknowledged existed only to himself, but he wanted to be rid of her. She kept calling about once a week. It was always something, a picture she had forgotten or she would like to have the bedspread. Nobody had not mastered the art of saying *'no'* yet and still afraid of confrontations. Nobody could not see himself or his needs as equal to someone else's. The *Girlfriend with the Armband Tattoo* often made comments about the situation and wished he would stop placating her.

Nobody had made a lot of progress in this area but still fell short in the fortitude department to push back. He could not see past the disagreement and weigh out different options. Nobody could not see he had a bargaining chip as well. He wanted to be rid of her and the only way he knew how was to push back slightly and ultimately give in. In the end from Nobody's perspective, he did not care. True his ability to push back was lacking, but most of the things she wanted only reminded him of her. Nobody knew from experience that he could always replace whatever she wanted within reason.

It was the watch that bugged him. He always saw the inscription promising *Church Girl's* never ending love. A portal to the past that called out to him, a beacon with only one message. Are you sure you need to let this one get away? The watch was handsome and Nobody did like wearing it, but her words touching his skin every day, not so much. Perceived by everyone as just a watch on a wrist, it symbolized a lost love that could be treasured or looked back on in times of trouble. A door to the past that should remain closed if his relationship with the *Girlfriend with the Armband Tattoo* was to flourish.

Nobody decided that placing it in a drawer would only keep its sphere of influence within arm's reach. No, he needed to severe the tie with this watch and what it represented. The symbolism of his grandfather's watch was protection and covering. The symbolism of this watch was pain and an unfulfilled promise. One was a key to his future and one to the past.

As he hopped on his Harley, the sun had started its final descent into the horizon. With the watch in his pocket and a new watch on his wrist, Nobody rolled down the road towards the lake. Taking advantage of the clear roads, he hit the gas and informed everyone within earshot he was on a mission. The lake which lay east west always provided for breathless sunsets during clear skies. Traveling across the east end of the Lake Murray Dam, Nobody drove to the other side and into the boat launch area with a small viewing platform over the water. The sky was breathtaking as the sun started to creep towards the water's edge. A light wind was blowing across the water and it produced a soft babbling sound when the small waves gently kissed the shore. The sun's glow was still in full view but only a finger's width from the horizon. It would only be a matter of time when the ball of fire would change its hue to the color of night.

It was here that the link to his former bride would end and the bond with the *Girlfriend with the Armband Tattoo* would be cemented in his heart. He called his sponsor's wife, who understood the meaning of this better than her husband. He told her that he was on the walkway over the water and in his hand the watch. After a short conversation on his intentions, he laid the phone down. With a wind up that would make Vida Blue proud, Nobody pitched his *time* he had had with *Church Girl* as far out into the lake as gravity would allow. A lake that sports a depth of 351 feet at one point only a few hundred yards from Nobody.

It splashed and descended into its watery grave with her words crying out one final time. The new replaced the old. The perception and symbolism matched. Every day when he would look at the time, it represented the future. He was free to live and love. Moreover, he knew the love he had for the *Girlfriend with the Armband Tattoo* was stronger than the history of the latter.

Similar to a baptism, a wedding vow or an oath, it is important to understand that the tradition of having witnesses to major events in someone's life is a sacred act which has been documented since the beginning of time. Today, by the witness of his sponsor's wife, Nobody had shut the door on a relationship born out of lust and rescue and opened one for love and commitment. You can't talk about fitness and eat cupcakes, nor can you talk about a relationship and mentally entertain a thought that will always remind you of the past in a way that will cause one to wonder 'what if' in times of trouble.

He did not know where this journey would lead him. What he knew with certainty was that for it to be successful, he needed to put it all on the table - drop his cards and call. God would call Nobody to endure many things in this relationship and admit things to her that would surely kill him, but today he made the promise in his heart to trust the path God had for him and not on one he had forged by his own will. He had to break from the past and trust that he did not need a lifeline to some memory.

As he looked over the water one final time, not remembering where the watch landed, which was now covered by the soft gentle waves, he climbed on his Harley, broke the cool sound of the waves with a thunder as he drove across the dam, trying to outrun the sun as it fell below the sky.

Episode 53

We are Family

It was mid-spring and life was moving along pretty well. Nobody had been drawn to younger women throughout his dating career, but the *Girlfriend with the Armband Tattoo* was just a tad older. Nobody just wanted someone who would appreciate him. Age probably doesn't have anything to do with it, but it was a change. When he was around her he felt like he could be himself - the part he knew, that is. He did not sport the obsessive *'want and need'* mindset and more importantly, he did not need a waltz partner in which he had to follow her every move for a sense of security.

They continued to talk about the future and how they would combine households. With a lot of differences in this relationship there certainly were a lot of similarities just beneath the surface. God was helping Nobody change inch by inch and even though he saw positive changes, it can take only a fraction of a second to go back to old thinking if you are not mindful. What is interesting to note is that while Nobody truly felt he was living in God's will, he may have been, but that doesn't necessarily mean in all aspects. Many of us have blind spots in our life that we have yet to see as contributing areas in our behavior that actually separate us from God at a deeper level. The Trinity is perfect is every way, but nowhere in the Bible did it say God expected us to be perfect. Yes there are laws to guide behavior but laws only govern external actions, not our thoughts. Just the opposite; He understands we are not perfect and He offered up the greatest sacrifice to bridge that gap. What He is looking for is progress in *His* direction with a willing heart.

There are spiritual principles at work around us and one of the famous one is that you will reap what you sow. This is important, because the effects of certain actions still have a bearing on your life whether you realize it or not. That is why recovery and a walk with God are processes and not events. God is with us on the journey and through a series of events and willingness on our part, more is revealed. As Jesus said so eloquently, "My Father is the vinedresser. Every branch in Me that does not bear fruit, He takes away; and every *branch* that bears fruit, He prunes it so that it may bear more fruit."

We are like the people entering the doctor's office, we know something is wrong and we go for treatment. We try following the directions given to us by the physician to get us on the path of better health. For instance, the doctor may say that for your wheezing to stop, you might want to consider not smoking. Seems clear enough and over a period of time the patient attempts to quit smoking a number of times only to fail one more time. The doctor reminds him on a follow-up visit, the patient says he is trying, but the doctor continues to encourage him to fight on and he manages to finally quit, but it may have taken him a year or two - it doesn't matter. The doctor doesn't care for him less; he just wants him to be healthy. The patient is getting better, the bouts between quitting and not quitting has improved his breathing. The patient had even started running to compensate for his behavior and was getting in better shape. However, he is still not quite healthy enough. Then, after a while, the patient is finally tired of smoking and realizes it just doesn't have any benefit in his life as it once had and, by some grace given to him, he stops smoking. He just had had enough of trying to hold on to the one thing that does absolutely nothing for him. Before the patient started going to the doctor, he only knew that he was wheezing and did not know why. He came to know the doctor and, after a few visits, he had a better understanding of what was going on. He tried other behaviors to compensate for it and though he was feeling better it still was there gnawing at him. But, he was determined to get better and that was the path he had to travel upon.

How many times have you heard someone say when in doubt read the directions? There are certain things that require a step by step process to obtain the proper finished product. If you try to bake bread too fast it will not rise and go flat. All the ingredients are there but if not done in the right order, then what you expected may not be obtained. When we truly give our hearts to God, He knows it. He loves us enough, however, to allow us to sit in our pain while we go through the process, a process that might be termed *pruning*. Maybe that is why so many turn away from God - they want a God who takes away the pain of the world instead of conquering the sin of this world, which He already has. The problem is a society with misguided desires. It has never been about a formula. If you are sincerely trying to live His will, He will walk with you through the pain and joy, the triumphs and the defeats. He does not love you because of all the things you do, God loves you, period!!! As you move closer to Him, more aspects of your life will present themselves for modification if you are honest and willing to change. Change will be easier and less monumental. Instead of saying this is too much to tackle at once or I will have to give up too much, getting on the path is sometimes all that is needed.

Our smoker picked up hiking and now has packed too much in his backpack. He is full of energy and is ready for the adventure, a weekend with God. A couple of miles into the trail he realizes that he has too much stuff and it has become a burden. He can't turn back, however, but it is too heavy and his breathing is labored. He starts getting rid of items he knows he will not need and he comes across the cigarettes. At first he wonders how he will get along without them and after looking at the pile of items, he finally decides what needs to be left behind because those are things hindering his progress.

Our hiker soon realizes he is the one carrying the load and God has had his arms open the entire time telling him to hurry along. God is walking and we are the ones falling behind. However, once we catch up and again realize that God just wanted us to quit smoking so we could keep up. He did not love us any less. When you walk with God, He will be able to point out things along the way and, if you are falling behind, you will miss the opportunity to see what God had for you at that stage of your journey.

That brings us back to Nobody. When they broke the news to the girls that they would be living under the same roof at his house, there was not a choir of angels singing with resounding joy. It was just the opposite;

they had a sudden fear for their mother that she would be hurt again. They believed she was rushing into this. They were against the move not because of Nobody, it could have been anybody.

Standing in the living room and hearing the commentary from missed conversations, it struck Nobody that he would have to prove that he was not going to hurt her. The *Girlfriend with the Armband Tattoo* held firm in her conviction and said they were going to move but unfortunately it was just the beginning of a long road. Nobody and she did not see what was in front of them. Within in a matter of weeks, once her house was rented, the girls decided to move back in with their father and stepmother. The oldest one put in the request, but the *Girlfriend with the Armband Tattoo* said that if one went the other would go as well. She did not want them separated and they could not bounce between households on a whim. They needed to stay through at least one school year.

It crushed her spirit. It dawned on Nobody that it seemed like history was once again repeating itself in a different form but still an issue had risen lying dormant just waiting for a time to spring to life. This opening could be the result of moving in with someone before getting married. The interesting part of this narrative is that the girls were afraid to see their *'mum'* get hurt. With coaching from the stepmother and the request from the father, they had been lured out of the home. They may have opposed their mother's decision to move in with Nobody, but this hurt more.

As Nobody started hearing about the history of the battle over the girls, it was striking, the behavior of the stepmother, was as if Nobody was listening to a conversation about his own mother. She obviously ruled the roost and the father did not try to buck the system. Without missing a beat, the father or shall we say the stepmother had to ensure that child support would be rendered unto them. The irony of the situation was that for years they claimed financial hardship as a means to argue for reductions in child support but now they needed more and they would try to pull as much as they could from an income less than $45K a year. Since the day the step-mother had the affair with the father when the youngest child was an infant, it was always her goal to punish the *Girlfriend with the Armband Tattoo* even though she had claimed her prize. She had always needed to grind the truth into submission at every turn. Even though he was an extremely successful veterinarian with a great practice, he was presenting a vision of declining income. The *Girlfriend with the Armband Tattoo* would have to prove to the court otherwise. Nobody heard all the stories of how the stepmother was always trying to pit the girls against the mother and have her choose which parent they should love. What a similar story to his own.

The girls had their regular visits and the *Girlfriend with Armband Tattoo* spent time decorating their new rooms with accents to personalize them. Deep into the summer, just before she was going to pick up the girls for visitation, they called and said not to bother. They would not go with her, they had a mother and it was not her. The world collapsed around her while Nobody was standing there trying to make sense of it all. Paralyzed, the life that they had planned seemed to swing in the balance and the bread was not rising.

Where is God in all this? They were trying. They were doing all the right things, meetings, even going to church, doing their best. He didn't want to believe it was a punishment but, in the back of his mind, he felt like it was. He thought that once you are on the right path it should all fall into place. That is what he heard. Why was it that life just seemed so hard, it was like you never got a break?

Nobody would pray for God to help her. He did not know what to do and all he could think about was what would happen to their relationship. Would they survive this, his immediate thought was that he would have to be everything for her and attempt to lessen the pain she felt. Her face was pale and her eyes displayed a sorrow so deep, it killed him. It was like watching someone riding on a bus looking out the window with no expression and shadows moving across the face as the world went by. How could you enjoy life with a major issue like this in the balance? How would they enjoy each other? One question continued to plague him: how did he get in this place one more time?

Nobody tried to comfort her but to no avail. The air had been let out of the balloon and he was powerless. He could not say or do anything. There was a history here that he thought had been resolved. The divorce had been final since the girls were infants and this was just another chapter in a horrid affair. The similarity looking over Nobody's life with his mom and relatives was extremely compelling. He had been strong enough to make changes, but he was also older. He chose to love all his relatives, regardless of his mother's wishes, he just hid his actions from her to save himself from the retribution that was always waiting to be administered - if she found out. The girls, on the other hand, if they did not choose wisely could submit themselves to a wrath far worse than what Nobody had.

The girls had been exposed to the same 'day in and day out' pressure from their stepmother. The stepmother had demanded that they show her they loved her and their father. The only way to demonstrate that sort of 'hostage taking love' was by not loving someone the stepmother despised. With the promise of private school, all 'stuff' teenage girls want and opportunities her father could provide, the deal had been struck and the *Girlfriend with the Armband Tattoo* was daughterless.

Nobody's relationship with his son was doing well and it was over a year since he had been gone. He and his ex-wife had worked from the context of the original divorce decree for visitation. In that decree Nobody had not requested child support from her. The less he had to do with her, the better. The guilt of his decision over the past months had diminished and there was great progress made with his son while in her care. She had a great husband; Nobody even sent him a Father's Day card thanking him for his efforts. All in all they tried to present a unified front to his son. However, there are always times when the wrong word can spark a series of events that nothing can be done to prevent the seed from sprouting.

Nobody was having an interesting conversation one afternoon during which they were talking about some of his son's issues and money was brought up. They were discussing how poorly his son managed money. Nobody, in a slightly sarcastic tone, proceeded to pontificate how he had always tried to instill the value of money into his son. Obviously, if some-thing was amiss in this area it most assuredly was something she and her husband were not doing properly.

His ex-wife responded with an, "Oh brother."

Two weeks later, by special correspondence from the Law offices of 'I'll Show You' was a petition for child support. Oddly enough, it was the same attorney who had processed his bankruptcy years ago after their divorce.

Smitten with rage, Nobody immediately called her to find out *'WTF'* was this about. He had spent years taking care of his son while she tried to find the right husband and got her act together. He dealt with all their affairs honestly and did not try to manipulate situations. He had been the sole financier for his son and never once demanded a single dime from her. It was only fair that she take over moving ahead. He had lived under that assumption when his son had moved. Since when was life fair? How could this be happening now? He was just getting his finances in order, didn't his previous contributions matter. He had let her off the hook all those years just to be hit with this. She had his son for over a year, she was claiming custody. What started out as a desire to help their son had now turned into an issue of *mon—ney*, slowly spoken and flicked off her forked tongue.

"Why God!" he exclaimed in his prayers! He was *doing* everything he thought was best.

His ex-wife just couldn't leave it alone. She had crushed him so many years ago only to reopen the wound afresh. She obviously wanted the last word. In a world that is not fair - no matter how many would like it to be - the lack of fairness is actually the natural order of things. Nobody was stung once again by reality. This was a changed circumstance and, if she wanted to file a petition, she could.

Truth #92 Nobody was powerless.

The idea that good behavior and prayer should produce good results as well is a half truth wrapped in a lie. This is the problem with assuming that, once you turn your life over to God, everything will be in perfect order. With the absence of love, evil exists in this world. It roams freely and has many disguises all used to try to trip us up. Some believe in a 'Sugar Daddy God' and the prosperity gospels that some preachers call them. This is a proposed secret formula to success that you can have your reward on Earth for obedient behavior and all your troubles will go away and you will be blessed here as well as in Heaven. Those preachers, who only preach portions of the Bible that suit their needs to gather tithes and offerings, have manipulated the Word in a way to demonstrate their prosperity through the gifts of others who want a life that is removed from reality or above reality. All the while these ministers lead the flock astray and make them believe they are following the Word of God.

It is true that a life centered on God will yield better results, but in some circles it has been skewed in a way to think materially instead of spiritually. Many have been led down a path that a life following God will bring a sense of comfort to their lives on Earth. It may be better stated that if you truly follow God with all your heart that you will find comfort from God regardless of how disastrous life may be around you.

The issue is that when one denies the existence of evil and it comes knocking on the door for any reason, the initial reaction that is described by countless stories is anger towards God instead of the true culprit. Many have been disheartened and believe they have been deserted by God in their time of need, similar to what we have seen with Nobody by his reactions.

There is prosperity in God's Word and He does fulfill our needs if we are true to His will. However, just because one reaches prosperity does not necessarily mean it is through the good graces of obedient behavior in God's eyes. There is always a price to be paid and the manner in which you obtain your 'wealth' will have a price associated with it. If you are not firmly grounded and mature on where your faith should lie, then His ability to reach you lessens. The promise is that if you truly submit to God, you will be given all that you will need to face what confronts you. The outcome, however, may not be what you desire for this life. If you truly follow the God of Abraham, the hardest lesson to learn is the willingness to venture the path you will be placed on to carry out His will for your life. The path He may put you on could bring you face to face with some sort of behavior or situation to actually demonstrate to the people around you God's love itself. There are those who are put off by God and love is not their core value. If the truth be told, when it comes to money which can be an idol, a majority of people will turn to money before turning to God.

Free choice has been spoken of before but let's quickly discuss an aspect of our relationship with God which is timely. Not only does God give you free will to choose love over evil (the absence of love,) God or No God. He also gives you free will to set the terms of His relationship with you. There are some in the Bible that God dramatically called into his service. The majority of us determine at what level to be bothered by God. Some show up once a week to church to check the box and show everyone that you at least attended, and by right you are a good person. Or, you carry your Bible everywhere you go and preach the Word but never have connected your heart to your head. What you have is an intellectual grasp of the Word of God, not a relational one. Then there are the people after God's own heart or somewhere in between - all of these or none at all. When the relationship with God is an intellectual one, your ability to speak into the spirit of someone around you will lack the passion required to pierce the soul. God has patience and forbearance and will allow us to loiter about while we try and get our act together. Many of us have good intentions and get lost along the way, and that does not make us bad, it makes us normal and is one of the challenges that we have been given through life.

Nobody believed he was after God's heart, but he did not know why. He never found the reason by going to church up to this point and as loosely defined as God is in the 12 step rooms, he yearned for that relationship. The only difference here was that he sincerely wanted it, but envisioned a result for it. He always had a feeling of God's presence from as far back as he could remember. A cosmic link, for lack of a better term, but his impatience got him lost along the way. Nobody's life was moving forward but he had not grasped that setbacks are not just a part of life but also the ability of God to help one move forward and a tool used to get closer to Him. Nobody retained an attorney and realized that he could not use his past contributions and her lack of them in the past to win his case. His counsel told him that the court only cared about today and that he would have to bleed money for six years. He loved his son, he was doing good, and there would be a document that laid out how they all would interact.

Was it a setback or was it a way to have this chapter of his life put to rest. Nobody and the *Girlfriend with Armband Tattoo* had made decisions to circumvent the ways of God while loving God. As a parent to a child, caught with their hands in the cookie jar, sometimes a slap on the wrist is what is required to capture their attention and cause them to ask first. God does understand the hearts of his children, he does not condemn them for mistakes but he will allow them to suffer the consequences of their behavior. They both made a decision that went outside the lines, what many know, as the covenant of God. The facts speak for themselves, every time Nobody rushed into relationships without following some of the tenants of God, trouble followed only happy to oblige.

Episode 54

My Girl

After the blow they had received, things started to settle down; the child support issue was behind him. The girls had meant what they said, or better yet, the stepmother had meant what she wanted them to say. The blossom of their relationship seemed to wither slightly. He was thankful that she had other women to talk to. Her struggle with God was apparent. He did not try to fix her or bring up the situation. The very limited phone calls were intercepted by the stepmother who answered or jumped in the middle of conversations to end them. The stepmother would call her out and tell her how bad of a parent she was. The stepmother would tell her that the girls did not love her and they were in bed sleeping or did not want to talk to her on the times she answered the phone. Each time the *Girlfriend with the Armband Tattoo* would get off the phone and hold her stomach as she walked to a chair to sit down. Nobody could sense her will to live teetered on the edge of a deep abyss. She was devastated. Nobody watched the woman he loved falling apart piece by piece in front of him. She tried to keep her spirits up but it was apparent this was not just a mother daughter spat, this cut to her core and the bleeding would not stop.

Nobody's divorce was finally cresting in the horizon and he would be free to pursue any course he chose for his life. However, every time his soon-to-be-ex-wife would call, she would still want one more thing.

Nobody was tired of fighting and knew that it was not important in the big scheme of things. The *Girlfriend with the Armband Tattoo* was always aggravated and questioned his sincerity towards their relationship.

The ways of God are so diametrically opposed to the world it is staggering. You must surrender to win, an odd concept but one that continues to breathe air into the fire of the spirit. However, during turbulent times, when you feel that you are walking with God and nothing seems to make any sense, a feeling of abandonment can make one ponder the validity of God in a cruel world. Nobody just wanted closure on all of these issues, but he was not patient enough to take them on in due time. Nobody always jumped in head first then hoped he would not hit his head. He knew his divorce would soon be over now that a date was set for the final hearing. As one part of the equation seemed settled, his girlfriend's side of the equation would not be resolved.

Nobody witnessed the good days and the bad days. He watched her pray and ask God to take away the pain as she tried to continue on with her life. He felt like he was all she had. There would be those times when he would find her sitting in a chair just looking into the distance. He would not ask about the girls for fear it would push her over the edge. Being one who shied away from pain and did not handle trouble well, he always tried to change the subject and take her focus elsewhere. Probably, as a way to fill the gaps inside as most people do, we tend to reach outside of ourselves and gather things to fill the one spot set aside for God's healing. Nobody felt badly for her but could not get a sense of her pain. All he understood was that when she was ill, Nobody was ill and if he was ill, he needed to remedy it quickly, since he had a low tolerance to any pain. He needed to keep things moving and place focus elsewhere.

They continued with meetings, motorcycle rides and they even found a church where the pastor was a member of Al-Anon. They felt he had an understanding of life on life's terms and it was wonderful to hear sermons from that understanding and apply the Gospels to it. Nobody kept his thoughts focused on God and not Jesus Christ, even though he had accepted Him in his heart years ago. He shuddered when he heard the Name, probably like the demons did upon hearing His name. There was too much animosity in that area with the Church and Nobody had yet to relate to the two actually being one. Nobody prayed and followed the God of his understanding and that was good enough for him. He picked and chose the parts he liked and tossed the rest aside. Nobody went to church because he loved her and would support her. He enjoyed the social aspect and the teachings he heard on how to deal with life. He had a passion for God, but not Jesus Christ at this time. The name Jesus Christ was like a barrier in his heart that prevented him from breaking through ever since the episode with the Baptist preacher.

There were too many things he held on to that prevented him from taking the step across that threshold, mainly his will to do as he truly pleased. This was not how he perceived it in his mind. He did not want to hear what he could or could not do. He wanted to keep an eye on God while trotting along his own path. He pulled his morality out on certain subjects and provided perfect rationalization for those things he might want to consider. He did not want to think more about others than himself. He did not want to contemplate the morality of others, because then he would have to question his. He did not want to let go of a life he wanted, without understanding where he was going.

Nobody wanted the life he had envisioned. He believed God had brought him this far and he would work hard to ensure he received his vision for his life, while giving God what Nobody thought was appropriate. It was easy, you prayed and that prayer deposited grace in an account that could be withdrawn at a later time when needed and at Nobody's convenience. This would be similar to the child calling the parent to get him or her out of jail in the middle of the night. Pleading for help, promising you would never do it again only to have your memory disappear after your visit to the grace bank and the withdrawal taken place.

This was the pattern Nobody was falling into, living his life as best as he could, giving heartfelt lip service to God, wanting the things of this world over the things God may want for him. He was in a delusional state that convinced him he was following God every step of the way. What he was actually doing was walking on a path of his choosing and wanting a God who would bless all his endeavors just because he acknowledged God. He asked for things one hundred percent of the time, he heard only twenty percent of the responses and listened to five percent of that.

While God, like a father who watches his child trip, stumble, and fall while learning to walk. The child still attempts to walk to the father. The child can only look forward and is not watching for what is directly underfoot. There was no doubt that Nobody and the *Girl with the Armband*

Tattoo were both walking towards the Father. They were just stumbling along the way and like a true Father, God was happy to see them try.

Even as Christ did the final night in Gethsemane, everyone wants to prevent the pain they see is coming without the understanding that pain is one type of vehicle used by God to transport us to Him. While the world tries to take the pain from the world, God uses pain to bring us closer to Him. We have discussed that one will reap what he sows and pain could be a byproduct of it depending on what type of seed that was sown. It does not diminish the fact that life on Earth is dangerous, frail and unpredictable by design. Our human condition tries to prevent and secure us from any sort of dilemma and we run from the thought of pain, all the while God encourages us to come to Him with our pain. This is a spiritual paradox that has caused many to curse God and others to embrace Him. Nobody was situated between the highs and lows in his life, but living inside the lows of his girlfriend. His life was in order by his standards, but effected by the circumstances of another. It made it hard to understand if she was with him because he was all she had left in the world or she truly loved him. Did God want him here? Would she love him because he stood by her or because he was the only one left?

Love is a commitment and lust is a feeling. Nobody had been guided by lust (feelings) his entire life. He also believed that to be loved, you must feel it coming back to you in order to sense or gauge the status of the relationship. Being hyper-sensitive by nature and conditioned to look at himself first when someone is in a bad mood or things didn't *feel* right, Nobody would say repeatedly, "I love you." The only reason he said it was to hear it said back and then if she was somewhat down he would ask, "Did I do something wrong?" All of these questions were about making sure he was acting appropriately and if there was something wrong that he was doing he would adjust himself to the situation and make it work.

When someone has not been guided through life by a good role model to help understand that people have their own issues, one would learn that one's needs do not have to be the absolute center of the universe. When Nobody felt alone or isolated even for a short amount of time he had to attempt to achieve acceptance by his actions. It is no wonder why Nobody's life was 'performance based' and he was insecure just underneath the surface. He looked to those around him for affirmation and it was a drug he had not given up. His affirmation came by way of relationships, son, job performance, his yard, his dogs, his motorcycle, and his house. The only thing he that he never accepted was himself for being who he was. In the confines of his soul, even though so many good things were happening around him, he still believed anyone given a choice would abandon him under the right circumstances. Nobody felt he was the last choice and any form of discomfort within those relationships was an indication that validated his position. He had yet to understand that pain or discomfort can be the fertilization required for something to grow.

Many people base their understanding of God by their surroundings; the horizontal plane instead of the vertical plane. The horizontal plane is based on feelings and logic based in a preconceived bias. If it doesn't make sense then it must be false. They affirm the world is a wicked place and thus probably that there is not a God after all, especially one in Jesus Christ.

Nobody believed in God, but deep down felt he had to depend on himself when the going got really tough. He couldn't believe someone would truly love him enough to stand by him during his darkest moments. That understanding translated to his relationship with God, trying to earn His love. So when the big day came, God would not leave.

Nobody was living with someone in one of her darkest moments, powerless to do anything about it. The only thing he could do was love her in her pain, without expectation, regardless of the outcome. In his past Nobody loved someone as a bargaining chip that he could cash in later. The big payoff was that his perseverance would make everything secure for him. This was new territory and being self-centered would make it worse.

With all these messages running through his brain, he continued to wonder where God was in all of this. Internalizing his world it was hard to watch her lament over the girls; he felt that this would be their undoing and there was nothing he could do to remove the isolation she felt inside. He just knew that one day she would wake up and say that he was a nice guy but, with everything going on in her life and her kids, that it would be better for both of them if she left. It wouldn't be fair to him.

Every day he thought this would be the day, never once considering that she actually loved him. He had no concept for what he had to offer in a relationship. He believed he was a place holder that could easily be tossed aside. Couple that with one's limited understanding of God, it is no wonder why so many believe God is not there for them. They base their understanding on their current surroundings drawing conclusions on feelings and or facts as they choose to interpret them.

How many times have you heard someone talk about God in a negative way and the first words out of their mouth is, "I don't believe God would. . . . . .!" or "If there really was a God he wouldn't. . . . . .!" They can only believe in a God that they can conjure up in their minds, not the one in the Bible. If there is pain it can't be of God. The ultimate shame is if terrible things are happening to or around you, then obviously you have done something wrong and deserve it anyway.

This was what Nobody was wrestling with and when he looked at his girlfriend, none of this was fair. How could this issue just sit in the middle of their relationship? Didn't God understand? Didn't God see that they want to do right by him? They were trying.

"God please help make this right, I want to get on with my life." The crux of the issue; Nobody wanted a God in his image that will guide him along the happy path of life. When the realities of life hit and love is truly put to the test, is it love that stands firm or the quest of a life one deserves that causes someone to take flight?

Nobody was learning something through this situation. Did he love her? Was her pain more than he could deal with? There would be no relief until he understood what it all meant to him. So while Nobody tried to separate her pain from his, he continued to pray. Nobody stood there by her even though he did not know why? He couldn't run from his discomfort, he didn't want to leave her and certainly did not want to hurt her. While trying to do the best they could given the current circumstances, she announced quite without warning she wanted her own Harley. Whether to fill the spot lost to her children or satisfy a lifetime desire, it was something new and a step forward. Within a period of a couple of weeks, she was the proud owner of an Aztec Red 1200 Custom Sportster. No words could describe the feelings in his heart when he saw her sitting on her bike for the first time in the driveway. She had a glow that propelled her beauty 1200cc fold.

Nobody could sense her fear and desire to ride. She had never driven before and she was apprehensive and within a short period of time it was evident that Nobody would not be her instructor. He did not have the patience to guide her through her anxiety to drive the Harley and she was not going to be rushed. He was from *"the just do it"* camp and she was from the *"when I am ready"* camp. He wanted to help her and be there for her, but this was her walk and what she needed was a supporter not a caretaker.

As he encouraged her to pop the clutch and take off, she asked him to leave her alone. She wasn't dealing with driving a motorcycle. She was overcoming a fear that only she could muster the courage to proceed. She was building upon her faith to propel her forward. She had rejected his assistance and guidance in this matter and Nobody's feelings were hurt. She not only did not want his help, she wanted to be left alone. He went inside their home and watched from a window. She sat on the motorcycle and time pushed forward.

As Nobody sat there, it was obvious that though he had a desire to be her one and only, there were things he had to step away from. He could not fix the issue with her girls, he could not teach her how to drive a motorcycle and he could certainly not take away her hurts. Nobody could not be her everything, but that did not mean she did not love him. It only meant that the *Girl with the Armband Tattoo* had her own walk in life and he would not be the one she turned to instead of God.

Nobody needed to make a decision and that was to love her for who she was and not what he wanted her to be. All his life Nobody wanted a perfect relationship that sailed into the night happily ever after. There was always a full moon, clear skies to navigate by and an enchanting sparkling sea to gaze upon. It was a vision of life and love that had disappointed him time and time again. This vision was part of life and like the seasons and the weather it was bound to change.

For this relationship not to end in failure he needed a change in attitude. Without understanding the spiritual dynamics of his decision, he calmly prayed to God to help him love her for who she was. Isn't that what God does with us? He loves us where we're at, but that doesn't mean he will bail us out. However, at some point we all sit in a driveway saying, "Leave me alone I will go when I am ready," or "I will do it my way," rationalizing our behavior, adjusting our values to make life more comfortable when prayers aren't answered in our time frame, then pleading with God to bless our little world while not truly following Him.

It is a delusional state when we stray from those values and morals God has place upon our hearts when we start turning towards Him. We start compromising our values to allow our desires to be fulfilled even while wanting to be closer to God. We introduce confusion by trying to convince ourselves our behavior is appropriate or acceptable. Then when things start to fray we wonder why this is happening again when we clearly believed God had blessed it and cry out to Him, "Why??"

For so many years Nobody believed he had to be perfect to be loved and also wanted perfection that could be loved. He loved someone that wasn't perfect. He knew in his heart, even though his girlfriend was independent that it did not mean that she didn't love him. She needed a place on Earth to turn when she was tired. The *Girlfriend with the Armband Tattoo* needed to be able to rest in the fact that Nobody was there for her. He needed to understand that he would not be perfect no matter how hard he tried. His thinking needed to shift and love her regardless if she would end up loving him in the end. He had to risk it all without knowing if it was a sure bet. Nobody had to love someone who was picture perfect in imperfection. He needed to believe it before he would see it, as he heard so many years ago in that small room with a bunch of strangers.

In the past he had only loved someone if there was going to be love in return after the initial chase. He needed for once in this life to love without a payback, just like God loved him. At the crossroads once again, opportunity was being played out through the circumstances in his life. From the outside looking in, it could be a sad story of a divorced mother who has lost her children and living with a guy in sin who was soon to be divorced (but allowed to act as unmarried per the separation agreement,) and the guy on the rebound living in sin afraid to face the world alone.

To God everything can be turned into good and it was an opportunity to understand love. By society's' standards they were the leftovers. In spite of the scars, God was calling and teaching them through the discomfort of the situation. Nobody was a divorced man trying once again to find a love that would last and The *Girlfriend with the Armband Tattoo* wanted to believe someone loved her and who would not abandon her. Two broken people struggling to find the truth of it all, calling on God not knowing why and finding out that though they are both stuck; one in the driveway and one by the window waiting for something to change, hoping that they would be chosen, by the other. As Nobody watched, she popped the clutch and the Sportster took off, he smiled knowing she had the strength to continue on. As she turned the corner and drove out of sight, he only heard the sound of the Harley in the wind. He was on a journey and so was she and he hoped that they could survive this and end up in the same place together.

Truth #93 Nobody had no idea where they were headed.

Episode 55

Happy Together

With all the gifts opened, Nobody announced that he had one more gift to present. Totally surprised to find a stereo, subwoofer, amp, crossover and speakers for her car, she had beamed with joy upon opening the gift thinking it was 'la piece de resistance.' Nobody had laid clues alluding to the gift throughout the holiday season which she could not guess and ultimately had to wait until Christmas Eve.

As he walked over to the Christmas tree, he said in a loud voice, "What is this, a Christmas tree in a Christmas tree."

As he reached his hand into the center of the tree, tucked away on a branch which had been in full sight throughout the month of December was a small ceramic green Christmas tree, with modest painted balls and garland, leaning against the trunk between two branches. Small enough to fit in the palm of his hand he walked over to the *Girlfriend with the Armband Tattoo*. He presented her the tree and a smile on his face that he could not hide with the straightest of poker faces. As she cautiously gathered the tree with both hands, and looked at the charming little tree, she noticed a latch and a hinge, after few seconds of thought she understood that the tree was not the gift but the package. As she worked the latch carefully, she pulled it opened. With the entire tree flipping back to expose the inside base, there was a space large enough for only one very small present. There perched on a scant piece of foam, with a sparkle that ignited the light of her soul, Nobody had finally decided what this relationship needed.

As she looked at the ring, Nobody bent down and looked into her eyes and proposed. The *Girlfriend with the Armband Tattoo* who started out as his friend, his Plan B for their first outing, his riding partner and the one who enjoyed an evening of discovery over the science of ear candles; the woman whose life was not perfect and struggled with God, family and life like he did; the woman who had talent and skills that seemed to compliment his, was now going to be his wife.

During our life we can see a gift in plain sight but at times we are too afraid to reach for it, not sure what might be in it or the actual cost. We want to see what is out there for us before making a decision. Nobody had heard that recovery was a gift left under the tree, but the journey to the tree seemed treacherous, but always worth the effort. For some the journey never starts, the fear of being hurt again can be too overwhelming. The visions of the past distort their view of the gift, or fear of the unknown will cripple someone to give up because it is too hard to imagine and cannot grasp the joy they might find.

Recovery is a gift from God for those people who have lost their way on very extreme paths that were easy to start upon but hard to turn back from once the feet have been firmly planted. They hold on to very possessive idols that keeps them trapped in a hopeless world. Recovery is one of God's beacons to reach his children. It is the gift left under the tree without a name tag. Anyone can retrieve it and only requires faith to open it and keep digging through it once opened.

Nobody embraced his recovery. He was learning that reaching for that initial gift provided him a multitude of continuing gifts, some easy to recognize and others painfully so. Marriage is a gift from God and an opportunity to experience what the joining of spirits truly means and on this night the next part of their journey would begin.

Marriage in his two previous attempts were a means to an end. It was an attempt to bring out the benefits of marriage without the proper ingredients. He looked for love in return through words of promise and wished that all of his feelings of inadequacy, fear, low esteem, would all disappear on the blessed day. Nobody left those marriages wondering why they turned out the way they did.

For those who watch from the bleachers, it can be easily seen that the faulty relationship foundations were built on fear, feelings, the desire for a problem-free existence and the lack of self-worth. Everything that God has sanctified on this world has been washed with *'grey water.'* Consumption, sex, personal achievement and financial gain have a place in this world but when the drive to attain these things thwart the will of God, dire results always follow. The biggest loser is the human spirit. Trying to find happiness through these things never satisfies the hunger.

Satan's biggest attack on marriage is to get people into as many beds as quickly as possible. Then, once two people are married, keep them separated. That way Satan can always remind each party of life as it was before. As the marriage starts demanding the true test of love, the past can offer an exit strategy. A couple can say this is too hard a road to venture on and walk into the arms of a memory where only ecstasy was experienced.

Having somewhat of an understanding of his failures, Nobody cautiously hoped he had approached this with a different set of standards. He had conferred with his sponsor and with her sponsor to get their blessings and share his intentions. Since Nobody had issues with his family, these people were the closest and most trusted people he knew. He had prayed to God that if this was not what He had intended for Nobody, to please kill the relationship before they traveled too far down the path. After he had done all these things he gave himself a few weeks to ponder his decision and ensure that this was what he wanted before he had purchased the ring.

He watched the *Girlfriend with the Armband Tattoo* and knew he could never intentionally hurt her and would not want to. More importantly, when he looked at her, he saw a woman that he knew he could grow old with. He had no clue what to expect and he could be traveling down the same road he had traveled three times before with his previous two wives and the girlfriend from hell that God ended up using to escort Nobody to recovery.

That night was perfect. The essence of marriage was felt by two people who believed in each other. She called her sponsor to share the news that everyone in their circle of supporters had waited anxiously for her to declare. Remembering the awe of children on Christmas morning, God, through the gift of marriage, can bring the same awe filled spirit to two adults with an innocence that could last a lifetime. When two people can look at each other deeply into their eyes and commit to love one another, there is no greater joy felt.

Why is it so hard then to understand that this is the same commitment God has for us? If it is true that what happens in Heaven is loosed upon Earth, then marriage is a representation of a greater love that none can truly imagine. The first gift given to man was a woman, no matter what path of understanding you believe in. The facts are that to survive one needs the other and try as the world may to attempt to discourage the message, the union of a man and a woman brings forth life just like the union between man and God.

May 27th, 2000, gathered on top of a stone pillar on the edge of the Saluda River, midway into the canopy of the surrounding trees, this spot provided excellent cover for a party of eleven on that hot spring day. Spanish moss hung from the limbs. The leaves redirected the light in various ways and the moss swayed yielding to the direction the slight breeze requested. Years ago this structure had been part of a bridge and it was by chance that they had found this little piece of history to conduct a small wedding ceremony. One member of the troop mentioned that it was one of the bridges General Sherman burned during the Civil War.

Off the beaten path, and not part of the Botanical Garden where they had planned to wed, it was apropos that Nobody and the *Fiancée' with the Armband Tattoo* would exchange vows in this wonderful setting. Found by chance as they walked a foot bridge across the river to the garden part of the zoo, someone had noticed a small foot path off to the left without any markings. Being adventurous, the group agreed it probably led to the edge of the river and they would find a spot there. However, to their surprise, the path led to the top of this once bridge support now overgrown. Due to its height in relation to the trees that grew below, it felt as if one was standing in the midst of the branches high above the ground and the little rays of light that broke through the leaves rounded out the beauty of the setting as though the light danced around the shade, saying, "Catch me if you can."

Surrounded by their family of choice, all from AA and Al-Anon, they exchanged vows and were supported by people who loved them and wanted their marriage to succeed. People would be there for them in a time of need. These friends; his sponsor (Best Man,) her sponsor (Maid of Honor,) the pastor they had met in the program, and a couple of friends, had all been there to wipe the tears and share in the joy of the blessed pair over the past year and a half.

It was striking that they were being wed on a stone pillar that ascended upward. One of Nobody's two previous marriages was conducted by a Justice of the Peace, who only upholds the laws of man and can be changed at any time to suit the masses. The second by a New Age minister and that ceremony was performed on the shifting sands of a beach. This marriage was performed on a pillar made of granite blocks, symbolizing God's strength. It stood the test of time and had a sense of tradition with God's blessing. It had not been swayed by the rush of the river. At one point, man had tried to destroy it, but it remained even against man's wishes. Overgrown with new vegetation, similar to the ideas of man which try to overshadow and cover up His existence, the strength of the pillar could not be overlooked. The pillar; silently watching, waiting for anyone to call on Him for support. Always present never wavering.

As the ceremony reached its crescendo, a roar of the lion from the zoo could be heard. How appropriate that a lion, a symbol of Jesus Christ who is called the Lion of Judah, would roar at that moment. Jesus referred to the church as his bride and was sent to Earth to claim His bride. With the gift of a river of life and a firm commitment, the stone pillar held the couple firmly above the river as a new day was dawning for the pair. Yes, each were getting married for a third time and each could tell anyone what not to do in a marriage, but today was different, the balance was shifting and they were starting to lean into God.

Marriage is the combination of two persons in body, soul and spirit and, over time in that order, they will become one. The man and woman are a counterbalance to each other. When God is part of the equation it can serve as a vehicle of healing even in the most intimate of places. As time passes and the core of a couple's spirit and soul start to move closer, the items that have been protected most by the individual become exposed to the other. This term is commonly referred to as the end of the honeymoon, but this is the most crucial part to its success and ultimate fulfillment of any marriage. If it is not handled properly and given the care and support needed, the growth and survivability of the union is in jeopardy. This is where the attacks on marriage begin and each must love the other in their weakness and set aside their wants and needs to serve each other. This is so hard to do in a world of messages that say, "You deserve to be happy," one can easily see why so many marriages do not invest in themselves and dissolve over time.

However, at this stage, things are somewhat new and our couple was starting a journey which will test their resolve and commitment. They were still two broken people, with a spirituality that still had toes on each side of the fence, but afraid to go either way for fear of making a wrong choice. Now that they are married they have at least mended one issue in an array of issues that marriage can heal with the help of God. In Asheville, NC, they enjoyed a simple honeymoon where they found a quaint Bed and Breakfast in which to start their journey. An affinity to hiking in the mountains was found and it would soon be a new hobby each would undertake in their own way. Each of them on their own journey with God, moving forward in search of the highest peak, our couple will find that love has a different meaning than what they were ever accustomed to.

When life returned back to the day to day grind, the marriage was the only change in the environment. The girls were still gone and birthday gifts were being returned that she had sent. Blocking and tackling was the preferred method, performed by the stepmother to limit conversations. Insight into their lives was nonexistent.

When she tried to call, his wife would hear a continuing barrage of attacks from the stepmother. She would take out the hot branding iron that seared the *Wife with the Armband Tattoo's* flesh with statements that described his wife as a whore with her head up every man's ass. She did not deserve her children. It was obvious that her attitude and behavior resembled Nobody's mother on so many levels. As he heard and listened to the yelling on the other side of the phone, Nobody knew the girls were being forced to choose who they should love and were held in a prison. It was also obvious that the father, like his own, had no strength to combat the stepmother and fight for his own children or himself. The only children that mattered were the boys he fathered with the stepmother.

A story of two women, one pleading to God for help and guidance while putting one foot in front of the other while the other playing a god of her choosing and passing sentence every time the real mother tried to reach out to her girls. Nobody could only stand by, watch and pray that this pain be lifted from his wife.

While his wife had her own issues, Nobody was still working on his and in the midst of all of this he decided they should go to Maine to visit his family when his son came home for the summer. Nobody had not been there in almost ten years; he wanted to see his grandmother, other relatives, introduce his wife to the *'fam'* and have his son visit as well. He was hoping that this would be a good trip.

Episode 56

V-A-C-A-T-I-0-N

As the preparations were being made for their trip, Nobody called his relatives and said that he would be coming to visit and he wanted to somehow visit them all if only for a short period of time. The anticipation was growing. He had not seen his favorite cousin in years and it was going to be great to see them all. One thing Nobody had always done was keep in touch, to the dissatisfaction of his mother.

Tensions were still present in the family and he had been plagued with questions from his mother off and on. She would ask if he had kept in contact with her side of the family. The disdain she had for her brother, Nobody's Godfather, had not subsided. His mother still had these cycles she went into. There was always someone else that she was mad at. Never liking the answer Nobody responded with, she always pronounced the same proclamation, "Why do you keep calling people that do not care about you?"

Nobody would always answer, "Because I love my relatives," a statement that baffled his mother.

The week of July 4th was finalized and the tickets were purchased. Nobody had only to wait. Keeping with some of the principles he learned in Al-Anon, he told his mother the basic plans they had for the week. There would a variety of activities that did not require his parents to entertain him or his family the entire week, but there would be adequate time to visit. A week before the trip, Nobody received a phone call from one of his aunts and she said that to save time from his vacation, all of his aunts and uncles would come down to Lewiston on the 4th. They would have a get together at her house and Nobody would be able to see everyone at one time. It would be a mini family reunion, in which everyone could meet his wife and son.

Caught off guard by her words, Nobody was somewhat speechless. Of course he said, yes. This touched him more than he thought and tears welled up in his eyes. He was special enough for everyone to come and see him and his family. When he got off the phone he told his wife. He sounded as though he had just gotten the bike he wanted for Christmas!

In his excitement, Nobody called his mother and told her about the get together on the 4th. Expressing himself like a young lad who just came home from a grand adventure, he would talk to whoever would listen. Nobody told his mother it was going to be great and that everyone was invited. His aunts and uncles were excited about meeting his wife and seeing his son and he felt like the 'Prodigal Son' returning home with everyone's arms open wide.

Not once had he thought what his mother's response would be and as he was sharing the news with her, she interrupted him and said, "We have plans that day and we are not going to change them."

Shocked! Nobody was dumbfounded. Standing in the kitchen with the phone to his ear, the color drained from his face, the joy that he had felt a few moments ago had disappeared in a flash.

"What?"

"Your father and I have plans for that day and we are not going to break them. You go right ahead and spend time with them. Is your uncle going to be there? When you are done with them maybe you can come and spend time with your PARENTS!"

"That is not fair. You have not traveled to visit me in South Carolina since 1994, I am coming to Maine and you can't even put away your anger against your brother for one afternoon to see me as well. I don't believe this."

"Why can't you just come to Lewiston and just see you parents. We are the ones that love you, not them!!"

It's hard making sense out of nonsense. The Prodigal Son may be returning home, but as he was running across the field with a smile on his face, arms open wide to the family that awaited him, pressure is felt, then he hears the shot and falls to his knees. The pain is delayed as he looks to his chest, and sees the blood flowing from beneath his shirt. He looks to where the shot came from and sees the person with the gun and asks, "Why?"

As he is on his knees, he pleads to God, "Why is this happening to me. I just want to be happy and do the right thing. I am not the person I used to be. I am tired of fighting, can't my mother see that? It's not wrong to love all my family. I can love them too; I won't hate them even if she does."

Anger and resentment is a very strong poison and it can taint the blood of anyone if not dealt with and resolved. The damage it can do, if left untreated, is like an infection that spreads. Nobody's mother's anger towards her brother had not subsided since he was fifteen, almost twenty years. It gets to a point you don't even know why you're angry after all that time. It just keeps fueling the emotion. Whatever their differences are, the path for healing can only be found by two willing participants, but Nobody refused to follow his parent's call to isolation from her brother and sisters. Nobody was almost ten years sober and his mother still did not know her son or choose to see him for who he was. It was almost like she saw him for who he used to be and not the man he was becoming. She had no consideration for his views as an adult.

His wife came over and hugged him. The little boy who was present a few moments ago had disappeared. The tapes were playing once again in his head. All he could hear was, "Why are you hurting your mother? No one loves you like we do."

She always did this. If it is not her way it was no way. A boy, who wants his mother to love and accept him, always left reaching out, pleading for her to love him in spite of their differences. She tells him she loves him like no one else, but the words don't match the actions. Nobody had married and lived with women like this. Pulling him in and then pushing him away. He always went back to be hurt again. Wanting to trust the words he so desperately wanted to hear, only to be disappointed time and time again.

His wife held him, he did not know if he was angry or sad. There were so many thoughts running through his head he could not corral them. He was speechless. Regardless, he would see his relatives and believe they loved him and wanted to see him.

As the 'Prodigal Son' got up from his knees, his heart still gushing with sorrow. He continued to walk towards the crowd of people waiting for him, encouraging him to come home, to the dismay of the shooter, who was walking away with the rifle perched on the shoulder. It was a good shot, but it didn't kill him.

The only thing he heard was his wife say, "I'm sorry."

The miracle is that God, had provided family who loved him, was attempting to heal the wound that continued to ooze.

The party, which was day one of his vacation, was a hit except for the comments about how shameful it was that his folks did not show up. One of his aunts insisted that she could not see how a mother could do that to her own children. It didn't matter how old they were, especially when they flew into town for a visit and hadn't been in town for ten years. His relatives told him they loved him and welcomed his wife into the fray. No matter what would happen with his folks, his aunts, uncles and grandmother all supported and loved him. They were the family he needed and the counterbalance to his parents.

Nobody talked about recovery, his job, kids and how God was important in his life. He saw a few of his cousins and planned a day with his favorite one. When the day had finished Nobody felt the love they had for him. He didn't have to prove himself worthy of love and he felt respected.

As they moved into day two, they went to L.L. Bean, went out to eat lobster with his parents. Not much was mentioned about the previous day and for the most part everyone was on their best behavior. Nobody had opted to stay at the Ramada Inn near his parent's house instead of staying there. It gave him a place to rest from all the feelings this trip had brought up.

He thought of the fights, the days of partying, high school and how different he was from before. He ran into people that he had not seen in years and it shocked him that it seemed like the town was caught in some sort of time warp. This was something he would confirm when he returned for his twenty year high school reunion. The town itself seemed tired and worn out and the people just existed. This town wasn't even fun to visit as a whole and, due to his past, it felt as though a cloud hung over it.

It was interesting that, after all these years, the moment Nobody was in the vicinity of his parents, he felt instantly transported back in time with his feelings. He had to pay such close attention to how he responded to even the littlest of comments, it was mind boggling. His wife started to get insight into Nobody's past as she saw how the interactions with his parents played out. The dance that Nobody continually got into was the 'repeated same question two-step.' His mother would ask a question, Nobody answered, a few moments later she would ask the same question again and Nobody would say, "I already answered it."

She would say, "Nobody why don't you just answer the question. I am your MOTHER if I want to ask the question again there is nothing wrong with that. Just do it for me?"

Then, when he refused to answer for the third time, the call out to his father occurred, "See how he is." Round and round they went. This was the catalyst for many more little quips that just seemed to put Nobody over the edge. Nobody refused to say, "*Yes mommy.*"

He knew he just had to keep his thoughts to himself, but when he was buying shoes at the Cole Haan outlet store, his mother asked if there was enough room for his toes and she watched him go through the shoe buying ritual we all undergo at some point in life. By all accounts a harmless question, to her it was innocent but to Nobody, in his mind he screamed, '*I AM AN ADULT. I CAN FIGURE IT OUT ON MY OWN.*'

The relief came when his father asked if Nobody would like to go to the candy store. He found pumpkin fudge 'to die for' at Wilbur's of Maine. The flavor just mesmerized his taste buds and for a moment eternal bliss was experienced. If this was Heaven, there was much to look forward to. They made their way to the shoppers at large, his mother, wife and son. The topic switched to the wonders of pumpkin fudge and samples were passed out. He just could not see his mother for who she was and vice versa. He had years of recovery under his belt, he prayed to God for help with his words, but the anger under the skin was applying so much pressure that just a scratch would let it out. This whole thing about honor thy parents tore him to pieces. He had such a hard time being around them. As the day wore on Nobody became more defensive.

He listened to her talk about how she takes care of the yard and how in the fall she is racking up bag after bag of leaves. All the work she does just to maintain the house. How she was perturbed that her neighbors would not rake their yards and how their leaves blew into her yard. It all had to be in perfect order. The house needed to be spotless and everything was in its proper place inside and out. Just like Nobody had done time and time again throughout his life.

If everything was in perfect order then it meant he was in order, but it was only a cover-up. As he listened to how everything should be from the opinion of his 'Madre,' he could easily see how he always needed approval to make sure he did the right thing.

He could see the pain on her face, but she was so disconnected emotionally from the pain that the anger kept it at bay and prevented any suggestions for healing. He would pray for her, but more than this Nobody was sad that his mother did not see what he saw.

Nobody was taken aback at the comments she made about people they knew and their children. Disregard would flick off her tongue about the decisions they had made and how their persona was a result of the children's behavior. It was like she took a picture and, from that one moment caught in time, a complete narrative was drawn from it. Without understanding the events that led up to it, his mother drew conclusions. The picture that was painted seemed to be always negative and in some way whatever happened, they deserved it or you should feel extremely sorry for them. Everything was negative except when the subject of his sister was raised.

When the issues of his sister would come up, everything was justified. Life was tough and they were doing the best that they could with what they had. Everything was understandable. She was living in Wisconsin, and they described their house and how they went and saw his new niece. Her description was that of a proud grandmother just like you should hear. As he sat in the car and was trying to piece it all together, yes his parents loved him in some way, but there was a big difference in the way it was delivered. He couldn't help but think how his sister went along for the ride with his parents all these years. It was telling how differently his parents saw each of their kids. She was the good one per se and he, well, he was the first born.

His parents seemed to understand his sister; they obviously couldn't or wouldn't understand Nobody. This is where the great divide existed.

Nobody wanted desperately for his mother to reconcile with her brother and address some of their issues face to face. His request, had always fallen on deaf ears.

Driving to their next destination, Nobody broached the topic again and, as always, was met with opposition. She would say that even in church they would not look at each other. However, it was always his uncle that didn't look at her. This prompted many other discussions about her sisters. As he listened he could see that a lot of her descriptions of these situations with her family would start in the middle of the story. When Nobody questioned if there was something that may have prompted these reactions by her family, she would say, "Why don't you just believe me and take up for your MOTHER? They are always trying to hurt me and all you do is believe everything they say."

Nobody silently shook his head and as he sat in the back seat of the car, his wife squeezed his hand. Nobody looked out the window trying to catch the countryside as a whole as the car sped along. He had heard about some of these incidents his mother was describing from his relatives the day before. Knowing that everyone plays a part in everything, he was amazed how differently she portrayed her siblings. There was a conspiracy and his mother couldn't understand why everyone wanted to gang up on her.

Remembering what he heard, he was dumbfounded how all the behaviors from her relatives came out of nowhere and not once did she see any part she played in it. Each incident started at the climax and it would appear that these were all random drive-by assaults on his mother who was only trying to be nice.

At one point during one of her stories as she was trying to convince Nobody that one of her sisters had screamed at her for no reason, Nobody asked a follow-up question. It was a small point that was left out which was that his mother had failed to mention her sister had come back and apologized. If this was true, why would his mother keep the issue alive? When this was brought to light, Nobody was chastised for putting his nose into things that did not concern him.

"YOU SHOULD BELIEVE ME AND NOT THEM! WE ARE THE ONES THAT LOVE YOU!"

What he had heard over and over again from his relatives was that, if you go along with everything she wants, then you are fine, but if you should happen to disagree with her, then all hell will break loose. He heard of her yelling and swearing, which Nobody understood all too well. There was a constant discussion about his family, but as he heard all of these things, the pieces started to paint a picture. Everyone in his family was at a point that they just couldn't understand why she acted this way. They were afraid that one day she would be alone and they all made every attempt to walk as lightly as they could around her.

One uncle had to tell his wife not to talk to her sister, Nobody's mother, because his uncle was tired of how she yelled and 'character-assassinated' his wife over the phone. Everyone described a time when his mother would not talk to them for a period of time and then come back into the scene as though nothing every happened. They all gathered that, once his mother felt they had been punished long enough, she would rekindle the relationship again. They would all try one more time and try to mend the wounds and continue on, but there was always someone she was mad at for some reason.

He heard how in public his mother was a charmer to people outside of her family. That she was pleasant and fun loving. His mother would say, "Just ask this person or that person they will tell you that I am a nice person."

She would relate how the people in the bank just loved her and would compliment her. That was all well and good but Nobody and his relatives knew that, if you angered her in any way, the wrath would soon follow.

Nobody had also picked up this trait of having someone in his life to direct his anger at. It could be work, a person at work, a person in the program, his ex-wife, or himself, but there was someone. It would be a while before he would get God's help to try and stop this cycle of behavior, but it was enough that he started to see it. This was why Al-Anon was so appealing to him, what he learned there addressed all the attitudes and behaviors that had separated him from a life he so desperately wanted.

When they finally made it to his parents' house and the moment Nobody crossed the threshold of the house, his whole demeanor collapsed around him. He felt smaller than everyone around him. It was as if a fog surrounded him. Everything looked larger or like looking in the side mirror of a car and the little note at the bottom that said, 'Objects are closer than they appear.' It was surreal. As he used the small bathroom under the stairs, containing only a commode and, if you were tall, your knees would hit the door if sitting upon the throne. The ceiling had an incline to match the grade of the stairs, and at 5'8"even he could barely stand in it. Nobody remembered how, as a teenager, he would come in here to smoke pot and blow smoke out the vent. Today he sought relief from God to help him maintain a sense of good will in a house that chilled his bones.

It was like a cloud enshrouded him. He felt as though he was going through the motions until he was brought back to reality when his mother told his wife that she had put some trash in the wrong trash can. It had nothing to do with recycling. He walked out in the back yard and saw the wood pile and reminisced of the days he would occupy himself and chop wood with an axe. That was such a relaxing time. Funny he always seemed to remember times of peace, isolated and away from everyone, whether it was in the toilet under the stairs, chopping wood, doing drugs, even by himself, all designed to escape the reality he was presented.

This was his family. Good, bad or indifferent this was where God had wanted him. Nobody wanted so desperately for his parents to see life differently. He wanted them to know God as he was learning about God, instead of some far away being. In his heart of hearts, he loved his parents but there was a lot of hurt here. A lot of history that seemed hard to ignore and just like his mother, he too was trying to drive a point home to her.

Her response to him was that he did not live there and anything that pertained to the family at large was none of his business. His intentions were good, but not for an audience that was not willing to change. She was justified in her anger and she said it and it was up to everyone else to get their act together before she would be OK with them.

Then it hit him. This was how he had thought about God. Nobody had once believed that he had to get his life in order first, then be worthy of God's love. He had to be a good boy before he drew the accolades from his mother growing up and if he wasn't good then love was withheld. It was a light bulb moment. He was still walking around still trying to get everyone's approval for everything he did, by running the narrative of all his accomplishments just to be able to hear, "Good job." His self-worth was dependent on man and not God even after all these years. When he could not feel God in his life he went to those around him for soothing.

When the week had past and they were finally on the way to the airport, he felt that 'cloud covering' leave that had surrounded him while in their presence, as they crossed the town boundary. He had learned a lot of things about himself and saw how many things he needed to work on.

His parents were his parents and they might never change or change into the parents he wanted. Nobody felt they were embarrassed because of him and they put up with him because he was their son but that was the extent of it. He still held out hope that they might acknowledge that they were proud of him in the manner he saw they held for his sister. Maybe one day, but for right now, he would have to rely on God as best as he could. No, he decided, he would not be obsessed with their approval as his final goal in life.

Episode 57

Midnight Train to Georgia

Traveling to the various sales offices within his region was part of his job. Covering the tri-state area of Georgia, South Carolina and North Carolina, Nobody spent a lot of time on the road. When he was not working, Nobody and his *Wife with the Armband Tattoo* enjoyed riding up to the foothills of Greenville, South Carolina on weekends to go day hiking and just thunder along the roads. The girls were still gone and there was no contact except the occasional phone calls his wife placed. His son had gone back to Arizona and the dog days of summer were still hanging around, but with football season fast approaching, they too would soon be behind them.

He asked his wife if she would like to move to Greenville. Her brother and mother lived there and they would be closer to the mountains they enjoyed so much. As far as work was concerned it was actually a better location for his travels and made for a central location. A lot of his time was spent behind a windshield and finding a way to make all his drives relatively the same distance seemed like a good plan. Much to his surprise she said yes.

Change is always good. When Nobody's mind gets idle and a routine sets in, boredom soon follows. Idle time tends to get Nobody in trouble. It was either from all the stimulants he did previously or his natural propensity for not being able to sit still. It's like watching a jack-in-the-box wind up and pop the lid on its own, because it was tired of waiting for someone to wind it up. He has to be doing, thinking, contemplating, or planning something. In proper balance, this is a desirable trait but when a person cannot find the time to sit still and just be, it raises issues when trying to hear the voice of God. Without truly waiting and listening we all tend to hear the first word and set off running without hearing the rest of the statement.

A perfect illustration is how David knew in his heart of hearts that he must get the Ark of the Covenant back to Jerusalem from the Philistines. In his haste, he ordered ordinary men to get the Ark instead of the Levite Priests. In the glory of God, everyone did as they were told and put it on a cart and off they went. They had some fan fare, but since they did not follow the custom and had ordinary men move it, one of these men was struck by God when he placed his hand on the Ark itself instead of the cart. Due to the death of that person, the Ark stayed in that location for three months until David realized how he must transport it back to Jerusalem. David had good intentions but in his haste, missed 'the how,' that had been passed down from generation to generation on how they were suppose to properly move the Ark from place to place.

In this busy world, with all the technology, when the God of Abraham wants to herald the message, the god of noise tries to subdue it. If one tries to listen it can be heard, but dedication to listening is an art one must learn over time. It was becoming a habit that whenever a major decision needed to be made, Nobody did pray. As we have learned previously, those prayers were always geared towards asking for a blessing on his plan, not an uncommon trait from those seeking God. We all want our prayers answered and this should be the proof that God is there. That is only half of the story though, and many expect that if we acknowledge His existence that should be enough. But, there is another side of the equation one must look for and that is the God side. What we need to understand is that God answers the prayers the way of his choosing and not always the way of our choosing. If you truly want to live God's will in your life, you need to come to grips with the fact that the answers do not always come in the form you'd expect them.

Somehow Nobody heard the word "*move*" in his mind and he went for it. Now, like most people when we make a decision, we want a plan, a vision and a direction. Nobody thought he had all these. So while in Atlanta at a

Braves game with his Senior VP and few of the regional sales managers, Nobody told his VP that he was planning on moving to Greenville and went on to describe how it would be beneficial to the company if he was more centrally located.

After a moment of pause the VP said, "I think that is a great idea, but I have a better offer. "If you move to Greenville, you pay for it. If you move to Atlanta, I pay for it."

Remember the saying to determine if you were walking out of the will of God in your life, it can be summed up in this simple phrase.

If it is God's will He'll pay for it and if it is your will you'll pay for it.

Even with the story of David it could be illustrated in the same manner. When David used the Levites, God helped them carry the Ark. God paid for it without incident as the Ark was returned to the Holy City. When David did it his way, he paid for it with someone's life.

Many times in life people pray to God for guidance. Their intentions are good, but that's the end of it, they pray and wait. They may even hear what they are supposed to do, but something inside them will prevent them from comprehending what they hear. It still comes down to our will versus God's will. We pray very hard, we look to the Heavens and beg for the answer. Since many of us try to fit God in our own 'life size' box, when we do hear an answer, many times, just like Nobody on numerous occasions, the thought that comes to mind is pushed aside only to say to oneself, *"That's crazy.*

This has to be the most frustrating thing about walking with God as the pathfinder. We continually want to see what He sees in the path ahead. We are still just kids in the car yelling, "Are we there yet?" and trying to get ahead of Him, calling out, "Let me see, let me see."

God is bigger than that and we just can't see past him. He did not give us that ability, but as men on this Earth trying to plan and find the path of least resistance, we try to ensure safe travels throughout life. We tend to look to the one thing we can grasp when something goes amiss—people, governments, insurance policies, retirement funds, social security, health insurance, jobs, cars, cell phones, and even churches through their services. We try to find comfort in something we can fall back on. The majority of the time we fall back on the promises made to us by men, in whatever shape they are. Then, when those promises are not fulfilled by man and we cry out against the injustice in the world for the broken promises, we blame God for our faith in men and the society we live in.

When turning to God, many are told that He would gently guide us as a tour guide would on an African safari. All people riding through life would be in the safety of a land rover while sitting in amazement at the wonders and beauty of the African plains. The ferocity of this small microcosm can make one shiver in awe. We are glued to the window as the power of nature demonstrated before us unfolds. When our bellies are full of the wonders of the plains, we sit back and relax in the comfort of our chosen surroundings and discuss it over dinner, and retire for the night dreaming of the wild adventure we endured from the safety of the vehicle.

No! God has placed us in the middle of the jungle. He tells us to have faith in Him through Jesus and follow Him on through to the other side. He says *trust* through every obstacle or crisis you may encounter along the way. If you walk behind Him He will lead you to the safety of His understanding where you can enjoy and relish the wonderful jungle called *life*. The trick is to stay on that path and when your path ends, He will turn and catch you before you fall.

Many of us want to check behind every bush or tree to see if there is another path that will lead us out of the jungle more quickly and/or offer a more beautiful alternative. We look for new places where we can sit and enjoy all that we see around us in the safety of our own barriers and of our own choosing. God has continued forward but you are moving in another direction, thanking God for bringing you this far as you blaze your own path in uncharted territory. We get side-tracked and, what was once beautiful somehow turns dark. We become lost. We yell, "God, where are You?"

The only problem is that when God turns around, you are not there. He calls out your name and, depending how far off the path you are or whatever pit you may have fallen down into on your quest for something more appealing, you may not hear His voice guiding you back to Him.

Then we cry, "God how could you let this happen, where are you?"

And, He says, "I never changed course."

The path was set and Atlanta was the destination. The mountains they enjoyed would still be close and the great adventure on the open safari was underway with God as their guide. Nobody had heard the word "move" and he acted on it. The vision he had was not the one he ended up with but they knew it was where they were supposed to go. They just acted on it and followed God and did not force a solution of their choosing and God paid for it. His wife called the girls to let them know of her intentions. The youngest daughter asked how she could do this? This had an effect on his wife but she had to move on and not let time stand still waiting for them to come home. She was tired of going to the mall, hoping to get a glimpse of them by some chance. Staying around hoping they would want to come back home tore her up inside and, even by the measures of the secular psychology; the change would do her good.

On November 3, 2000, they rolled into the northern *'burbs'* of Atlanta. Their support system was now three and half hours away. For the first time in Nobody's life, he would have to rely upon someone: in this instance it was his wife. She, in turn, would rely upon him. And, they were to do it in a land that was new to both. To borrow a scene from the Bible, they had left their Garden of Eden and must now face whatever was in front of them.

Prior to their departure, they were thrown a 'going away' party. It had been peppered with very touching moments for both of them. His sponsor over the years - a man of few words and someone who had been with him throughout the good and bad - had presented a gift. It was a small desk picture with the word "Risk" on it and the picture itself had a sloop with three masts venturing out from beyond a high walled outlet to the sea with the following caption.

"A Ship is safe in a harbor, but that's not what a ship was built for." (1)

At that moment, Nobody knew that his time had come. At thirty-six years old, ten years under his belt in the twelve step recovery - including three years or so of being in Al-Anon - he was no longer the prodigal son going out to spend his fortune. No, he was going out to find it.

As he looked at the picture with a tear in his eye, he realized that the man who had helped guide him to this point with grace, love and under-standing, had blessed him to move on. This was a tradition seen throughout the Bible, but trivialized in the modern western world. Neither of them understood the true significance of the act, but were assured that God has a way of getting His message out to those whom He is calling. God calls all of us; are we willing to listen and act?

As with every walk with God, there are highs and lows. Days you feel God's hand on your shoulder and other days gripped with absolute bitter cold of isolation wrapped with fear. As you look around for God, you embrace yourself with whatever skills you have to stay warm. Those with a shaky foundation use old tricks to sooth themselves, commonly known as the seven deadly sins. Looking for God all around in desolate open frozen tundra and believing He is not there only means He is not in your field of vision and your lack of patience is changing your outlook. He just might be behind you all the time, allowing you the dignity to walk in faith with the struggles that come with that.

It is in these times that God can use this semblance of separation not to test you - though many think life is nothing but a test - but grow you up and learn the art of resourcefulness as we all try to gain some form of identity in this world. It is then, where the 'rubber meets the road' that we test ourselves unwittingly as we battle with our thoughts and motives.

Nobody and his wife got settled and immediately found meetings to attend and very quickly they found themselves being introduced to new friends. They found a Saturday night couples meeting and a routine was beginning to take hold.

The craftiness of delusion is that while you think because you are doing one good deed and all is well, other areas of your life might be exposed that will affect other areas of your life that we have not comprehended yet.

Nobody's *Wife with the Armband Tattoo's* attitude towards him was getting increasingly sharp. She was dealing with many issues; separation from her kids and her own childhood wounds were starting to surface now that she was in a new place. The once comfortable surroundings could not be used to suppress the pain from her past. As her feelings around these issues were being brought to the surface, it's quite understandable that Nobody might be a focus of an increased scrutiny.

One of the areas that was under constant debate was what Nobody did at work. She couldn't understand that in a sales environment, a manager had to go on sale calls with sales reps and lunch was part of the equation. The problem was that sometime these lunches involved going out with a female. The debate raged on with neither of them giving in.

"No, you go ahead and eat lunch without me; I'll wait for you in your car until you are done to make my wife happy." said Nobody in his head as he would argue with his wife.

When it came to sex, Nobody's drive seemed to take a dive, in a way. He wanted more from his wife in this area to increase his level of excitement. What did not help was the increasing available content on the internet. Nobody secretly fed his appetite for sex while waiting for his wife to come home from work, when she went out to run errands, or when he was on the road. It was also triggered when she was mad at him and things were rocky and that silent cold chill ran through the house.

In Nobody's mind, the lie was that it helped with the anxiety he felt. As time progressed, in the discussion of their sex-life, they had even made a purchase that would help them along to meet the pleasure he thought they were both looking for. With the order came a short video montage of X-rated film excerpts that Nobody insisted they watch together during those times they came together as husband and wife. He also watched alone as well, always feeding that anxiety but always in secret. He enjoyed it but was ashamed at the same time. Once his appetite was satisfied, and guilt set in, he would pray to God for help only to fail again and again.

Being surrounded by a culture that says it is OK, over time can lessens one's resolve to maintain abstinence from such sources. Being in AA or church, does not mean that you are surrounded by holy people that have the same spiritual desires that you might have. You are surrounded by people who need not do a lot of things that are harmful. It is when you try to gain something from the wrong source, like going to the hardware store for a loaf of bread, that one can mix values and be confused of what a true life dedicated to God can mean. The steps and religious practices can be spiritual in nature, but anyone can fit their lifestyle into a faith of their choosing and remain spiritual. If one begins to allow destructive behavior in one's life and then rationalize it away, by saying as long as I am not drinking, it is OK. While there is some truth to that, it is only one piece to a puzzle. Anyone can easily view pornography in a religious manner and pray to God thinking all is well.

Many famous people have fallen due to one area in their lives that they did not attend to while maintaining a stellar community presence. It does not make them bad people or their behavior as a reason to discredit God even if that person was a preacher, it only means that we are all human and susceptible to all sorts of influences. Without the right focus, everyone can be caught in the *snare*.

The anti-God crowd says that Christians should not force their morality on them, especially if they cannot live up to their own standards. So while the anti-God crowd tries to find incidents that prove their case as to why Christians are nothing but hypocrites and should not be listened too, they continue to prove, through the actions of others, why God is not real or religion should not be followed. They miss the point with these incidents. God is in the resurrection business and while the world may focus on the sin, God focuses on the person and how to bring him back to life in spite of his sin. Not what the world tries to do by crushing them out of existence and hoping they are ruined forever because of it.

However, if all of this was OK as the culture says it is, why do so many people hide their behavior and feel ashamed for it when they are by themselves. Could it be that deep down inside they know that this was not how God intended sex to be viewed - as an animal instinct that should be satisfied at all cost?

Nobody was introduced to pornography early in his life and now trying to use it as a way to spice up their marriage during their intimate moments and attempted to get buy in from his wife. In some sort of way if she would find it acceptable, then this might just be the rationalization he was looking for. The problem was Nobody always hid his behavior. On the outside it was "harmless" by the world's standards, but it was used by Nobody to calm his anxiety and feed his nature in moments of boredom, or better yet, when he was alone with himself and his thoughts. This was a new drug that had gained a hold over him.

Nobody, at a certain level, hid this from his wife. When she would return home, he was always paranoid. Did he remember to hide his tracks? Will she see that something is wrong with his behavior or ask him any questions? He will have to be more loving and attentive so that she will not think anything is wrong. If there is something wrong with her mood, Nobody would ask if anything was wrong with the intent to see if he was in trouble, not necessarily to give her support because he had compassion for her.

This was the cycle he was in and for many years it had crept in ever so slowly. What used to be magazines his second wife had allowed him to purchase, he hid his true behavior under the cloak of secrecy to a new secret life of sexual 'quick hits' with the Internet. He never spent any money on the secret life to make sure he would not get found out but, in the shadows, he was surfing free sites, ever watching and looking out behind his shoulder.

The tragedy was that when he walked into any room whether at work or home, the thoughts that always plagued his mind was that he was a 'sick-o' and a 'pervert.' If the people he came in contact with only knew how demented he was, he would be cast out. If his wife ever found out, he could not stand there and take in the evil gaze he was sure to see from her. He would rather be dead then endure that look. Some days he just wished he would get caught so the lid could be blown off. Instead he worked harder and did more things in an effort to hide.

The *Wife with the Armband Tattoo* felt and requested repeatedly the need to feel a bond with Nobody. As his wife, she was clamoring for more attention while Nobody was working and satisfying his own needs. Whether the hobbies were darts, the motorcycles, the next meeting, the next movie or the next project their time was filled with stuff to do.

He worked all week in a stressful sales environment. His wife complained that they were just roommates. Nobody did not know how to address this and felt trapped. He could not be her *everything* and he did not know what to be. He had run out of ideas to keep her happy and he himself could not reach inside to find out why he could not respond to her. He had so much to say to her about how he truly felt, but as the words flew by, he could not put them in any order and his lack of response drove her anger into deeper depths.

This anger towards each other had reached new heights and it was readily seen when they went to the couples meeting on Saturday nights. That was the one thing they did not give up. Being around the program, they both knew and had developed the habit to show up even if the world was falling in around them.

After the meetings everyone went out to eat and usually the husbands huddled at one of the tables and the wives at the other. Nobody was drawn to one tall bald headed 'dude' who wore a bandana most of the time. He was also a member of a local United Methodist Church. He was a very imposing character with a soft demeanor. Over time, they started talking and gradually got to know each other better. There was another couple who attended that seemed to have been through quite a bit in their marriage and Nobody asked them if they would talk to them. There was no doubt that their marriage was in trouble, what could it hurt? Nobody didn't want this marriage to end up like his others. It was tough and without either one of them being totally honest, the root cause could not be easily ascertained.

So as the laundry list of crap was thrown about the living room at this couple's home, they both went back and forth with each other in the presence of this gracious pair. The husband looked at The *Wife with the Armband Tattoo* and at one point said to her, "You are not talking about what you are talking about. This is not about Nobody is it?"

She said, "No." Over the course of a few minutes, a barrage of pain crept out from inside of his wife and she discussed some of the issues that 'recovery' was bringing to the surface. Relief swept over Nobody's face, knowing that it wasn't completely his fault and, at this point, that was all that mattered. He just needed some air.

When they moved to Atlanta, attending church was not on anyone's agenda. On Sunday mornings, Nobody attended a men's AA meeting, where he got his dose of 'God inspired' conversation, however seemingly from the Good Orderly Direction department and Nobody was satisfied with that.

When Spring rolled around, Nobody decided that he would paint his house himself to save the money, learning the hard way that these projects might take a bit longer than anticipated. He was into week four of a planned one week vacation project, on his ladder in the front of his house, his neighbor walked by and asked when he thought he would be done. Nobody laughed and said that when he was done, the first weekend free, he would surely go hiking to make up for lost time. Not losing an opportunity, his neighbor said he enjoyed hiking as well and was looking for a partner he could do the Appalachian Trail with. This wasn't day hiking, this was all out backpacking and the wheels were turning.

The deal with hiking was something he and his wife enjoyed together. It was day hiking so at the end of the day you end up in a bed and have the luxury of a normal bathroom. Backpacking was a completely different sport - you stayed out in the woods, slept on the ground and crapped behind a tree.

His wife quickly added this all up and said, "If you go, you're going without me."

"OK." Nobody said.

Nobody was always afraid to do things by himself even if it meant to go away and do something with other people. A night with the guys was almost unheard of. The fear of losing something within the relationship or to have the other person think you did not love them had cultivated a smothering effect on all his relationships.

His wife, on the other hand actually encouraged him and with the level of trust he had with her, Nobody felt he could venture out and try things she did not particularly care to share in. This seemed to be one of those things he could spread his wings and take off with.

Additionally, growing up, Nobody would walk in the woods to get away to sooth his soul as a child and even in the Army, he would go into the woods for a respite. To Nobody, he could enjoy nature and commune with his Maker.

As he planned his first adventure, gear needed to be bought and REI was just the place. With a list in hand and credit card to boot, Nobody hit the $2000 range in short order. There was the backpack, the rain cover for the backpack, trekking poles, stove, sleeping bag, hiking clothes, smart wool socks, water filter, the right tent, pans for cooking, the head lamp, the sleeping pad, and water containers. When all this stuff couldn't fit in the backpack, he purchased an additional storage compartment that latched on quite easily. This went on for a month and his wife watched and finally asking when the madness would stop.

Nobody would say, "Soon" and continued the quest for hiking equipment perfection and the proper method in which to pack all the gear he had - over and over again.

What was funny, as most hikers learn when the big day finally came and he and his neighbor were at the trailhead, he took Nobody's pack and emptied it in the back of the truck and proceeded to sort his gear.

"You don't need this, or this, or this, or this and you definitely don't need this" his neighbor said with a grin on his face.

"All that planning and money and now you say I don't need this."

"You'll see," he said.

As he donned his pack and began to proceed up the mountain with pep in his step and adventure on his mind, he heard the words, "Move'm out." After fifteen minutes, he wondered if he had made the right choice and was wondering how he would make it one mile to the campsite let alone seventeen more over the course of the next two days.

The pack was below his rear quarter, it was pretty heavy, he was leaning forward and sweat was dripping from his face. With his coffee pot, couple of books, twice as much water than required and other items he swore he needed, he would not let on that he wasn't sure if he could make it. He just kept moving.

Like a walk with God, at first we are all excited of the great adventure. Some of us come with Bible in hand and riding a pink cloud, only to find that, once you are on the path, all that you had envisioned isn't what you had expected. You soon realize that if you go it alone you might not continue. You need friends with you to help sort your pack so you don't have to carry such a heavy load and this trip is always better done with someone who has been there before.

Before settling in, Nobody learned that his neighbor attended the same United Methodist Church some of the folks from the Saturday night group attended as well.

"These folks are popping up everywhere," Nobody thought to himself.

Laying in his sleeping bag, Nobody, who was restless and heard every noise imaginable, was fearful and excited all in one. There was a little mouse that tried to scratch his way in all night right next to his head and the rustling of leaves as the wind blew through. The distant call of the owls, reminded Nobody that on the other side of this piece of fabric was a world that he would have to do more than just enjoy. He would have to walk through it and he was up for the challenge.

As morning broke and everything was packed, his neighbor readjusted Nobody's pack so it rode higher in the small of his back. The weight seemed to be cut in half, as they looked around to see if they had forgotten anything. They started walking. One foot in front of the other as Nobody took in a deep breath and absorbed the beauty of the forest.

Midway through the day, they crossed the Georgia line into North Carolina just south of Bly Gap. There was a small mud puddle of water and as they looked at the map, it seemed as though there might be a better water source just up the path, so they blew by. Within ten minutes, and steadily going up, it was obvious that that was the water source they needed so they dumped their packs and returned the way they came to fill up.

Laughing at themselves for not believing what they saw as a water source. It just proved that you might just want to look with your eyes and not your brain, sometimes. The map said there was water further up the trail, but their eyes saw water and ignored it thinking it would be better if they pressed through.

Funny, it seems you always want something better than what you have right in front of you. They retraced their steps, which took about twenty minutes, on the path already traveled. His neighbor, who was ahead of him by about twenty yards, all of a sudden yelled out and a rattlesnake, was heard.

Within the course of twenty minutes, on a portion of the path they had already traveled, a timber rattler had ventured on the path. In all this beauty and wonderment, there was still danger lurking in God's world, reminding them they still needed to pay attention.

Similar to everyday life, which we seem to understand because we walk the same path every day, if we are not careful, we just might step into something if we're not paying attention. Our two heroes looked upon the snake with awe. It was beautiful in a dangerous sort of way knowing that it is best to steer clear of the snake but still drawn to it.

As his neighbor, was trying to prompt the snake with his trekking pole, Nobody urged his partner, "Hey, just leave it alone."

Nobody had always loved snakes, but he knew this one had better be left alone. His partner agreed and they watched it travel back into the thicket.

Rattlesnakes come in different shapes and sizes. Some are more dangerous than others, but they all bite if given the chance. Warning someone to keep away from a poisonous snake or something that might not be good for them, is advice many take and given the situation, many adhere too. But when the snake takes the form of a morality issue where the wisdom is pursuing a certain behavior is not altogether wise. Others will say, "I know what I am doing, leave me alone and keep your morality to yourself."

Even in the extreme, John the Baptist was eventually killed because he confronted Herod about sleeping with his brother's wife. Everyone knows that Herod's behavior was not wise, but as more and more people are told and start believing they can have all they deserve, what was once a sin that people did in secret is now just a way of life. Maybe, just maybe, they rationalize God and the church had it all wrong. That is why all these little issues that seem harmless and "hurt no one" are sometimes a slow acting poison that decays the soul. After a while, when you tell someone you don't have to warn me of the snake, people will stop announcing the danger and one day when no one is around, you will end up bit.

We still need people along the way to tell us to steer clear of danger when spotted and it doesn't matter who sounds the alarm. Occasionally, it can be the babe in the woods and not the experienced hiker that can see the forest through the trees.

It wasn't long after the first hike that Nobody totally jumped in with both feet. He started swapping out gear, which was lighter. He planned weekend hikes with co-workers and his goal was to cover the same ground on the Appalachian Trail his neighbor had already covered. That way, they could move north together on the trail in unison.

Episode 58

In Your Letter

As Nobody spent time with all of his new friends, his marriage was slowly suffering. Nobody was completely obsessed with backpacking and the little fun he and his wife had enjoyed together day hiking was now a thing of the past. They went to the movies, out to eat and ran little errand things together. In the middle of all this marriage was a big chasm. Nobody gauged the health of the marriage by what the *Wife with the Armband Tattoo* was or was not doing or saying. Was she not talking about things that bothered her - check; were they still having sex - check; if she hadn't found out about the things he was doing in secret - check. Nobody would run down this list every day in his mind. If she is not talking about anything, then everything must be good. Problem solved.

However, that was Nobody's limited world. His wife was going through her issues and being more of a loner, she spent more time by herself. By her very nature she was not a socialite with the girls. Nobody had no idea what she did when he was hiking over the weekend but he did trust her and didn't give it a second thought. While this was certainly a new attitude he was in possession of, it had its draw backs. Since he did not care what she did, when he burst through the door speaking of his grand hiking adventures, he acted like the child coming home from camp telling his folks all that happened. It never dawned on him that she too may have had a grand adventure. Still living in a self absorbed world, it was all about him.

The *Wife with the Armband Tattoo* would complain that he did not care and that when he came through the door, the first thing he did wasn't to come over and kiss her and say 'hello,' it was to talk about himself.

She complained about the hiking money. From Nobody's point of view, he didn't golf and wasn't dropping fifty to seventy-five bucks a shot. Once he got all of his hiking gear straightened out it was all reusable. Plus, once he managed to hike the same portion of the Appalachian Trail his neighbor had already hiked, he wouldn't go out as much, which was about a couple of times a month during this time period.

Though he knew it was true, he would just have to remember to kiss her once he came through the door. It has been said that the hardest part of flying is the landing and taking off.

Nobody needed to learn how to land from one of his adventures, but he also had a hard time taking off as well. Let us remember that if someone isn't doing anything wrong and it doesn't hurt anyone, then it must be that there's probably nothing wrong with it, so it would seem. One of the hardest parts of Nobody's leaving the house for an extended period of time, was the continuing nagging thought that he may have left clues behind that his wife would know he had been viewing porn.

As Nobody would drive away, he would sometimes turn around to go back to the computer to make sure the history was cleaned in the browser. He would break out in a cold sweat thinking that some virus might be lodged in the computer from a questionable site he might have visited. That would surely spawn a question. Even worse, he may have left the computer on and all she would have to do is hit the back button and behold his *sin* on display.

Driving away, he would be in absolute fear and terror over this. Playing out all the possibilities in his head, hoping that when he did call her on the phone, to check in, the tone in her voice would reassure him his tracks had been covered well. What would he walk into when he got home, how would she respond if she did not let on that she knew over the phone. Why did he have to even look just one more time before he left? There were many times going through this ritual that he had wished he would just get caught so he wouldn't have to hide anymore, as previously stated.

Her job was pretty tough, working for a tile company that was family run. The owner cut corners where they could on their jobs and the whole family dynamics with the wife, father, son, daughter in-law were all center stage. It would be safe to say that she had to stay out of the line of fire, she was treated like family but that is not saying a whole bunch. So with her daily perils, she needed to dodge carefully, it wasn't hard for her to look at Nobody's actions and pick out things that bothered her.

One afternoon as he had just returned from home with more items from REI, she looked at him and said, "Are you all done buying gear?"

"As a matter of fact I am." He exclaimed.

It wasn't a week after this little exchange, that Nobody realized he wanted *'one more* thing.' He had always enjoyed maps and he had purchased map software to make his own maps. Everyone wants to know where they are and Nobody wasn't any different. On the trail backpacking, he liked to know where he was. He had his maps, but he wanted to know where he was as well as where he was going.

Similar to all of his relationships, he always asked poignant questions to take a reading of his standing at any given time. He did not trust his own instincts in this regard. If things did not feel right it had to be something he did. He would always say, I love you to his wife to hear it back or ask his boss if he was doing OK. Life for Nobody was about living in fear. Nobody needed the affirmation of those around him to settle his spirit. If he was able to calm himself, then he could continue on.

This sort of behavior was a constant force in his life and in a way faithless. It was one of those techniques he learned as a child that never left him into adulthood. Now, just like with his relationships, Nobody needed to know where he was in the woods and that could only be accomplished with a GPS. For whatever reason, Nobody needed to understand exactly where he stood in all of life's surroundings.

As he broached the subject about the GPS, he was quickly rejected by his wife. The *Wife with the Armband* Tattoo succinctly reminded him that he said he was finished and held him to it. This infuriated Nobody that he had been caught in his own trap.

Nobody continued going to his Sunday morning AA meeting and his wife started going to the United Methodist Church that his neighbor attended. It hadn't been a month when the *Wife with the Armband Tattoo* asked if he would go with her at least every other Sunday.

Being a wonderful husband and still wanting his GPS, maybe if he went he just might get some cover and be able to buy this thing and so he agreed and went to church with her.

It had been a while since he set foot in a church. When he walked into the lobby he saw his big bald friend, Mr. Clean, from the Saturday night meeting. He got the proverbial hug and greeting. Mr. Clean told Nobody that he would like the pastor since the pastor was like them and had ventured into the rooms of AA.

Another hook that had been laid, he now couldn't use the excuse that the preacher was out of touch if he didn't like what he heard. Still, for whatever reason, he had a chill run through him. It was like everyone could see everything bad about him. He was bound and determined not to conform so he had shown up in shorts and a polo, but there were others in the same attire. The music was contemporary and they had a real band and for all that it was worth, the sermon was pretty good and he had survived.

He always cringed when the name Jesus Christ was spoken, instead he prayed to God fervently. Nobody was a *'spiritual'* guy, who just wanted to be blessed by God for all the things he was doing while he honored God with his thoughts. There are a lot of people in this world that have bought into this sort of faith. Thinking their way through and not actually walking through it. This went on for a couple of months, and he was still bent out of shape over the stupid GPS. He couldn't believe she still held on to this. He was a grown man and bringing in a paycheck! He felt like a kid and 'wifey' was the parent. He just couldn't figure out a way to get this GPS, until one day he was looking over the internet and found a hiking watch complete with compass, altimeter, thermometer and every other little gizmo except a GPS in it. But hey, it was close enough for government work.

As his plan was being laid out, he slowly dropped hints that he needed a new watch at perfectly timed moments. He said it would be something he could wear hiking not to damage his normal watch. He was keeping his eye on EBay, her favorite shopping venue, ready to pounce. He finally got her to buy in it. When the watch was at a price that sort of fit into his budget of $130, he bought it under her account. Now if Nobody wasn't hiding anything, like a small boy who was caught with his hand in the cookie jar, it should have been the end of it. However, after he purchased it, he deleted the listing from her list of purchases.

He kept his mouth shut and acted as though nothing was wrong. Out of site out of mind was his motto, until the next weekend when his buddy came over to help him change out the valve cover gasket on his truck. As they were yucking it up, his wife came outside and asked if she could speak to Nobody for a second.

"No problem, Babe."

"How come the watch is not on my list of items bought?"

"I took it off the list."

"Why would you do that and how much was it?"

"It was $128."

"What kind of watch is this?"

"Just something I can wear when hiking or bounce around in."

She left the two alone and went back into the house. "Close call," he said to his friend.

He jokingly cast aside his wife's questions in front of his friend only to have her return fifteen minutes later with a look that could have fried an egg in its shell instantaneously.

"Excuse me, I'll be right back" as he followed her into the house.

"I know what you did now. I can't believe you lied to me. What a fool I have been, to be duped into thinking that it was a 'bang around' watch."

After thirty seconds of her talking, and the anxiety level starting to reach a fever pitch from within the house, Nobody casually strolled back outside and told his buddy that it was probably a good idea for him to leave.

When he left, Nobody chimed in and started telling her that she was not his mother and the afternoon went downhill from there. That night they still attended the couples meeting, but the air could be cut with a knife and Nobody asked the husband of the couple, who saw them previously, if they could talk in the morning. He was not going to church with her, that was a given, and he agreed.

Nobody met the man at a Huddle House. Nobody spewed how aghast he was about his wife's behavior as he laid out his case in front of his de facto sponsor for the morning. Silently waiting for Nobody to finish pleading his case as though preparing for trial, once he made his closing argument, his de facto sponsor simply looked at Nobody and said, "You are wrong."

"What?"

"You are right about the parent child thing, but as far as the watch goes, you are wrong. You manipulated the situation and got caught. As a matter of fact you need to apologize."

The feeling inside of Nobody was one of absolute rage. *'He was wrong!!! He was a grown man, how dare she say what he could or could not buy. He was responsible, he brought in most of the money, and he was the only one trying to save for retirement.'*

The de facto sponsor continued to talk about how, in his marriage, they share only one bank account. There was no way they would even do that, Nobody explained. His wife had spoken about how in the past bank accounts had been cleared out by a former husband and Nobody, well he needed control as well. He would offer it up as a suggestion, which he knew she would refuse. Thinking about what was said, he couldn't grasp the fact that in this argument there were parts he was right and wrong. His whole life he had to be right, to prove his case.

Then, the de facto sponsor said that he needed to keep his word and not buy the GPS. This was like being told he could not eat a cookie that was on a plate right in front of him. I just need one more cookie and I will be OK after that.

Nobody was told he needed to apologize to his wife for his part and it would be best to write it all down. In the heat of the moment when the emotions are high, a man will lose his way in discussion with a female, he was told. While logically, it might all be very clear in Nobody's mind, once emotion and feelings were part of the discussion all bets were off.

The fact was that at 10:30 AM, while his wife was at church and he was in a Huddle House, Nobody was being crushed. Not into submission, but the tough veneer that he wore proudly. It wasn't a preacher telling him he needed to mend his ways or go to Hell, it was just another Joe, who also believed in God and was able to deliver another message to Nobody in a manner he could hear.

'Why do these messages always come in the form of a 2 x 4?'

Driving home with a multitude of feelings: remorse, anger, fear, and dread, Nobody decided he would write this stupid note to her and do what he was told.

Sitting in a rocker, what he thought would be bullet points, turned out to be a letter to his wife. As the words moved from pen to paper he couldn't believe how clear it all became and his anxiety started to subside. As he wrote down his thoughts, a deep feeling hit his gut that was a combination of hurt and pain so deep that it was like something was buried in his chest somewhere past his heart and was being uncovered.

When she returned home, she asked how his breakfast went and he said "fine." He asked her if they could sit down in an hour to go over something. The anger was still in the air between the two of them, and though the words were few, they were still amicable.

Tending to minor chores, prior to this sit down, through clenched teeth, Nobody prayed, "God's words not mine."

He still held on to that prayer his DC sponsor gave him many years ago. He went and sat down in the living room. This was a "seat belt moment." A place you are not comfortable in, you want to leave and, last but not least, listen to what someone might want to say to you. More often than not, you might have to change and he never knew where the conversation would lead. Without these moments, change will never occur in a marriage.

As she sat down, Nobody rocked almost aggressively in his favorite glide rocker. He had paper in hand. She sat on the couch and only looked at him. He started reading and as he was describing how he felt about the issue over the watch, the parent child relationship they had, and apologizing for his sneaky behavior, the tears started to fall and emotion erupted out of his chest. All this emotion was bellowing out as he continued to read. He felt like a complete baby, a total 'wuss' and surely not a man she wants to be married to. It was like a waterfall pumping water out of his chest, a feeling he hadn't felt since he was in treatment in El Paso. He was completely vulnerable in front of his wife. He looked up once he finished reading; she was just sitting there with no emotion. Nobody sat there with nothing else to say. It was all right there. Their relationship was in trouble, he was out of ideas and all he had was his honesty about the situation, but they had a chance and then real conversation began.

Instead of a joint bank account they agreed that any purchases over a hundred dollars needed the other's permission. She asked if he would go to counseling and he cringed. It is funny how loud a house can be when there is so much anger in the atmosphere, but now as they were sitting there, the house was in a state of utter calm, you could hear your own heartbeat. They seemed sheltered from the outside noise. Nothing could be heard but their own breathing. It was as if they were in a time capsule and time stood still all around them.

A few days later the watch arrived. To put this watch in perspective, as Nobody opened the box, he swallowed whatever moisture was in his mouth. This watch was a honking monster. It was Army green with a huge face outlined in a black compass dial, three quarters of inch thick, with some orange lettering and a big orange button to light the dial. Not your everyday watch to bounce around with. When he put it on to see how it would look, it was almost too big for his arm even just for hiking. There was no way this issue could have been thwarted. When his wife saw the watch she just rolled her eyes and walked away.

Episode 59

Viva Las Vegas

With the holiday season right around the corner Nobody, always the perfect gift giver, decided he would try something they had never done together. They would fly somewhere for a trip, Las Vegas! This would require the perfect planning because delivery is key.

He started going to church with his wife more often and he kept his word on spending money. During this opportune time he started dropping hints for a hiking GPS as a Christmas gift. It wasn't long and coupled with the looks he received from his beloved; this was too hot an item and carried a lot of emotion with it. This was one gift he would never receive from his wife. However, still being the opportunist, he asked for gift certificates to *REI* from his relatives instead.

Less than a month out from Christmas, Nobody lined up new luggage and a few small gifts that would lead up to the actual trip as she opened gifts on Christmas. He figured the tickets would be placed in the luggage. It was still a long ways away but Nobody planned very well and he wanted it to be perfect. It was all about the planning to get the desired effect. He started getting packaged travel quotes and it looked like he would be better off to fly out the weekend after New Year's.

Nobody started calling Mr. Clean more often and pretty soon, Nobody asked him if he would be his sponsor. They held some of the same beliefs and Mr. Clean went to the church they were going to.

It was also about this time, that the issue of counseling came up again. She had found out the church had a counseling center called the Haven of Hope. It was staffed with Christian counselors and, wouldn't you know it, they had a husband and wife team who said they would see them.

The dread inside his soul cannot be described. All the crap he went through with his second wife and counseling continued to plague him as he thought about it. It was always what *he* had to do to change. What *he* was doing wrong and if *he* would change then the marriage would succeed. What about *her* crap, she has plenty too?

This was, however, his third marriage and they were right around this mystical time frame when it was cut and run time. He had been in this place before and he didn't want to go through it again. He had said yes even though he didn't want to go. It was a couple of weeks out until their first meeting, the counselors worked for donations and his wife said she would pay for it, so he couldn't use the *"I can't afford it"* excuse. As the time drew nearer she started commenting again on who he went to lunch with at work. This infuriated him, because he wasn't doing anything wrong.

He had his typical response at the ready, "Don't you trust me, it is just work and there is nothing to worry about."

She usually just turned and walked away, a chill was left in her wake and Nobody tried to reconcile the feeling he had inside.

The following day driving home from work, Nobody received a call from the travel agent as he was pulling in to the subdivision. She had all the plans laid out for their trip to Las Vegas. The agent had a few options that she wanted to go over with Nobody. As they were discussing which trip itinerary to book, he was approaching his house and his wife had beaten him home for the first time in a long time. Since this was a surprise gift, he couldn't talk about in front of his wife, he drove by the house and went around the neighborhood until he was done.

With all the plans finalized and beaming with excitement, he tried to keep his poker face on as he walked into the house. She was in the kitchen next to the sink and she did not look well.

"Who were you were talking to on the phone?"

"What are you talking about?"

"I saw you drive by the house on the phone with someone, who was it? If it isn't a secret, then it should not be a problem. It is obvious you are hiding something from me, so who was it?"

Completely shocked, he was trapped and he hadn't done anything wrong, but he couldn't tell her about her Christmas gift.

"I can't tell you who it was, it is confidential," hoping the AA code could get him through this.

"I knew it," she yelled and then her whole demeanor imploded and her body contorted inward.

In a manner of seconds she had completely lost voluntary control of her body, she was moaning and holding her stomach as her knees seemed to buckle underneath her weight as she slid down the counter. She had a faraway look in her eye staring into the nothingness of life.

He moved towards her and grabbed her below the arms and tried to keep her up and console her, but she pushed him away. He moved forward again and this time held on tight. He wanted to make sure she didn't try and hurt herself. He had not witnessed anything like this since his first marriage, when he thought his first wife was going to hurt herself after his DUI. She kept crying, moaning and then she bent over at the waist. His arms around her mid-section were the only reason she was not on the floor. He didn't know what to do but keep his hold on her.

"I promise you, there is nothing going on, I just can't tell you who I was talking to."

The crying and moaning continued for what seemed like hours and then it started to subside. The house went very quiet and she moved upstairs to the bedroom without saying a word. When she was settled, Nobody called Mr. Clean. He needed help, and he did not know what to do without risk of ruining her Christmas gift. They talked for a bit and he was given advice on how to behave.

It was a good thing the counseling session was two days away, there was no doubt they needed it. Mr. Clean said that this was probably deeper than just talking on the phone and he needed to start praying for his wife. Listening to his wife share in meetings, it was clear things were starting to bubble up and it was going to be a tough road for a while and Nobody had better be prepared.

Counseling day arrived and they sat in the hallway waiting to meet the counselors. It was eerily quiet, the door opened and the previous session left. Then, out from the door a short elderly man, who looked like everyone's grandpa, walked out.

'Oh great, just what I need, an old man who doesn't get it,' he thought to himself.

He invited them into the room and they all sat down, the happy four-some. Introductions took place and they were allowed to describe why Nobody and his wife were there. The *Wife with the Armband Tattoo* went first and he heard the list of things he was doing or not doing. There was the non-intimate house they lived in, the lunches with female co-workers, the secret phone call, it's only sex and that stupid watch. Nobody chimed in and brought up the parent child relationship issue and he had his list of other issues as well. He was glad she didn't have anything up her sleeve that would have surprised him. He just wouldn't know how to deal with the pornography if it was brought up.

After this went on for a while, Grandma looked at both of them and said, "Do want this marriage to work?"

They both nodded. "OK then, are you willing to take divorce off the table?"

It was a questions neither of them, had expected. They both had their cases ready to prove who was right or wrong and they had hoped this couple would make sense of it all.

"Well, are you both ready to take divorce off the table?"

It was don't make promises you can't keep time, "I am willing to take the D-word off the table."

The *Wife with the Armband Tattoo* nodded and agreed as well.

"OK then a couple that prays together stays together. Do you two pray together?"

"No we have our own programs," and they went on to discuss their involvement with AA/Al-Anon and God as they understood Him.

"That is nice, but if you want this marriage to work, you are going to have to pray together. Can you try and pray together?"

"We can try," Nobody said, with a sheepish voice. He looked over to his wife and she did not look very thrilled with the idea. This was not what they had expected.

Grandma then leaned in and said, "Without God in your marriage the outlook is not good." They were given a few other instructions, like for now don't talk about big issues together. Keep to the simple stuff like what's on TV and would you like something from the fridge, how was your day and don't ask questions you do not want an answer to.

All of this took about an hour and it was just about quitting time, when Grandma said, "Can we close in prayer?"

Nobody bolted upright in his chair and said, "As long as you do not use Jesus' name."

He didn't know where that came from. He was okay praying to God, but not Jesus Christ. It was something that just drove him batty. Every time he heard someone use Jesus' name, it made his skin crawl. He believed in God and knew Jesus was a real person one time, but pray in His name, no way. He would just come here take what he liked and leave the rest.

Grandma didn't miss a beat, she prayed as he requested and they went on their way. The ride home was different. The only thing they got out of this meeting was to pray and don't talk about any deep subjects. This was going to be interesting; since there was nothing to talk about. The only things they ever talked about was what they were or were not doing and how there was no intimacy in the house. Then, if they were not talking about that, they watched TV or they did their own thing. Being a football fan kept him occupied, to her disgust.

They went to bed that night without praying, she didn't bring it up and neither did he, but he did think about it until he fell asleep.

The next night, as they were getting ready for bed, Nobody said he would like to pray if she didn't mind. He got on his knees next to the bed for what had seemed like centuries, said a loud, "God, I do not know why we are here at this place. I have no answers and I do not know what to do to help save this marriage. I just know that I am praying because I have no other options. I pray for my wife and our kids. I pray for the willingness to work together to make this marriage work and I pray for Your Will in my life."

She did not pray and said goodnight. This was true for the next night as well. It wasn't until the third night that she offered up a prayer. It wasn't much, but it was something. They continued to pray every night until the next session and no one died in the process.

During counseling, a variety of topics came up and it was discussed that she needed to see Grandpa separately. It was obvious to Grandpa that, she needed to deal with some issues privately for a bit then they would all get back together in a joint setting. Finally, Nobody had a little reassurance that it was not all his fault and, at this point, he needed something to hang his hat on.

Nobody started spending more time with Mr. Clean and, as they were talking, Nobody asked him if he could share with him his Higher Power.

Nobody was sick and tired of trying to figure out who God was. He had been down so many paths that he had a topographic map with plenty of roads, paths, trails, peaks and valleys but they all led nowhere.

Mr. Clean reached into his bookcase and pulled out a paperback, it was titled, *The Case for Christ* (2) written by Lee Strobel who was once an atheist. He said this was the book he read that put him on his current path.

This was not what he had pictured. He thought they would get into a discussion on who he thought God was and how he interacted with him in his life. Then he could say why he didn't believe in God the way he did. He was handed a book to read. He never read books about Jesus Christ; he read novels and traveled to unknown worlds he could get lost in. The books he read like this were 'New Age' stuff or from some guru somewhere that taught good orderly direction and tried to bring in cockeyed views of Christianity that were easier to grasp. Even though he now had adopted a more mainstream view of God, a watered down version, one that could be easily digested.

Nobody took the book from his hand, and with a big 'sigh,' said he would read it. He was out of options and he was tired of trying to find the perfect Higher Power to suit his needs. He would again do something he did not want to do. And there was that name again, Christ, plastered over the cover of the book. He had asked the question and this was what he got.

Christmas was a couple of days away and life was getting better in the house. It was funny that at a meeting, his wife said that because he had opened himself up in prayer and was vulnerable in front of her that became the reason she began to pray out loud in front of him. It felt good to hear her say in front of everyone that he was courageous. He had felt he was a coward and thought he only talked a good game while silently always scared - similarly to the '*Cowardly Lion*.' He had never been described as courageous by any of his wives in the past or friends for that matter. It was quite a boost for him and it made him feel more like a partner to her than a person she was stuck with.

He had not cracked that book yet and with the holidays and social events to deal with, he was reading the Rings trilogy and that had to be finished first. The extravaganza that he had planned was set, he had the luggage, the tickets were perfectly planted, he had called her boss about the time off she would need, and it was done in the most minute detail. A well orchestrated delivery system.

Soon she would know who that person was on the phone and hope he would get a bit of a reprieve for that day. His sponsor, Mr. Clean now, said the *Wife with the Armband Tattoo* would need to go through this healing process herself and not place the focus of her past hurts on him. She would need to see how she had placed her insecurities on him.

His son did not come this year so it would be just the two of them. They would go to the midnight service and hopefully she would want to open gifts when they got home. He still felt like a kid inside when Christmas rolled around.

He kept in touch with his parents, but that was it. They just called and discuss things like news, sports, and weather - that was all they spoke about mostly. He did his part to be the good son by sending cards on special occasions and call regularly. His mother would still try to bring up her brother and why Nobody shouldn't call him. She would always bring up some incident that happened just to prove that he was a 'schmuck.' However, at this stage, they both were wrong, but her unrelenting anger towards him was too much to listen to.

Nobody still spent a lot of time in counseling to go over the issues with his parents. He had gone to see Grandpa individually and there was still a lot of anger inside of him. All his mother did was try to convince Nobody that no one loved him and that he was wasting his time keeping in touch with his relatives. He should only be loyal to his parents. This conversation always angered him, especially when her words never matched her actions.

It was on one occasion that Nobody exclaimed quite forcefully that if his mother continued to force him to choose who he should love, she might not like his answer. If she wanted to continue speaking with him, this constant discussion about her brother had better stop.

It never occurred to him that all these years always hearing over and over that nobody loved him, could attribute to the fact that he never believed he should be loved. He picked women who loved him for reasons other than love. Watching porn, trying to get some sort of connection to love in a perverse manner that only the Father of Lies can craft in a way to leverage self-fulfillment all the while drowning spiritually. Always believing he had to work harder to prove himself worthy of love and when he did not feel love, he would turn to other means to gain satisfaction. He had to feel loved, because he did not believe he was loved. Everything in his life revolved around this. That was why he cared if people liked him or not.

He had gotten off the phone, and his wife looked over to him and said, "Have you ever asked your mother why she is so mad at him?"

Nobody said, "I know why. It was due to the time I was a fifteen and I wanted to move in with my uncle." However it was a good point and he immediately dialed back his mother to just to make sure.

"Mom, hey it's me again. I have a question for you. Can you tell me why you are so mad at your brother?"

As he listened on the phone, the color drained from his face. He could not believe what he was hearing. He heard his mother relay a story about his uncle, an incident that had occurred that was totally unrelated to him. They (his mother and her siblings) had all decided to show up at his grand-mother's house. He did not hear the entire recanting of the story because he only heard the words *"my brother"* and *"cheesecake."*

"Are you telling me that I have had to put up with this loyalty bullcrap for years over a freakin' pound of sugar? I can piece together being mad at him over wanting me to move into his house when I was fifteen, but this is absolutely ridiculous."

His mother relayed the story in a completely justifiable manner. All the pieces lined up perfectly to prove why her anger was justified and why he should be hated. Dumbfounded, he hung up the phone and just sat there. His wife came over and placed her arm around him and he heard her say, "I'm sorry."

As he sat there, he knew the real root cause of her anger towards her brother. If she admitted that it was about Nobody it would mean something was wrong in the house. However, to say it was over the cheesecake made it someone else's issue and not hers. Whatever it was that his mother needed to do to sleep at night killed him. All this sneaking around for years to make sure his parents would not get mad at him for talking to his Godfather. The constant questioning he underwent. How Nobody needed to be loyal to his family only, the fear he lived with if his parents were to reject him. In his heart he knew it started back when he was fifteen, but the seething anger she had towards her brother had clouded her vision.

He sat there and told his wife that one day he would have to address his family and get his mother and uncle in a room so they could mend fences. His mother, who always played the victim, who was always sick and her sickness was always rooted by the actions of others, needed help. In his anger, he still wanted her to live a happy life but would she ever listen to him? Could he ever get his dad or sister to pay attention to the way his mother acted? This was not normal!!!!!

Christmas was a smash and the gift went over well. Their relationship had been going great since they started going to Christian counseling. The counselors weren't trying to keep them there forever milking the bank account, they addressed issues straight on and instead of asking them how they felt about something, it was all about action. They had to bring God into the relationship to heal the tough places that could not heal by talking it out. On a wedding day, everyone proclaims to God and the world that they will hold true these vows and once they are pronounced man and wife, God is conveniently tucked away into a corner after the event. At least that was how it was for Nobody, but today they were inviting God into the marriage and they felt the difference.

During his Christmas break, he popped the book given him earlier and it captured his attention immediately. The author, through investigative reporting, wanted to prove Jesus was just a man who thought he was God. The author wanted to finally be able to live life the way he wanted and prove there was no reason to believe in Him for salvation. He interviewed men with pedigrees from here to eternity. Some were theologians, forensic scientists, historians etc., not your everyday barracks lawyer who will argue a case based on pseudo evidence. The more the author asked these guys the tough questions that were used to discredit Jesus' life as the Son of God, the more he was astounded at the logical way in which the scientific method was applied to show that it must be true based on the actual evidence. Nobody was a smart guy and he knew it would be very hard to argue against what he was reading. The only way to deny the proof was to say the facts are skewed based on an anti-Christ bias and hope one day that the argument can be proven in your favor.

Now Nobody understood why it is so important for the science community to find the missing link. All those pictures he saw growing up as a kid were not based on fact, but on a hope that it was true, that we evolved from apes. If it could be proven once and for all, then we can revert to our animalistic roots and behave anyway we want without fear. Once you die it's over, forever more!

As they were flying to Las Vegas, he read the chapter about the beating Jesus underwent prior to the long walk. When you look at the history books that depict this event, including the Gospels, there was no way that he could have hopped off the cross and gathered his disciples to follow him as some of his detractors would like you to believe. This was, by Roman custom, a true thrashing that was meant to lead to a point of death. If the soldiers did not carry out the sentence to the victim's death, they were subject to punishment as well. It would behoove them to carry out their orders so they themselves would not die. It actually turned his stomach as the book went through each phase that Jesus went through that day to His death, even the puncturing of his chest where the water ran out of His lifeless body.

Could he have been wrong all this time? As he sat in the plane, he silently prayed to God to help him understand more.

However, the attention span of anyone can be diverted instantly from God, especially as they were getting ready to land in Las Vegas, commonly known proudly as 'Sin City.' From the moment they landed, Nobody's eyes looked at everything, the women, the lights, buildings, everything needed his attention, while trying to spend time with his wife. He wanted to play the slots, eat, walk, and go to the shark tanks. There was so much to do, it never dawned on him that, as they moved through the day, it was more about what he wanted to do than what his wife wanted to do. As he looked around, his wife started getting mad at him for looking at other women, but it was hard for him to stop. He knew he needed to stay focused on her but his brain was so drawn to everything it was like a drug in its own right. It was all so alluring; this place was actually dangerous for someone like him. It had been years since he had been here, and today if he was by himself, he knew trouble would soon follow. This place was not safe, but even in the face of danger many will venture forward without the proper respect given to the things which can be bad.

The day had been uneventful as they visited many sites, bought souvenirs, watched Sinbad at Bally's and topped off the night as any couple might do on their honeymoon. This still wasn't enough. The night was young, and though his wife was tired, there was more to see. So to the dismay of his wife, who would have preferred he stay in the room, he went out to gaze at the sites within his hotel.

He walked the property, played slots, watched others play cards and saw the stream of humanity walk by him, too concerned with their own lives to pay attention to him. Even the hookers paid no mind to him, just as well, he was too chicken anyway. He may think of all the things he would do, but never follow through. As time wore on he planted himself on a machine and won close to a hundred bucks before retiring for the night.

The room was cold upon his return, they still had issues and even though they had made headway, it had not been a smart move to go out without his wife, even if nothing had happened. She did not care about the money he had won. It was like he had left her alone on their wedding night. Leaving the hotel room at 11:30 PM at night in Las Vegas isn't a smart move especially if you both are trying to fix a marriage that is wounded.

After three days, they left without further incident. Overall, it was a good trip, but there was still much to learn. The book he had started before the trip was finished within days of their return and he would never look at Christ the way he did before. It was time that he started doing his own reading. So he made a list of all the people that were interviewed or cited in the book, and he bought books by those authors and a new literary journey had begun. He was going to understand once and for all the truth about God, Christ and the church and draw his own conclusions. This was too important to let someone else dictate his eternity by the opinions of people who truly do not care what happens to him after he is out of their sight. He was responsible for his own life and the direction it should take, and this was one area he did not want to get wrong.

Episode 60

Love is a Battlefield

S o the literary journey began, with famous authors like Ravi Zacharias, Norman Geisler, C.S Lewis and Peter Kreeft. These authors have spent their lives arguing for God's and Jesus Christ's existence. They debated the tough questions presented by non-believers used to trip up Christians who want to hold onto their faith in a world that will easily discount the Bible and Jesus' claim that He is the Son of God and rose from the dead. These modern day prophets, with the gift of word, could clearly articulate that God is here. The challenge, is to spend the time to find out for yourself what the truth really is. On an intellectual level, non-believers have painted a picture in a way that the truth can be easily covered up with supposition and half truths. Nobody had no idea where this quest for information would lead him but, as he read, a whole new world opened up for him. At first, he was angry for being so stupid to automatically believe the non-believers of Christ over the believers. These were not just run of the mill Bible thumpers; these were highly intelligent men who very clearly laid out their case in the midst of carefully laid traps by the secular community.

As Nobody read, he saw how some of the arguments from the secular community, easily fell apart. Even the theory of evolution and intelligent design gave him pause when the historical and fossil evidence was outlined.

He was now fighting for his relationship with God and would not easily roll over just because someone said there can be no God or Jesus Christ.

Everything in this world requires maintenance. Industries are built around home and auto repair. You cannot just buy something and hope that it will work forever. Everything requires a check up every so often. Isn't it funny that when we ignore this, one day something will happen and we will be forced to take action. Likewise relationships need to be checked under the hood and if you find that something needs repair, repair it. It is just that some are just afraid to look.

We have all heard of a relationship that falls apart due to irreconcilable differences. This means that the work was too hard and both parties would prefer to walk away. If a major item in a home breaks, would it be left broken? A repairman would be called. When it comes to relationships, many hope the problem will go away and fix itself. The reason for this is that while homes and cars can be fixed with a check, a call and a little time, relationships are conversationally two way streets. Even if someone makes a mistake, both parties have a responsibility in healing. If a relationship is looked at by one of the partners as an appliance, it only means that if you fix the appliance, then all will be swell. The issue is if each partner is an appliance, both need to be fixed.

You can't just read self help books in a marriage and hope that what you learn will rub off on your partner. You can't badger each other into good behavior. Each side must be present and the challenge isn't that a husband must understand every woman's needs for the relationship to flourish, but each must understand each other's needs. That is where the expression 'if it's worth having its worth fighting for' came from.

If you believe in Satan and his only goal is to keep people away from God, wouldn't it seem plausible that breaking up marriages would be top on his list? This goes deeper than marriages between a man and woman; it would also seem the marriage between God and his people. There needs to be as much protection placed around a relationship as a bank that guards everyone's money.

Nobody and the *Wife with the Armband Tattoo*, finally understood that their relationship was worth fighting for. As they started fighting for their marriage, each of them started fighting for their relationship with God in their own way. They attended couples workshops put on by the counseling center. They met with other couples who were on the same path and were also in the program.

It was during one of these workshops, held at a lake house, that Grandpa put in a DVD titled, *The Ledger*. This was a twenty minute two person play between a husband and wife. The scene opens with a couple who are arguing over something. As the scene unfolds, each pulls out a ledger of items to prove to the other they are right. The wife starts pleading for her husband to read her ledger. He ignores her ledger and asks her to read his since his ledger is more important. The wife says no and tries to force the husband to read hers. Within ten minutes, the wife is on her knees begging her husband to read her ledger. The husband places his to the side and says the ledger doesn't matter. What matters is their relationship. The wife is weeping on the floor and the husband tries to hold her. All she has is the ledger to hold on to. She is so afraid to let the husband pull the ledger from her hand that she becomes more distraught. How many times have we held on to something thinking it was what we needed to feel secure?

Nobody, watching this scene unfold before him, triggered something inside that was extremely raw. He thought of the day in the kitchen, when his wife saw him on the phone with the travel agent. What started out as a tear turned into him sobbing. The emotion in this short play had touched a nerve. He was the wife, wanting to be loved and trying to prove why he should be loved and when no one is listening, he pulls out his ledger to prove to the world he is worth loving. Then, he saw his wife in the same role. When someone is actually trying to us love differently, we tend to respond out of habit. This is where understanding and compassion enter. Embarrassed, Nobody couldn't stop his own weeping. He looked to his wife, speechless, but the look in his eyes told the whole story. They both had their own ledgers and when the chips were down, they both pulled them out. The ledgers needed to be put away and the love for each other needed to be the focal point.

Sitting out on the dock during a break, another couple who attended joined them. They discussed marriage and how they were building a better relationship in and out of the bedroom. It was here the husband said that he prayed to God before they came together as a couple. This made Nobody squirm a bit. This was one of those areas that, even though he enjoyed, he also felt ashamed and dirty after. He was embarrassed about his body. He was equally embarrassed when he wanted to try new things in the bedroom.

Nobody wanted to talk about it with his wife but was always afraid to ask. Nobody had a fear he would be seen as a pervert for liking something in this area of their marriage even though it was permitted. Now praying to God, about something that Nobody felt was dirty, raised the stakes.

Sex was God given and therefore good, but the beauty of it has been cheapened in this world. It has been marginalized in every marriage and brought down to an animalistic behavior instead of a representation of God's love.

At this stage, sex was just an act now to be enjoyed by Nobody that they needed to perform as a matter of duty. If he got his, he was good. However, to hear these words about praying was a fearful proposition. The husband said it with such conviction that it made him stop and ponder the weight of their words.

As he thought about this during the rest of the day, Nobody could not let go of the fact that he was dirty himself. The drive to look at porn, kept him trapped in a vicious cycle of repeated failure and only short term successes. He was too afraid to tell anyone, but for his wife's sake, he would pray ahead of time. She was worth it, even though he felt he wasn't.

As in *Dante's Inferno's* second circle, always seeing never touching, this vicious cycle played out in other ways. Since his senses were dulled by the frequent viewing, as with all addictions, tolerance levels increase and what excited him yesterday required more to satisfy today. It is easy to see how this can get out of hand, but the world says it can be controlled. However, while Nobody knew he would be condemned by women, he was caught in a trap. He wanted more from his wife, who never performed to the exact need he was anticipating, but Nobody never verbalized his wants and he was inevitably let down. Nobody was not enjoying the *Wife with the Armband Tattoo* for who she was, but for what Nobody wanted out of the rendezvous. Once over, as Nobody would attempt to sleep, he would feel dirty. He would recall their time together and his thoughts of his behavior performing sex repulsed him. The most beautiful act that God gave his children was being thwarted by Satan and were caught in his web of deceit.

The battle raged on, he was learning about Christ on an intellectual level. He was praying with his wife daily. He would now pray before having sex with his wife and ask for God's blessing over his own creation. These new behaviors and study were never tried in the past and the results would speak for themselves, by putting forth an effort that few indulge in.

They didn't want to be roommates; they wanted to be husband and wife. No longer was running away an option and every time Nobody would think about the grass on the other side of the fence, he remembered his vow in that office with Grandpa and Grandma. This seemed more important than their wedding vows, because they were asked a direct question and Nobody did not make promises he would not keep. He would ask God to help him love his wife for who she was and not what he wanted her to be.

It wasn't long after this workshop, the term *"Walk to Emmaus"* kept popping up all over the place. He would hear Mr. Clean talk about it, the couple who were with them on the dock, and people in passing at church. Nobody asked what the term meant. He was familiar with the Biblical reference, but everyone was talking about it as a place to go. Mr. Clean said it changed his life, others said it was the best three days they ever spent. That was about all he would get out of anyone, so he dropped it.

But this issue with porn was just gnawing at him. He had no relief and he needed to address this. Nobody was a fairly open individual, and he had started talking about, in so many words, his little computer problem in the rooms of AA. He heard a variety of remedies, but nothing that he tried helped. He was very guilt ridden over it. One night, after a meeting, a guy from Jersey that he had come to know, pulled him aside and said that God loved him and that he too had the problem. After a long weekend on a church retreat, he knew he was forgiven. This was not your ordinary run of the mill 'you are loved by God' speeches. This guy was forgiven! He had the demeanor that went with a man who was at peace with his soul.

How Nobody wished that he could have this sort of peace in his soul. Jersey Guy told him not to give up. The victory was in the fight for purity in an impure world. He looked at him with eyes that spoke volumes; it was as if he could peer into Nobody's soul. This man had traveled his path and knew the struggle and more importantly, looked upon Nobody as an equal and not as an ugly soul.

It just so happened that Nobody's inquiry into the *"Walk to Emmaus"* perked a few ears along the way and the couple from the dock asked them if he and his wife would like to go. They learned that it was a two weekend event where the men went on weekend number one and the wives on weekend two. They were told that they did not need to worry about anything just be ready to go in about a month.

When God starts knocking on your door a lot of things happen, Paul went blind so Jesus could get his attention, Jonah got swallowed in a whale so he would finish out his duty, David had to face Goliath, Joseph was sold in slavery for delivering a vision and Abraham was told to pack his things and get moving.

This was not as severe, but Nobody and his wife each had issues that started springing up before this new adventure. Satan is true to his word and the only truth Satan will acknowledge is to derail those who want and need God in their life. The issue for Satan is not to pester the people who are separated from God but the ones who want to be with God. However, when life starts dishing it out, one can easily forget that Satan is still out there tormenting and beating us down until we will hopefully relent to the pressure and give up.

Obstacles may be placed in your path in an attempt to thwart your plans. In the book of Daniel, Daniel had a vision and prayed to God for understanding but an angel was held up by one of Satan's appointed. It wasn't until the angel Michael was sent that Gabriel was able to get past this force that held him up for twenty-one days. Same here, once God tries to reach one of his children, the call is out. A big neon light soon resonates over that person, and angels or demons are called to protect or destroy. Similar to the parable of the soils, and in this case, the soil was good and their people were around to encourage Nobody and his wife to persevere.

It was as if every problem was amplified leading up to his departure. Customer issues, his wife was just in a bad place, and with all the work related problems that were mounting, he contemplated postponing the weekend to a time that had less stress around it. Everyone told him to ignore it and pray, so pray he did. When it was time to go, he had no idea what he was in for. He just knew that something special was about to happen, and when they asked him for his watch, he knew the jig was up. He was going to be isolated from the outside world.

During the three days, Nobody felt and understood the love of Jesus Christ in his life for the first time. It was no longer a knowledge debate, but a heartfelt understanding. When the time came for him to face the man he was, he openly admitted his porn addiction to a person from his church, that was there supporting the event. This person looked at him and said, "You are not alone. I too have this issue and I only got relief when I admitted to my wife the essence of my sin."There is no way I can admit that to my wife. You have no idea, it will crush her. It is better for me to find men like you to share with and be held accountable."

When the weekend ended he was a changed man. He understood what Jersey Guy had said that night after the AA meeting. He was forgiven and more importantly, he admitted his devotion to Jesus Christ. The hounds of Heaven had been after him all these years and with the patience only the Father can offer, he was caught in the fold. He wasn't told what to do, how to do it or why he should do it. He felt the love of Christ that weekend and that was all it took. The one thing Nobody had searched for his entire life was to be loved, and it happened that weekend and through the love of a bunch of strangers, Nobody felt Christ's presence in way he had only dreamed of.

Nobody, as it has been said, works very hard to not make promises he could not keep. During the weekend he watched the music team play, he had such a desire to sing and play guitar, it was overwhelming. This was something he had always wanted to do but could never find the time, or felt he would never be good enough. However, it played on his heart and on the last day, he went up to the lead guitar player and said, "I am going to learn how to play guitar."

He and the guitar player talked for a few minutes and said their good-byes since the weekend was almost over.

As Nobody walked away, he thought in his head, *"Surely this guy has heard this a thousand times before, but today this was one time it would turn out to be true."*

When Nobody arrived home, he was one hundred pounds lighter and was told not to share his experience with his wife. So when he walked through the door, she immediately saw something in him she had never seen before. He hugged and kissed her. There was a love inside of him that transcended all other feelings he had ever experienced. He saw the beauty of his wife in front of him.

As her departure was approaching, she became very angry and fearful. Their disagreements, since his return, were sparked by little things and she was accusatory. He wanted to be at the church to send her off and give her a kiss goodbye before her three day Walk to Emmaus. However the pressure at work was mounting and he was afraid to ask for the time off. Afraid, he told his boss that it was extremely important and he needed to be there for his wife and he was allowed to go. Now, Nobody wanted it to be a surprise.

He did not commit to her that he would be there to kiss her good-bye, but it would be OK and his friend's wife from the dock would make sure she was taken care of but, she was very angry. She was making claims and saying things that were not true. She claimed he didn't care about her and that work was more important than her. She had no idea that he was driving towards her.

How many times have we cried out to God saying he didn't care only to find out he was on His way? What we thought about God turned out to be our own impatience and fear clouding our faith in Him.

When he got to the church, Mr. Clean's wife was there in the lobby. Nobody told her all about his wife and her emotional state. She looked at him and said, "It is OK, she is scared and does not know what God has in store for her. She will be fine, this is why she needs to go. Her spirit is responding to the call and because this is a new feeling and there is a lack of understanding, she is acting out. I was the same way, you'll see."

Waiting in the lobby behind the tinted glass of the doors, Nobody saw his wife arrive and park her car. She was alone and he could not help but feel for her. How he wanted to run to her and carry her across the lot, a wounded soldier being carried to safety. He loved her so much, but even on this day, the depth of his love for her could still not penetrate the inner depths of his soul, but he knew one day that barrier would be broken with God's help.

There she was a lost soul in a desolate parking lot, having no idea of the love she was going to feel and the joy that she would experience when touched by Christ. As she walked towards the door, which she could not see through due to the tint, Nobody saw the pain in her soul written all over on her face. She had no idea that she was being watched with the most loving eyes the world could produce, just likes Christ does.

It took him back to one of their counseling sessions with Grandpa a couple of months back. They had been discussing the things that made each of them happy and sad in the marriage. Nobody spoke about his adventures and the thrill he got when he went hiking or drove his motorcycle and how he liked to try new things. When his heart was touched like this, it was like his chest exploded with a sensation and he just wanted to run through the fields. He liked the newness of the adventure.

His wife, on the other hand, started sharing and saying that everything Nobody spoke about had to do with things that did not involve her. He was excited to do new and wonderful things apart from her. His heart sank when he heard that. It was not what he meant, but before he could defend his statement, Grandpa hushed him.

She continued describing her fear that one day something new and exciting would be another women and this just scared her to death since she was seven years older than him. It was like they were equal opposites and what made him happy scared her to death.

As he listened and watched his wife, something in his heart changed. She was crying a cry he had not seen from her before. She was emotionally naked in front of him and for the first time in his life, he understood what the word *'compassion'* meant. He sat there and his heart felt like it leaped from his chest, with arms open in a way that would cradle hers.

When she finished crying and had gone silent, not a sound could be heard. The stillness in the room was intoxicating. When he was allowed to share, he looked her and said, "Having lunch with women at work is not important and if you don't want me to do that anymore, I won't. I love you and you are more important than any of them."

Standing there he had that same feeling as that night in counseling as she walked towards him. His heart was lurching from his chest as she made her way closer. As she reached for the door, he pushed it open. As she realized what was happening, she dropped her bags and fell into his arms. She sobbed uncontrollably and each sob produced an entire body reaction as he held her entire weight.

The world had once again stopped and not a sound could be heard as he kissed her head and said, "I love you."

As they stood there and the world started coming back into view, he gathered her bags and they passed through the doors together.

Episode 61

While My Guitar Gently Weeps

E ight Hundred and sixteen days later in early November, they decided they would attend a conference on *'Love & Respect' (3)*. Over the past two years they had been working on their marriage. They attended various marriage workshops and conferences and worked hard to fulfill their commitment to each other. They both spent time working on themselves and got involved and supported each other through their struggles. No longer alone to deal with life, they had crossed a barrier they felt they would never cross. The book Nobody read on this topic, was the best biblical representation of what marriage should be and since there was still a lot of ground to cover, he insisted they attend, when the conference made a stop in Atlanta.

There were so many examples of issues in their marriage they still had a hard time overcoming, it boiled down to how God made a woman and a man. Once a couple understood what their spouses needed, as God had made them, then a lot of the fighting subsided and each could look at each other differently.

They had made great headway, but his wife still insisted that he did not love her the way she wanted and Nobody insisted that she did not look up to him. He wanted to be her protector, but she always held him away at arm's length.

His *Wife with the Armband Tattoo* rekindled the relationship with her girls and the healing was well under way and they were a part of her life once again. Nobody learned how to play the guitar and actually started playing in a community service at their church. He vowed that he would only play for God and worship Him with the music. He found that so many times when he was hurting that he could play to God and find himself weeping while playing either through practice or even on stage.

As hard as he had tried to purify his own altar, there were still areas in his life that he did not make headway in. He approached other men in his bible group that struggled with the computer and no matter how many men said they wanted to be part of an accountability group, they always seemed to slip away after time. Nobody was tired of failing and tired of empty promises made by other men. To Nobody this was a life and death issue that he held close to his vest.

Nobody felt like a fool up on stage after a bout with the computer, singing and playing for everyone at the church service, knowing that everyone would scoff at him and call him a pervert if they really knew what happened behind his façade. He was tired of admitting to his Bible study group of his failing, when everyone seemed to have their act together. Nobody was tired of the way he felt after an episode. It was like an unholy spiritual residue that covered his mind for days after. He felt dirty and ashamed and had a hard time looking people in the eye. When he practiced his guitar in his room and was singing, he felt like a fake and fraud. These were words used by his father to describe him. The words stuck. Maybe it was true, maybe this was all his imagination, but deep down he wanted to believe God would help with this and remove it.

He kept referring to that Bible passage that describes how a man does what he doesn't want to do, but still loves God with all his heart. It was the merry go round of endless repentance. Some days he just wanted to give up and die - what was the use? He would never get it right; he would probably be *left behind* if the rapture happens, no matter how hard he tried. Then there was the hiding he did from his wife. He could recognize the triggers and was able to combat it about fifty percent of the time. The men in his group empathized with him but they did not seem to want to be bothered.

Then during prayer one morning before church, Nobody broke down in front of the pastor. The pastor recommended a book he should read called *Every Man's Battle (3)*. He said that finally someone was willing to put it all on the table and tell men like him (the author) that there was hope and with God's grace that men can overcome this once and for all. That Nobody, who felt he was alone was far from the truth, it was a serious problem with all men.

So he bought the book and kept it from his wife so she would not see what he was reading. Other times when he had books like this out, she had thought he was having an affair and it opened up a can of worms he was unwilling to open. He felt he was a coward. He should be able to handle it. There were guys he met with outside of church circles who blew this off and told Nobody that he needed to give himself a break. He heard some women in the church speak about this and from their little self righteous perch, considered men who looked at that as shameful perverts, who truly did not love God.

How wrong they were and right at the same time. If they could only understand the pain that is felt and it was one of the reasons he could not tell his wife, because it would tear her apart. This was his issue and like the step nine said, you only made amends if it did not hurt another person in the process. This would hurt her, so he needed to make a living amends and get out of this vicious cycle.

That's where they were in early November, as they readied themselves for the first night of a two day event. They ran into another couple from their Saturday night couples meeting, but the focus was on the speaker. He came out and was a quirky sort of guy, and after he set the crowd at ease he started outlining how God made women. The women all applauded; finally someone understood where '*they*' were coming from. They wanted to be loved and men didn't have a clue on how to do it. The speaker spent the night describing the differences between men and women with the focus on the women. The *Wife with the Armband Tattoo* was happy they had gone. They left that night with a good feeling that this guy knew what he was talking about and it was great to see someone very biblically connected.

Day two on the other hand discussed men and what they are looking for. It was as if the speaker was reading from Nobody's internal script. Respect was what a man needed. Yes he needs love, but a man needs respect more than love. He went on to say, in world of feminism that says men should be more like women with their feelings, men are left holding on to a set of emotions they do not know what to do with. They are meant to feel ashamed when they have needs or look at things differently than their female counterparts. Since the world is saying that the way he feels is wrong, they are left isolated in marriages without any hope. God made him that way, who are you to say that God made a mistake.

He further elaborated that those men sitting next to you are programmed by God to lay their lives down for you. Would you for him? When he said those words the auditorium when silent and the speaker had their attention.

The speaker went on to say that women are conversational creations, men are not. They process information differently and if men had to process their feelings like a women, nothing would get done, (the audience chuckled).

Then he held up his hand and said, "The fact of the matter is a man can tell you, better yet, he can count on one hand his sins. He knows what is wrong in his life and what is wrong with his spirit. Women can be dangerously self-righteous when they start thinking they understand how a man thinks from their perspective when gossip is a sin that women can easily slide into."

Nobody turned to his wife, she was looking up at him with the most loving eyes he had ever seen her have and said, "I understand now."

Tears flowed and Nobody was beside himself. He hugged her, but he knew what that man on the stage had said. He knew his sin. He was right. Nobody was the most afraid he had been in his entire life, because he needed to tell his wife. She thought he had tears of joy, but Nobody was crying out of absolute fear.

They took a break, and Nobody grabbed the speaker's book and ran down front. He needed to speak to him and used the excuse of having the book signed. He waited patiently and hoped he would not turn him away. The tears and emotion gripped his chest. There was one more person in front of him, *"Please God let me speak to him?"*

When it was his turn he was in full tears, he looked at the speaker and said, "I know what you meant up there about the sins on one hand. I need to admit to my wife about my addiction to pornography but I am afraid of her reaction. I am so scared and ashamed."

As he was crying, the speaker placed his hand on his shoulder and said, "It will be alright, you will have an opportunity to do that today."

He signed the book and said good-bye. Nobody took in a deep breath and turned around, his wife was walking up to him and asked if he had gotten the book signed.

She got a better look at him and said, "Wow, are you alright?"

Like a dead man walking, "Sure, he just hit a spot I can identify with."

When the conference was over and they were walking to the truck, (they had to get home so they could turn around and go to an annual dinner they were to attend - it was a formal affair and they needed to get dressed and, on top of that, they needed to pick up a treadmill on the way home.) As they got in the car and he looked at his wife, she was absolutely beaming with beauty. This conference was the ultimate marriage conference. How gracious was God to this speaker to give this message for couples who want a better marriage, for better or worse. His wife got it and he was happy for it. She looked at him and asked what was wrong.

He looked at her and said, "Can you ask me what my sin is?"

"I don't understand your question."

"Can you please.....ask me.....what.....my.......sin.....is?" Nobody said, as he was opening up his entire soul to the women he loved. She had the power to destroy him at that moment.

She was no longer beaming but looked deathly afraid, "Nobody what is your sin?"

As his throat tightened, he looked at his wife. In his truck nowhere to run, he said, "I......have.....a problem.......with.....pornography."

Not sure if it was relief that he wasn't having an affair or just a momentary pause, her look went blank and then the redness increased. Short of words, nothing was said. They drove in silence towards the exercise equipment store. After a quick bite to eat at Arby's and on their way to his truck she said, "I can't help you, it is between you and God."

They loaded the treadmill and went home. The air was frigid and Nobody was as naked as a man could be. He was no longer hiding, but at what cost? He had no more secrets from his wife, she now knew the man she was married to. After they got home they changed and went to the dinner, where they mingled with friends throughout the night. On the way home they exchanged notes about the speaker and the dinner, but nothing else was said about his question he poised to her earlier in the day.

He did not know how to act, what to do, or what to say. They were home and after a long day with many activities in the midst of this bomb he unloaded, he did not know if he could even approach her. He loved his wife and God, but he felt completely alone. Nobody was standing next to the bed when she came out of the closet and walked toward him as they were getting ready to retire. She moved towards him, without any anger in her eyes, she went to him gave him a hug and with a gentle kiss said, "I love you."

There they held their embrace and Nobody finally understood why he was searching for God. He was searching for God because deep down he knew that God had not given up on him, even though Nobody had. He had been on this quest ever since he was a kid. Earlier in the day, she said that it was between him and God. She believed God loved him even in his worst moment. For better or for worse were not empty words, they had weight and substance behind them. In the past this was where he felt everyone should run to greener pastures because he was a piece of crap. But she stood there holding him, fighting for him, standing for him in his most vulnerable position. *She was God with skin on representing the Father, just like Christ did.* He could continue with his life knowing that God and his wife loved him, even though he was not perfect.

He was forgiven!

Episode 62

The Final Countdown

S even years later and a lot growth in his walk with Christ, it was now six weeks past the birth of Nobody's grandson. Nobody had written a letter to his son giving that fatherly advice that can only be shared between a father and son. He and his wife touched down in the hot Arizona desert, and as they exited the airport the rush of heat blew across their faces. There was a moment of anxiety, curiosity and a slight feeling of apprehension. Nobody was not too sure how the day would play out. They had no plans except they would go out to eat and shop for items his son and his wife said they needed for the baby. There was a part of Nobody that did not want to go near the feeling that was slowly burning inside his heart. The feeling was nestled in the very deepest recesses of his chest, firmly planted, connected to his tear ducts and the roots of his hair.

It was during visits like this in the past with his family, even though they had nothing but good intentions, that Nobody was fearful he would say the wrong thing and cause someone to get angry at him. The difference now was that he had spent many years with God's help to undo the myths and fallacies that had played such a large part of his life. As easy as it sounded to him the best thing he could do was to remain as quiet as possible and not offer an opinion unless he was asked. Nobody should love his son and family right where they were. It was probably the most important time in his son's life. He was a man with a family and if Nobody did not want to repeat history, the best thing he could do was keep a door open, by not giving anyone a key to lock. As Nobody and his *Wife with the Armband Tattoo* were driving to his son's in-laws' house, they stopped and got the last minute gift bag and tissue to place in his grandson's New England Patriots baby survival gear, (bottle, pacifier, bib and 'onesie.') There was sort of a numb feeling inside of him. Part of him did not want to feel the emotion but the other side was yearning to get there as quickly as possible. On the highway, getting closer by the minute, Nobody prayed to God that though he was far from perfect, to please bless this trip and visit. His life was passing in front of his eyes and he knew that in his weakness, Christ's strength would endure.

As they made the final turn into the dirt driveway, the wind formed little dust devils off to the left and small white rocks outlined the path a car should travel amongst the dust and sand. Prickly pear cacti, desert grass and a variety of spiny plants, reminded Nobody of a life past when he used to live here. It drew him in, and his inhibitions fell away as the door opened. A new chapter was about to begin, hugs were exchanged and in the middle of the living room, in a mechanical rocker, lay asleep one of God's miracles.

Speechless and paralyzed, Nobody could only gaze upon the six week old infant. He did not know what to do, so he did nothing but watch. Nobody's wife, after a few moments, picked up the child like a pro and did what every mother instinctively knows how to do; comfort and soothe. This was a trait Nobody only hoped he would feel one day.

It wasn't long when it was time to hold his grandson. Small and fragile, afraid he would break if he did something wrong, he slowly took him in his left arm and cradled him. Fussing and crying, it did not matter. Here in his arms, the son of his son, he had such a feeling he could not remember or somehow sense. Nobody remembered when his son was born, he wept with joy. Yet on this day, he could only feel this precious child in his arms and a need to protect him as his God given duty. His grandson had such a serious look upon his face as he gazed toward the ceiling. It dawned on Nobody that children are spiritually sensitive to God and his angels. Without a second thought Nobody whispered to him, "God loves you. Do you know God? Do you see his angels above you?" As if on cue, his grandson smiled. It seemed as though his grandson knew who Nobody was referring to. Speaking God's name over him settled him down.

After a packed schedule of shopping, eating, visiting his son's church and home they decided to end the visit with a final dinner. A long day in a carrier, his grandson was not in the best of moods. The bottle worked for a time and bouncing on the knee also had a limited shelf life. Dinner was served, Nobody's wife, took the child outside and tried to comfort him. It wasn't long before Nobody finished his meal and went outside to relieve his wife. The baby was crying and upset; she looked at him and asked if he could handle the baby in this state. For a moment Nobody wasn't sure because all his life he never handled situations well where people were upset. He did not know how to make it better. Even though this was only a baby, his learned behaviors where trying to tell him not to go through with it and if he did, it would only be for a short period of time until the reinforcements came in. But all he could say was, "It is my turn, you go ahead and finish your dinner, we will be OK."

The baby was crying, fussing, and wriggling about, not happy on his shoulder or in his arms. Nobody walked, back and forth rocking gently, his grandson, cradled in his arms. No one was around to say what a good job he was doing. No one telling him he was doing it wrong. No one was questioning his faithfulness or loyalty. Not scared he would make a mistake. He was just there with this child cradled next to his heart. Holding him close, the tears welled up in both of their eyes for different reasons. As he gazed upon the wonder that God gives so many people but many don't realize, especially when his son was born twenty-five years ago. At that time Nobody was happy but he had been numb and did not understand then what he knew now.

With absolutely no fan fare, as only God would have it, Nobody sang to his grandson, one of his favorite John Denver songs, *Sunshine on my Shoulders*. After a few bars, the boy started to close his eyes and fall asleep in the comfort of his grandfather's chest safe and secure, not realizing that the man who held him had a life of pain, joy, wonder, fulfillment and awe. He had once doubted that God had even loved him and he thought he was a nobody that was not worth loving. He had many times wanted to end his own life, because of the fear he had held sacred. He had made so many mistakes, but '*this*' day was different. As he continued to sing and held the baby close to him, he could sense the faith this child had in him if only for this moment. As Nobody continued to weep the song out of his swollen throat, though this child would not remember this moment like Nobody did. Nobody was reminded that he too had a moment like this as a child, resting comfortably on his aunt's chest in that old metal rocking chair. The look on his grandson's face was peaceful as he slept.

"God loves you."

A small smile broke through like a small ripple from a drop of dew on a glass covered pool of water. As Nobody thanked God for this gift, he knew that his life was now changed. He finally understood what nurturing and compassion was. He knew his son would be OK. He would make mistakes, but in the long run, if he knew to turn to God, the answers would come. He just had to keep searching and not give up because he was human.

Making his way back into the restaurant to join the rest of his family, Nobody looked to God and then to his grandson. His life was not a failure, but only a journey back to God. He knew he would play a part in this child's life and it was important that this child, as well as his own son, understood they were loved and that God loved them as much as anybody else. It would not be easy, but many have gone before them and succeeded. Nobody was *somebody*, and knew that his job would be to make sure the message of God's love would forever ring in his son's and his grandson's life. He was the man he always wanted to be. He was no longer a nobody. He was always somebody that God loved and blessed and wanted him to return home.

As he looked upon this child before entering the restaurant, the only thing that came to mind was what his prayer partner Mr. Clean told him every day after their daily prayers; "And remember, God loves you and so do I."

Epilogue

Eulogy
Yvonne Masse
4/11/2012

I t has often been said that funerals are for the living. That being said, Funerals clearly are a time of reflection: on the loved one, on life and on death, and they are a time of introspection for many of us. Many times in the past as I sat in a memorial service, I wondered what people might say about me when my day comes. Will the room be packed or will it only be those who feel obligated to be there? I have been to both types of funerals. What will the banner of my life announce to those I have left behind? Will that one person show up who I had a brief encounter with and pass along some profound moment in time when I was the help they needed, or that I simply walked by them, indifferent.

Was I God with skin on or was I a prude who only thought of himself and did not care for his fellow man? Will I finally hear God speak those words, "Well done my good and faithful servant."

Before I share my thoughts on my grandmother I would like to relate a short story, bear with me and I promise you will understand. I want to speak first of Pepere, because not only did Memere have an extreme impact on my life but so did he and it was a tandem event.

A short time prior to his death, I was told my grandmother asked my grandfather what he would like to do with his watch. He said please make sure Roland gets it. To an 11 year old boy that was a nice gift but at that age I did not appreciate the value of this watch I possess today.

When I picked up this watch this morning it started ticking after thirty-six years without any human intervention.

In my mind's eye I can still see Pepere praying by his bed, on his knees, a humble man in front of his Maker. It did not matter who was running around that small apartment, when it was time for bed, down on his knees he went. I remember how as a child the only thing I wanted to do was sit between Memere and Pepere in the front seat of his Impala whenever we visited. It was the best place in the world to me as a kid.

As I grew older and time passed, it is not a secret that I took a temporary path that lead to a variety of, shall we say - shenanigans. Memere was always there for me with open arms until I left Lewiston, but as I did the things I did and through the years leading up to my revelation, I would pause and feel in my heart that Pepere was watching me and for a brief moment felt the guilt and shame of my actions. But I was not able to stop the downward spiral, even though deep down I wish I could have made him proud. It's a curious thing, to be caught up like that, knowing you need help but not sure how to ask for or to get it.

Fast forward eighteen years from his death. I was getting ready to be baptized as an adult and I was close to three years of sobriety. I had called Aunt Lillian to share with her my joy in finding Christ again in my life and my upcoming AA birthday. I had a recent interest in finding the watch my grandfather had left me and that my mother was going to send it to me. I will never forget that call because that day God revealed his awesome wonder to me.

When I mentioned my sobriety date was the 18th of October, there was silence on the other end of the line.

I said, "Hello, Aunt Lil, are you there?"

"Roland, what did you say?" "I am going to be 3 yrs sober."

"No, no, the date." "Oct 18th."

"Roland, did you know that was the day your grandfather died?"

All of a sudden, every memory of him, thinking about how I felt when I thought he was watching over me all came to a point. In an instant I was reliving the shame I had felt to know that he had witnessed my lowest and most shameful moments, moments I would never think of sharing in public. But he had seen it all and I knew from the bottom of my heart, he had been watching over me the whole time and even in my sin he loved me. Just like Christ loves each one of us, all of the time.

On Oct 18th 1990, I thought my life was ruined forever, but on the anniversary of his death I was given a gracious death blow to my old life of addiction. I had no way of knowing that his prayer was being fulfilled and my life was being given back to me. How grateful I am that one of his last acts on Earth was to profess his watch over me and even in his death his spirit continued to capture my attention for the life God truly had in store for me.It came not with a gentle promise but a loving spiritual 2x4 up alongside my head.

With the watch ticking this morning, I know he is here but now with Memere.

Now my grandmother, who has carried the mantel for this family since his departure, continually pledging her love for Claude Masse until the day she died.

We are here to honor her life today; I can only hope that my life can represent the love she had for everyone in this room, including me.

When I was in Memere's presence I always felt safe. I was the focus of her attention; it was like no one else mattered. Memere loved me for who I was at any given time. She took me where I was and did not bother to ask about the past or say you should not have done that. We both knew and no words needed to be spoken. In her eyes she was simply glad I came back to her, just like Christ does.

She was there for me, wild and eighteen, trying to figure out who I was. She never questioned what I was doing; she just loved me. Later, when I came to grips with my addictions, she never shamed me for what I had done. She just said she was just glad I was safe and on the right path. Her only wish was that I would become a Democrat. Sorry, Memere. . .

Her love for me and the love Pepere had for me that presented itself over the years, propelled me to do better-not because they asked me to but because I wanted to in order to not disappoint their love for me. They both helped deliver the one-two punch in my life without one angry word, just loving heartfelt encouragement and a yearning that I would stay true to myself.

She never talked bad about anyone to me over the years. She just wanted to see everyone together, resolve their differences and have everyone spend time together, just like Christ does.

It is hard sometimes to figure out what Christ wants from us if all we do is watch the actions of other Christians, because though they might mean well, they are still imperfect and eventually we all get let down. However, Memere always said she was praying for those around her. She knew her Maker and she gave me one of the best representations of Christ's teachings through her many loving and forgiving actions. She prayed faithfully and acknowledged God which is an example I follow. Pepere may have knocked me over the head with God's help, but she was there over the years to help pick me up whenever I called.

Memere always showed me love and respect. She never tried to manipulate my actions with her words. A man's core need is to be respected by those around him. God made men that way. Even when men do not deserve respect, a man responds to someone who treats him with respect even in his failings. It propels him to do better.

In my lowest moments, she still respected me as a man who needed to make his own decisions, whether right or wrong, but allowed me the dignity to come to my own realizations and love me in spite of all my spots and blemishes.

In the Bible, Jesus always demonstrated his respect to those he came across. He did not shame them, rather he just presented the truth and they were free to choose their path in hopes they would choose wisely. In every event he loved them, and had compassion and empathy towards them regardless of their choice.

Memere was not afraid to talk about God and she never tried to stifle the extreme joy I have in my heart to that end. When you see the workings of God in your life and you can trace it back to a point in time, it is no wonder why I proudly stand here today a man of God my grandparents can be proud of. So much so the last time I visited her she asked if I was a preacher yet. I can only say that I have a heart for God and the message of my life is open to all. I am reminded of what St. Francis of Assisi said, "Wherever you go, preach the Gospel. Only when necessary, use words."

Finally, during my last visit I shared with her the final chapter in the book I have been writing for over a year. I wrote the last chapter 9 months ago on an airplane flying back from seeing my grandson for the first time, and since then I have been writing towards that end.

As we held hands and I read to her, I couldn't help but weep. The words on the page reflected the love of God I possess in my heart and I can attribute that love based on the actions of these two people. How it touched her and me as the words were spoken. As I looked up from the pages into her eyes, she knew I was baring the soul of my life I have lived in the past, and the joy and redemption I have today. Her eyes became misty as I read into her spirit. When I was finished I looked up at her. There was no painful look on her face, only one of peace and she said, "That was beautiful." And, we hugged in silence.

1 Corinthians 13:4-7 says is best. *Love is patient, love is kind and is not jealous; love does not brag and is not arrogant, [5] does not act unbecomingly; it does not seek its own, is not provoked, does not take into account a wrong suffered, [6] does not rejoice in unrighteousness, but rejoices with the truth; [7] [bears all things, believes all things, hopes all things, endures all things. Love never fails. . .*

Memere was not ashamed of her life or the possessions she did not have. She focused on the important things; she loved her family, she loved Christ and last of all, I knew she loved me, and that knowledge helped me out of the grave I was in for so long. . .

That is why My Memere will always be my Valentine.

By
Roland Jutras
Faithful Grandson

Bibliography

1. **Risk Harbor Card**. *Corporate Impressions*. s.l.: Successories Inc., 1998.
2. **Lee Strobel**. *The Case for Christ*. s.l.: Zondervan, 1998.
3. **Dr. Emerson Eggerichs**. *Love & Respect*. s.l.: Integrity Publishers, 2004.
4. **Steve Arterburn, Fred Stoeker, Mike Yorkey**. *Every Man's Battle*. *a.l*.: Waterbrook Press, 2000.

Appendix

The Myths

Myth #1 Nobody needs to be a good boy all the time.
Myth #2 Nobody needs to be careful all the time.
Myth #3 Nobody thinks being different is bad.
Myth #4 Nobody needs to make sure his parents love him.
Myth #5 Nobody needs to ask permission every time.
Myth #6 Nobody learns he must be extremely careful not to get hurt.
Myth #7 Nobody is afraid to tell the truth.
Myth #8 Nobody is hurt by their parents.
Myth #9 It's Nobody's fault they are not happy.
Myth #10 Nobody needs to be careful not to say the wrong thing.
Myth #11 Nobody needs to apologize all the time.
Myth #12 Nobody needs friends to make him feel better.
Myth #13 Nobody believes self-worth is based on accomplishments.
Myth #14 Nobody needs to be noticed all the time.
Myth #15 Nobody manages fear of pain.
Myth #16 Nobody should be rewarded for doing good work.
Myth #17 Nobody needs to have a girlfriend people think is pretty.
Myth #18 Nobody tells the truth and gets in trouble.
Myth #19 Nobody knows that to feel special you need someone to love you.
Myth #20 Nobody believes everyone is trustworthy.

Myth #21 Nobody feels safe if other people are fighting.

Myth #22 Nobody thinks to be someone you must be liked.

Myth #23 Nobody believes you can convince someone to love you.

Myth #24 Nobody gets punished for getting hurt by accident.

Myth #25 Nobody thinks loves is based on outside appearances only.

Myth #26 Nobody believes relationships should be absolutes.

Myth #27 Nobody's world would be perfect once they move.

Myth #28 Nobody needs to do things others are doing to be accepted.

Myth #29 Nobody was proving that drugs are not harmful.

Myth #30 Nobody's worldview can't be wrong.

Myth #31 Nobody should make sure he never gets hurt.

Myth #32 Nobody believes he is unlovable just the way he is.

Myth #33 Nobody believes he needs to be accepted by a drug dealer to prove self-worth.

Myth #34 Nobody has to try harder to be liked and accepted.

Myth #35 Nobody must have sex in high school to prove his manhood.

Myth #36 Nobody needs love to feel complete.

Myth #37 Nobody believes that absence makes the heart grow cold.

Myth #38 Nobody believes if someone says they love you forever, they mean it.

Myth #39 Nobody needs to be who he thinks someone wants him to be.

Myth #40 Nobody thinks he must keep his word to marry even if he does not love someone.

Myth #41 Nobody believes love is a feeling and you should follow it.

Myth #42 Nobody completed her.

Myth #43 Nobody thought he was a smooth operator.

Myth #44 Nobody's relationship was made in Heaven.

Myth #45 Nobody believes based on his accomplishments he is the best.

Myth #46 Nobody believed if the outside looked good then the inside would be.

Myth #47 Nobody believes he is untouchable.

Myth #48 Nobody was weak and pitiful.

Myth #49 Nobody had a chance if he just stopped taking drugs only.

Myth #50 Nobody had the best made plans.

Myth #51 Nobody thinks good behavior equals an easy life.

Myth #52 Knowledge, mediation and good intentions through spiritual means would help Nobody.

Myth #53 Nobody looks sober.
Myth #54 Again, it's Nobody's fault they were not happy.
Myth #55 Relationships are meant to satisfy all needs for Nobody.
Myth #56 Nobody sees sex as a commitment.
Myth #57 Nobody was inadequate as a man.
Myth #58 Nobody's unlovable.
Myth #59 Nobody felt sex healed all ills in a relationship.
Myth #60 Nobody felt a new beginning would change everything for the better.
Myth #61 Nobody thinks tweaking instead of all out change will solve an ongoing problem.
Myth #62 Nobody believed everything would go according to plan.
Myth #63 Nobody believes pain can somehow be removed from his life with Good Orderly Direction.
Myth #64 Nobody is told that right thinking produces a positive life.
Myth #65 Nobody was unworthy of God's true love for him.
Myth #66 Nobody believed deep inside God would eventually punish him.
Myth #67 Good Christian behavior always equals earthly rewards.
Myth #68 Nobody believed that this might be the woman sent from God.
Myth #69 Another match made in Heaven for Nobody.
Myth #70 Nobody was less than a man.
Myth #71 Nobody had abandoned his son.
Myth #72 Nobody wasn't man enough to keep a woman happy.

The Truths

Truth #1 Nobody has parents that fight all the time.
Truth #2 Nobody's mother lies.
Truth #3 Nobody's mother would abandon her son.
Truth #4 There were angels close by.
Truth #5 Nobody has to lie to protect himself from others.
Truth #6 Nobody voted for him.
Truth #7 Nobody's father was ashamed of his son.
Truth #8 Nobody feels special because of a kiss.
Truth #9 Nobody wanted to be good in God's eyes.
Truth #10 Nobody should be wary of the Priest.
Truth #11 Nobody is betrayed.

Truth #12 Nobody lies to protect himself.

Truth #13 When it comes to other people's feelings, Nobody is clueless.

Truth #14 Relationships have varying expectations not absolutes.

Truth #15 Nobody was noticed.

Truth #16 Nobody's mother blames her oldest kid for her marriage problems.

Truth #17 Nobody wants to get away from the family.

Truth #18 Nobody wishes he was truly loved by his family.

Truth #19 Nobody's father despises his son.

Truth #20 Nobody's parents do not understand that they have isolated him.

Truth #21 Nobody believes he cannot cope with life without marijuana.

Truth #22 Nobody knew what lust was, but not love.

Truth #23 Nobody's girlfriend had a great family.

Truth #24 Nobody's mother lies to protect herself.

Truth #25 Nobody turns from God because of the church.

Truth #26 Nobody's coping behaviors were learned from his parents.

Truth #27 Nobody repents for the hurtful words spoken.

Truth #28 Nobody has a moral fiber that cannot be denied.

Truth #29 Nobody made a mistake and somebody is going to get hurt.

Truth #30 Nobody hurts another person without remorse.

Truth #31 Nobody is surviving by being needed.

Truth #32 Nobody relies on laws to cope with a moral decision.

Truth #33 Nobody smothers the life out of a relationship.

Truth #34 Nobody experiences the serenity which surrounds a self-less decision.

Truth #35 Nobody judges his insides by people's outsides.

Truth #36 Nobody's marriage was blessed by worldly affirmation and not God.

Truth #37 Nobody brought his past into his present.

Truth #38 Nobody had nothing to believe in but himself.

Truth #39 Nobody felt love from God..

Truth #40 Nobody witnessed what a true man was.

Truth #41 God sent a messenger to Nobody.

Truth #42 Nobody's world was shattered and he did not have faith that it would turn out well.

Truth #43 Nobody's world was spinning out of control.

Truth #44 Nobody had gone astray from God.

Truth #45 Somebody finally heard what he was saying.

Truth #46 Nobody felt a level of companionship that filled that hole in his gut.

Truth #47 God had sent another angel.

Truth #48 Nobody replaced mumbo-jumbo with the God of Abraham.

Truth #49 There are forces out there keeping Nobody from the one true God.

Truth #50 Nobody was on a hill with God.

Truth #51 Nobody was lost in a relationship illusion.

Truth #52 Nobody failed to listen to God's messenger.

Truth #53 Nobody wanted HER to love him.

Truth #54 Nobody plays Russian Roulette.

Truth #55 Nobody decides not to listen to another one of God's messengers.

Truth #56 Nobody made sure everything was where it was supposed to be, ALL THE TIME.

Truth #57 Nobody crapped out.

Truth #58 Nobody had met his match.

Truth #59 God's love was being orchestrated for Nobody.

Truth #60 Nobody learned what mercy was.

Truth #61 Nobody wanted a God on his terms.

Truth #62 Nobody had to believe in something other than fear.

Truth #63 Nobody saw the pain that denial brings how it is soothed with the truth.

Truth #64 Nobody walks in faith.

Truth #65 Nobody saw God's messenger intercede for him.

Truth #66 Nobody saw the truth being presented.

Truth #67 Nobody could run from the past no longer.

Truth #68 Nobody comes to terms with his life.

Truth #69 Nobody's faith was building a bridge to God.

Truth #70 God met him where he was and Nobody was listening.

Truth #71 Nobody received what was needed.

Truth #72 Nobody saw another one of God's angels.

Truth #73 Nobody had left no baggage behind.

Truth #74 Nobody agreed he lived by most of the teachings of Christ but not the faith in Christ.

Truth #75 God had never deserted Nobody.

Truth #76 Nobody finds comfort at God's house.

Truth #77 Nobody tries to bargain with God.

Truth #78 Loose lips sinks ships.

Truth #79 Nobody was afraid of losing what he wanted.

Truth #80 Nobody was living a lie.

Truth #81 Nobody was granted his wish.

Truth #82 Nobody loved the thought of marriage.

Truth #83 Nobody thought love was physical attraction, even in marriage.

Truth #84 Nobody made an informed decision.

Truth #85 Nobody realized he was somebody.

Truth #86 Nobody had repeated history at a different level.

Truth #87 Nobody was painted into a corner.

Truth #88 Nobody felt vindicated.

Truth #89 Nobody saw the truth, a possible repeat of history.

Truth #90 Nobody saw a person weighing out facts instead of feelings to make a proper decision.

Truth #91 For the first time ever, Nobody had hope.

Truth #92 Nobody was powerless.

Truth #93 Nobody had no idea where they were headed.